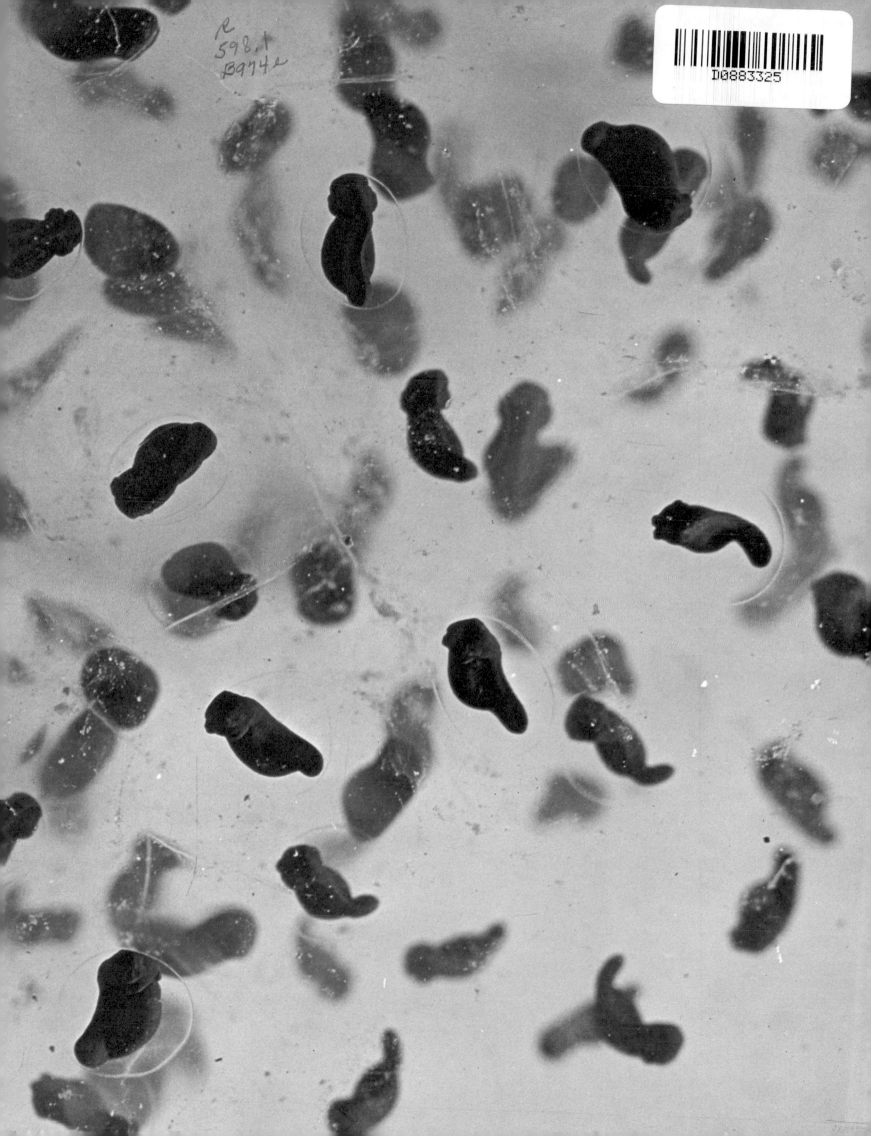

ENCYCLOPEDIA OF
REPTILES,
AMPHIBIANS & OTHER
COLD-BLOODED ANIMALS

Introduction by

Dr Maurice Burton

octopus

in association with
Phoebus

Contents

First published 1975 by
Octopus Books Limited
59 Grosvenor Street, London W1

© 1968/69/70 BPC Publishing Ltd
© this compilation 1975 BPC Publishing Ltd

This book is adapted from 'Purnell's Encyclopedia
of Animal Life', published in the United States
under the title of 'International Wild Life'.
It has been produced by Phoebus Publishing Company
in co-operation with Octopus Books Limited

Text by Maurice and Robert Burton

ISBN 0 7064 0458 0

Distributed in USA by
Crescent Books
a division of Crown Publishers Inc.
419 Park Avenue South
New York, NY 10016

Produced by Mandarin Publishers Limited
22a Westlands Road, Quarry Bay, Hong Kong
Printed in Hong Kong

Introduction

Evolution is the sum total of change whether it be in the world of living things or in the design of an aeroplane. When applied to the living world it should properly be spoken of as organic evolution. Nobody can deny that plants and animals do change, from generation to generation, because such changes can be seen to occur. We know also, from fossils, that they have occurred in the past. The disputation has largely arisen about the way the changes have been brought about and about the continuity of the changes.

The gaps in the continuity in organic evolution are, perhaps, the most perplexing feature of the study of evolution. In animals it is possible to trace, in theory, a satisfactory succession from the microscopic, single-celled animals to the mammals, which contain the largest known animals as well as the most highly-organised. There are, however, two large gaps, as well as several smaller gaps, that have so far proved unbridgeable except in imagination, or by extrapolation, which means much the same.

In this book the warm-blooded (or homoiothermic) animals, the birds and mammals, are ignored and attention is confined to the evolution of the cold-blooded (poikilothermic) animals, especially of the amphibians and reptiles. The step from the poikilotherms to the homoiotherms is relatively a very short and simple one. There are some so-called warm-blooded animals which are capable of giving up their temperature control and becoming temporarily cold-blooded. Hibernating animals do so seasonally, others, such as hummingbirds, do so each night. Many so-called cold-blooded animals can, in fact, raise their body temperature above the level of the surrounding air at times.

The two big gaps are between the single-celled Protozoa and the remainder of the animal kingdom, the multicellular animals or Metazoa. Between them there is a small subdivision, the Mesozoa, animals with the body composed of about 20 cells, without gut or nervous system. When first discovered the Mesozoa were thought to represent a possible link between the Protozoa and the Metazoa. The current view is that they represent degenerate flatworms.

So the next stage up from the Protozoa, the bulk of which are unicellular (with a very few forming small colonies of cells), are the Cnidaria, formerly known as Coelenterata, and the Porifera or sponges. The position of the latter is highly problematic. In many ways they behave like colonies of Protozoa, and some zoologists have regarded them as such. The prevailing view is that they are aberrant animals and some authors have taken the view they are not animals at all but something midway between plants and animals.

The Cnidaria include jellyfishes, corals, sea anemones and related forms characterised by having bodies composed of two layers of cells. So they are referred to as diploblastic. They have a simple nervous system and the rudiments only of a muscular system and sense-organs.

The next step in the evolution of animals came when the embryo developed a third layer of cells, giving rise to the triploblastic animals. This third layer lies between the original two and is the origin of the muscle fibres that conferred the power of active locomotion on their possessors. All that was needed was the evolution of limbs, to be actuated by muscles, so carrying the animal freely about. The first equivalent of limbs so far known were the setae or bristles, such as are found in the ringed worms, or Annelida, of which the earthworm is the best known.

The Cnidaria were originally known as radiated animals. They are radially symmetrical, which means any line through the long axis of the body divides it into roughly equal halves, as in a sea anemone with its tentacles arranged like the spokes of a wheel. The other form of symmetry is the bilateral symmetry in which a line through the long axis of the body divides it into two halves each the mirror image of the other. Movement

the Arthropoda and the Echinodermata, as well as the Annelida which includes the host of marine bristle-worms in addition to fresh-water worms and earthworms. There are a number of smaller phyla: Polyzoa (or Bryozoa) or moss animals, Brachiopoda or lampshells and several groups of 'worms'. They occupy subordinate positions so far as numbers are concerned but each adds its quota to the general picture of the progression of animal life from the relatively simple single-celled Protozoa to the more highly organised animals.

Numerically the strongest, and the most diversified, phylum is that of the Arthropoda or jointed-legged animals. This includes the classes Crustacea, Insecta, Arachnida (spiders, ticks and mites), Diplopoda (millipedes) and Chilopoda (centipedes) and several smaller classes. The number of insect species

but nothing an impartial examination would regard as vitally important.

The truly big gap in the evolutionary sequence, greater than that between the Protozoa and the Metazoa, is that which separates the invertebrates from the vertebrates. To appreciate this fully it is necessary to be sure about the definition of a vertebrate.

It is usual to say the animal kingdom is divided into invertebrates and vertebrates. It is more correct to say it is divided into invertebrates and chordates (phylum Chordata), but chordates is an unfamiliar term, so the more familiar word 'vertebrates' is used. The Chordata is divided into four subphyla, the Hemichordata or acorn worms, the Urochordata, including sea squirts and salps, and the Cephalochordata or lancelets. The three subphyla are often referred to collectively as the protochordates (i.e. primitive chordates) as a matter of convenience. The fourth of these subphyla is the Vertebrata.

The backbone, which characterises the vertebrates proper, is a series of bones, the vertebrae, forming a flexible supporting rod for the body and tail. It appears fairly early in the embryo but it is preceded by a continuous solid rod of cartilage known as the notochord. The bony matter of the backbone is laid down around it and in the end the notochord disappears, its substance being incorporated in that of the backbone.

Included in the protochordates are a small number of diverse animals which either have a notochord or a structure that can be interpreted as the forerunner of the notochord. The protochordates therefore bridge the gap between the invertebrates and vertebrates, at least in theory. Indeed, one eminent zoologist a quarter of a century ago committed himself to the statement that the gap between invertebrates and vertebrates had been satisfactorily bridged.

The truth is that as the years have passed since then, scientists have become less sure. Thus, the notochord is formed from the dorsal surface of the primitive embryonic gut, in the true vertebrates. The acorn worm is one of the protochordates. It looks like an invertebrate, being worm-like. It has gills like those seen in baby fishes and in the embryos of other vertebrates, and it has a hollow finger-like outgrowth of gut which has been interpreted as the forerunner of a notochord.

Were all these convincing, the acorn worm could be accepted as a true missing link, part invertebrate, part vertebrate. This supposed notochord of the acorn worm never was very convincing and opinion is veering away from this view.

This aspect of the subject will be dealt with more fully later. For the moment, it should be recalled that this century-old search for transitional forms between invertebrate and vertebrate has become a sort of zoological quest for the Holy Grail.

There are deep fundamental differences between the two groups. One of these is that in invertebrates the main nerve cord is ventral and the main blood vessel is dorsal to the gut. In vertebrates the reverse is true. One suggestion made was that the chordates arose from invertebrates that took to living upside-down, a theory that was quickly abandoned.

in true radially symmetrical animals is up and down instead of forwards and backwards.

Once bilateral symmetry was achieved together with some form of limbs the maximum efficiency in movement demanded segmentation of the body. This is seen to best effect in the body of an earthworm which is divided into rings or segments each with its set of muscles. The gut can run lengthwise from a head-end with its mouth and around the mouth can be positioned the specialised sense-organs, eyes, ears and nose. Since movement is essentially forward the head with its battery of special sense-organs is in a commanding position to put the animal in touch with the surroundings. The nervous system, with a central nerve-cord and nerves running into each segment, is controlled by a brain lying in the head where the main sensory equipment is located.

From earthworm-like ancestors sprang the main groups or phyla of the invertebrates, or animals without backbones: the Mollusca,

is conservatively stated as 750 000. The rest of the arthropods number just over 100 000, and the total for the whole animal kingdom is 1 240 000. So approximately two of every three species are insects.

There is a minor gap between the molluscs and worms and the arthropods, on the one hand, and the worms and the echinoderms (starfish, sea urchins etc), on the other. The first of these is partly bridged by the centipedes and millipedes, which are worm-like with legs, and possibly the caterpillar-like animal known as *Peripatus*, although the latter does not have the significance in this respect that it was formerly credited with.

If by virtue of a phenomenal patience, almost limitless time and the rich collection of specimens such a task would involve, all the species of invertebrates could be laid out in order of increasing complexity of the muscular, nervous and locomotory systems, a convincing picture of invertebrate evolution would be apparent. There would still be minor gaps,

The Invertebrates

From the figures given on page 9 it is clear that the vertebrates represent only a minor part of the animal kingdom numerically. They total 42 350 out of a total of 1 240 000 or approximately 3 per cent. Of this small percentage only 12 700, the birds with 9 000 species and the mammals with 3 700 species, are warm-blooded, representing one per cent of the whole. If we were able to take account of all the species that have ever existed these two percentages would be still further reduced until they would sink into insignificance. For example, there are only 260 species of lampshells still in existence but 30 000 extinct species have been discovered and this represents only a small part of those formerly living. There are 800 species of octopuses and squids but at least 11 000 are known to have existed in past eras and to have died out.

The remaining 99 per cent of all living species, the invertebrates, belong therefore to the overwhelmingly dominant section of the animal kingdom. They are, however, mainly of smaller size and more lowly organisation than the vertebrates especially in the development of their nervous system. Only in one class of the phylum Mollusca, the Cephalopoda (which includes the octopuses, squids and cuttlefishes), is there anything like a close approximation to the vertebrates. The largest known squid is some 60 feet long, but that length is mainly made up of a pair of long, slender arms. The cephalopods also have the nearest approximation to a vertebrate brain, the remaining invertebrates have either no concentration of nerve cells that could possibly be called a brain, or have a pair of cerebral ganglia, or knots of nerve cells, that are usually referred to as a 'brain'.

The huge preponderance of invertebrate numbers is evidenced in another striking fashion. The vertebrates make up only a single subphylum of one phylum, the Chordata, as we have seen. The invertebrates comprise 22 phyla, a phylum constituting a group of plants or animals forming a primary division in classification.

There is another broad difference, too often slurred over by the glib phrase 'invertebrates and vertebrates'; whereas the ground plan of structure is moderately uniform throughout the vertebrates, the invertebrates are highly diverse. Leaving aside the

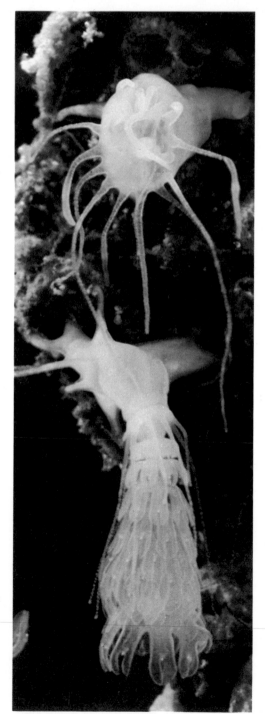

Protozoa, with all their life processes contained within a single cell, an invertebrate may be anything from a jellyfish to a worm, snail, insect or starfish. Strikingly different though these may be in outward appearance, there are even greater differences in their internal structure and behaviour.

It is simpler to visualise the changes needed to convert a fish into a salamander or lizard, or even to a bird or mammal, than to envisage the changes required to convert a jellyfish to a beetle. The early thinking that led to the first formulating of a theory of organic evolution was based on a study of vertebrates.

The successive major steps in this course of evolution, some of which have already been touched upon, can be briefly summarised. First, the original unicellular units must aggregate and organise themselves into tissues, probably in a single layer. Secondly, the double layer (diploblastic) is formed, probably on a radial plan. Thirdly, the intervention of a third layer (triploblastic) allows for the development of a muscle system in a bilaterally symmetrical body. Fourthly, the body must become segmented. Fifthly, the acquisition of limbs for locomotion is necessary. Sixthly, there is the elaboration of a nervous system and with it the specialisation of primitive sense receptors into organised sense organs.

These stages can be traced reasonably and satisfactorily through the invertebrate series, although there are gaps and dead ends. To that extent it is possible to visualise a genealogical tree such as zoologists are fond of making – although they have little value unless they can be translated into three dimensional models!

If the theory of organic evolution is to hold together, at some point on that tree must be found the starting point for vertebrate evolution. Insects, molluscs and others of the higher invertebrates are unlikely to have afforded such a starting point, since they are already specialised. *Peripatus*, for insects and arthropods generally, and *Neopilina* for the molluscs, show that a segmentation, similar to the ringed structure of the earthworm, is a prerequisite to further advance. So we have to assume, in the absence of evidence to the contrary, that the vertebrates sprang from an invertebrate that had basically an annelid construction as typified by the earthworm.

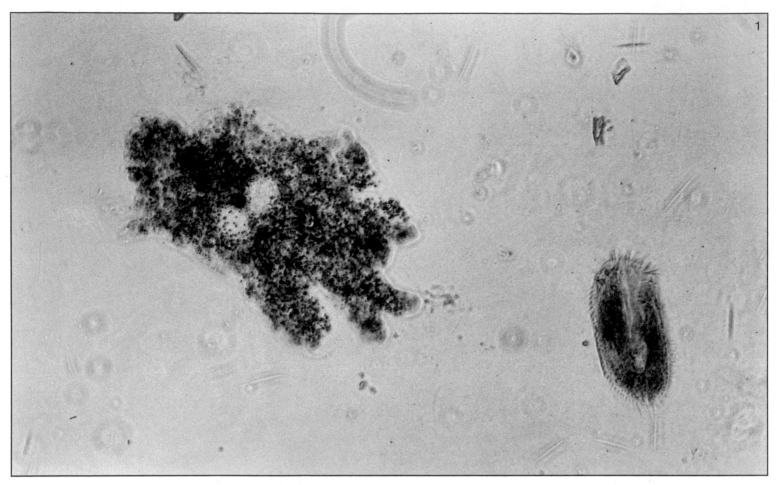

Amoeba

Amoebae form a group of the single-celled organisms called Protozoa. Protozoa means 'first animals'. These organisms have affinities with plants – some of them photosynthesise.

Like any cell the amoeba consists basically of an envelope containing the substance protoplasm. In the middle of the cell, surrounded by the protoplasm, is the nucleus, a body which can be thought of as a blueprint for the organisation of the cell's activities. If an amoeba is cut in two the half with the nucleus may survive and reproduce; the other moves around for a while but cannot digest its food, and when its reserves are gone it dies.

The protoplasm is not, as was once thought, a jelly; it has a very complicated structure, and consists of a cytoplasm divided into a granular endoplasm and at the ends of the pseudopodia, and elsewhere under the surface, a clearer layer known as ectoplasm.

Many amoebae

The name amoeba is applied not only to members of the genus *Amoeba* but to a range of different types of Protozoa with pseudopodia (see below) living in the sea, in fresh water, in damp soil and in the bodies of larger animals. They include some with shells, like *Arcella*, and also the half-dozen species that live in the human mouth and digestive system, one of which is the cause of amoebic dysentery *(Entamoeba)*. Some amoebae contain many nuclei, among them the giant *Chaos carolinensis*, which may measure up to $\frac{1}{8}$ in.

Amoeba proteus, the textbook amoeba, measuring about $\frac{1}{50}$ in., is just visible to the naked eye and may be found in fairly still fresh water. It moves about by extending a finger of protoplasm, called a pseudopodium ('false foot'). As the pseudopodium enlarges, the cell contents – protoplasm and nucleus – flow into it, while the rest of the cell contracts behind. Though it has no definite shape, the amoeba is not a shapeless sac of protoplasm, for it has a permanent hind end and forms its pseudopodium in a characteristic pattern according to the species.

Feeding

The amoeba feeds mainly on other Protozoa and also small rotifers. It does so by 'flowing' around them, the protoplasm completely surrounding the food to enclose it in a 'food vacuole' containing fluid in which the prey was swimming. Digestion is a similar process to that occurring in many other organisms: digestive juices are secreted into the food vacuole and the digestible parts are broken down and absorbed. The rest is merely left behind as the amoeba moves along.

This process is known as phagocytosis, from the Greek 'eating by cells'. In a similar process called pinocytosis, or 'drinking by cells', channels are formed from the cell surface, leading into the cell. Fluid is drawn into the channels and from their tips vacuoles are pinched off. The fluid is then absorbed into the protoplasm in the same way as the digested contents of the food vacuoles. This is a method of absorbing fluids in bulk into the cell.

1 *The well known one-celled animal, amoeba, showing large water excreting vacuoles. This picture includes a Stylonychian which belongs to another, ciliated, group of protozoans. (Magnified 150 times.)*

Water is continually passing in through the cell membrane as well as being brought in by phagocytosis and pinocytosis. Excess is pumped out by contractile vacuoles which fill with water and then collapse, discharging the water to the outside.

Reproduction

The amoeba reproduces itself by dividing into two equal parts, a process known as binary fission and taking less than an hour. It begins with the amoeba becoming spherical. The nucleus divides into two. The two halves move apart and the cell then splits down the middle.

Some species of amoebae can reproduce in a different manner. The nucleus divides into hundreds of small ones and each becomes surrounded by a little cytoplasm and a tough wall – all within the original cell. The resulting 'cysts' can survive if the water dries up and can be dispersed to found new populations. Larger cysts may be formed without reproduction taking place, when the whole cell surrounds itself with a thick wall. Though some amoebae reproduce sexually, *Amoeba proteus* has never been seen to do so.

Pushing or pulling?

The story of the amoeba illustrates not only the advances made in the last few decades in the techniques of microscopy but also

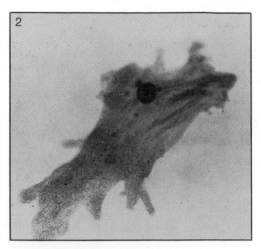

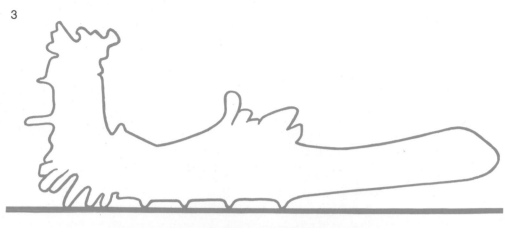

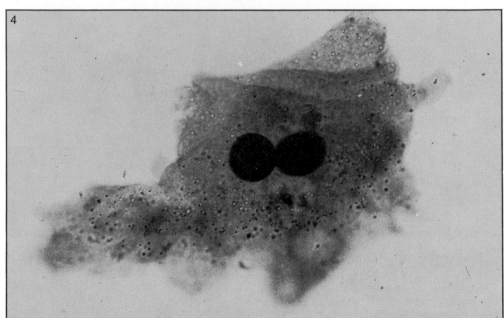

2 *Amoeboid movement – showing pseudopodia in action, from above.*
3 *Diagram of modern microscope's side view of amoeba moving to the right on small protoplasmic pegs with pseudopodium, or false-foot, extended.*
4 *Amoeba with nucleus, which controls cell, divided, prior to cell splitting into two.*
5 *Special light phase contrast microscope gives this beautiful view of amoeba showing food in vacuoles.*

the difficulties involved in research.

Years ago microscopists could watch amoeba only from above in the usual manner of looking at very small objects. From this angle one could see the pseudopodia advancing over the surface of the microscope slide and apparently in contact with it. In recent times a technique has been devised for watching it from the side and a new detail has come to light. In fact, when each pseudopodium moves forward it is supported by an extremely small peg of protoplasm which remains attached to the ground at one spot while the rest of the animal, raised just above the ground, advances over it. Finally, the pseudopodium is withdrawn and reincorporated into the body of the amoeba.

A number of theories of 'amoeboid movement' have been proposed over the last 20 years but its mechanism is still not thoroughly understood. One can see, under the higher powers of the microscope, the protoplasm streaming forwards along the centre of the pseudopodium and moving out to the sides at the tip in what has been descriptively named the 'fountain zone', and there acquiring a firmer consistency. At the same time the reverse change occurs at the 'tail', where the protoplasm resumes its forward flow.

What is still in doubt is whether the advancing protoplasm is being pushed forward from behind, like toothpaste in its tube, or pulled by changes in the proteins in the fountain zone. The problem is by no means trivial, for some of our own cells move in an amoeboid manner and its solution in terms of the behaviour of protein molecules could cast light on one of the basic properties of protoplasm.

phylum	**Protozoa**
class	**Sarcodina**
order	**Amoebida**

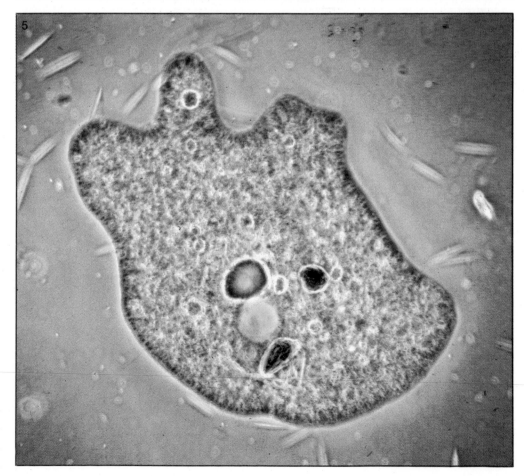

Jellyfish

Jellyfish are free-swimming relatives of sea anemones, corals and hydroids, all belonging to the phylum Cnidaria. In the life cycles of many cnidarians there are two distinct phases. One is a free-living jellyfish, or medusa, that reproduces sexually, while the other develops from an embryo and is an anchored, or sessile, polyp, or colony of polyps, that in turn buds off jellyfish. One or other phase may be dominant and the other less important or even non-existent. The large jellyfishes make up one class, the Scyphozoa (or Scyphomedusae), in which the polyp stage is very small. Attention will be concentrated here on this group.

Upside-down hydra
The typical jellyfish is umbrella-shaped, globular or conical with 4 or 8 tentacles around the margin, or many tentacles may form a ring around the margin. Under the umbrella, and like a handle to it, is the mouth, leading into the digestive cavity. The mouth is drawn out at the corners into four long lips. The basic form of the body of the jellyfish can best be understood by comparison with that of hydra. The body of hydra consists essentially of two layers of cells forming a sac and separated by a very thin layer of non-cellular material, mesogloea. In the jellyfish the mesogloea is very thick. Although the body of a jellyfish is more elaborate than that of hydra it still has the same two-layered structure and ring of tentacles around the mouth.

Some common jellyfish
A jellyfish found in seas throughout the world and which is common off the coasts of Europe is *Aurelia aurita*. It grows to nearly 1½ ft across, with many very short tentacles. The blue, yellowish, reddish or brown jellyfish *Cyanea*, also known as sea blubber, can reach 6 ft across in Arctic waters but is usually less than half that. The jellyfish *Chrysaora* has 24 tentacles, and these may be 20 yd long in one species. Around the centre of its white or yellowish disc there is often a brownish ring from which streaks of the same colour radiate. Another common jellyfish is *Rhizostoma*, or 'the root-mouthed', named for the shape of its lips. It is a whitish dome, about a foot across, with a deep purple rim. It has no tentacles but is easily recognized by the cauliflower-like oral lips. In the United States it is called 'cabbage blebs'. Some jellyfish are luminescent and one of the most intense, which is occasionally found in north European waters, is *Pelagia noctiluca*.

Different ways of feeding
Jellyfish swim by rhythmic pulsations of the umbrella or bell. The movement is very like an umbrella being opened and shut slowly. It is co-ordinated by a very simple nervous system and by sense organs around the edge that are sensitive to light, gravity and chemicals in the water. Jellyfish are carnivorous and many of them capture fish, shrimps and other animals on their trailing

*The polyp generation of **Aurelia aurita**, like all other jellyfish, is a small sedentary phase passing the winter hanging from a rock. In spring the polyp becomes divided by transverse grooves, a process known as strobilisation, until it looks like a pile of saucers.*

tentacles, paralyse them with their stinging cells and transfer them to the mouth. *Aurelia* catches fish when young, but once grown to about 1 in. across feeds in quite a different way on small planktonic animals. These are trapped in sticky mucus all over the surface of the body and are driven by cilia to the rim. There the accumulating blobs are licked off by the 4 long oral lips. Further cilia propel the food in currents of water into the digestive cavity, from which a system of branching, cilia-lined canals radiate out to the rim, carrying food to all parts of the body. *Rhizostoma* feeds in the manner of a sponge, drawing in small planktonic animals by means of ciliary currents through thousands of separate mouths on the greatly elaborated oral lips. It is these mouths and the many little sensory palps on the oral lips that give the

jellyfish its characteristic cauliflower appearance. Another plankton feeder is a tropical jellyfish *Cassiopeia* which lies mouth upwards on the sea bottom in shallow water, pulsating its bell gently and capturing plankton with its lips as it is wafted by. It has symbiotic algae in its oral lips which benefit from the sunlight falling on them (see also anemone *Anthopleura*, page 16).

Piles of saucers
The common *Aurelia* is readily recognised by the four nearly oval purple or lilac reproductive organs, ovaries in the females, testes in the males. These lie in pouches in the digestive cavity but show through the transparent bell. The male sheds his sperm into the sea and these are wafted to the female and taken in along with her food. The eggs are fertilised and develop for a

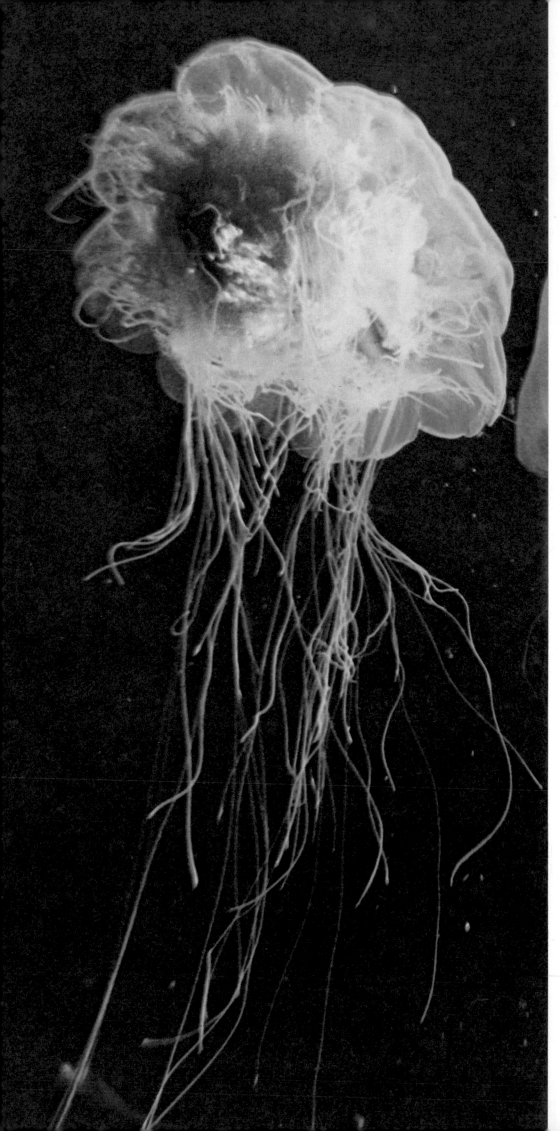

while in pouches on the oral lips. They are eventually set free as tiny planula larvae which soon attach themselves to seaweed or stone and develop into small polyps, known as scyphistomas or hydratubas, each with 16 tentacles. From the base of each, stolons, like runners of strawberry plants, grow out and new polyps develop on them. Each polyp eventually gives rise in the following winter to a number of young jellyfish called ephyra larvae, not round like the adult, but with the edge of the bell drawn out into 8 arms, notched at the tips. To do this, the polyp becomes pinched off into segments so it resembles a pile of lobed saucers. Then the tissue connecting these saucers contracts and snaps and each one swims off as a little ephyra. The growing ephyras transform gradually into adults by filling in the spaces between the arms.

An alternation of forms like this is typical of these jellyfish, though, in *Pelagia*, the egg develops directly into ephyras.

Sea wasps

Jellyfishes are practically all water. A jellyfish stranded on the shore will soon vanish under the hot rays of the sun leaving little more than a patch of water in the sand. Their bodies are nearly 99% jelly and the whole body contains less than 5% organic matter. Yet jellyfishes can be extremely venomous as anyone knows who has hauled on a rope covered in long trailing tentacles. The stings of jellyfishes come from the many stinging cells or nematocysts which shoot out a poisonous thread when touched. The severity of the sting depends very much on the number of nematocysts discharged and also on the type of jellyfish. The most venomous jellyfishes are those living in the coral seas and the least troublesome are those in temperate seas, but even these, if enough tentacles are allowed to touch our bodies, can sometimes lead to a loss of consciousness and, in the case of one bather, to drowning. This kind of accident is happily very rare. The most venomous jellyfishes belong to what are known as the Cubomedusae, so called because of their somewhat squarish shape. They range in size from as small as grapes to as large as pears and have four tentacles or four groups of tentacles. Some of these, like bathers, seem to prefer quiet shallow waters in the warmer seas, and are particularly troublesome around the northern Australian coasts, the Philippines and Japan. They have been called sea wasps and they can kill in as short a time as half a minute, usually in a quarter of an hour, the victim dying in excruciating pain.

| phylum | **Cnidaria** |
| class | **Scyphozoa** |

◁ *Young* **Cyanea** *or sea blubber. This is the giant among jellyfish, sometimes 6 ft across with trailing tentacles 200 ft long.*

Anemone

'Anemone', from the Greek for wind, was first used for a flower in 1551. At first the marine animals that look like flowers were called plant-animals. The name 'sea-anemone' was not used until 1773. Today, marine zoologists almost invariably speak of the animals as anemones. That they are truly animals is no longer in doubt although the order to which they were assigned is still called the Anthozoa, that is, plant-animals. The basic differences between plants and animals are:

1 A plant manufactures its own food, by photosynthesis, using the green chlorophyll in its leaves; an animal takes solid food.
2 A plant is incapable of locomotion; an animal can move about.
3 A plant has no obvious sensitivity; an animal usually has recognisable sense-organs

There are exceptions to all three principles, especially among the lower plants and the lower animals, but these are good working guides.

A sea-anemone has simple sense-organs, takes solid food and, surprisingly, is capable of locomotion.

The most outstanding feature of sea-anemones is the variety of their colours and, in many species, the beauty of the patterns these make. Colours and patterns in higher animals are known to serve as camouflage, warning coloration, recognition marks and other utilitarian purposes. Sea-anemones neither need nor could use any of these; their colours and patterns consequently appear as pure art-form.

Long-lived and motile

Anemones are found only in the seas but there they are world-wide, from between tide-marks to the great depths of the ocean. They are most abundant in warm seas where they can reach up to 3 ft across. The smallest are little more than a pin's head, but this requires some explanation. Voracious feeders, anemones will eat any animal flesh they can catch and swallow, and they may swallow prey of large size relative to their own bulk. It is not unknown for one anemone to swallow another and they are not immune to each other's poison. They can, however, survive for a long time without food, gradually dwindling in size until quite minute. This may be one of the secrets of their long life—anemones have been kept in aquaria for as much as 100 years.

Sea-anemones are by no means 'rooted to the spot'. There are even burrowing anemones. Those that are normally seen fixed to a rock move by gliding on their base. Others somersault, bending over to take hold of the substratum with their tentacles, then letting go by the base and slipping this over to take hold beyond. A few species lie on their side to glide along, or blow themselves up, let go with their foot, and float away.

Stinging tentacle feeders

An anemone is a cylindrical bag with a ring

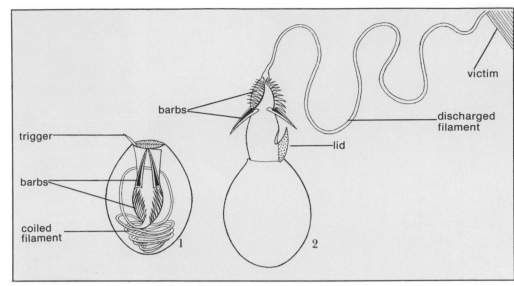

1. *Bag-like stinging cell of cnidarian full of paralysing poison and with coiled filament inside.*
2. *When the cell is activated by having its trigger touched or by food chemicals, the lid flies open and the coiled contents turn inside out, shooting the poison-filled filament into the body of its victim, which is also retained by the barbs.*

Plumose anemone, **Metridium senile***, can be quite large, up to 9 in. high and 6 in. across the head.*

of tentacles surrounding the mouth on the upper surface. The opposite end is flattened and forms a basal disc, or foot, by which the animal sticks to a solid support. The interior of the bag is one large stomach, subdivided by curtains of tissue, or mesenteries, which hang down, partially dividing the stomach into eight compartments. Food is caught by the tentacles, which are armed with stinging cells. When a small animal, such as a shrimp or a fish, touches a tentacle the stinging cells come into action, paralysing and holding it. Adjacent tentacles also bend over to continue the stinging and holding until all begin to move towards the mouth, where the prey is engulfed. Indigestible remains from a meal are later voided through the mouth.

Stinging cells are a characteristic of the phylum Cnidaria to which sea-anemones belong, and included in the phylum are jellyfishes, the stinging cells of which are more familiar to most people. The Cnidaria are accordingly spoken of as stinging animals or, better still, nettle animals. Sting-cells, or nematocysts, are double-walled capsules, filled with poison, set in the outer surface of the tentacles. Each contains a coiled hollow thread, sometimes barbed at the base. At the outer end of the capsule is a thorn-like trigger. When this is touched the coiled thread is shot out. It turns inside-out as it is ejected, its fine point pierces the skin of the prey, and the paralysing poison flows down the hollow thread. Some kinds of nematocysts stick to the prey instead of piercing the skin, and in a third type the thread wraps itself around the victim. In addition to being triggered off by touch some nematocysts come into action as a result of

Left: Anemones can have little use for warning coloration or camouflage, so their colours appear as nature's art. This red anemone is **Tealia crassicornis.**
Right: **Anthopleura xanthogrammica,** *the giant green anemone, is one of the few anemones to live in direct sunlight. Its green colour is due to minute one-celled green algae living in its cells and photosynthesising.*

the presence of certain chemicals.

The body-wall of an anemone is made up of two layers of cells. There is, however, a good series of muscles. One set is longitudinal, running from the foot to the bases of the tentacles. The other is circular, running round the body. By the lengthening and contraction of these muscles the body can be drawn out or pulled in. There is also a series of retractor muscles which assist in the sudden withdrawal of body and tentacles. There are only very simple sense-organs and there is only a simple nerve system, a mere network of nerve-cells.

The action of the nematocysts is automatic, the result of the trigger being touched—it is a reflex action. A nerve strand also runs to the base of each nematocyst and it is these nerve strands that control the concerted action of the tentacles once a nematocyst has been discharged. The nerve network comes into action to cause the contraction of an anemone when it is touched. It can be made to expand again by adding a nutrient solution to the water. The slime from a mussel, for example, in the proportions of one part in a million, will make the body expand, and the tentacles extend, very slowly, perhaps taking an hour to come full out. Then the body sways slightly and the tentacles wave as if groping for food.

Sexual and asexual reproduction

Most anemones are either male or female, but some are hermaphrodite. In some, eggs and sperm are shed into the surrounding water, in others the larvae develop inside the parent body. The eggs vary in size, the largest, only $\frac{1}{25}$ in. wide, being a thousand times larger than the smallest. The fertilised eggs sink to the bottom and divide, or segment, to form oval larvae. These move about the seabed but finally each comes to rest, fastens itself to the bottom of the seabed,

grows tentacles and begins to feed.

An anemone can reproduce in other ways. It may split longitudinally to form separate individuals, or grow a ring of tentacles half-way down the body, after which the top half breaks away to give two anemones where there was one before. Young anemones may be formed, in some species, by fragmentation, or laceration. In fragmentation small anemones, complete with tentacles, arise from the base of a parent, become separated and move away. Laceration occurs in some species with a roving disposition. As the anemone glides over the rocks pieces of the base are ripped away and, being left behind, regenerate to form very minute but otherwise perfect anemones.

Enemies

Enemies are large sea-slugs, sea-spiders, fishes and sometimes starfishes and crabs.

Restless anemones

Aside from their diverse methods of locomotion, which are used but sparingly, anemones are always on the move, in a kind of slow-motion ballet. This led to an important discovery, the subject of which was the plumose anemone, 3–4 in. high, with a feathery crown of numerous small tentacles. When several scores of these are living in a large aquarium they are seen, at any given moment, to be in different attitudes. The body of some may be stretched up, others shortened and thickened; perhaps it is shortened and slender, its surface thrown into wrinkles, or it may be bent over to one side. The tentacles also will be in various stages of extension and retraction. Sometimes one or more anemones will be dilated and their tentacles withdrawn, so that they look like balloons anchored to the rock. Others may be so withdrawn that they look like buttons on

the rock. They may be watched for some minutes and no movement seen; but when anemones are watched closely and continuously against a black background, and their shapes drawn at intervals, they can be seen to be in continuous movement. This has been confirmed by other experimental methods, including a speeded-up film. Even when anemones are kept under conditions of constant temperature, in water free of food or undisturbed by vibrations the rhythm of activity continues. It can be interrupted by the presence of food or other disturbing factors, when the anemones react by more purposeful movements. One effect of this inherent rhythm of activity is to keep the animal in a state of constant preparedness for feeding, defence and other activities essential to the maintenance of life.

This movement is called the inherent rhythm of activity because it is self-starting and self-maintaining. It is common to all living organisms, as we now know. Obvious manifestations of it are seen in such processes as the beating of the heart, as well as in less obvious ways. When we sleep, for example, we do not simply lie still. Our bodies are in constant, if slow movement, in much the same way as the bodies of plumose anemones were shown to be.

phylum	**Cnidaria**
class	**Anthozoa**
order	**Actiniaria**
genera	**Actinia** **Anemonia** **Metridium** *and others*

Ragworm

Ragworms are marine relatives of earthworms. They are colourful worms, in browns, reds and greens, living mainly on the shore or in shallow seas, throughout the world. Ragworms have more bristles on each segment than earthworms and so, together with many other kinds of marine ringed worms, are known as bristleworms. They are active, often bulky and well known to sea anglers for their use as bait. They range in size from 1 in. long to as much as 3 ft. Their bodies are divided into segments, which may number 200 or more in the longest ragworm. Each segment is flanked by a pair of parapodia, flat, lobed outgrowths bearing bristles. The first two segments do not have these: the foremost segment having instead two short tentacles, which are also light sensitive, and two sensory palps; the second segment has a group of four tentacle-like 'cirri' on each side. The first segment also has four eyes. In North America the names mussel worm, clam worm and pile worm are used for ragworms because of their associations.

Brain unnecessary for swimming

Zoologists know ragworms by the more flattering name of nereids—the Nereids of Greek mythology were beautiful sea nymphs. Ragworms swim by side to side undulations of the body. These undulations pass forwards, instead of backwards as in most serpentine animals, and in doing so allow the parapodia to act as paddles, pushing the worm forwards. If the restraining influence of the brain is removed, by cutting off the head segments, swimming may become continuous and it also continues if the worm is cut into short lengths. Each length continues the swimming actions, so it is not the brain that co-ordinates the movements of swimming but the nerve cord which runs along the body and thickens in each segment to form a compact mass or ganglion. The brain controls whether movement takes place or not. The worms need be no more than inefficient swimmers since they spend most of their lives in U-shaped burrows, in mud or sand, or under stones between tidemarks. Gentle undulations, up and down this time, in contrast with the side to side swimming movements, serve to draw currents of water through the burrows. When a ragworm crawls out of its burrow to feed, slow movements of the parapodia suffice, but, as the worm speeds up, the whole body begins to undulate, much as in swimming. One ragworm, *Nereis fucata*, is noted for its habit of sometimes living in the shells occupied by hermit crabs. It lies on the right upper side of the crab and in the inward water currents that it sets up.

Net of mucus

Most ragworms are carnivorous, eating small invertebrates such as crustaceans. Some ragworms feed in various other ways, browsing on mud or filtering small particles from the water they draw into their tubes. *Nereis diversicolor* may catch its food by spinning a net of mucus over the mouth of its tube and drawing water in. Particles of food get caught in the net and after about 10 minutes the worm pushes its head up to gather the net in its mouth and swallow it. The mouth has a proboscis that is turned inside out as it is protruded. At the end of the proboscis is a pair of sharp horny jaws, like those of a beetle. A large ragworm can give the human finger a nasty bite with these, but they are more often used to grab prey of various kinds, including small fish and other worms. As well as these jaws, the protruding proboscis has groups of other much smaller teeth or denticles on the sides which help to secure the prey.

Courtship dance

In many ragworms breeding involves such great changes in the adults that the breeding worms were once considered as belonging to a separate genus, *Heteronereis*, a name that still survives as a descriptive term. The hind end of the body becomes swollen with eggs or sperm and the parapodia become more elaborate and develop fans of long, oar-shaped bristles, more suitable for swimming. The eyes, especially in males, usually become larger and the tentacles and palps smaller. Now the worms leave their burrows, generally at night, and swarm near the surface of the water where they release their sex cells, sometimes in the course of a sort of nuptial dance in which the males swim rapidly in small circles around the females. The eggs are released by the rupture of the female's body wall, which is stimulated by the presence of the sperm in the water. In the American *Platynereis megalops* fertilisation is internal, the male wrapping himself around the female and introducing his sperm into her mouth. At this stage in the lives of both sexes the wall of the gut has disintegrated so there is no obstacle to the sperms reaching the ovary. The assumption of the heteronereis form occurs only at certain times of the year and, like swimming, is under the control of the brain. If its brain is

▽ *A good relationship – at least for the commensal worm* **Nereis fucata** *that lives with the hermit crab* **Pagurus bernhardus** *in the empty shell of* **Buccinum.** *The worm lives in the upper spirals of the shell, only coming out to eat the left-overs of the crab's meal.*

removed a young worm will turn into a heteronereis without more ado. Moreover, the heteronereis stage can be suppressed in an adult worm by implanting in its body the brain of a young worm.

From the fertilised eggs hatch little spherical larvae propelled by cilia and bearing bristles grouped in three pairs, representing the parapodia of three segments. The number of segments gradually increases and the larvae eventually settle on the bottom.

In some species of ragworms mating occurs in the tube, the female dies soon after she has laid the eggs and the male then eats her and tends the eggs himself.

Survival value of worms

Among the ragworms that do not pass through the heteronereis form is a species that lives in the sand and mud of estuaries and shores. It has been studied in great detail because of its ability to survive in brackish or even fresh water. This species is *N. diversicolor,* a burrowing worm 2−5 in. long with a red line down its back where its dorsal blood vessel shows through the skin. It can, however, be variable in colour: green, yellow, orange or red. The habit of swarming in the surface waters and producing free swimming larvae would hardly be appropriate in the flowing water of an estuary, so it is not surprising that *N. diversicolor* does neither of these things. Spawning takes place in spring as the temperature of the water rises above 5°C/41°F and at this time tangles of several females around single males are sometimes to be seen. Both sexes are very fragile and likely to burst if handled. The eggs hatch a little over a week after being fertilised and the larvae, without bristles at first, stay on the mud surface or in the parental burrow. Having depended on their yolk stores for the first few weeks, they start to feed when about ½ in. long and make their first burrows when twice that size.

The larvae of ragworms generally are less able to survive in water of low salinity than are the adults and it is this that limits the spread upstream of *N. diversicolor.* In the freshwater Lake Merced in California, however, lives a ragworm *N. limnicola* very closely related to *N. diversicolor*—possibly both represent one species. This is only possible because the eggs are fertilised inside the mother and the larvae emerge only when able to stand the fresh water.

phylum	**Annelida**
class	**Polychaeta**
order	**Phyllodocida**
family	**Nereidae**
genera	*Nereis* *Platynereis*

◁ *The head and tail regions of two* **Nereis diversicolor** *show the uniform structure of a ragworm. The body is fringed with many paddle-like parapodia used in swimming; the red stripe down the body is the dorsal blood vessel (× 11).*

Earthworm

The earthworm, so familiar to gardeners, has many varieties, and the two dozen British earthworms are not all easily recognised at a glance. The brandling **Eisenia foetida** *has alternating bands of red-brown and yellow and a strong smell, and has always been sought by anglers as a potent worm bait. It lives in dung and compost heaps, as does the gilt-tail* **Dendrobaena rubida.** *Another distinguished by its colour is the green worm* **Allolobophora chlorotica.** *The species usually referred to as the earthworm is, however, the large* **Lumbricus terrestris,** *up to 10 in. long (rather short by comparison with the 11ft earthworms of Australia). The reddish tinge of this and other earthworms is due to the oxygen-carrying pigment haemoglobin in the blood. The long body is divided into ring-like segments (150 of them in* **L. terrestris**) *and some of the internal organs, those for excretion for example, are duplicated in most of these segments. At the tapering front end is the mouth with its overhanging prehensile lip, but with no teeth or jaws. Around the body, like a cigar band (segments 32-37 in* **L. terrestris**) *is what is sometimes taken for a scar, where the worm has been cut in two and healed again. It is in fact a special gland, the saddle or clitellum, which secretes the cocoon.*

How the earthworm burrows

An earthworm moves along by waves of muscular contraction travelling back along the body. Each body segment acts as a unit lengthening as it becomes narrower under the action of circular muscles, becoming broader as it shortens, pulled in by longitudinal muscles. When a group of the segments are pushing out sideways into the wall of a burrow, holding the worm firm at that point, elongation of the foremost segment of the group pushes forwards the segments in front. At the same time another segment, in the group at the rear, becomes shorter and fatter. This continues until the whole worm has moved forwards.

Extra grip is given during crawling, especially on the surface of the ground, by short, backwardly-directed bristles, which can be pushed out as required. There are four pairs on each segment except the first and last. These can be felt on the underside, more easily than seen, by drawing a worm backwards through the fingers.

Tree-climbing earthworms

Although a worm burrows partly by pushing soil aside, it also eats much of it. In some species, swallowed soil is voided at the surface in the familiar worm casts, though this is not true of *L. terrestris* which seldom makes casts. Some earthworms, like the gilt-tail, climb trees and may sometimes be found under the bark. The brandling, too, often scales trees and fences. After heavy rain in India, earthworms have been seen

△ *Worm casts – soil drained of humus and nourishment by the earthworm's gut – on a lawn.*

▽ **Lumbricus terrestris** *is the familiar garden 'lobworm', the angler's heavyweight worm bait.*

19

migrating uphill and even up trees, presumably to avoid immersion. They were, however, probably in no danger of drowning, since earthworms can be kept under water for months and still survive. Those found dead in puddles have probably died from other causes. Getting too dry is more dangerous for a worm than getting too wet. In dry weather and in winter, worms may burrow as much as 8 ft below the surface. At such times, they may pass into a state of inactivity in mucus-lined chambers in the ground.

Fleeing from moles
Earthworms have no ears or eyes but their surfaces – especially the upper – are sensitive, even to light. A worm can detect the vibrations from a mole digging, and large numbers of earthworms will come to the surface, as if in panic, when a mole is working nearby. Pushing a stick into the ground and wriggling it about also brings worms to the surface. Should an earthworm fall foul of a predator, it may lose only part of itself, torn or cast off by reflex action (autotomy). The remaining portion of worm can often regrow the lost part. The amount of this regrowth varies from one species to another, but it is usually limited to a few segments at the front end and slightly more at the hind end.

Rudimentary intelligence?
The chief food of earthworms is decaying plant matter although they sometimes eat small dead animals, such as other worms, and droppings. Some food is taken in with soil swallowed in burrowing, but vegetation lying on the ground near the mouth of the burrow is also important. This is pulled into the burrow and to some extent pre-digested by digestive juices from the mouth before being eaten. Charles Darwin in *The formation of vegetable mould through the action of worms,* a book published in 1881 just before his death, showed that leaves, pine needles and even paper would be drawn in and used to line the upper parts of the burrows. In spite of the fact that worms are blind, the leaves and paper triangles with which he experimented were usually drawn in by their pointed ends. Clearly it is easier to

draw in a leaf by the tip than by the edge, and Darwin reasoned that this behaviour showed rudimentary intelligence. Several biologists have since looked into this and it seems clear now that leaves are pulled down in the way which is mechanically most efficient, that is, by the tips. The worms reach from their burrows, grasp leaves at random, and pull. If the leaves meet with resistance they let go and try again. Success comes when they happen to grasp the tip of the leaf, and so they do this largely by simple trial-and-error and not by intelligent action. There is, however, more to it than this, for worms respond to some of the chemicals in the vegetable matter, showing a preference for the chemicals of the leaf tips rather than those of the bases and stalks.

A worm's castle
It is not unusual to find heaps of pebbles on gravel paths, as if torrential rains had washed the gravel uneven. This is probably the normal interpretation. But if one takes a closer look it is possible to see that around each hillock there is bare earth, and in this are impressions of the outlines of pebbles on the heap nearby, showing that something has lifted the pebbles up carefully and placed them on the heap. If one of these heaps is carefully taken apart we find a worm-cast at the centre and beneath it a small mound of earth forming the core of the heap. The heap will consist of up to 200 pebbles of a total weight of about 22 oz, the pebbles ranging from pea-sized to $1\frac{1}{2}$ in. across and weighing $1\frac{1}{2}$ oz.

The best way to see what is making these heaps is to go out after dark after a light shower of rain with a red lamp, walking carefully so as not to cause vibrations in the ground. From each heap a worm will be seen stretching out, anchored by its tail in the centre of the heap, and with luck one may see a worm pressing its mouth against the surface of a pebble to form a sucker. It is not easy to catch the worm actually in the act of moving the pebble but one can hear, as one stands silent, the occasional chink of a pebble being moved, and there is the impression in the surface of the soil, already mentioned, showing the outline of a pebble now lying on top of the

heap, to give evidence that it has been moved gently.

We know that worms will pull leaves into the burrow, and they will also drag in small sticks, feathers, even pieces of wool lying on the ground. We can only surmise that it is necessary for the worm to clear part of the earth's surface to feed. On a piece of ground without pebbles it is possible with care to watch earthworms feeding by stretching out from the entrance to the burrow and running the mouth over the surface of the earth rather like the nozzle of a vacuum cleaner while swallowing movements can be seen, as if the worm were sucking in minute particles of soil or food material as part of a meal.

Economical breeding
A visit to a lawn on a warm, still night that is not too dry will show worms joined in pairs, each with its hind end in its burrow. Some species pair below ground. Each worm is hermaphrodite and sperms are exchanged during the three or four hours in which the pairs are united, held together by slime from the clitellum and by certain of the bristles.

Egg-laying begins about a day after mating, and this may continue for several months without further pairing (belying the view of Gilbert White, the 18th-century English clergyman and naturalist, that the earthworms are 'much addicted to venery'). As they are laid, the eggs become enclosed in a cocoon secreted by the clitellum and are fertilised by sperm stored in it—not, as one might expect, from inside the body. The cocoon of *Lumbricus terrestris* is pea-sized and dark brown. Although several eggs are laid in each cocoon, together with a thickish albumen, only one embryo usually survives. The young worm emerges after 1–5 months and is ready to reproduce after another 6–18 months. How long worms usually survive is uncertain but *L. terrestris* has been kept 6 years in captivity and *Allolobophora longa* $10\frac{1}{4}$ years.

Churning up the soil
Estimates of earthworms to the acre have been as high as 3 million, or 15 cwt. Without their continual action in aerating and drain-

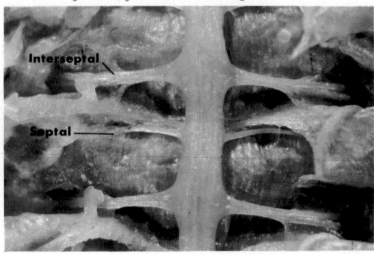

An earthworm's main nerve (centre) branches off into each segment of its body. Septal branches run next to each dividing wall; interseptal branches run into the middle of each segment. The 'brain' (not shown here) consists of 2 knots of nerve cells above the gullet.

Interseptal

Septal

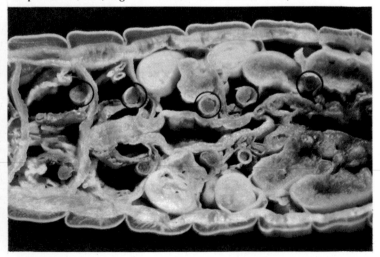

Two blood vessels run the length of a worm, one above, one below. Connecting these like the hoops of a barrel are circular vessels; 5 pairs of these (in segments 7–11) are dilated and pulse rhythmically forming the 'pseudo hearts' (ringed in the horizontal section below).

△ *Earthworms mating; the process takes 3–4 hours, during which the couple both keep their hind ends in their respective burrows.*

▽ *Sweating it out; to conserve moisture in a dry spell, an earthworm coils itself in a small chamber which it lines with its own mucus.*

ing, pulling down leaves and throwing up worm casts, the earth, or at least uncultivated land 'would soon become cold, hardbound, and void of fermentation; and consequently sterile', as Gilbert White wrote in 1777, a time when 'gardeners and farmers express(ed) their detestation of worms'.

Darwin pointed out, however, that the action of earthworms may be harmful on sloping ground and assist in denudation, the soil brought up from below the surface being washed or blown downhill.

Worms occur in the highest numbers in grassland, where there is plenty of food and no disturbance, and the population declines drastically if the ground is dug or ploughed. There is a limit to the earthworm's toleration of soil acidity and, if this is exceeded, vegetation accumulates on the surface as a mat which eventually becomes peat.

From the weights of daily collections of worm casts, Darwin estimated that $7\frac{1}{2}$ to 18 tons of soil can be thrown up per acre each year, equivalent to $1-1\frac{1}{2}$ in. over 10 years. One result is a very fine surface layer of soil and, at the same time, large stones tend not only to be buried under the collection of casts but also to be undermined. This is why some of the outer stones of Stonehenge have started to disappear—the present rate of covering there is estimated at about 7 in. per century, a rate considerably exceeded in some of Darwin's experiments. This also explains why so many Roman remains are now buried. In a ditch at Verulamium (St Alban's) which had been sealed over by the floors of successive buildings during the first 4 centuries AD—with no apparent way in or out – have been found certain 'mud worms' *Eophila oculata*. These require very little oxygen and had plenty of food.

phylum	**Annelida**
class	**Oligochaeta**
order	**Prospora**
family	**Lumbricidae**
genus & species	***Lumbricus terrestris*** *others*

To add to the worm's grip while tunnelling and crawling, pairs of bristles (setae) grow through the skin (top left). The central gut is buckled, increasing the surface area.

An earthworm strains liquid waste through tubes (nephridia) inside the body wall, one pair per segment. Also shown below is the ventral nerve cord below the central gut.

In the worm's 13th segment the ovaries flank the ventral nerve cord (centre, with one of the two main blood vessels above it). Eggs are laid in a cocoon already containing sperm.

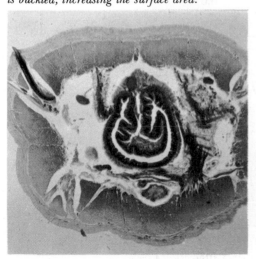

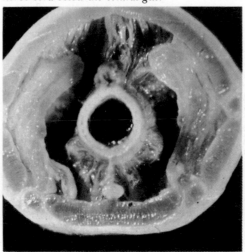

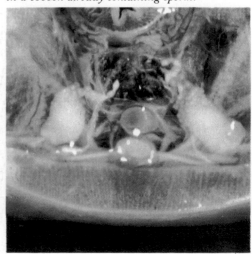

Neopilina

In the eyes of a non-scientist neopilina is a somewhat uninteresting animal—just another limpet. To the scientist it is one of the most exciting discoveries of the mid-20th century. Apart from the fact that it is yet another living fossil, the whole circumstances of its discovery are astonishing.

In 1952, when the Danish research ship Galathea *was nearing the end of her cruise in the Pacific, her dredge was hauled up from a depth of 11 878 ft off the coast of Costa Rica. In it were 10 living limpet-like animals and 3 empty shells. They belonged to a new species, of a group of molluscs known as the Monoplacophora, which seemed to have died out 350 million years ago. Each empty shell was spoon-shaped, thin, fragile and semi-transparent, coloured pale yellowish white. The largest was 1½ in. long, 1¼ in. wide and ½ in. high. The top of the shell rose to a peak the apex of which tilted over at one end. The inside was a lustrous mother-of-pearl.*

The body of the living neopilina was like that of an ordinary limpet at first sight. When the shell it was in was laid on its back there was the usual fleshy foot, not so large as in the common limpet and it was bluish round the edges and pink in the centre. Either side of the foot was a row of 5 gills, and the mouth was at the centre of a fleshy triangle situated at one end.

Which way up?

Nothing quite like neopilina had been seen before the mid-20th century, and because it had been brought up from the deep ocean bed, it was not possible to do more than speculate about neopilina's way of life. The stomach was filled with radiolaria, tiny single-celled animals with jewel-like siliceous skeletons. The floor of the ocean where it had been living was dark muddy clay. Dr Henning Lemche who examined these first specimens formed the idea that they normally rested on the clay with the foot uppermost and collected the radiolaria that drifted down onto them. Sir Maurice Yonge, the leading British marine zoologist, takes the view that it could not feed this way. He agrees the foot is smaller than one would expect to carry a limpet-like animal over the soft clay bed. But he believes it moves the 'right way up', gathers its food from the seabed as it moves along helped by the gills which act not only for breathing but for locomotion. There is a pair of fleshy tentacles just behind the mouth, and these may perhaps help in gathering food into the mouth. Yonge's view is supported by the fact that each of 4 specimens caught off the coast of Peru, in 1958, had a layer of mucus on the foot, as if neopilina laid down a track of slime on which to crawl, like a garden snail.

Four species discovered

The importance of the discovery of neopilina lies in two things. The first is that it should have been followed so quickly by the findings of other species in other parts of the world. The second is that it vindicated forecasts made by scientists about the relationships of the mollusca to other phyla of invertebrates. Concerning the first of these it is surprising, in view of what happened later, that neopilina remained undiscovered for so long. Since about 1850, when ocean dredgings began in preparation for the epic voyage of HMS *Challenger*, there have been dozens of voyages by ocean-going research vessels, some covering small areas with intensive dredging, others covering much wider areas of the ocean but not so intensively. Nothing like this remarkable mollusc was brought to the surface in that century of searching. Yet 6 years after neopilina had been found off the coast of Costa Rica, another species was caught in 19 200 ft off the coast of Peru, and 4 years later 4 specimens of a third species, each ⅔ in. long, were brought up from 8 250 ft off the coast of California. Then, in 1967, only 9 years later, a single specimen of a fourth species was caught in the Gulf of Aden in 9 000—11 850 ft. From these figures it seems a fair assumption that these animals have a much wider distribution than is represented by these finds.

Missing link found

It has long been supposed that the ancestors of molluscs must have been some kind of ringed worm, like the marine bristleworms such as the fanworms. Yet if we put the two animals side by side they look very different. Moreover, when we look at their anatomy we find two very marked differences. A worm has a segmented body. It is also bilaterally symmetrical. That is, if we cut a worm through the middle lengthwise, the right hand half will be the mirror image of the left hand half. By contrast, a mollusc is not segmented and its body is not bilaterally symmetrical or only slightly so. Instead, it has become twisted, and this is especially true of its internal organs. So altogether molluscs and ringed worms seem to be very different kinds of animals and yet there are some things about them that suggest they must be related. Scientists studying this took the view that if ringed worms and molluscs had a common ancestor, then somewhere along the line there must have been a mollusc with a bilaterally symmetrical body, gills in pairs and a shell like a limpet. They made drawings of what this 'missing link' mollusc ought to look like. When neopilina was found it turned out to be almost identical with these drawings.

phylum	**Mollusca**
class	**Monoplacophora**
order	**Tryblidioidea**
family	**Neopilinidae**
genus & species	*Neopilina adenensis*
	N. ewingi
	N. galathea
	N. valeronis

Neopilina galathea. The top of the shell rises to a peak which tilts over.

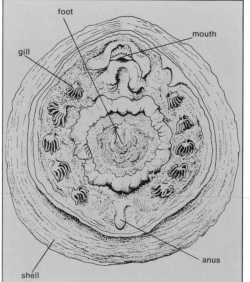

Diagram of underside of **Neopilina galathea** *shows the five pairs of gills, mouth and anus.*

foot

mouth

gill

anus

shell

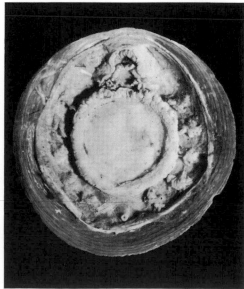
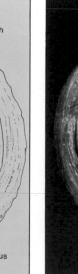

On its back—the fleshy foot of **Neopilina galathea** *is smaller than the common limpet's.*

Peripatus

Peripatus is one of the most extraordinary animals living today. A relict from the past, it was once thought of as a link between the soft-bodied ringed worms, such as the earthworm, and the hard-bodied arthropods, which include insects, spiders and crustaceans.

Its body is rather worm-like, tapering towards the hind end. It is 1—3 in. long but can be extended or contracted, and is sinuous in movement. The colour of peripatus is very variable, ranging from dark slate to reddish-brown in the various species, and there is usually a dark stripe down the back. The skin is dry and velvety to the touch and there are 20 or so pairs of short baggy legs each ending in a pair of hooks and ringed like the body. There is a pair of flexible antennae on the head with an eye at the base of each. The eyes are simple although each has a lens. They are directed outwards and upwards and probably do no more than distinguish between light and darkness. The sensory hairs clothing the antennae and most of the body are organs of touch and taste.

Must live in damp places

Peripatus is dependent on moist conditions, being found only in damp forests in South Africa, Australasia and South America. It lives under stones, rotting wood, the bark of fallen trees and similar damp places, being unable to withstand drying. In a dry atmosphere it will lose a third of its weight in less than 4 hours and will dry up twice as fast as an earthworm, and 40 times as fast as a smooth-skinned caterpillar its own size. The cause lies in its breathing system. An insect breathes through branching tubes or tracheae. Because the openings are few there is little loss of water and, moreover, there is an efficient mechanism for closing the openings when necessary. Peripatus has unbranched breathing tubes so it needs far more of them, with an opening to each tube, which means a rapid loss of water from the body when the surroundings are dry. As a result peripatus is found in 'islands', damp localities separated from other colonies by dry country.

Sticky threads for defence

The moment peripatus is disturbed it throws out one or two jets of a milky-white fluid from little nozzles or oral papillae, on the head, one either side of the mouth. On contact with the air the fluid solidifies immediately into sticky beaded threads of slime 3—12 in. long. The fluid is in reservoirs, one each side of the head, shaped like the rubber teat of an eye-dropper. Although the threads stick to one's fingers they do not stick to the velvety skin of peripatus itself, but insects and other small animals become entangled in them.

This entangling seems to be accidental because the threads serve more as a defence. Their food is mainly small insects such as termites and they also eat other small animals such as woodlice.

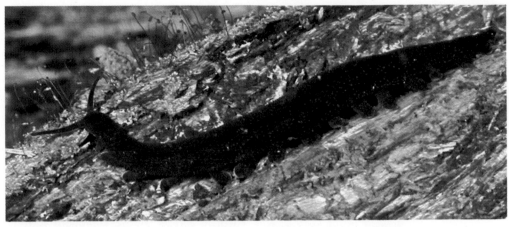

Going for a stroll: a peripatus from New Zealand **Peripatoides novaezealandiae.**

Haphazard mating

The mating of peripatus can only be described as casual. The male places capsules containing sperms on the female, apparently at random since he will place them even on her legs. He may place them at times on another male. For a long time it was not known how the sperms reached the ova. Then it was found that white blood corpuscles in the female body migrate to the skin immediately beneath a capsule and break through it by digesting the cells of the skin. At the same time the lower wall of the capsule breaks and the sperms enter the female's blood stream and find their way to an ovary. There in large numbers they force their way through the wall of the ovary. If an immature female receives sperms the young egg cells feed on them and grow for a year before they are ready to be fertilised by a second mating. Except in a few species which lay eggs the embryos develop in the uterus taking in nourishment from the mother through its walls. In one South American species special tissues are formed, making a kind of placenta, to pass food from the mother's body to the growing embryos. Development takes 13 months and as young are born each year there is one month in each year when a female is carrying two sets of embryos, one just beginning to develop, the other nearly ready to be born.

Evolutionary bridge?

The theory of evolution, in which it is assumed life began in water, requires two main invasions of the land. One, by the vertebrates, meant a change from gill-breathing to lung-breathing and indications of how this may have taken place are seen in the lungfishes (page 60), the coelacanth (page 56) and the various newts and salamanders. Among the fossils, also, there is an almost complete series showing how this came about. The other invasion is that which brought the invertebrates on land, and the most important change was that from the aquatic ringed worms, such as the fanworm, and the crustaceans, leading to insects and spiders. If one were asked to draw a hypothetical animal to bridge the gap between the ringed worms and the insects, one could not fail to draw something very like peripatus. Moreover, in its internal structure as well as its outward appearance, this animal looks like the forerunner of both millipedes and centipedes, and they in turn look like forerunners of modern in-

sects. We know from fossils that insects, millipedes and centipedes, in the form we know them today, were already in existence 400 million years ago, so any ancestors linking the two must have been in existence even earlier. It is of interest therefore to find there is a fossil *Xenusion* in the rocks of over 500 million years ago that looks almost the same as peripatus. It is little more than a rusty coloured stain in a piece of limestone rock, yet its shape and the structure of its body and legs can be seen clearly enough to leave little doubt that the peripatus living today and the *Xenusion* of 500 million or more years ago could be closely related. From it or from animals very like *Xenusion* began the line which, through numerous changes, led to the millipedes, centipedes and insects, while another line of descent was continued, almost unchanged, in peripatus.

Theory devastated

This represents the views held a few years ago. It reads almost like a scientist's dream, for everything falls so neatly into place. Then two things happened. First, fresh fossils have come to light from Australia, southwest Africa and England, which are clearly related to *Xenusion* but are much more complete. Together, this fresh evidence leaves little doubt that this supposed missing link between worms and insects was, in fact, a near relative of the sea pens, of the phylum Cnidaria, that are related to corals and jellyfishes.

The second event was hardly less devastating to the cherished idea that peripatus is a worm-insect, a bridge between the Annelida, and the Arthropoda (insects, spiders, crustaceans, millipedes and centipedes). Dr. Sidney Manton, the leading authority on the Onychophora, leaves us in no doubt that in its structure, mode of development from egg to adult and in its movements, peripatus is wholly arthropodan. Although it is undoubtedly primitive in many of its features, such as the simple head, the long series of similar limbs and, in certain features of its internal anatomy, peripatus is utterly unconnected with the ringed worms.

phylum	**Arthropoda**
class	**Onychophora**
genus & species	***Peripatus capensis*** **P. moseleyi,** *others*

Crayfish

The crayfish is a freshwater crustacean. It looks like a small lobster, 4 in. or more long, and coloured sandy yellow, green or dark brown. The head and thorax are covered with a single shell, or carapace, which ends in front in a sharp-pointed rostrum. Its eyes are compound and stalked. On its head is a pair of small antennules which are richly supplied with sense-organs, and a pair of long antennae, which are organs of touch. These have excretory organs at the base. The crayfish has a pair of strong jaws and two pairs of smaller accessory jaws, the maxillae. The second pair of maxillae drives water over 20 pairs of feathery gills on the bases of the thoracic limbs.

On the thorax there are three pairs of appendages, which are used to pass food to the jaws, a pair of stout pincers and four pairs of legs, which the crayfish uses to walk forward. The abdomen is divided into segments and has five pairs of limbs on its underside. The first pair are grooved in the males and are used to introduce sperm onto the female. The other four are swimmerets. The crayfish can swim speedily backwards with forward flicks of its abdomen, which ends in a fan-shaped tail. It does this to escape.

Preparing to carve: a freshwater crayfish about to feed off a male stickleback.

Crayfish in cooler waters

The two families of crayfish are confined almost entirely to temperate regions: the Astacidae in the northern hemisphere, the Parastacidae in the southern hemisphere. There are no crayfish in Africa, but they are present in Madagascar. There is none in the greater part of Asia, but they are found in Korea and the northern islands of Japan. The largest crayfish *Astacopsis franklinii* lives in Tasmania and may weigh up to 9 lb. Another large crayfish related to it is sold as Murray River Lobster in southeastern Australia. One of the Tasmanian crayfish, known as a land crab, habitually leaves the water and burrows in damp earth in forests. In the Mammoth Cave in Kentucky, in the United States, there are several crayfish living in the underground waters. They are colourless and blind; the eyes are gone, leaving only the stalks.

Naturalized aliens

Only one crayfish *Potamobius pallipes* is native to Britain. It is known as the white claw. A larger European crayfish *Astacus fluviatilis*, reared on farms especially in France, has been introduced into the Thames, and is known as the red claw. An American species, introduced into Germany, has become established there. The three species have similar habits. They live in rivers and lakes, especially those with hard water which contains the lime needed for their shell. They feed mainly at night, resting by day in burrows in the mud or under stones, but can sometimes be seen moving about by day.

They eat smaller aquatic animals such as insect larvae, snails, worms and tadpoles, and a small amount of plant food. In the Mississippi Valley they graze on rice during the night. This infuriates the local farmers who regard them as pests.

Unusual breeding habits

Crayfish mate in the autumn. The male turns the female over and sheds milt through the first pair of abdominal appendages onto her abdomen, where it sticks. The female then goes into a burrow to lay her hundred or so eggs. These become attached to bristles on her swimmerets where they are fertilised by contact with the milt. The eggs hatch the following spring. Unusual for a crustacean there is no larval stage. The newly-hatched crayfish are transparent, and tiny replicas of the adults. They remain attached for some time to the female's swimmerets, which they grasp with their claws.

Life and death in crayfish

In many parts of the world, crayfish are considered a delicacy. Sometimes they are eaten raw although this can prove to be hazardous, because crayfish carry a fluke larva. If this is swallowed with a crayfish it will migrate through the wall of the gut to the lungs, where it matures to the adult parasite. In time the adult lays eggs which are ejected with the sputum. From the eggs hatch first stage larvae which infest snails. The cycle of parasitic infection is completed if a snail is eaten by a crayfish.

One interesting aspect of the life of a crayfish is that it grows by periodic moults. This is common knowledge and is often stated in books on natural history. Most crustaceans and insects grow like this. But although it is always stated simply, the process itself is complex. In crayfish it takes place in four stages. First the calcium salts, the chalky matter in the old shell, are taken back into the blood, ready to be laid down again in the new shell being formed beneath the old one. Then the old shell, or such as remains of it, now merely a tough cuticle, is shed and the body takes up water and swells. Then the calcium salts are laid down in the new cuticle and this takes time to harden.

The moult of a crayfish takes 6 hours. During this time the crayfish fasts and stays in hiding. It is a very dangerous period for it; not only is it vulnerable especially to enemies, but it is also in danger from the many attendant difficulties of the process itself. It has only recently been realized, in fact, that many crayfish die during this complicated moulting process.

phylum	**Arthropoda**
class	**Crustacea**
order	**Decapoda**
families	**Astacidae** **Parastacidae**
genera & species	*Astacus fluviatilis* *Potamobius pallipes* others

Pastoral ant

The pastoral ants do not represent a natural classification but an ecological grouping of those species of ants which indulge in a form of husbandry. It has long been known that some species of ants regularly visit aphides, otherwise known as greenfly or blackfly, to take the honeydew from them. The story is so well known today that there must be few people who have not heard it. Yet, as we shall see later, it was once thought unbelievable. What is not so well known is that not only do ants 'milk' the aphides, much as we milk cows, but they tend, herd and shepherd them, much as livestock are cared for by human herdsmen. Moreover, other insects such as scale insects, leafhoppers and the caterpillars of many butterflies, are also used by ants because they give out either honeydew or some other sweet fluid. The caterpillars of these butterflies are taken into their nests by ants solely for the sake of the sweet fluid they give out. Here we shall deal with some of the more remarkable ways in which ants make sure of a continual supply of honeydew from aphides.

Honey farms

In aphid farms the ants shepherd the aphides to the more tender parts of the plant, so the improved 'pasture' results in the aphides giving a greater supply of honeydew. Some ants take honeydew only when they happen to come across aphides. In others, it is less haphazard and when the ant strokes an aphid with its antennae the aphid responds by increasing the flow of honeydew. Further, some aphides have a special structure, a sort of drinking vessel, into which the honeydew flows and from which the ant can drink. The link between the two insects is so close that if the aphides are threatened the ants will pick them up and carry them away to safety. Some ants, it is said, take the aphides into their underground nests for the night and bring them out again the following morning, placing them back on the leaves from which they were taken the previous evening.

Battery farming

It is not only green leaves that serve as pasture. There are ants which take aphides underground, excavating cavities for them, to feed on the sap in roots. Others build special shelters on the stems of plants which may be just roofs or may be complete 'stables', entirely enclosing the aphides. Various materials may be used; earth is made into a cement with saliva, chewed plant fibres make a form of paper, known as carton. This paper is manufactured in much the same way that wasps make their paper nests. The making of carton is a feature more especially of certain tree ants *Crematogaster*, which also use it for making brood chambers in their nests for their own eggs and larvae.

A big occasion—winged males and females of **Camponotus ligniperda** *engage in a nuptial dance surrounded by other members of the colony.*

Egg marketing

Some ants carry their pastoral activities a stage further. In the autumn aphides lay their eggs on the stems of shrubs. They remain there all winter, hatching the following spring. Not all the eggs survive because of the many predators, including some of the small insectivorous birds that are forever searching the crevices in the bark of trees and shrubs for anything edible. There are, however, some species of ants which in autumn, when the aphides are laying their eggs, carry these eggs down into deep underground nests, tending them throughout the winter. Then, when they hatch in the spring the ants carry the larvae up above ground and place them on plants to feed. They may place them first on one plant then on another as the spring succession of green shoots unfolds, so providing them with the best possible pastures.

Over-grazing

In spring the foliage of a climbing rose, a peach tree or other shrub or tree sometimes suddenly becomes infested with aphides. One day it is, to all intents clean, then two or three days later it is covered with these plant lice. In England, at least, it is not unusual to hear someone say: 'Look how the blight has struck this rose (peach or plum tree, as the case may be). It came in with the east wind (or the southwest wind, or whatever wind had been blowing).' These visitations are partly the results of the high rate of reproduction of the aphides, so one day they are too few to be noticeable, then 2—3 days later they are everywhere on the bush or shrub and the leaves are curling. In some instances, the original cause may be pastoral ants carrying the aphides and planting them there. This is especially true of young peach trees, and if we look carefully we shall see the ants streaming up and down the stem and along the branches, among the hordes of aphides.

The ant-aphid relationship may have begun by the ant mistaking the aphid's abdomen and back legs for the head and antennae of a fellow ant.

A North American ant *Lasius americana* is notorious for tending the aphid *Anuraphis maidi-ridicis*, which feeds on the roots of cotton and corn. The ant looks after the aphid eggs in winter and plants the young aphides on the crop in spring. But for the ants, the aphides in some places probably would not survive the winter, or would do so in such small numbers as to be negligible. As it is, the intervention of the ants can sometimes result in serious damage to the crop.

'Ant-cows'

Linnaeus, the Swedish botanist, 200 years ago named the aphides 'ant-cows' and spoke of ants milking them. A century later we find William Kirby and William Spence, in their famous *Introduction to Entomology*, speaking about this in curious terms. Having described the slave-making ants they say: 'That ants should have their *milch cattle* is as extraordinary as that they should have slaves. Here, perhaps, you may again feel a fit of incredulity shake you:—but the evidence for the fact I am now stating being abundant and satisfactory, I flatter myself it will not shake you long.' The subject was more fully studied later in the 19th century by Sir John Lubbock (later Lord Avebury) and the incredulous became fully accepted. Some writers have used the name dairying ants, others pastoral ants, and Alexander B and Elsie B Klots, in their *Living Insects of the World,* published in 1959, comment that no human could take more care of his domesticated stock than these ants do of their aphid 'cattle'.

phylum	**Arthropoda**
class	**Insecta**
order	**Hymenoptera**

Black widow

This name is given to a number of species of spiders widely distributed over the warmer parts of the world. The North American species **Latrodectus mactans** *is especially noted for its powerful venom, a reputation which is not fully justified. The female is about ½ in. long, a shiny velvety black with a red hour-glass mark on the underside of her almost spherical abdomen. The male is much smaller. The size and colour of the female has led to the alternative names which include shoe button spider, red mark, red back, jockey and also hour-glass spider. The more familiar name of black widow is based on her colour and on the reputation she has for eating her mate as soon as he has fertilised her. It seems possible that the strength of the venom varies with the species and the one inhabiting the southern United States seems to be the worst.*

△ *Black widow, sitting on its web with the feet touching the silken strands, waits for a victim (× 6).*

▽ *The spider begins to wrap and secure its victim by using quantities of silk from spinnerets (× 18).*

▽ *Often it is only at this stage that the victim is stabbed with the fangs and paralysed, then the back legs are skilfully used to enshroud almost completely the ant victim in the viscid silk (× 6).*

Painful but not fatal

The black widow spins a coarse irregularly designed web which often has a short funnel of silk, usually in the more elevated area. The male spins a similarly textured web but much smaller. Cool dark places are chosen, in cellars, outbuildings, ruined or abandoned houses, under doorsteps and porches, beneath floorboards or in piles of rubbish. Among the outbuildings must be included the primitive latrine where, it seems, most human victims have been attacked. Proportionately with the large numbers in which it exists the number of people who fall victim is surprisingly small. The known cases of injury or death in the United States for the 217 years between 1726 and 1943 are 1 291, only 55 of which are known to have been fatal. That is, one death in every 4 years and half a dozen injuries per year. Moreover, the evidence suggests that a high percentage of injuries have been sustained in rural areas where the plumbing is primitive, and even there the victims are mainly children or elderly or unwell people. Above all there seems a strong suggestion that when death does occur shock is a contributory factor if not the sole cause. Nevertheless, the non-fatal consequences are unpleasant enough. The poison is a neurotoxin which attacks the nerves to cause severe pain, muscular cramp, paralysis and hypertension. Fortunately the spider itself is retiring and more concerned with avoiding people than with attacking them. And only the females are troublesome as the male is too small to have enough venom to have any significant effect on humans.

With the exception of one family all spiders have poison glands. These lie in the cephalothorax, the smaller and front portion of the two parts that make up a spider's body, and the poison passes through slender ducts to the fangs. In all but a few spiders, the black widow being one, the venom is effective only against small animals such as insects. It is introduced into their bodies by a stabbing action rather than a bite since no jaw mechanism is involved, the mouthparts of a spider being capable only of sucking.

Paralysed victim enshrouded in silk

As with other web-weaving spiders the black widow sits on the web with her feet touching the silken strands. When an insect flies into the web and starts to struggle the vibrations are detected through the feet of the spider who immediately runs out, and by skilfully using her rear legs and quantities of the viscid silk from the spinnerets, quickly binds and secures it. Often it is only at this stage that the victim is stabbed with the fangs and paralysed, subsequently to be almost completely enshrouded in silk. Meanwhile a drop or two of saliva containing a protein-splitting ferment is exuded from the spider's mouthparts into the insect's body, the contents of which are therefore digested externally. This takes an hour or two, at the end of which the spider, by using its muscular stomach as a pump, sucks out the 'soup', leaving behind only the husk of its prey. This the spider finally cuts away and lets fall to the ground.

Pedipalp sperm reservoir

When adult, the male seeks a mate but before doing so he spins a very tiny web, rubs his abdomen against this and ejects on to it a drop of seminal fluid. This he then takes up in his pedipalps, a pair of specially adapted appendages situated near the mouth and resembling short legs. In mating the male merely transfers the sperm from the reservoir in the pedipalp to the female's body, only one mating being necessary for several bouts of egg-laying, since the female stores the sperm and uses it over a period, often of months. The eggs are laid in silken cocoons and the spiderlings hatching from them are, apart from colour, more or less replicas of the parents and independent from the start.

Self imposed widowhood

Almost everyone believes that the female spider invariably eats her spouse after mating. Even some of those who study spiders join in the chorus possibly after having occasionally seen this happen. This, it is said, is the reason for naming this most venomous spider the black widow. Certainly few people have ever sat down and watched hundreds of spiders mating to see whether the male is invariably eaten. Therefore this idea that the female always eats her spouse is based on this act of cannibalism being occasionally seen. There is, however, a more reasonable explanation. For example, we are told by one expert after another that when the male spider has transferred his sperm to a female he replenishes the reservoir in his pedipalps and will do so several times. This is consistent with the accepted and oft-repeated statement, that male spiders are polygamous—a polygamous male obviously cannot meet his death at each mating. The more likely explanation, and one consistent with the facts, is that after several matings the male becomes enfeebled, is indeed moribund, and then it is that the female devours him, as she would any similar small animal that came her way.

It is a fact that in the insect house at the London Zoo where black widows have been bred in large numbers for many years, individual male spiders have often been mated many times.

phylum	**Arthropoda**
class	**Arachnida**
order	**Araneae**
family	**Theridiidae**
genus & species	*Latrodectus mactans*

Black widow with her completed cocoon. On hatching the spiderlings, apart from colours, are more or less replicas of the parents and independent from the start. The name widow comes from the belief that the female eats the male after mating. This does happen, but only occasionally.

The Forerunners of Vertebrates

It is not possible to fix the point at which the original stock that gave rise to vertebrates left the main trunk of the evolutionary tree. Therefore the better method for tracing it is to work backwards from the most primitive of known vertebrates. These are the so-called jawless fishes or Agnatha, which includes the lampreys and their degenerate relatives the hagfishes.

The eel-like lamprey is limbless, has a row of gill-openings along each side of the forepart of the body and its body is supported by a backbone that is little more than a rod of cartilage surrounded by a membranous sheath. More important for our present discussion is its larva.

This is small, elongate and lacks the sucker-like mouth of the adult lamprey. Instead it has a sort of hood over the mouth and a mechanism for filtering fine particles of food. It is blind and shuns the light, and for up to seven years or more leads a burrowing life in the fine sand at the bottom of the river. The lamprey larva is so unlike the adult that it was once thought to represent a totally different kind of animal and was given the name of *Ammocoetes*.

Living in sand off the coast at various points throughout the world is an animal very like the ammocoete larva, in both structure and habits. This is called the lancelet, of the subphylum Cephalochordata, originally given the name *Amphioxus*, now changed to *Branchiostoma*. The lancelet is usually about 1½ in. long, though the largest species known is 3 ins. long and lives off the coast of California.

The lancelet has primitive eye-spots but is otherwise blind. It is a filter-feeder, has a spinal cord with a swelling at the front end which represents the forerunner of a true brain, and has a notochord similar to that of the ammocoete and, indeed, to the backbone of the adult lamprey. In most ways the lancelet resembles the ammocoete larva and clearly is of similar stock. It has, however, primitive features of its internal anatomy reminiscent of the invertebrates. For example, its excretory system is quite unlike that of vertebrates and like that of the flatworms. It therefore can be regarded reasonably as a first plank in the bridge between invertebrates and vertebrates.

The next plank, in descending order in the animal scale, is the subphylum Urochordata. This includes 3 000 species of sea squirts, salps and related forms. The adults of most species look like typical invertebrates of a low order. The sea squirts especially look like discoloured lumps of firm jelly. Much of the anatomy and physiology of the Urochordata is typical of that of invertebrates, and in particular of the Cnidaria. There is, however, a hollow main nerve cord, as in vertebrates, and a notochord in the tailed larva, usually called a tadpole from its shape.

The acorn worm, representing the subphylum Hemichordata, is worm-like but has gill-slits like those of the ammocoete. The blind diverticulum of the gut, once thought to represent a primitive notochord, is now regarded as nothing more than a finger-like extension of the gut. The position of the acorn worm is now highly problematic and can be said to offer little in the search for vertebrate ancestors.

The Pogonophora are even more problematic. They are currently regarded as representing a whole new phylum of over a hundred species of tube-dwelling, worm-like marine animals, often 500 times as long as they are broad. They have no mouth or gut, a well-developed heart and blood system, with haemoglobin, and an ill-developed dorsal nerve cord. The Pogonophora remained undiscovered until 1950 although, as is now known, they are very numerous on the seabed in several parts of the world. This is perhaps their most remarkable feature and it gives grounds for hoping that some day another animal discovered unexpectedly will provide a more solid clue to the ancestry of the vertebrates.

In this section dealing with the ancestry of the vertebrates are included the Echinodermata, a phylum which includes starfishes, sea urchins, brittlestars, sea cucumbers and sea lilies. Fifty years ago the position allotted to the echinoderms in the animal scale was below that of the ringed worms. Then they were elevated following the discovery that their physiology had much in common with that of vertebrates. Their larvae are similar to that of the acorn worms, so the echinoderms were placed near the protochordates. Now, it seems, second thoughts are tending to prevail.

Acorn worm

*The name for numerous similar animals of the subphylum **Hemichordata**. In its natural habitat an acorn worm appears as a bright orange or red 'acorn' sticking out of the surface of muddy or sandy shores. If this is carefully dug out a fragile, earthworm-like animal is revealed. Its length varies from 2 in. to 6 ft depending on the species.*

The 'acorn' is in fact the proboscis, which is attached to the body by a stalk. At the front of the body, surrounding the stalk, is a cylindrical collar. The mouth, which is covered by the collar, opens into a straight intestine running the length of the body. Behind the collar are two rows of gill slits that connect the intestine with the exterior. In the proboscis is a very simple heart that pumps blood first through a kidney then to the intestine and gills. There are no sense organs, only simple sensory cells in the skin.

Tunnel dwelling marine animal

Acorn worms are to be found from the shoreline to the depths of the sea, down to two miles or more. Most species live in U- or V-shaped tunnels in the sea bed, while others construct tubes of mud or sand particles glued together with slime. A few that live in deep water move freely over the bottom.

Movement is effected by the proboscis and the collar. These are water-filled bags surrounded by muscles which contract to elongate the proboscis and so force it forward. Then cilia—minute whip-like proto-plasmic hairs – drive water through openings in the walls of the proboscis and collar so that they swell up. This anchors the front end of the animal while the rest is dragged forward by muscular contraction. Acorn worms can also move over the sea bed propelled by the concerted beating of the cilia covering their bodies.

Mud for food

As the acorn worm moves around, sea water with mud and sand in suspension is forced into its mouth. The water is filtered out through the gill slits and the solid material is passed on down the gut where any organic matter is digested. The undigested sand is bound up in mucus and ejected from the terminal anus to form a 'worm cast' like that of the lugworm.

Some species of acorn worm also secrete slime over the body. The slime is swept towards the mouth by the cilia and picks up particles of organic matter on the way.

Tornaria larvae

The reproductive organs lie in pairs behind the gills. The eggs are laid either along the sides of the parent's tunnel or directly into the surrounding sea. Some species, living in deep or cold water, lay a few large eggs, rich in yolk, which develop almost directly into baby acorn worms. Others, in warm

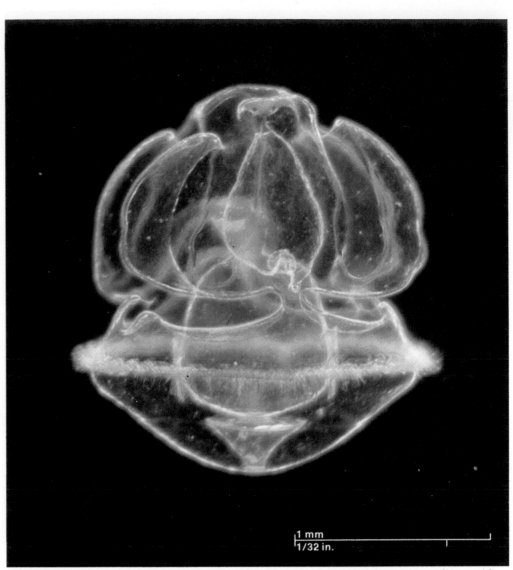

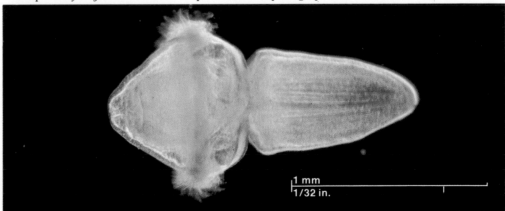

These unique pictures show how the minute acorn worm larva, swimming at the surface of the sea with its millions of tiny cilia, changes gradually into an adult (overleaf) which crawls on the sea bed. This is probably the first time the metamorphosis has been photographed.

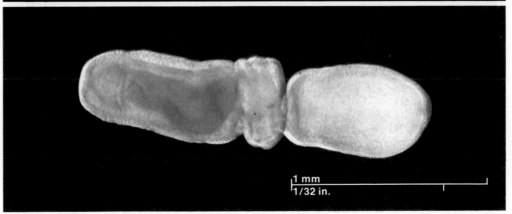

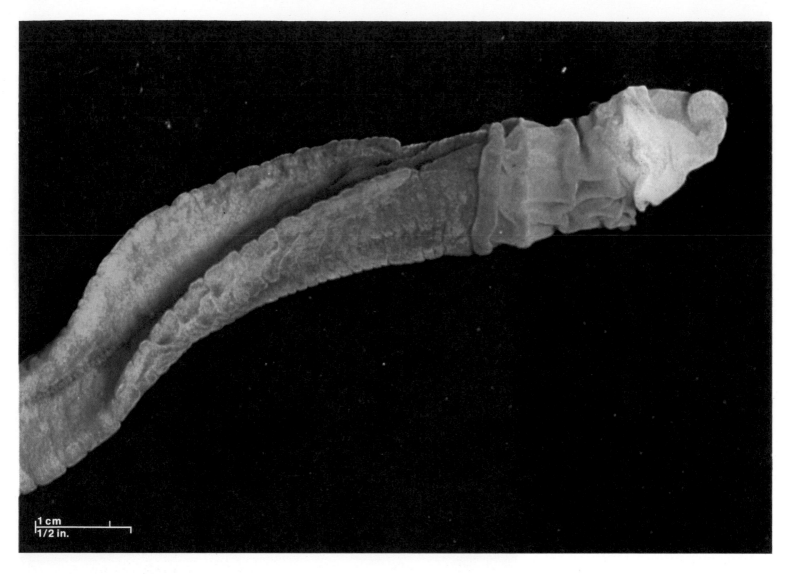

or shallow water, lay large numbers of small eggs with little yolk. These develop into larvae that swim around in the surface waters before settling to the bottom and becoming adult and worm-like. The larvae, called *tornaria,* have bands of cilia around the body which by their beating keep them from sinking and, as in the adults, sweep food into their mouths. As they grow larger more bands of cilia are developed; but eventually the larvae become too heavy even for these additional swimming organs and sink to the bottom to take up their adult way of life.

Spawning takes place in most species of acorn worm when the tide is out. The sexes are separate and as the breeding season approaches the gonads, producing either the eggs or the sperm, appear as a series of bulges along each side of the trunk behind the region of the gill slits. The eggs are laid first, in coiled masses covered in mucus in the shallow puddles left by the receding tide. These egg masses stimulate the male to shed sperm. After fertilisation the egg masses break up and the young larvae are dispersed by the returning tide.

Missing link found

Superficially acorn worms look very much like earthworms, but the internal structure of their bodies is of special interest. Certain features give acorn worms an apparent affinity with back-boned animals, the vertebrates, to which group man belongs. First

there is a stiffening rod, rather like a notochord, in the proboscis. A notochord is found in the early embryos of all vertebrates, and it is around this that the backbone is first laid down. The notochord is also found in primitive creatures such as the lancelet. The presence of this structure puts an animal in the phylum Chordata. Acorn worms, with only a short notochord, are put in the subphylum Hemichordata.

Other features which have been said to link acorn worms with the Chordata are the structure of the nervous system and the rows of gill slits. The latter are also found in the embryos of vertebrates.

On the other hand, acorn worms are also linked with certain groups of invertebrates. The larvae, the *tornaria,* are very similar to those of the sea cucumbers, relatives of the starfish and sea urchins. So these insignificant-looking worms could be an evolutionary link between the two main divisions of animals, the vertebrates and the starfish group of invertebrates.

Fisherman found the link

During the second half of the 19th century, when the scientific world was excited by the new Darwinian theory of evolution, it was realised that there was a deep gulf between the vertebrates and the invertebrates. So a search began for either a theory to explain or a missing link to bridge the gulf. The discovery of a number of animals, which scientists have now grouped together as the

A 1 ft long acorn worm which uses its acorn shaped proboscis and collar to burrow a U- or Y-shaped tunnel in the mud, lining it with mucus. It will usually hide by day, emerging at night to creep over the sea bottom.

Protochordata, provided the link.

One of the more important of these was the acorn worm. It was first discovered by a Neapolitan fisherman, ignorant of science, who found fragments of a strange animal in his net and took them to a zoologist in Naples who, after a careful study, was able to recognise that here possibly was one of the missing links.

Hidden seashore treasure

Shore-collecting had already become widespread following the pioneering efforts of Philip Henry Gosse in the 1850's, so it is surprising that a fisherman brought to light this unusual animal. There are several reasons for this. The acorn worms are pale and soft-bodied and even when fully exposed look not unlike, at first glance, one of the many different kinds of marine worms. For the most part the acorn worms remain within their burrows in the sand, with just the tip at most exposed. Normally they do not leave the burrow except at night. In addition their distribution is very patchy.

phylum	**Chordata**
subphylum	**Hemichordata**

Lancelet

A semi-transparent, elongated marine animal usually under 2½ in. long, the lancelet is shaped rather like a fish; it swims like a fish, too, by sideways undulations of its flattened body, which is pointed at each end. But it lacks the paired fins of a fish and—for other reasons—cannot qualify as a vertebrate. The various species are widely distributed in the seas throughout the world. On the coast of Amoy, China, 35 tons of lancelets are harvested for food each year.

*Lancelets are found in tropical and temperate seas, generally close to the shore. Originally they were given the scientific name **Amphioxus**, which means 'sharp at both ends', but this has now been changed to **Branchiostoma** for reasons given at the end of this article, and amphioxus, the anglicised form of the scientific name, is now used as an alternative common name, especially in biological laboratories.*

Taking evasive action

Most of the time, the lancelet lies with its hind end buried in sand or gravel, the head pointing more or less vertically upwards above the surface. The beating of cilia around its mouth creates a current drawing water in through the mouth and thence through a sort of sieve, known as the branchial basket, in the front half of the body. The water passes through the sieve and out through a pore near the middle of the body, on the underside. When disturbed, the lancelet leaves the sand, zig-zags rapidly around in the water above and then dives back into the sand a few seconds later.

Curtains of food

The branchial basket is an elongated oval in shape with vertical slits on either side. It serves as a set of gills for taking oxygen from the water flowing through it, and also for capturing food. Along the floor of the basket is a groove known as the endostyle. This constantly secretes mucus that is carried up the internal sides of the branchial basket by the beating of cilia lining the walls, in a kind of curtain. This curtain of mucus contains many minute gaps through which water can flow through the gill slits and so to the outside. Food particles, such as diatoms, are, however, trapped on the inside of the mucus curtain which continues to be driven upwards by the cilia until it reaches another longitudinal groove in the roof of the basket. There another set of cilia drive the mucus backward into the stomach where it is digested.

Lopsided larvae

The lancelet lives 1—4 years, varying with the species. The eggs and sperm of the lancelet are released into the sea to be fertilised. About 8 hours after the egg is fertilised a ciliated embryo has been formed which swims about and then changes into an elongated, lopsided larva. This eventually develops into the adult. The lopsided larvae is ⅓—⅔ in. long but sometimes it grows much larger than this and becomes sexually mature without changing into an adult. This process is called neoteny. These giant larvae of the lancelet were once regarded as a separate species and given the name *Amphioxides*.

Vertebrate/invertebrate?

In 1774 a strange little animal was picked up on the coast of Cornwall and sent, preserved in alcohol, to the celebrated Russian naturalist, Pallas. There seems to be no record of who picked it up or why it was sent right across Europe when there were many competent naturalists in Britain who might have examined it. At all events, Pallas described it in a footnote in a book he was publishing, giving a very brief description in Latin and naming the animal *Limax lanceolatus* under the impression that it was a slug. Half a century later, on December 21, 1831, Jonathan Couch, one of the leading English naturalists of that time, was walking along the shore near Polperro, in Cornwall, after a storm. It is the practice of some naturalists to go beachcombing after a storm to see what specimens may have been thrown ashore. Apparently Couch turned over a flat pebble lying on the sand about 50 feet from the ebbing tide and saw a tiny tail sticking out of the sand. He dug out the rest of the animal and was able to watch it in a sea-water aquarium and see how active it was. Couch sent the specimen to William Yarrell (the English zoologist) who in 1836 described it in a book *A History of British Fishes* as a fish of very low organisation to which he gave the name *Amphioxus*. He also recognised it as the same animal that Pallas had looked at. Previously, however, in 1834, the Italian naturalist Costa had published a description of the same animal collected from the shore at Naples and had given it the name *Branchiostoma lubricum*. This brief history accounts for the changing of the animal's name. It had become generally known as *Amphioxus* because Costa's description had been overlooked and was not brought to light until 45 years ago. The international rules of nomenclature state that the first name proposed for an animal must be the one used even if it has been overlooked for years. So the name given by Costa had to take precedence over Yarrell's *Amphioxus*.

The relationship of the lancelet with the rest of the animal kingdom remains one of the most interesting features of the animal. Amphioxus resembles the vertebrates in having a dorsal nerve cord lying above a stiffening rod, the notochord, and an arrangement of muscles along its tail much as in a fish. At the same time it lacks a backbone, jaws, or indeed any bone, and a brain as well as the eyes and other sense-organs associated with the brain. So it is not a vertebrate, yet comes very near to being one. The current view is that both amphioxus and the vertebrates evolved from the same ancestors as the sea-squirts or tunicates, which feed in much the same way as amphioxus but are anchored to a solid support when adult and look most unlike amphioxus. They do, however, have a free-swimming tadpole-like larva. If this were to become sexually mature without taking on the sessile adult form, like the 'amphioxides' larva, then we should have something like both the ancestral amphioxus and the ancestral vertebrate.

phylum	Chordata
subphylum	Cephalochordata
family	Branchiostomidae
genus & species	*Branchiostoma lanceolatum* *B. californiense* others

Heads upwards, a pair of lancelets sift the water for food. The fish-like muscle blocks can be seen along the body. The squares showing through the skin of the belly are reproductive organs.

Pogonophore

The name of these marine animals means literally 'beard-bearers', and if the name sounds mildly ridiculous, this is in keeping with the whole history of the group. The pogonophores represent a branch of the animal kingdom that was completely unknown until 1914, and which attracted little attention even among marine zoologists until little more than 15 years ago. Yet they seem now to be the most widespread and abundant sea animals.

The 100 or more known species of pogonophores are worm-like and extremely slender; a 5in. individual being ⅒ in. thick. Most are a few inches long; the largest is just over a foot. Each lives in a transparent horny tube little wider than itself, but five times as long, which has ring-like markings at intervals along its length. The animal itself is made of different sections, each having a slightly different shape. In front is a long tentacle or tentacles—there may be as many as 200 or more in some species—fringed with pinnules. At the rear end are spines, or short bristles, like those on the bodies of earthworms and marine bristleworms. They probably help the animal to move up and down inside its tube. No mouth or other special organs have yet been identified.

These animals have now been found in all oceans, mainly at great depths, down to 25 000 ft, but in recent years some have been discovered in shallower water.

Mystery tube-dwellers

Dredged up and kept alive for only a few hours, living pogonophores are difficult to observe. Their way of life has to be deduced from what can be seen in the dead animal. They live only where the seabed is fine mud, and seem to spend most of their time inside semi-permeable tubes, through which water can pass. This may be important to the animal inside the tube because incoming water would bring oxygen for breathing. Studies at very high magnification with electron microscopes have shown a complicated body structure, including a nerve network and blood vessels containing red blood with haemoglobin. No digestive organs have been seen. The nearest thing they have to a brain is a group of nerve cells, the ganglionic mass. Tests made with living pogonophores showed that they reacted only slightly to being touched.

A question of feeding

There has been much speculation about the way pogonophores feed, as to whether they take particles of food from the water by gripping them with the pinnules on the tentacles or whether the pinnules give out a sticky secretion to which the particles adhere. Another suggestion has been that the tentacles may sweep the surface of the mud for particles. Where there are many tentacles they form tubes or complicated spirals, and it is believed food may be caught and digested in these, as in a sort of external stomach. These tentacles may also secrete fluids which digest the food externally, the food then being absorbed through the skin. The most favoured view is that these animals absorb nutrients dissolved in the seawater through their skin, but all these suggestions are no more than inspired guesses.

▷ *The single tentacle of* **Siboglinum** *often coils up into this helical shape. Along its length is a double row of fine unicellular pinnules.*

▽ *A rare photograph of the recently discovered species* **Oligobrachia ivanovi** *from the north east Atlantic. This large pogonophore is seen partly removed from its tube, its seven tentacles coiled up into an orange mass (× 10).*

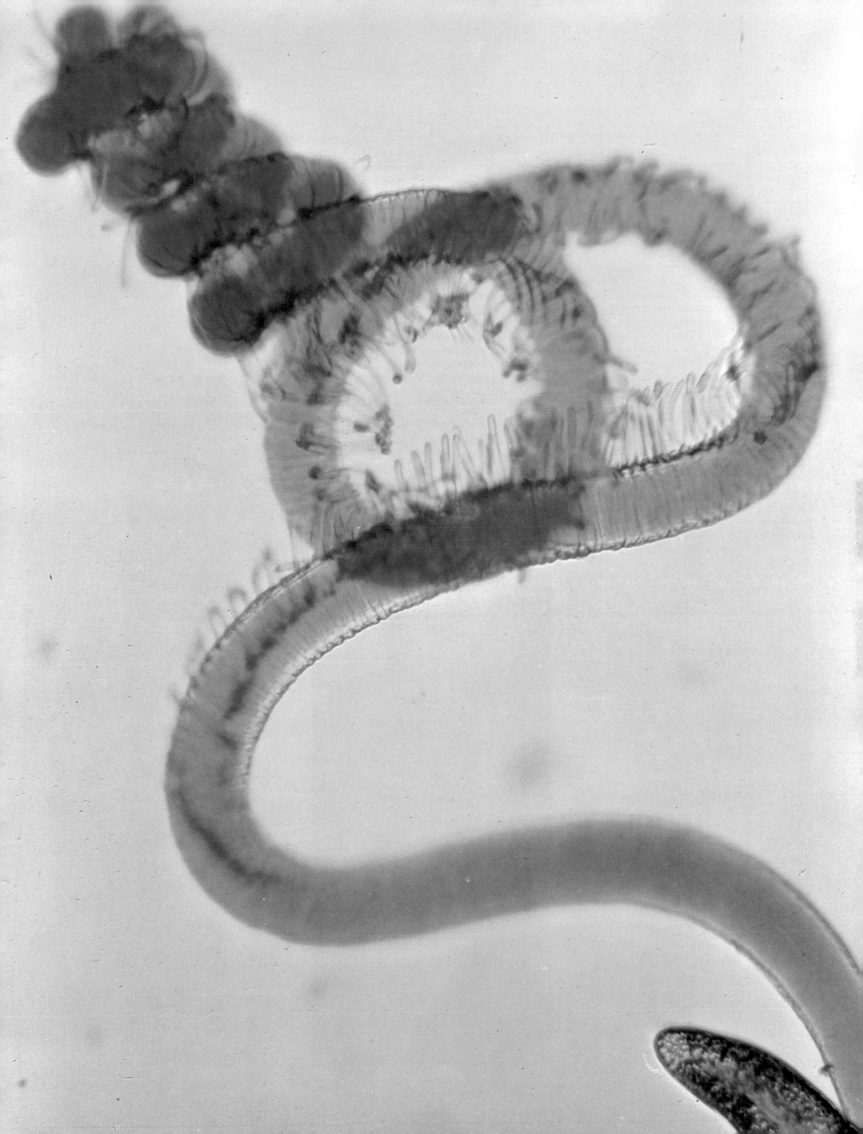

Unknown breeding habits

Some pogonophores that have been examined have contained large yolky eggs, others have had sperms enclosed in capsules, or spermatophores. There is nothing to show whether the sperms are merely liberated into the sea to find their way to ova in other individuals, or whether pogonophores join together in some simple form of mating. Estimates have been made of how densely they live. These vary from 50 to 500 per sq yd, but even the more densely crowded would have difficulty in contacting each other. The most reasonable assumption seems to be that the sperms are liberated into the sea, yet the fact that they are in a capsule, would suggest that the male places them on the female, or in her tube. Embryos and larvae have been found in some of the tubes. The embryos are rounded, with two girdles of cilia around the front and the rear ends. As the cilia beat in a wave-like action the embryo slowly revolves on its axis. Later, the embryo grows longer, into what may be called a larva, in which the future hair-like adult pogonophore is foreshadowed.

The youngest phylum

The very existence of the phylum Pogonophore was entirely unknown and wholly unsuspected until 1914, when specimens were examined by the French zoologist Professor M Caullery. These had been collected by the Dutch research ship *Siboga* dredging in the seas of the Malay Archipelago. He worked on them from 1914 to 1944 but was unable to find any relationship between them and other animals. He named them *Siboglinum* after the Dutch ship, *linum* being Latin for flax or linen thread. Then, in 1933, more were dredged up in the Pacific, and the view began to be taken that they were degenerate bristleworms. Soviet research ships began to find large numbers of pogonophores in the Sea of Okhotsk and later in the Indian Ocean, Antarctic and Atlantic Oceans. The Russian zoologist AV Ivanov decided, in 1955, that they represented a new phylum, which he named the Pogonophora. In plain terms an entirely new section of the animal world had been discovered.

The pogonophores have been described as looking like threads, like bits of string, or like trawl twine—or even contemptuously as looking like chewed string! We know now that research ships at sea had been finding masses of these tangled threads in their dredges. They cluttered the decks when the dredges were emptied onto them and on a British research ship they were given the name of the Gubbinidae—and shovelled back into the sea ('gubbins' is a slang name, often used by scientists, for unidentifiable 'insignificant' rubbish!). This alone shows how abundant they are on the ocean bed. It also shows why nobody took any notice of them; they looked like fibrous rubbish.

There is a great deal yet to be learned about the pogonophores. Some of it may shed light on the evolutionary history of the vertebrates. The current opinion is that they are most closely related to the supposed forerunners of the vertebrates, such as the acorn worm (page 29).

phylum	**Pogonophora**
order	**Athecanephria**
order	**Thecanephria**

Ancestral pogonophore—the tapering tube of the fossil **Hyolithellus**, *buried over 500 million years ago in Cambrian rocks in Greenland. The indentation above the tube probably marks the position of the animal when feeding (× 8).*

A developing ciliated embryo of **Siboglinum** *removed from its mother's tube. There is a broad ciliated band on the protosoma below the apical cone, and another smaller band at the end of the body on the metasoma (arrowed) (× 160).*

Tree-like tube of **Polybrachia**, *this middle section has membranous frills. Like many small pogonophores it has ring markings and is divided into segments. The rigid tube is composed of chitin and proteins (× 5).*

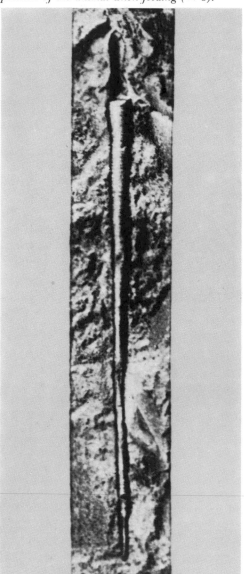

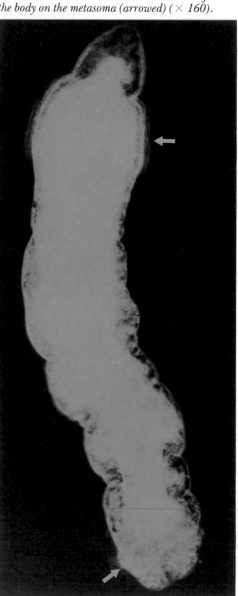

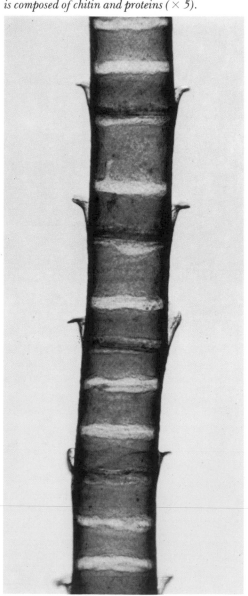

Salp

*Salps are barrel-shaped, transparent animals living in the plankton. They are very simple in form, with an extraordinary plant-like method of reproduction. They are one of a group of animals that are thought to be a link between vertebrates and invertebrates. Others are the acorn-worm (page 29) and the lancelet (page 31). The scientific name **Salpa** has been adopted as the common name. Salps float at or near the surface. The transparent jelly-like body, ranging from less than an inch to 4 in. long, has muscle bands forming irregular or partial hoops round the body, somewhat like the hoops of a barrel. By the alternate contraction and relaxation of these bands the barrel-shaped body pulsates like a heart. Water is drawn in through an opening at one end and is driven out through an opening at the other. This current brings food and oxygen at the front and creates a sort of feeble jet-propulsion at the rear.*

Salps are usually found well away from land, on the high seas, especially in the warmer waters of the world.

Curtain feeding
The internal organs of a salp are simple. The gills are little better than large openings in the gullet, the digestive tract little more than a simple tube, and the nervous system merely a knot of nerve cells with slender nerve fibres leading away from it. There are no special sense organs. A salp feeds on small particles in the water which are trapped in a curtain of mucus, like an irregular spider's web, that is continually drawn up from the floor of the gullet.

Alternation of generations
Salps are found in two forms, one solitary, the other in aggregation in which several individuals are linked together. The first is asexual, the second is sexual, and because these two regularly alternate there is said to be an alternation of generations. The sexual salp is hermaphrodite, carrying both eggs and sperms, but as these do not ripen at the same time, a salp is not self-fertile and its eggs must be fertilised by sperms from another salp. There are only 1–3 eggs at a time, connected to the mother by a kind of placenta through which they are nourished. When these eggs have grown into new small salps they break away from the mother and become solitary. The solitary salp grows a sort of tail on its underside, in line with the body. A chain of new individuals which forms the aggregate or sexual generation buds off from this.

Complicated reproduction
A close relative of the salps, which looks very like them, is *Doliolum*, another barrel-shaped jelly-like animal. Its muscle bands are more regular so they look even more like hoops on a barrel, and its way of life is essentially the same as in the salps except for its method of asexual reproduction, which is remarkably complicated. It begins

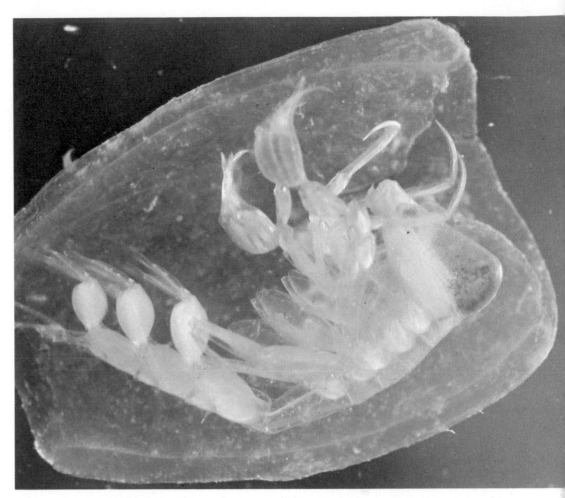

*Having eaten the internal organs of this urochordate, the shrimp **Phronima sedentaria** floats about luxuriously inside the empty barrel.*

with buds appearing on the underside of the barrel. The buds then creep up the sides of the barrel in a continuous procession, because as fast as one bud moves away a new bud appears in its place. The procession makes its way to a small fin-like tail at the rear of the parent body, and from there the buds creep onto a long continually growing tail which sprouts from the hind end of the barrel. The never-ending stream of buds settles on this long tail in three rows, one on top and one on each side of the tail. Each bud in the top row grows a stalk and new buds settle on these stalks. The buds in the side row start to feed and they supply food for all the other buds as well as the parent body, which now becomes no more than a vehicle towing a chain of multitudinous progeny.

The sequence is broken when the buds in the top row break away and become, like the parent, vehicles for towing rows of developing buds. At the same time the buds on the 'tails' of these new individuals multiply by further budding, but these new buds break loose, swim away and become sexually mature, producing ova and sperms. They form the sexual generation. The ova and sperms are later shed into the sea and from each fertilised egg hatches a tadpole-like larva that turns into an asexual barrel with its procession of buds, and the cycle begins all over again. It is not surprising that in places the sea is crowded with *Doliolum*. For other examples of such prolific asexual reproduction we have to turn to the plant kingdom.

Shrimp predator
Little is known about the enemies of the salps or its relatives like *Doliolum*. We know that a number of animals such as turtles, the ocean sunfish and others feed on jelly-fishes, in spite of their stinging cells, and it seems fair to assume they also eat the jelly-like salps that have no stings. There is, however, one predator on these barrel-shaped 'jellyfishes' that deserves special mention. This is a shrimp, *Phronima*, which also preys on the salp's relative pyrosoma or 'firebody'. It is an inch or so long with large compound eyes and exceptionally big claws. It enters the barrel and eats all the internal organs while using the barrel as a kind of luxury coach in which to travel. The female shrimp, having scraped out the transparent barrel then lays her eggs in it. Then she pushes this adopted brood chamber in front of her rather like a baby carriage, until the eggs are ready to hatch out and the larvae eventually swim away.

phylum	**Chordata**
subphylum	**Urochordata**
class	**Thaliacea**
order	**Salpida**
genus	*Salpa*
order	**Doliolida**
genus	*Doliolum*

Sea cucumber

In spite of their name sea cucumbers are animals, related to starfishes and sea urchins. Aristotle, the Greek scholar, first gave them the name over 2 000 years ago. Many of them look like cucumbers; but a few of the 1 000 species have extremely bizarre shapes indeed.

As with their relatives, the starfishes, the parts of the body are in fives or multiples of five. At the front end surrounding the mouth is a crown of tentacles: usually 10 or 20 but sometimes up to 30. The long almost cylindrical body of a typical sea cucumber may be slightly flattened underneath. It has five longitudinal ambulacral areas, each containing two or more rows of tube-feet. Often the tube-feet are scattered over three of these grooves on the underside and are used for creeping over the bottom. The tube-feet on the upper side, running along the back, are small, fewer in number, and are often degenerate. In a few species the tube-feet have been lost altogether.

Most sea cucumbers are several inches to a foot long but a few are several feet long. They are mainly uniformly coloured, occasionally paler on the underside, sometimes with darker markings. The colours are usually greys, browns, black or some shade of purple, rarely red or orange, but some small burrowing forms may be pink or violet.

There are five orders differing mainly in the shape of their tentacles and tube-feet. Sea cucumbers are found in all seas usually at depths of less than 600 ft, but a few live at greater depths down to 33 000 ft. A few species may be found at times on the shore at extreme low spring tides.

Shapes for all situations

Sea cucumbers creep about, mainly over sandy bottoms, some burrow in sand. Some of the latter have the two ends of the body upturned so that the animal is permanently U-shaped. This leaves the mouth and tentacles at the surface for feeding and the hindend at the surface for voiding waste. Some burrowing forms have a long 'tail' that curves up to the surface for getting rid of waste. One sea cucumber *Thyone* buries only the middle part of its body, and takes several hours to do so, whereas others, using more conventional methods, such as entering the sand headfirst, disappear from sight in a few minutes.

The sea cucumber *Rhopalodina* departs radically from the usual shape in having a bulbous body and both mouth and anus at the end of a long stalk, which may be three or four times the length of the body. Some sea cucumbers are flattened with spine-like processes around the margins of the body, looking in outline like a pressed holly leaf. *Psolus diomediae* looks more like a large slug. Nearly all sea cucumbers live on the seabed but one species *Galatheathuria aspera* is flattened and swims freely in the sea. Another *Pelagothuria natatrix* is shaped like an octopus with a dozen arms, and probably swims about near the surface. At the other extreme is the extraordinary deep-sea *Scotoplanes globosa* with a rounded, oval

body, almost like a giant tick, and with two pairs of bent 'fingers', one pair pointing forwards, the other pointing backwards.

Light anchors

Most sea cucumbers move over the seabed using the ventral tube-feet in each of the three lowermost ambulacral areas. Some have no tube-feet and these drive themselves along by muscular contraction and expansion of the body somewhat like an earthworm. To aid this movement they may grip the bottom with the tentacles and use the spicules in their skin. These are microscopic calcareous rods and plates, often having delightful shapes. The rods may be branched or they may form anchors, the plates may be perforated or form wheels, baskets or tables. Many of the spicules make the skin rough, giving it a grip on the sea-bed. A sea cucumber 3 in. long may have up to 20 million spicules in its skin.

Sticky tentacles

Sea cucumbers feed on small plants and animals or on detritus, that is small particles from the breakdown of dead plants and animals. A common European species *Cucu-* *maria saxicola* lives in burrows in rocks made by other animals and stretches out its tentacles into the water to feed. The tentacles are slimy and small floating plants and animals get stuck on them. Each tentacle is then bent back to the mouth in turn and the trapped food is licked, as we might lick jam from our fingers. Other sea cucumbers, such as *Holothuria*, with only short tentacles use them to scoop sand and mud into the mouth. The burrowing sea cucumbers simply swallow sand or mud as they plough through it, digesting any edible matter it contains and voiding the rest. Studies of sea cucumbers living on coral reefs have shown there may be 2 000 to the acre; between them they pass 60 tons of sand through their bodies each year.

Free-swimming larvae

Most sea cucumbers shed their eggs and sperms into the water where the eggs are fertilised and develop into free-swimming larvae known as auriculariae. The auricularia is semi-transparent, almost jelly-like, with an irregular shape as if much folded, and it has a number of lobes or arms with a simple gut at the centre. Around the margins of the body and arms is a continuous band of cilia which drive the larva through the water. Later the arms are withdrawn giving the body a barrel shape and the cilia form bands like barrel-hoops around it. Then the bilaterally symmetrical larva, instead of swimming straight forward, spins like a top. After a while the larva sinks to the bottom, five tentacles grow out, the symmetry taking on some radial features, and becomes a small sea cucumber.

Some female sea cucumbers carry their eggs each in a separate pocket along the back; others have larger pouches with several eggs in each, the eggs being pushed into the pockets or the pouches by the tentacles. There are a few species in which the females incubate their eggs inside the body, and one species that carries the eggs in special pockets in the stomach.

▽ *Sandwiched between two corals, the sea cucumber* **Stichopus variegatus**. *Although eaten in the Far East and Australia it is only second class food because its body contains limy spicules. Others are prized for their succulent flesh and are eaten raw or boiled then dried.*

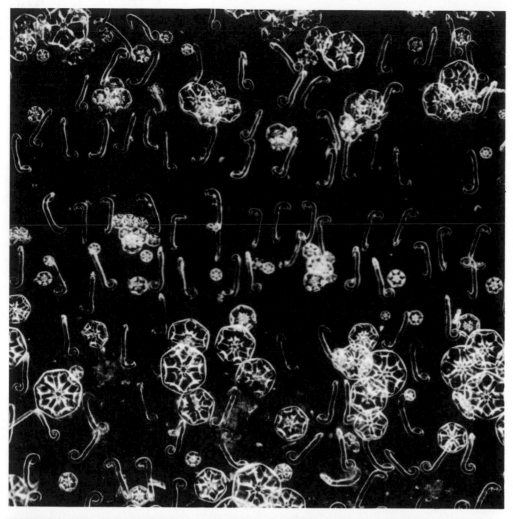

Battery of defences

The main enemies of sea cucumbers are probably starfishes, although they are also eaten by bottom-feeding fishes. They have, however, several ways of protecting themselves as well as having tough, slippery skins. Some give out a poison. Others can squirt out sticky white threads through the anus, and one species *Holothuria forskali* is known to fishermen as the cotton spinner because of this habit. The threads are slender tubes branching from the gut. They entangle the animal attacking the sea cucumber and once used they cannot be drawn in again. The sea cucumber merely grows a new set. Some sea cucumbers throw out the whole of their internal organs at an attacker, and grow a new set. In spite of these unpleasant qualities the larger sea cucumbers are caught in the Far East and off the coasts of northwest Australia and eaten raw, or else boiled and dried and later eaten, as *trepang* or *bêche de mer*.

Cucumbers as homes

A notable animal partnership is that between sea cucumbers and pearlfishes. These are not the only animals to use the cucumbers as homes. Several peculiar kinds of bivalve molluscs live permanently in the intestine of some species of sea cucumbers and there is a bivalve *Devonia semperi*, living in the seas around Japan, in which the foot forms a suction cup and the mollusc, using this, clings to the surface of a sea cucumber as a hitch-hiker. Around Japan also there is a sea snail that has literally carried parasitism to enormous lengths. It has no shell, or internal organs except those for reproduction, and it takes nourishment direct from its host. Its name is *Parenteroxenos dogieli* and it lives inside *Cucumaria japonica*. It is worm-like, much coiled, and when stretched to full length measures 4 ft against the 4 in. of its host.

phylum	**Echinodermata**
class	**Holothuroidea**

△◁ *Hooks and diadems—calcareous spicules from the skin of* **Taemogyrus allani** *(×70).*
◁ *Defending itself,* **Holothuria forskali** *squirts sticky white threads from its anus.*
▽ *Diagram to show pentagonal symmetry in different members of the echinoderm group, the position being stylised.*
▷ *A sea cucumber with a crown of blue tentacles, a bright Great Barrier Reef member.*

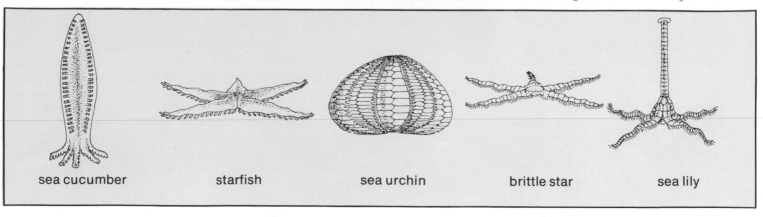

| sea cucumber | starfish | sea urchin | brittle star | sea lily |

Sea lily

Of all animal survivors from the past probably none has a greater claim than the sea lily to being called the fossil that came to life. It has other claims on our attention as well, for although related to starfishes, sea urchins and sea cucumbers, and decidedly animal in every way, it is very plant-like in shape. In a typical sea lily the body is at the top of a long slender stalk. At the bottom of the stalk in some species the rooting processes, which anchor the sea lily to the bottom, are slender and branching, looking uncommonly like the roots of a land plant. The body itself is small and bears five arms each of which has a row of pinnules so that the sea lily looks more like a miniature palm tree than an animal. In some species the arms are much branched, each branch having its rows of pinnules. In others the stalk is plain, while in yet others it carries throughout its length many tentacle-like processes, known as cirri, the use of which is unknown. The colours of sea lilies are mainly yellow, pink and red. The smallest sea lily living today is only 1½ in. high and the largest is not much more than 2 ft high, but fossil sea lilies were sometimes as much as 70 ft high.

The closest relatives of sea lilies are the feather stars, which are found mainly in shallow seas. In contrast sea lilies are found in most oceans but rarely in waters of less than 600 ft depth. They are most numerous at depths of 3 600 ft and some are found as deep as 27 000 ft.

Bodies mainly chalk

Although there are few fossils in rocks earlier than the beginning of the Cambrian period, which began 600 million years ago, at the start of that period there are many remains of sea lilies. From then on, down through the geological ages, they continued to be numerous, so much so that in some places in the world the limestone rocks are largely made up of their skeletons. Usually these are broken up but many fine fossils have been collected of sea lilies in an almost perfect state of preservation so even the fine details can be studied.

The sea lilies living today are, like their remote ancestors, almost 90% chalk, which makes their alternative name of stone lilies particularly apt. The stalk is made up of joints made of calcium carbonate which look almost like simple vertebrae, although sea lilies are invertebrates, that is, animals without backbones. The resemblance to higher animals is, however, only superficial. The small body is strengthened with chalky plates and the arms and their branches have a skeleton of smaller, vertebra-like joints, running through their centres. The living tissue makes up only a small percentage of the total bulk of the animal, and the internal organs, although so small, are similar to those of a starfish. Like the starfish, the

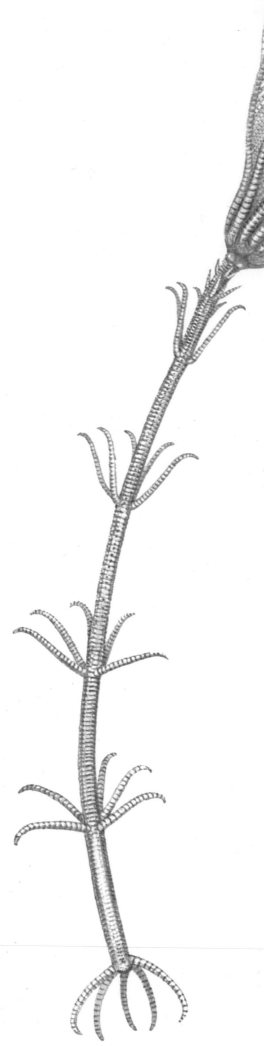

*The sea lily **Annachrinus wyville-thomsoni** consists of a stalk at the top of which is the theca or cup with branching arms covered with pinnules.*

sea lily also has nerves and muscles. This can be appreciated from the words of Louis Agassiz, the famous American oceanographer, who was probably the first to watch a living sea lily brought up from the depths. 'When disturbed the pinnules of the arms first contract, the arms straighten themselves out, and the whole gradually and slowly closes up. It was a very impressive sight for me to watch the movement of the creature, for it not only told of its own ways, but at the same time afforded a glimpse into the countless ages of the past, when these crinoids, so rare, and so rarely seen today, formed a prominent feature of the animal kingdom.'

Sensitive to change

One reason why we know so little about the way of life of sea lilies is that they are deep-sea animals, so that we cannot make direct observations of them. On the rare occasions that living specimens are brought in, they last very little time in aquaria. Unless conditions are absolutely right, and are kept that way, the sea lilies die. The slightest upset makes them break up, and it is probably because they are so sensitive to the slightest change or disturbance in the water that they do not live at depths where there is any turbulence. Probably the only thing we know about their natural history with any certainty is the way they feed. Even this is more by deduction than direct knowledge. The arms are grooved and lined with cilia. We can imagine the sea lily, spreading its arms and pinnules to form a sort of net which catches small dead animals and plants or particles from the decaying bodies of small animals slowly raining down from the surface waters above. These, trapped in the grooves, are passed onto the mouth by the cilia. Although it is a meagre living, sea lilies do not have a lot of tissue to feed.

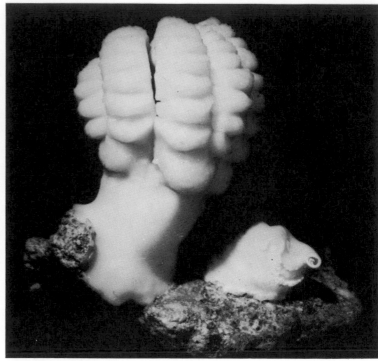

△ *The feather star* **Antedon bifida** *viewed from below. The five forked arms, making a total of ten, are jointed and have grooves lined with cilia which sweep the food towards the mouth.*

△ *Complete contrast to the slender sea lily opposite: the squat* **Holopus.**
▽ *The sea lily is often referred to as the fossil that came to life. This fossil, from the Silurian, means it is about 420 million years old.*

Sensational discovery

For a long time it was thought that the sea lilies were extinct. Even when the first living specimens were found they were thought to be rare until the ocean-going research cruisers, following the voyage of the *Challenger,* began to haul their dredges up filled with sea lilies. The USS *Albatross,* for example, made a haul on one occasion of 3 tons of sea lilies in one sweep of the dredge. A later American expedition organized especially to search for them, in the early years of this century, found such forests of them in the ocean depths of the Pacific that at one time the decks of the ship were piled high with sea lilies. The first sea lily found was in 1755 in deep water off Martinique, in the Caribbean. It was sent to France and in 1761 was exhibited before the French Academy of Science as the *Palma marina,* or sea palm. The second specimen was brought up from deep water off Barbados a few years later. This was exhibited before the Royal Society in London. Not for a hundred years did another come to light, when one was dredged up from deep water off the Lofoten Islands, off Norway. This really made European scientists sit up and take notice. It caused as great a stir as did the coelacanth fish (page 56) 70 years later.

phylum	**Echinodermata**
class	**Crinoidea**
order	**Articulata**
genera	***Holopus, Metacrinus, Rhizocrinus*** *others*

41

Sea squirt

Sea squirts live in the sea, always permanently fixed, and when touched they
contract, suddenly squirting out two long
thin jets of water. Some sea squirts are
solitary, others live in clusters, and there
is a third group that lives in colonies. In all
the body is enclosed in a firm jellylike coat or
tunic, from which they also derive the name
tunicates. The two jets of water we see when
we touch a sea squirt are ejected through
two openings, one at the top of the animal,
the inhalant opening, the other on its side,
the exhalant opening. So long as the animal
is not disturbed water is drawn in by the
beating cilia through the inhalant opening,
bringing food and oxygen, and it is driven
out through the exhalant opening, carrying
away waste products.

Inside the tunic are the vital organs. The
inhalant current is drawn into a capacious
gullet which leads into a short intestine that
ends near the exhalant opening. Except for
one side of the gullet these organs lie free in a
body cavity, the atrium. The walls of the
atrium form a muscular layer known as the
mantle, which is enclosed by the jellylike
tunic. The walls of the gullet are perforated
by a thousand or more small vertical slits
arranged in rows. Fine blood vessels run
through the bars separating these slits, so the
walls of the gullet act as gills. The bars are
coated with cilia which, by their concerted
beating, set up a current drawing water in
through the inhalant opening and driving
it through all the slits. Lying in the atrium
is a simple heart from which blood vessels
run to the various organs. Those going
to the wall of the gullet break up into a
fine network to run through the numerous
bars separating the gill slits. A small knot of
nerve cells, the nerve ganglion, lies in the
mantle between the inhalant and exhalant
openings, and serves as a brain. A few simple
nerves run from this ganglion, and except
for the reproductive organs there are few
other organs, and those which are there are
simple in structure.

▷ A galaxy of sea squirts. **Botryllus schlosseri**
forms beautiful encrustations on rocks often
exposed at low tide. It is a colonial form,
each star being composed of from three to
twelve individuals which have a common
exhalant aperture at the centre. The whole
colony is enclosed in a jelly-like tunic, and is
found in a variety of colours. Coiled white tubes
of the worm **Spirorbis** and the red encrusting
alga **Lithothamnion** add to this picture.

Fouling buoys and ships

Sea squirts are found in all seas, from between tidemarks, where they can be numerous on pier piles, to the depths of the ocean. The solitary forms hang from the undersides of rocky overhangs, the bottoms of boats left anchored for a long time, and on the submerged parts of buoys or pontoon piers and wharfs. Those that grow in clusters, and also some of the solitary forms, grow on rocks and pebbles, on bivalve shells or the backs of large crabs, and many species are partially buried in sand or have incorporated into the outer layers of their tunics small pebbles or sand grains. The colonial forms encrust the surfaces of rocks or other hard surfaces, and in these, scores or hundreds of individuals are enclosed in a common tunic. The individuals may be grouped in circles, ovals or stars, each individual having its own inhalant opening but all members of a group sharing one exhalant opening at the centre. In very deep water, down to 16 000 ft or more, sea squirts settle on manganese nodules or other solid objects or else have long stalks with the lower part of the stalk buried in the mud or ooze, as in the aptly named *Abyssascidia*.

Cleansing the sea

Together with sponges and bivalve molluscs sea squirts are living pumping stations, constantly passing water through their bodies, extracting small particles of food from the water. Sea squirts living on the shore and in shallow waters feed on microscopic fragments formed from the breakdown of dead plants and animals. They probably also take in very small members of the plankton. Sea squirts living farther from the coasts, where the water is cleaner, feed mainly on plankton. The method of trapping the food, however, is the same in all types. The cilia on the bars between the gill slits waft the particles to one side where there is a groove bearing cilia and glandular cells giving out mucus that traps the particles. The cilia then drive the food-laden mucus up towards the top of the gullet, along a groove that runs on either side round it, to another ciliated groove, the dorsal lamina. From there it is passed down that side of the gullet and finally goes into the stomach.

Tadpole larvae

Each sea squirt is both male and female. It sheds its eggs and sperms into the water, where the eggs are fertilised by sperms from another sea squirt. There are, however, some species in which the eggs stay in the parent body and are fertilised by sperms carried in on the inhalant current. In either case the larva swims freely in the sea and looks like a tiny longtailed tadpole with a sucker on the front of the head and a mouth just behind this. In the tail is a notochord and a nerve cord, as in young vertebrates, and the internal organs generally are better developed than in the adult, which is degenerate. After a while the tadpole settles head-down on a solid surface, absorbs its tail with the notochord and nerve cord, grows two openings at the end where the tail used to be and becomes a baby sea squirt.

There are features of the anatomy of the tadpole larva which bear comparison with the structure of the vertebrates. The tail, as we have seen, contains a notochord and a hollow nerve cord and on the outside of these are three rows of muscle cells. The nerve cord shows no sign of a thickening in the front that could be interpreted as a brain but it does contain a sense organ, a small eyespot. The body has a short gut with a single pair of gill slits and a simple ventral heart. At best these features do no more than suggest or foreshadow the vertebrate structure and they have given rise to considerable academic discussion regarding their significance.

Prolonged larval stage

Nearly related to sea squirts are animals known as appendicularians. They are like the tadpole larva of a sea squirt but they never grow up. Instead they become sexually mature as juveniles, and the adult phase of the life-history has been lost. This kind of juvenile reproduction is known as paedogenesis and is similar to neoteny (see Axolotl, page 68) in which the larval state is unduly prolonged. An appendicularian has a special way of feeding. It secretes mucus over its head which traps small plankton. These are eaten, but small inedible particles also fall onto the mucus and after a while the mucus becomes cluttered with these, so the appendicularian throws off its mucus cap and spends the next half hour secreting a new one.

phylum	**Chordata**
subphylum	**Urochordata**
class	**Ascidiacea** *(tunicates)*
genera	**Amaroucium, Botryllus, Ciona,** *others*
class	**Larvacea** *(appendicularians)*
genera	**Appendicularia, Oikopleura,** *others*

◁ *A species of sea squirt from the Great Barrier Reef, off the coast of Queensland, Australia.*

Sea urchin

Sea urchins—or sea hedgehogs—are the spiniest of the Echinodermata or 'spiny-skins', the group that includes starfishes, brittlestars, sea lilies and sea cucumbers. Their internal organs are enclosed in a test which typically takes the form of a more or less rounded and rigid box made up of chalky plates fitting neatly together. There are, however, sea urchins with leathery, flexible tests. In sea urchins with the rigid box the shape may be nearly spherical, rounded and somewhat flattened, heartshaped, or like a flattened disc, as in the sand dollar (p 2015). In most sea urchins the test is covered with spines, which may be short and sharp, long and slender or thick and few in number. When the spines are removed knobs can be seen on some of the plates. These form part of the ball-and-socket joints on which the spines move. Also seen when the spines are removed are the double rows of pin-holes arranged in a series of five, forming a star in the heart urchin or running from the bottom to the top of the test when this is spherical. In the living sea urchin the tubefeet project through these pinholes. Among the spines are small jointed rods with two or three jaws at the top, which act like tiny pincers. These are known as pedicellariae, and each moves like the spines on a ball-and-socket joint. Sea urchins are not only attractive in appearance when living, but their tests, cleaned of their spines, are collected because of the beauty of their design. In life they are attractively coloured from greens to yellow, red, orange and purple. The smallest sea urchins are barely $\frac{1}{2}$ in. across, while the largest are up to $1\frac{1}{2}$ ft across, including the spines.

The 800 species have a worldwide distribution, mainly in shallow waters, usually at less than 600 ft although some live down to 1 500 ft.

Burrowing through steel

In addition to the spines and the pedicelliariae, the teeth of a sea urchin play an important part in its life. These too are objects of beauty. Over 2 000 years ago Aristotle wrote of the teeth as resembling a horn lantern with the panes of horn left out. There are five vertical teeth supported on a framework of rods and bars, and the whole structure, teeth and supporting skeleton, is now called Aristotle's lantern. Some sea urchins move freely over the seabed using their tubefeet to pull themselves along. When walking the tubefeet are pushed out, their suckers take hold and then the tube-feet shorten, pulling the body along. Its course is usually an erratic one, as first the

△▷ *Pink pin cushion: an edible sea urchin* **Echinus esculentus** *on* **Laminaria**. *Only the ripe ovaries are eaten, raw like caviare, or cooked.*
▷ *Sea mine: small spines surround the bases of the larger primary spines of a* **Cidaris cidaris**.

The dramatic development of Echinus esculentus

Eggs and sperms, one egg lacks the fertilisation membrane.

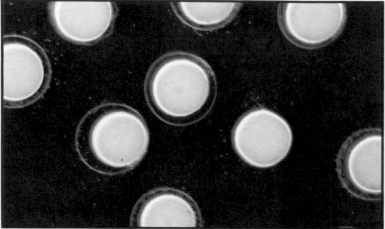

The first cleavage, the eggs divide into two equal cells.

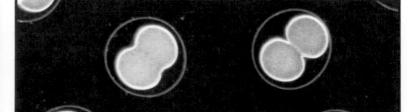
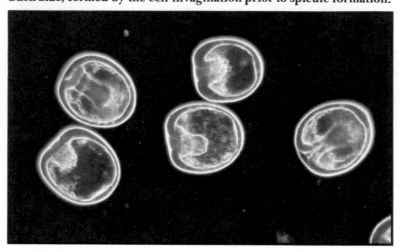

Hollow balls, the blastula at 18 hours, composed of 800–1 000 cells.

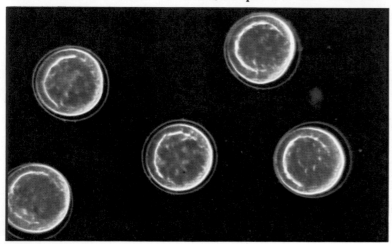

Gastrulae, formed by the cell invagination prior to spicule formation.

If food is scarce at this stage the pluteus larva may be retarded.

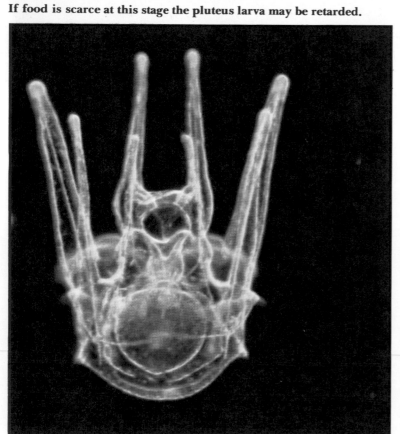

A complicated development – the larva metamorphoses at 7 weeks.

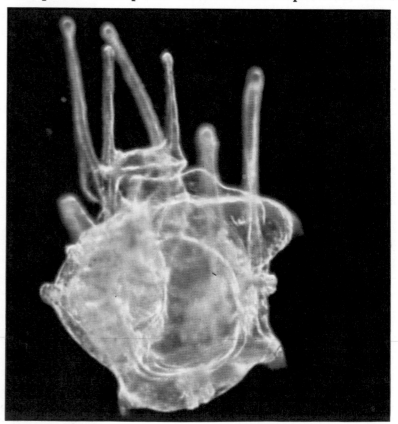

The 4-celled stage at $3\frac{3}{4}$ hours. Cleavage is equal to the 8-celled stage.

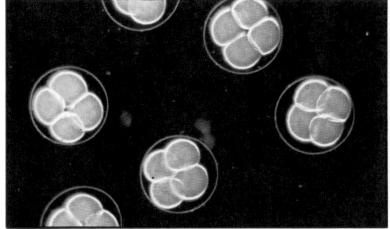

32-cell to 64-cell stages. Unequal division gives two sizes of cells.

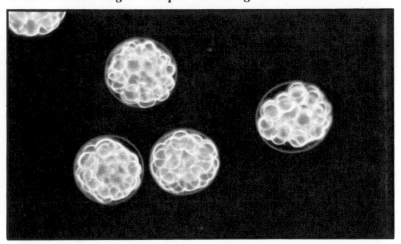

Gastrula elongates into a conical shape, plutei larvae at 3 days ($\times$ 90).

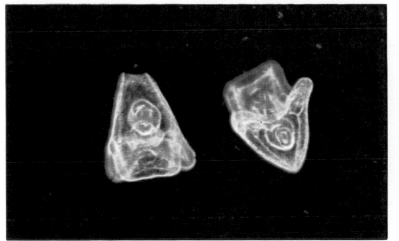

Planktonic 4-armed pluteus larva feeds by tracts of cilia on its arms.

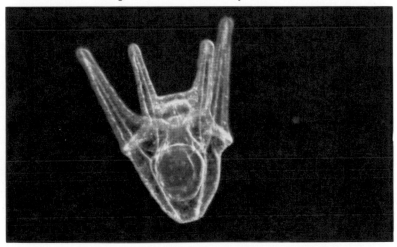

The larval arms are lost and the tube feet are formed ($\times$ 80).

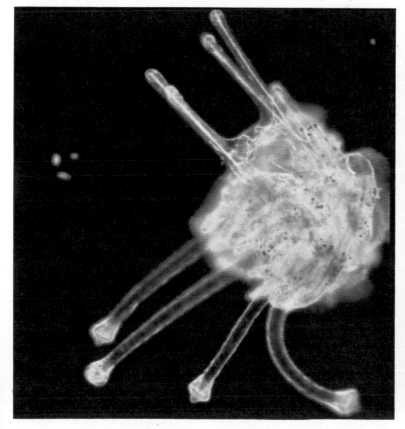

'Ice crystal'—a young sea urchin all spines and tube feet ($\times$ 60).

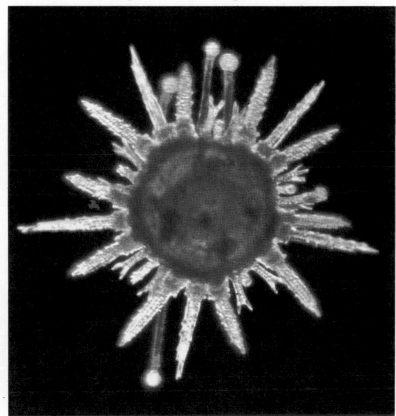

47

tubefeet on one side are pushed out, then the neighbouring tubefeet, each side pulling the sea urchin in a slightly different direction. Other sea urchins use their tubefeet, assisted by the spines, while yet others walk on the spines in a deliberate way, pursuing a steady course, and when viewed from the side the animal appears to be walking on many stilts. There are also sea urchins, including the heart urchins, so named from their shape, that plough through sand and burrow into it, using their spines. *Echinocardium* sinks vertically into the sand, to a depth of 8 in.—twice its own length or more. It lines its vertical shaft with mucus and pushes several very extensible tubefeet up the shaft to the surface of the sand to breathe. It also keeps a horizontal shaft open behind it with other tubefeet, to receive its excrement, while tubefeet in front are picking up particles of food and passing them to the mouth. As the *Echinocardium* moves forward it abandons the vertical shaft by withdrawing its tubefeet, then pushes them up through the sand, making a new vertical shaft to the surface.

There are sea urchins that burrow into soft rock, using their spines to scrape away the surface, some using their teeth as well. *Echinostrephus molaris* of the Indo-Pacific makes cylindrical burrows several inches deep. When feeding it comes up to the mouth of the burrow. Should anything disturb it, it merely drops into the burrow and wedges itself in with its spines. On the Californian coast steel pier piles put in position in the late 1920s were completely perforated by the sea urchin *Strongylocentrotus* in 20 years, the steel being ⅜ in. thick. In other places the anti-corrosive surface layer of the steel piles was abraded and polished by the sea urchins' spines.

Surface cleaning pincers

Sea urchins are mainly vegetarian, chewing seaweeds with the teeth of their Aristotle's lantern. Burrowing forms eat fragments of dead plants in the sand, but probably also take animal food. All get some food as a result of cleaning their tests. The pincers of the pedicellariae are constantly moving about picking up grains of sand that fall on the skin covering the test and also any tiny animals that settle, such as barnacle larvae. These are passed from one pedicellaria to another to the mouth.

Free-swimming larvae

Male and female sea urchins shed their sperms and eggs respectively into the sea where fertilisation takes place. The larva, known as an echinopluteus, is like that of other members of the Echinodermata, with slender arms covered with bands of cilia. Before it settles on the seabed it already has a mouth surrounded by a few tubefeet and spines and the arms are shorter. It is when the arms are too short for swimming that the tiny sea urchin, barely half-formed, settles on the bottom.

Protected from predators

Sea urchins are eaten, especially when small, by bottom feeding fishes but have relatively few other enemies when fully grown. The roes of *Echinus esculentus* have long been eaten in Mediterranean countries and other species have been fished in the Caribbean, South America, Malaya and Japan. Off Barbados they are fished by naked divers with handnets. Most echinoderms have unusual powers of regeneration which sea urchins lack. They can re-grow tubefeet and pedicellariae and if one of the plates in the test is cracked it will be cemented and healed. If a part of the test becomes pushed in, however, the damaged plates will be merely cemented together but will not be pushed out into their normal position. Nevertheless, what sea urchins lack in healing powers they make up for in armaments. In many species the spines are sharp, hollow and brittle, and readily break off. Bathers getting such spines into their feet can sustain painful wounds, and in some places sea urchins are so numerous on the seabed it is practically impossible to put a foot between them. We can be fairly sure that most animal predators treat them with as much respect as the human bather or diver. Many, as we have seen, burrow in sand or rock. Others hide by day under rocks coming out at night to feed. This is purely a reaction away from the light but the practical effect is to keep the animals hidden. Those that do not hide from the light, including the European *Psammechinus miliaris*, hide by holding pieces of seaweed over themselves with their tubefeet. *Diadema* of the Caribbean has light-sensitive cells scattered all over its test. It also has long needlelike spines. Any shadow falling on its body makes the spines in the shaded area point towards the object causing the shadow, thus presenting a formidable array of weapons to a potential attacker.

phylum	**Echinodermata**
class	**Echinoidea**

◁ *Natural radial symmetry—a section through the spines of various sea urchins (approx × 20).*
▷ *Close up of **Toxopneustes pileolus**, a venomous sea urchin. The numerous pedicellariae produce a flower-like effect intensified by a white border of spicules that edge the valves.*

Starfish

No animal is more clearly symbolic of the sea than the starfish or sea star. Artists making drawings of sandy beaches seldom fail to include a starfish, yet a starfish lying on the shore is bound to be dead or dying. Starfishes are found in all seas. The typical form is made up of five arms radiating from a small central body with a toothless mouth on its underside. The number of arms may, however, be from 4 up to 50, and some of the common starfishes that normally have 5 arms may have from 3 to 7. The smallest starfishes are less than ½ in. across, the largest 3 ft. The commonest colours are yellow, orange, pink and red, but there are some starfishes that are grey, blue, green or purple. Some of the smallest, known as starlets or cushion stars, have very short arms, so their outline is pentagonal.

The body wall of a starfish is reinforced and supported by calcareous plates, or ossicles, more or less exposed at the surface but always with at least a thin covering of skin, although this may wear through in places. They may occur as closely set plates or form an open network. Spines of the same material project from the surface singly or in groups, each spine moved by muscles at its base. The surface may also bear many little pincer-like pedicellariae, like those of sea urchins (page 45). The pedicellariae take various forms. Some consist of a pair of tiny jaws mounted on a short stalk while others consist simply of three spines with their bases close together. They play an important part, seizing small organisms, so preventing the surface becoming encrusted with algae and sedentary animals. The pedicellariae are aided by cilia distributed over the surface. The material of the ossicles, spines and pedicellariae of echinoderms is unique in the animal kingdom as each element is a single crystal of calcite growing in the form of a three-dimensional network, to combine both lightness and strength.

Besides a general covering of sensory cells there is a light sensitive optic 'cushion' at the base of a short tentacle, which is a modified tube-foot at the tip of each arm.

There are 2 000 species, most of which live in shallow seas but some live in deep seas. The species are most numerous in the northern part of the North Pacific.

▽▷ A starfish can lose all its arms but one and still survive by using its efficient powers of regeneration. The top starfish is regenerating a third arm. As regeneration results in an increase in population it can be classed as a form of asexual reproduction.
▽ Not only rare but also beautifully symmetrical. This starfish **Archaster typicus** is the only one that shows anything approximating to copulation. Other starfishes merely release millions of eggs into the sea during the one breeding season of the year.

△ *Highly magnified pincer-like pedicellariae of* **Asterias**. *Lethal-looking contraptions, they help prevent the surface of the starfish from becoming encrusted with algae* (× 230).

One arm leads the way

Starfish move about by means of numerous tube-feet arranged in two or four rows along a groove on the underside of each arm. The tube-feet are hollow, muscular cylinders connecting at their bases with a system of tubes, the water vascular system which is filled with water. The 'feet' are pushed out hydraulically by the contraction of muscular sacs which lie at intervals along the system of tubes. At their tips there are usually suction discs, which also have sticky secretions which aid them in sticking to rock or prey. In the burrowing starfishes the tube-feet lack suckers. The water vascular system connecting the tube-feet opens to the out side through one or more porous plates on the upper surface. These madreporites, usually single, are situated off-centre of the body disc. In some species one arm nearly always takes the lead when the starfish is walking, but it is more usual for the arms to take turns in leading the way though there are differences in the extent to which each arm is favoured in a given species or individual. One species has been known to travel at the breath-taking speed of two yards a minute, but the more usual speeds are 2—3 in. a minute.

Multiplying by dividing

Irregular starfishes are sometimes found. They are those that have lost one or more arms and are regenerating new ones. Starfish have good powers of regeneration. They are also pests on oyster and mussel beds and those whose job it was to dredge the starfishes to get rid of them used to tear them apart and throw them back. This was a waste of time. The damaged starfishes merely grew from the torn parts, at least part of the body being necessary for regeneration. One genus *Linckia* is, however, known to be able to regenerate just from a piece of arm ½ in. long. *Linckia* actually uses its arms to propagate itself—the arms pulling in two directions till the animal pulls itself in two. Any bits that get broken off add to the numbers of new individuals.

Protrusible stomach

Starfish are generally carnivorous, feeding on molluscs, worms, crustacea, fish and other echinoderms. Those, like *Asterias,* that prey on bivalves open them by arching over them and pulling on the shell valves with their tube-feet. The mollusc may resist for a long time, but the starfish eventually overwhelms it and the bivalve, due to muscle fatigue, has to allow its valves to part a little. The starfish then protrudes its stomach and inserts it inside out into the mollusc – a slit of $\frac{1}{400}$ in. is enough for it to make an entry. The stomach then secretes digestive enzymes into the mollusc. It has been said that the starfish gives out a poison to make the muscles of the mollusc relax. It now seems there is no firm evidence for this. The burrowing star, *Astropecten,* feeds differently, by taking food in whole. Shells or skeletons are later ejected through the mouth, for this genus has no anus. The cushion star *Porania pulvillus,* sometimes thrown up on the beaches of Europe, is unusual in that it feeds on microscopic organisms, propelling them towards its mouth by means of the cilia on its underside. Another species *Ctenodiscus crispatus* feeds on mud drawn into its mouth in strings of mucus along the grooves under the arms. *Asterina gibbosa,* one of the cushion stars, eats sponges and ascidians.

51

Born in a stomach

Both male and female starfish have two reproductive organs in each arm, each one opening by a pore at the base of the arm. There is usually one breeding season in a year, when millions of eggs may be released into the sea. *Asterias* may release 2–3 million within two hours, but as many as 200 million are released by some species. In *Asterias*, a bipinnaria larva hatches from the eggs. It has two circlets of cilia and is bilaterally symmetrical. The front end later becomes drawn out into three arms, the larva then being called a brachiolaria, while a curious asymmetrical development results in the growth of a young starfish mainly from the left side of the larva of which it still remains part. After about two months of drifting on currents with other plankton, the larva

anchors itself by its three adhesive arms and the young starfish breaks free from the rest. Some cushion stars attach their eggs to the undersides of stones, the brachiolaria stage being omitted. The change into a starfish therefore occurs at an earlier stage of larval development. Several species brood their eggs and these hatch as young stars instead of as larvae. In these species, which mostly live in colder waters and particularly in the Antarctic, the eggs are large and yolky and less numerous. In some species, like the scarlet starfish *Henricia sanguinolenta,* the mother arches herself over her sticky eggs until they hatch. Meanwhile she goes without food. Amongst other methods of brooding, perhaps the oddest is that of *Leptasterias groenlandica* in which the eggs are kept in pouches in the parent's stomach.

Incredible story

Starfishes raid oyster and mussel beds and feed on the shellfish. These raids are, however, insignificant compared with the dramatic largescale destruction of coral reefs that began about 10 years ago, which may have serious effects on fisheries and cause dangers of land erosion. The arch villain is the 'crown of thorns starfish' *Acanthaster planci,* so named for its covering of spines. It has 16 arms and averages 10 in. across, although it can reach two feet. It feeds on coral polyps. It was once thought a rarity, until 1963, when swarms were reported on the Great Barrier Reef. At the same time it was implicated in the destruction of coral in the Red Sea. A population

▽ *Madagascan starfishes* **Protoreaster lincki**, *a sea urchin and a hermit crab.*

explosion took place in many widely separated areas of the Pacific and other oceans and it is killing off coral at an alarming rate. In 2½ years it killed nine-tenths of the coral along 38 kilometres of the shoreline of Guam. As the polyps are destroyed, the dead coral is overgrown with weed and most of the fish depart, their habitat ruined. The areas affected include the Great Barrier Reef of Australia, Fiji, Truck and Palau. Just why the crown of thorns is flourishing in this way is not clear though it is suspected that human interference is to blame, possibly through dredging or blasting. No effective control for these starfish has yet been found.

phylum	**Echinodermata**
class	**Asteroidea**
orders	**Phanerozonia, Spinulosa, Forcipulata**

▷ *Cutting a swathe through the Pacific coral by eating all the live polyps, the crown of thorns starfish **Acanthaster planci** has reached plague numbers. Its feeding habits create a vicious ascending reproductive cycle; where it has killed coral, beds of algae form – ideal sites for the starfish to lay more eggs.*

▽ *Common starfishes of all shades and sizes congregate in a dark crevice.*

▽▷ *A common starfish **Asterias rubens** demonstrates the suction power of its tube feet.*

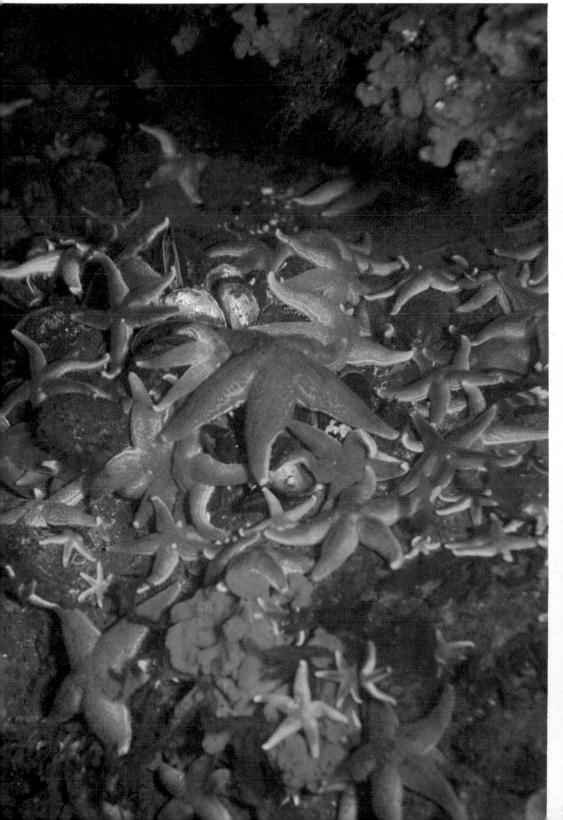

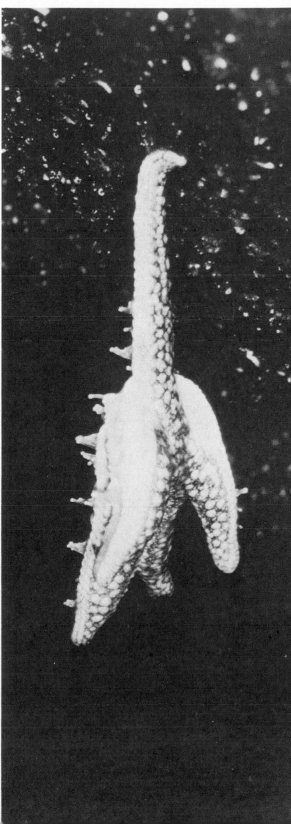

The Emergence onto Land

The evidence on which the theory of evolution is based is drawn from the study of fossil as well as living species. Nowhere in the whole field of this study is there such a complete series as in the transition from fishes to amphibians. Such gaps as there are in our knowledge are small and can be filled in by imagination or, better still, by extrapolation.

Fishes are gill-breathing, aquatic and have two sets of paired fins used for balancing, manoeuvring or swimming. Amphibians, such as newts and salamanders, are gill-breathing when young (some retaining gills all their lives), then develop lungs, and they are typically only partially aquatic and have two sets of paired limbs for walking and for balancing and manoeuvring when in water. In swimming they use a wriggling motion of body and tail (as in most fishes).

The picture presented to us by scientists of the invasion by vertebrates of land from water is as follows. Millions of years ago there were certain fishes that could live in stagnant pools by gulping air, which supplemented their ordinary breathing by gills. At that time, the climate had become warmer and as more pools dried up the only hope for survival was for the fishes to progress over land to find a pool that had not dried up. The more the fish was able to use its fins as legs and the more limb-like its fins the better was it able to travel in search of a fresh pool.

This may read like a flight of fancy but it could be near the truth, although the greater likelihood is that there is no need to invoke the severe climatic conditions. Many fishes living today can breathe or gulp air as well as using gills. Outstanding among these are the lungfishes, but there are others such as the mudskipper, climbing perch and the whole group of labyrinth fishes. Even the common eel is capable of surviving extended periods out of water, and also of moving over the ground although it is virtually without paired fins.

When it comes to fishes using their paired fins as limbs for locomotion over a firm surface the choice is only slightly more limited. The mudskipper is an excellent example since it spends more than half its time out of water, moving about over the mud. The climbing perch may not climb trees, as was

originally supposed, but it can travel relatively far from water using its fins and spines on its gill-covers as crutches and surviving on aerated water carried in its gill-chambers. Climbing perches survive so long out of water that the local people carry them about with them as a supply of fresh fish.

Interestingly, one of the most convincing displays of walking on paired fins is given on the seabed by the toadfish, which does not leave the water and does not gulp air. What the toadfish does emphasise for us is that evolution rarely proceeds in a straight line. One fish develops leg-like fins, another develops lungs. Neither can leave the water but the two together allow us to visualise how, if another species were possessed of leg-like fins and could make use of atmospheric oxygen for breathing the main obstacles to leaving the water for life on land would have been surmounted. This emergence onto land could occur without necessarily any great changes in the environment but simply as a response to competition from other species of fishes.

In 1939, when news of the discovery of the coelacanth reached Europe there was great excitement among zoologists. This was not solely because it belonged to a family of fishes that were believed to have become extinct a hundred million years ago. It also combined in its anatomy a number of unusual features the most obvious of which was the lobed fins that look so like legs. What is more, when the eighth coelacanth was caught alive and kept in captivity for 17 hours it was observed to be capable of turning its fins through an arc of 180°. Yet the coelacanth probably never uses its fins as walking limbs nor can it gulp air nor survive very long out of water. Although it lives in fairly deep water it is, so to speak, half-way to being prepared for a life on land.

The coelacanth was hailed by some zoologists as a sort of missing link that would tell us much about the evolution of the vertebrates, even of man himself. These hopes were only partially fulfilled. What is now realised is that it is a primitive member of the bony fishes, with a spiral valve in the intestine, as in sharks, a very small brain, a simple linear heart, and a backbone that is little more than a notochord!

Climbing perch

*Although long familiar to scientists under the name **Anabas scandens** the name of this fish is now **Anabas testudineus**. It is 9 in. long, perch-like, grey-green to greyish-silver with brown fins, and there is a dark patch behind each gill-cover and another at the base of the tailfin. Climbing perch extend across southern and southeast Asia, from India and Sri Lanka to the Philippines.*

In the water with spiny dorsal fin lowered. It 'walks' on land by digging the spines of the gill covers into the ground, using the pectoral fins as props and pushing with its tail.

Overland wanderer

Little would have been heard of this ordinary looking fish but for its habit of travelling overland to find a fresh pond when its home water is drying up. It does this using the gill-covers, pectoral fins and tail. The gill-covers have spines on their hind margins which are dug into the ground with a side-to-side rocking motion. The pectoral fins are used as props to help the forward thrust from the tail-end. It is half a wriggle and half a seal lollop enabling the fish to travel at about 200 yd an hour.

The ability to breathe out of water is due to a large gill cavity, divided into two compartments. The smaller and lower of these contains the normal gills. The larger upper part contains a rosette of concentrically arranged plates with wavy edges, the whole richly supplied with a network of fine blood-vessels. In fact, the rosette works like a piece of lung. Air is swallowed and passes by an opening on either side of the throat into the rosette chambers, the opening being controlled by a valve. The spent air leaves through the gills' exit, in the usual way.

A drowning fish

It is not only while the fish is out of water that this accessory breathing apparatus is used. Like the true lungfishes, and others that have lungs or lung-like organs, the climbing perch can live in water low in oxygen—water polluted and foul from rotting vegetation. In such water it can rise to the surface and gulp air. Indeed, the climbing perch is one of several fishes which drown if held under water.

Although the overland speed of the climbing perch is slow, the fish can stay out of water for a long time. The people of India and Malaya carry them for days on end in moistened clay pots. It is one way of ensuring a supply of fresh fish.

There is no difficulty in catching climbing perch in the right season. At the beginning of the dry season the fish burrows into mud and goes into a resting stage, like the well-known lungfishes. At other times, and usually in the early morning or during a rainstorm, the fishes travel over the ground in troops. Climbing perch are tolerant of sudden temperature changes, and feeding offers few problems since they take a wide variety of animal and plant food.

Casual parents

It is surprising, in view of their wide diet, that climbing perch do not eat their young, as so many freshwater fishes are prone to

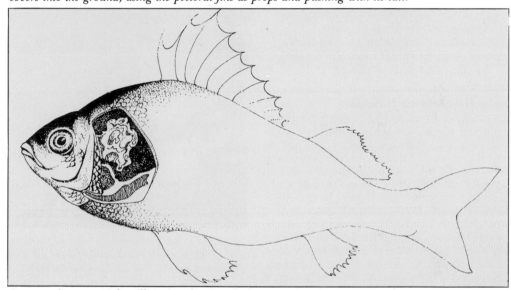

Cutaway diagram of the gill cavity, showing the large air-breathing rosette section.

do, after nursing them through early infancy. The female climbing perch lays her eggs at random; these float to the surface and the parents show no further interest in them. The eggs hatch in a day or so.

End of a legend

The western world first learned of the existence of the climbing perch in 1797, when Lieutenant Daldorf of the Danish East India Company, stationed at Tranquebar, wrote a memoir on it. In this he pointed out that the local legend was that the fish climbed palm trees and sucked their juices. Daldorf confirmed the story by saying he himself had found one in a slit in the bark of a palm tree that was growing near a pond.

For nearly 250 years the perch was called 'climbing' and nobody questioned it. Possibly this was due to two facts that appeared to bear out the fish's reputation. One was that the perch will climb the trunk of a tree leaning well over, just as the marine fishes known as mud-skippers will. The other fact is that the perch is sometimes found well up a tree, in a crotch or a fork

or even in a slit in the bark, as Lt Daldorf found his.

Then, in 1927, Dr BK Das, the Indian expert on fishes, discovered that perch in trees do not get there under their own steam. When troops of perch are travelling in search of fresh ponds crows and kites swoop and carry some of them off, and they park their catch in various places, including trees. The perch can live for days out of water so it must often have happened that people have found live perch high up in trees. What more natural than to draw the obvious conclusion, which fooled us for 250 years until Dr Das took a closer look?

Now it is becoming fashionable among students of fishes to call it a walking perch —but even this is an exaggeration.

class	**Pisces**
order	**Perciformes**
family	**Anabantidae**
genus & species	***Anabas testudineus***

Coelacanth

First made known to science in 1938, and belonging to an order previously thought to have become extinct 70 million years ago, the coelacanth is a 5ft long, 120lb primitive fish. Coelacanth means hollow spines, referring to those of the fins. The fish, first caught off the coast of Natal, and later off Madagascar, is of robust build, brown to dark blue, and outwardly shows several peculiarities. The first is that each of the pectoral fins, instead of coming straight off the body, is carried on scaly muscular lobes and seems to be halfway between a normal fin and the walking limb of primitive land animals. The rear dorsal and the anal fins are similarly lobed. The second peculiarity is in the tail. Instead of the junction between the body and the tail fin being marked by a constriction, the body merely narrows rapidly and evenly, and then continues backwards as a narrow strip, dividing the rays of the tail fin into two equal parts, one above and one below it. Another peculiarity is its scales. Each scale is a bony plate covered with dermal denticles (small tooth-like points in the skin) like those of sharks.

Scientists' clever forecast

In addition to its strange external appearance the coelacanth has a number of peculiar internal features which are just as significant as its ancient ancestry. Although it is a bony fish, the backbone is made up almost entirely of a large, tough cartilaginous rod, the notochord. In an evolutionary sense, the notochord came before the backbone, and in the developing embryo of vertebrates it appears first and is later enclosed by the vertebrae and lost, except in very primitive vertebrates (for example, lampreys). The heart of the coelacanth is very simple, even simpler than that of other fishes. Interestingly enough it is like the heart predicted by anatomists when trying to explain how the heart evolved.

The kidneys, instead of lying just under the backbone, are on the floor of the abdomen, and instead of being a pair they are joined. This is unique, and it is hard to see any explanation. It is not so much a primitive character as one quite unexpected. The stomach also is peculiar; it is just a large bag. The intestine has a spiral valve, a feature shared with sharks and other primitive fishes.

Armoured 'lungs'

Perhaps one of the more perplexing features of the coelacanth is the swimbladder (an elongated silvery bag, an outgrowth of the gullet). This probably arose in the first place as a breathing organ. The fossil coelacanths, which flourished 450−70 million years ago, had a swimbladder and lobed fins. It was largely among these fishes that scientists looked for a possible ancestor to the land vertebrates. That is, the coelacanths seemed to be distant ancestors of man, with the beginnings of lungs and of walking limbs. One drawback to such a theory was that the

*Highlight in natural history: Professor Smith poses with **Malania**, the second coelacanth to be discovered, together with South African Air Force personnel, Captain Hunt's schooner crew, and the French governor of the Comores (at right). The date is December 29, 1952.*

swimbladder of coelacanths was sheathed in bony scales, so it could not have served as a lung and it would have made a very poor hydrostatic organ.

Hopes frustrated

When it was realised that an actual living coelacanth had been found, the more sober scientists hoped it would shed light on the puzzle of the rigid swimbladder. The more excitable ones began to talk about the living coelacanth shedding light on man's ancestry. Some of them broadcast to this effect and the coelacanth became, in the minds of many listeners, a missing link of supreme importance. That proved, however, a nine days' wonder. The swimbladder was also a disappointment. The first modern coelacanth was almost decomposed before being examined by an expert. In addition it had been gutted in the hope of preserving it. When more living coelacanths were caught and dissected, the swimbladder was found to be slender and filled with fat. It, also, cannot function as a lung and even more certainly is not a hydrostatic organ.

There are a number of other features of the anatomy which are peculiar, and which are of interest mainly to the expert. To-

gether they suggest that the coelacanths were an aberrant offshoot of the early fishes, having gone off at a tangent from the main line of evolution. They show relationships with sharks, chimaera, lungfishes, and other primitive fishes. Above all, they indicate that the coelacanths, following an independent evolutionary line, were a dying race, with the living coelacanth as the last survivor, so far as we know.

One of the peculiarities, which has an interesting lesson to teach, is the skull. This is hinged midway, as in fossil coelacanths. The brain cavity in it is large. It has long been a puzzle how the brain managed to work if the skull containing it was hinged. The living coelacanth shows that the brain is small and confined to the rear portion of the skull, behind the hinge. It lies embedded in fat and cushioned on two large blood ducts. The brain itself is therefore very small by comparison with the cavity of the skull.

It is common, in studying fossil animals, to take a plaster cast of the cranial cavity in the skull to reconstruct the shape and proportions of the brain. The living coelacanth teaches us that this could well be misleading.

Trawler's lucky catch

A considerate and curious seaman, a quick-thinking curator of a tiny museum, and a scientist who let nothing stand in his way: these three people brought to light one of the most exciting animals of the century. On December 22, 1938, a fishing boat shot her trawl off the mouth of the Chalumna River, west of East London, in South Africa. It was not the usual place for the trawlers to fish. On this occasion the ship stood 3 miles offshore, her trawl dragging the seabed at 120 ft. It came up with 3 tons of fish, which were emptied on the deck in the usual way. Half an hour later the trawlermen came to the last fish, 5 ft long, blue, and with unusual scales, a fish they had not seen before. It lived for 4 hours.

The skipper, Captain Goosen, realising he had something unusual, sent the fish to Miss Courtenay-Latimer, curator at the East London museum. She wrote to Professor JLB Smith at Grahamstown, 400 miles away. But it was now Christmas Eve, the mail was choked, and so Smith did not see the fish for some days after its capture. Nevertheless, although it was in poor shape he realised its importance, and it is to the credit of Smith, Miss Courtenay-Latimer and Captain Goosen that a priceless scientific treasure was brought to the notice of the world's scientists.

On December 20, 1952, a fisherman, Ahmed Hussein, landed a 5ft, 100lb fish with a hook and line, from 65 ft of water off the Comores Islands, west of Madagascar. Professor Smith was informed, and flew to the Comores in a South African Air Force Dakota placed at his disposal by the then Prime Minister, Dr Malan. Although Smith gave it the name *Malania anjouanae* after the Prime Minister, it was later realised this was the same as the first coelacanth, which had been named *Latimeria chalumnae*, after Miss Courtenay-Latimer. This second fish was the culmination of a 14-year campaign in which Smith flooded East Africa with leaflets in English, French and Portuguese, offering a reward of £100 for the first two specimens caught.

A lucky find

Madagascar, including the Comores, was then under French administration, and French scientists now took up the search. A third was found in September, 1953, and in 1954 two more were caught: on January 28 and January 31. Since then others have been caught, which suggests that the one caught off Natal in 1938 had wandered from its normal habitat.

This, one of the most interesting of living fishes, is known therefore almost entirely from a dozen dead individuals examined by scientists, or watched for the very short while a few survived in aquaria. Brought to the surface they have soon died due to the combination of decompression and exposure to warmer waters.

class	**Pisces**
order	**Crossopterygii**
family	**Coelacanthidae**
genus & species	***Latimeria chalumnae***

△ *The leaflet which offered East African fishermen £100 for the first two coelacanths caught. Skin divers have looked for the fish off the coasts of Madagascar and neighbouring islands, and some have caught a glimpse of large fishes believed to be coelacanths along the steep slopes where the rocky sea-bed suddenly dips in a vertical wall to very deep water.* ▽ *Skeleton of a coelacanth tail. The characteristic double tail has fins made up of hollow rays of cartilage. This is a link with the Rhipidistian fishes of 320 million years ago, the supposed ancestors of land animals.*

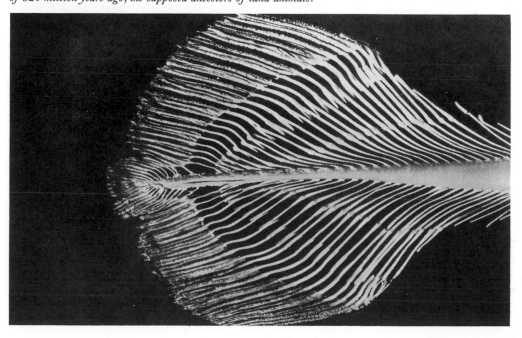

Lamprey

Lampreys look like eels and have some-times been called lamprey eels or lamper eels. They are, however, jawless like the hagfish which is their nearest relative, and, like the hagfishes, lampreys are not true fishes but direct descendants of the jawless Ostracoderms. There are about 30 species, both marine and freshwater. Some are parasitic on fish, others are not. Lampreys live in temperate regions of northern and southern hemispheres. The sea lamprey, the best known, lives on both sides of the North Atlantic. Members of the genus **Lampetra** *are found in Europe and Asia as well as North America. In the southern hemisphere, species of* **Geotria** *and* **Mordacia** *are found off the coasts of Chile, Australia and New Zealand.* **Geotria** *has a large fleshy bag, of un-known function, almost hiding its mouth.*

Pump-like gills

The eel-like body of a lamprey has a slimy scaleless skin. Its fins are found along the centre-line of the body. There is a single nostril in the middle of the head, which leads behind into a blind sac. The eyes are well-developed. The head ends in front in a large funnel-like mouth with horny teeth lining the funnel, some of the teeth being on the muscular tongue protruding at the base of the funnel. Behind the head is a row of small circular gill openings running along each side of the body. Inside are seven pairs of gill pouches lined with blood-red gill-filaments which open into a tube that is blind at one end and opens into the back of the mouth in front. A lamprey can breathe by taking in water through its mouth to pass across the gills. More often, because the mouth is so much used as a sucker, a lamprey breathes by contracting muscles around the gill-pouches, driving the water out. As the muscles relax water is drawn in. This pumping action seems to be helped by movements of the sinuous latticework of cartilage, the branchial basket, surrounding the gill-pouches.

The lamprey feeds by pressing the circular edge of its mouth against the side of a fish which it finds by eyesight, not by smell as in the hagfish. It protrudes its tongue and punctures the fish's skin by rasping the teeth on it; the fish starts to bleed and the blood is sucked in by the lamprey. It sucks in a few fragments of flesh as well, but it feeds more on the blood than on the flesh. Not all adult lampreys feed in this way; some species do not feed as adults.

Lampreys barricade their nests

There are three species of lamprey in Europe. They are usually spoken of as the sea lamprey, river lamprey and brook lamprey. It is better to use the second's alternative name of lampern, because it also spends its adult life in the sea. The brook lamprey is also known as the pride. It lives all the time in freshwater. Those lampreys living in the sea enter rivers to spawn. The migration begins in winter and

△ *The hooded larva of a brook lamprey.*
▽ *Lamprey skeleton showing branchial basket, which supports the gill pouches, and the viciously toothed, circular mouth cartilage, which serves instead of jaws.*
▽▽ *Powerful sucker of a brook lamprey.*

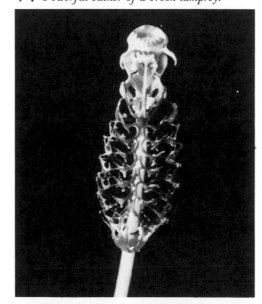

by spring the lampreys are in the rivers and building nests. They swim strongly and can make their way over rocks or up vertical walls, hauling themselves up with the sucker mouth. The male lamprey makes a nest by holding pebbles in its sucker mouth and moving them downstream to form a barricade. In a depression made upstream of this, the eggs will later be laid.

The females arrive later than the males and then help build the nest, the two sometimes combining to move large pebbles. After spawning the adults drift downriver to die. The eggs are $\frac{1}{25}$ in. diameter and they hatch 2 weeks later. The larva, or ammocoete, was once thought to be a different species. It is small and worm-like, and lives by burrowing in the sand or mud and coming out at night to feed on particles of plant and animal bodies. These are strained through fleshy tentacles (cirri) on a hood-like mouth and passed into the gullet where they are caught by sticky secretions on a special groove, the endostyle. This endostyle becomes the thyroid gland—the chemical controller of growth—in the adult.

After 3–5 years of larval life the ammocoete, now 4–5 in. long, changes into an adult lamprey. The hooded mouth becomes funnel-shaped, the cirri are replaced by horny teeth, the nostril moves from the front of the snout to the top of the head, the eye grows larger. The sea lamprey becomes silvery and goes down to the sea, as does the lampern, but the latter does not parasitize fishes. Instead it feeds on molluscs, crustaceans and worms. The pride or brook lamprey, which remains in rivers, does not feed when adult.

Surfeit of lampreys

It is often said that King John died of a surfeit of lampreys. It was, in fact, Henry I. It was King John who fined the men of Gloucester 40 marks because 'they did not pay him sufficient respect in the matter of lampreys'. American history is more recent and has to do with a surfeit of lampreys in the Great Lakes. Gradually, over the years, the lampreys made their way up the New York State Barge Canal and the Welland Canal and became firmly established in the Great Lakes. There they ruined a commercial fishery that had been yielding a yearly catch of 11 million pounds of lake trout and other fishes. A big research programme was set going to find ways of killing off the lampreys. Weirs were built to stop further migrations into the lakes, the lampreys were poisoned and electrocuted. Some success was achieved but now that a poison that kills the larvae has been discovered lampreys are being wiped out and the fisheries are recovering.

class	**Agnatha**
order	**Petromyzoniformes**
family	**Petromyzonidae**
genera & species	**Petromyzon marinus** *sea lamprey* **Lampetra fluviatilis** *lampern* **L. planeri** *pride* *others*

Loach

The two dozen species of loaches and spiny loaches live in the fresh waters of Europe and Asia, including the Malayan Archipelago, as well as a small area in Morocco and one in Ethiopia. They are small, seldom more than 1 ft long, and while a few have a fairly normal fish-shape apart from a flattened under-surface, most are worm-shaped. Most of them have a conspicuous pattern of dark bands on the body or it may be broken up, or otherwise altered, until only a marbling remains. They have small scales in the skin. There are three or four pairs of barbels around the toothless mouth which is set back beneath the snout. The single dorsal fin, the anal fin and the paired fins are all much the same size. The spined loach is named for a spine, which may fork at its tip, below and in front of the eye.

Except for three species, the stone loach, spined loach and weatherfish, all belong to southern and southeast Asia, and these include two well known to aquarists, the coolie loach and the clown or tiger loach. The common name coolie is derived from the scientific name **Acanthophthalmus kuhlii**. The most colourful of the family is the clown or tiger loach, brilliant orange-red with velvet black bars.

Automatic air-conditioning

Loaches are bottom-living. Those living in streams have rounded bodies, somewhat flattened from above down in some species, while those living in still water have bodies flattened from side to side. They use their barbels to hunt for food—mainly insect larvae and worms—and some species burrow into the sand or mud at the bottom, either to escape enemies or to pass the winter. Loaches sometimes eat algae and were often kept by aquarists to clear the aquarium walls of green coatings. Their usual method of feeding, however, is to comb the surface of the sand or mud, swallowing edible particles and passing solid grains out through the gills.

Two features of the behaviour of loaches are particularly impressive: the way they breathe and the way they react to changes in the weather. Loaches have gills, and a swimbladder whose front part—in some species at least—is enclosed in a bony capsule. Many loaches breathe through the intestine. When the water becomes impure they come to the surface and gulp air which they swallow. They also gulp air if the pond dries up and, burying themselves in the mud, wait for rain. The wall of the hind end of the intestine is rich in small blood vessels and works like a lung, taking in oxygen and giving out carbon dioxide, the spent air being expelled through the vent.

Experiments in aquaria show a direct relation between the air gulping and a rising temperature of the water. The warmer the water the less oxygen is holds. At 5°C/41°F a loach breathes solely through

△ An affectionate pair of clown loaches. This orange coloured loach with its velvet black bars is a hardy species renowned for its habit of uprooting rank vegetation. It has been known to live for 25 years in captivity.
▷ With its sensitive barbels extended the stone loach hunts for food. A toothless fish, the loach eats mainly insect larvae and worms and occasionally algae. Obviously a useful fish to keep aquarium walls clean.

its gills. At 10°C/50°F one bubble of air is swallowed every 2 hours. At 15°C/59°F five bubbles are swallowed in an hour. At 25°C/77°F ten bubbles are swallowed an hour. If, however, a loach is placed in water that has been boiled to drive out oxygen, and is then cooled to 25°C/77°F it will swallow 67 bubbles an hour, coming to the surface every minute or so to gulp.

Switch from gills to lungs

In some species most of the intestine is used as a lung. This is true of the stone loach and spiny loach as well as the weatherfish, an Indian species *Lepidocephalus guntea* and a Chinese species, the mud loach *Misgurnus anguillicaudatus*. After gulping air, the Indian loach turns a somersault, at the same time driving out the spent air through its vent. A stream of 8—12 bubbles are ejected with force producing a distinct clicking sound. When these bubbles are collected and analysed they are found to contain only a small percentage of carbon dioxide, the rest being nitrogen and some oxygen. In fact, most of the carbon dioxide is got rid of through the gills.

The Chinese loach is remarkable because it has a seasonal lung. It uses gills only in winter, when there is more oxygen in the cold water, but in summer it becomes an air-gulper. Moreover, as the fish resumes its gill-breathing the 'lung' part of the intestine reverts to digestive tissue.

Famous for fecundity

Although loaches have been popular aquarium fishes little is known of the breeding habits of most of them. They have only occasionally spawned in captivity and accounts of what happens are conflicting. One writer has spoken of the eggs being laid on sand, another in a bubble nest. More is known about the stone loach, which has a reputation of being a prolific breeder and

in Shakespeare's Henry IV there is the phrase 'breeds fleas like a loach', which is supposed to refer to its fecundity. Izaak Walton claimed that the loach is usually full of spawn and breeds three times a year. It spawns indiscriminately on stones and pebbles in April to May, the eggs being laid at night. The eggs are large for so small a fish, $\frac{1}{25}$ in. diameter, sticky and numerous. They hatch in 8—11 days, the fry lying on the bottom at first and beginning to feed at 8—10 days after hatching.

Weather prophets

Several species of fishes are supposed to foretell weather changes. One of the most famous is a loach known in continental Europe as the weatherfish, but other loaches are said to do much the same. The name 'loach' is said to be from the French *locher*, to fidget, and, loaches are said to grow restless 24 hours before the approach of a thunderstorm. They are said to be sensitive to changes in barometric pressure although there have been no experiments to test this. A theory put forward in 1895 is that the Weberian ossicles function as a barometer. These bones connect a fish's swimbladder with its inner ear.

class	**Pisces**
order	**Cypriniformes**
family	**Cobitidae**
genera & species	**Botia macracanthus** clown loach **Cobitis taenia** spined loach **Misgurnus fossilis** weatherfish **Noemacheilus barbatulus** stone loach others

Lungfish

The earliest fossils of lungfishes go back over 350 million years. These and other fossils show that lungfishes have at some time or other lived all over the world. Today only 6 species survive: one in Australia, four in tropical Africa and one in South America. Having lungs for breathing air they can live in stagnant water. Some of them can also survive the drying out of rivers. The lungs are essentially pouched branches from the gut which in most fishes have modified into flotation organs or swimbladders. Modifications and improvements in their efficiency during the course of evolution have led to the true lungs of active land animals.

The Australian lungfish **Neoceratodus** is the most primitive of the six. Originally it was found only in the Burnett and Mary Rivers in Queensland but has since been introduced to lakes and reservoirs in that state. Its alternative name, Burnett salmon, shows that it is a full-bodied fish and it may be as much as 6 ft long and 100 lb weight, although usually only half that length. The body is covered with large scales and the paired fins are flipper-like. The largest African lungfish **Protopterus** may measure 7 ft but is usually 2—3 ft. Like the South American species **Lepidosiren,** the African lungfishes have more eel-like bodies with small scales embedded in the skin. The paired fins of **Protopterus** are long, slender and flexible, those of **Lepidosiren** are short and slender. The four African species range over a wide area of tropical Africa, the South American lungfish is widely distributed over the Amazon basin.

Buried in mud

The African and South American species have a pair of lungs and they must gulp air to live no matter how good the water they are living in. The South American lungfish tunnels into the mud as the stream dries out in summer and two of the African species burrow into the mud and give out quantities of slime which hardens to form a cocoon with a hole in the upper end. This resting state in hot weather, the reverse of hibernation, is called aestivation. During aestivation the fish continues to breathe at a reduced rate. The cocoon of the African lungfish, embedded in mud, has an opening to the surface and the fish lies doubled up with its head and tail at the lower end of this 'breathing tube'. While aestivating the lungfish absorbs its own muscles for food, and one examined before and after 6 months resting had dropped from 13¾ to 10½ oz and its length had decreased from 16 to 14¾ in. Once out of aestivation it had more than made good these losses in 2 months.

Another problem for the lungfish is the disposal of body waste. Its kidneys separate water from urea—the poisonous end product of food breakdown—the water goes back into circulation and the urea is stored.

△ *Part of the eggs of spawn laid by an Australian lungfish. Spawning is mainly in September and November. The development of the embryos is more similar to that of the frog tadpole than a fish.*

△ *The African lungfish has small embedded scales and very narrow pectoral and pelvic fins.*
▽ *The South American lungfish has an eel-like body, also with embedded scales, and slender fins.*

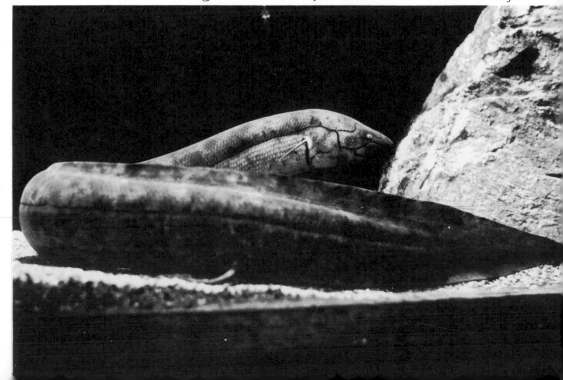

△ *The Australian lungfish, unlike the other two types, has a flatter and broader body covered with very large overlapping scales. The paired fins are broad and powerful and capable of supporting the fish by resting them on the bottom of a stream or pool.*

In most vertebrates 10 parts per million of urea in the system would be fatal. A lungfish can survive 20 000 parts per million. As soon as aestivation is over the urea is discharged and the kidneys cleared of it in a few hours.

The fish comes out of its cocoon when the rains return and the streams fill up once more. Usually the aestivation lasts only a few months, but African lungfishes dug out still in their cocoons embedded in a block of dried mud have been kept for over 4 years before being immersed once again in water. Although emaciated they soon recovered and began to feed.

The Australian lungfish has only one lung and lives in water with plenty of oxygen so does not need to come to the surface to gulp air. Moreover, it cannot survive drought and dies if kept out of water for any length of time.

A taste for snails
The Australian lungfish eats both animal and plant food, the others are carnivorous and the plant food they take is swallowed by accident as they grub for crustaceans and molluscs. A detailed study has been made of the food of one species of African lungfish by Philip S Corbet. This shows that the bulk of its food when fully grown is freshwater snails. It also takes a fair proportion of insect larvae and a small number of cichlid fishes. Moreover, the diet alters with size. Up to a foot long the lungfish eats insect larvae only, from then until it is 2 ft long its food is a mixture of insect larvae, snails and the occasional cichlid, but beyond 2 ft, it eats only snails.

Tadpole-like babies
The primitive state of the Australian lungfish is also seen in its breeding. The female lays her eggs at random among water plants and neither parent pays any further attention to them. Both African and South American species dig a cavity in the mud in which the female lays some 5 000 eggs. The male tends these, wriggling his body to drive over currents of water to aerate them. He also chases away anything coming near the nest. The larvae hatching from the eggs climb up the sides of the nest cavity and hang vertically with the head upwards for

1—2 months. The larvae have four pairs of external gills which they gradually lose. The first pair is lost at the end of the first month, the rest being lost during the next month in the South American lungfish while the African species take several months to lose theirs. The larva of the Australian lungfish does not have external gills. The other species grow their permanent gills as their larval gills are being absorbed. In one African species vestiges of external gills persist through life. The South American species has 6 gill arches and 5 gill clefts. The African species have 5 arches and 4 clefts.

The pelvic fins of the male of the South American lungfish grow filaments during the breeding season. These contain many small blood vessels. Opinion is divided on whether these give out oxygen to help the developing eggs or whether they act as extra gills, helping him to stay with the eggs rather than rise for air so often.

Few predators
One of the main advantages for a fish to be able to live in stagnant waters is that there will be few enemies to contend with. That the present day lungfishes have persisted more or less unchanged for millions of years suggests that they have not had great pressure from predators. The main losses are among the young, and some of these may be from adult lungfishes themselves, especially in the African species which are apt to be pugnacious even to fishes their own size, judging from their behaviour in aquaria and the way they attack other fishes when netted. The adult lungfishes are eaten by crocodiles as well as by fish eagles who take them as they come to the surface to gulp air.

Swallows air
Land-living vertebrates breathe by lungs and take in air through the nostrils. The nose acts, therefore, as an organ of smell and supplies a passage for air used in breathing. Fishes have nostrils and a sense of smell. Most of them have no lungs, so the nostrils lead into blind cavities containing the olfactory (smell) membranes. Water is drawn in and driven out, merely to bathe the olfactory membrane. It had long been assumed that lungfishes, which have nostrils and lungs, breathed through their noses. Some 20 years ago JW Atz showed that they did not. Among other things, when a lungfish breathes air it swims strongly to the surface, pushes its snout well out, opens its mouth wide and movements of the mouth and throat show it is swallowing air.

class	**Pisces**
order	**Dipnoi**
family	**Ceratodontidae**
genus & species	*Neoceratodus forsteri*
family	**Protopteridae**
genus & species	*Protopterus aethiopicus* others
family	**Lepidosirenidae**
genus & species	*Lepidosiren paradoxa*

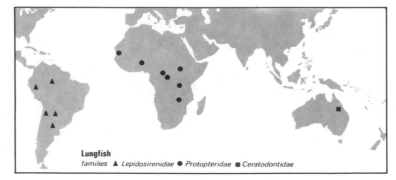

Lungfish
families ▲ *Lepidosirenidae* ● *Protopteridae* ■ *Ceratodontidae*

The six species of lungfish were once more widely spread but are now confined to three countries. One in Australia, one in South America and four in Africa, very similar in form to the American species suggesting the continents were once linked.

61

Mudskipper

Mudskippers are fish which, instead of retreating with the falling tide, usually remain on the exposed mud. They can breathe air and move quickly over the mud, using their pectoral fins. Among some of the largest members of the goby family, they live on mud flats and mangrove swamps from West Africa to southeast Asia and the southwestern Pacific.

Mudskippers are 5—12 in. long, almost tadpole-like with a heavy head and long body compressed from side to side. They could well be described as pop-eyed, with their conspicuous eyes, placed well up on the head. These eyes can move

Three mud dwellers

Mudskippers show a zonation from the depths of the mangrove swamps, even up in the trees, through the mud of the forest floor down to the mid-tide level. There are three basic types of mudskippers. The eel-skippers *Scartelaos* so called because they have long slender bodies, live in the very soft mud at mid-tide level in the estuaries and are never far from water. Little is known of their habits. The second group, genus *Boleophthalmus*, live in large numbers on the mud at the seaward edge of mangrove forests. They may move into the margin of the forest, under the trees, but no more. They move their heads from side to side as they skitter over the mud skimming diatoms and algae from the surface. In a way not yet understood, they sort these

△ *Mudskipper profile: these are quite common in tropical parts of coastal Australia.*
◁ *Gill-chambers full of water, Malayan mudskippers* **Periophthalmus chrysopilos** *on mud.*

about in all directions. The front dorsal fin is high and spiny. The pectoral fins are fairly large and somewhat limb-like. The pelvic fins are joined to form a kind of sucker. The colour of the body varies from blue-grey to brownish, often with many small blue spots. The fins, especially the two dorsals, are decorated with coloured spots which vary according to the species.

In western Africa they live on the Saharan shores to the north and the Namibian shores to the south. In eastern Africa they range from East London to the Red Sea, and from there around the shores of the Indian Ocean and into the Indo-Australian region.

out from the water in the mouth, swallow the diatoms and algae and spit out the water. The third group includes the genera *Periophthalmus* and *Periophthalmodon*, the commonest mudskippers, found along the banks of creeks and throughout the mangrove forests. These feed on insects that have fallen into the mud, on crabs, worms and the smaller mudskippers.

The species of *Periophthalmus* fall into two groups: those represented by *P. kalolo* in which the pelvic fins are still separate, and those represented by *P. chrysospilos* with the pelvic fins joined and forming a sucker. Mudskippers of the first group can climb only onto the exposed roots of mangroves whereas those of the second group are able to climb the vertical shoots and trunks by means of their suckers.

In these Malayan species the pelvic fins have moved anterior to the pectoral fins and joined to form a sucker which enables them to climb the vertical trunks of mangroves.

Living in air

All mudskippers spend much of their time out of water, but they constantly return to the pools left by the tide. The gill chambers are much enlarged to carry a supply of water but this has to be continually renewed in the pools although they can breathe air through the membranes lining the back of the mouth and the throat which are richly supplied with blood vessels. Mudskippers are said to dip their tails in water because they breathe through them. This is not so at all. They need to keep their skin moist, so they often splash water over themselves with one of the pectoral fins. They also have to keep their eyes moist. We have a supply of fluid on the surface of the eye supplied by the tear gland, and every time we blink we draw the lids over the eyes and moisten them. Fishes have no tear glands and a mudskipper cleans and moistens its eyes by pulling them back into the head.

Double vision

The eyes themselves serve a dual purpose: the retina of the upper half is rich in rods, which means that it can detect small movements; the lower part has cones, which give colour vision. Presumably with the upper part of the eye they look down to detect insects and other small animals but watch other mudskippers for their colours, since these are used for signals. Eelskippers, when they meet, open their mouths at each other, showing the dark indigo blue inside. They also raise and lower the long spine of the dorsal fin. These movements are a challenge which may end in a pushing match, after which the two separate.

Most, if not all, mudskippers have some form of signal which is often used while they are moving about over the mud. Usually it is a matter of raising and lowering the brightly coloured first dorsal fin every few seconds. One species throws itself in the air at frequent intervals, seeming to stand for a split second on the tip of its very thin tail before flopping back on the mud. This appears to be a matter of making those around keep off its territory, so all have their own feeding ground.

The mudskipper's pectoral fins are broad and mounted on a stubby limb, a sort of arm. In moving over the mud it uses these as crutches. It anchors its body with the anal fin and presses downwards and backwards with the pectoral fins, so it moves

with a similar action to a sealion. In the water it swims in the usual way, that is by wriggling its tail, usually keeping its head above water.

Gymnastic courtship

Except in the breeding season, when the male has brighter colours, it is impossible to distinguish the male from the female except by dissection. At the breeding season in *Periophthalmus chrysopilos,* the only species whose breeding behaviour is at all well known, the colours of the male intensify and he has a brilliantly golden chin and throat. He displays this by doing 'press-ups' at passing females until he attracts one. She then follows him to his burrow. Mating seems to take place in the burrow, and the eggs are also laid there.

Mud sappers

Although it is generally believed that the first fishes to come on land, the ancestors of the salamanders, were probably of the coelacanth type (see page 56), the mudskippers show us some of the ways in which these ancestral land-water vertebrates must have lived. They are truly amphibious, some species spending most of their time on land, others most of their time in water, being able to stay submerged for up to 2 hours. They have overcome problems of breathing and movement on land, and have also solved the problem of shelters, by burrowing in the mud. The burrows are made up of a saucer-shaped depression leading into a vertical tunnel, with a rampart of mud round the saucer. The saucer may be anything from 6 in. to 2 ft across. One species makes a Y-shaped burrow with twin turrets of mud at the surface. The burrow is dug with the mouth, the fish bringing out mouthfuls of mud and spitting them on to the rampart to build it.

Leaping as well as bounding

The actions of any mudskipper out of water are quite remarkable, as we have seen. There is, however, one species which does more than probably any other to justify the common name of these relatives of the gobies. This is *Periophthalmus koelreuteri*, which is the most widespread species, round the shores of the Indian Ocean. It spends a great deal of its time, when the tide is out, perched on the margins of small pools in the mangrove swamps with the tip of its tail just in the water. The usual size of this mudskipper is about 5 in. in length. When disturbed it jumps to the next pool, which may be anything up to 2 feet away. Moreover it seldom misses its target. Such jumps are made by curving the body and then straightening it suddenly.

class	**Pisces**
order	**Perciformes**
family	**Gobiidae**

▷ *A giant mudskipper **Periophthalmus** displays by raising and lowering its dorsal and tail fin. This species lives on the banks of Malayan rivers where they dig 'castles' for themselves. This is a small pool with a muddy wall and perhaps a tunnel in the pool for the fish to retreat into. This species is about twice the size of **Scartelaos** being about 9 in. and also much fatter. It will sit on its 'castle' wall and defend its territory, evicting all rivals.*

▷▷ *Tail standing. This mudskipper **Scartelaos viridis** was filmed at the mouth of a small river near a Chinese hamlet in Malaya. It lives on the mud flat and is exposed only at very low tide. Every so often, as the series of frames show, it throws itself upwards until it is almost standing on its tail before flopping back onto the mud. This appears to be a matter of showing itself to warn those around to keep off its territory so all have a reasonable amount of feeding ground.*

Open-mouthed, an oyster toadfish swims around, ready to snap up anything edible that it can take in at one gulp.

Toadfish

As its name suggests, the toadfish's looks are extraordinary; it has a head like a toad and the tail of a fish. Toadfishes have large heads, broad and somewhat flattened, with wide mouths armed with many blunt teeth. Tags of skin decorate the lower lip as well as other parts of the face. The eyes are large. The short, front dorsal fin is spiny and in some species the spines are hollow and poisonous. The second dorsal fin is long and soft-rayed. The pelvic fins lie well forward of the pectorals. Toadfishes are usually 1 ft long but may be up to 1½ ft. The scales are very small and are embedded in the slimy skin, usually a dirty brown colour with darker mottlings.

There are about 30 species living mainly in shallow water in tropical and temperate seas, but some may enter brackish water, and a few live in freshwater.

Generally lethargic

Toadfishes are solitary, slow-moving bottom-dwellers, usually sheltering among stones or rocks or in cavities. They are strongly territorial, each keeping to a fairly small area from which it drives away intruders of its own species. Toadfishes are also pugnacious towards almost any moving object. Some toadfishes make limited migrations from deeper to shallower waters to breed, but as a family they are lethargic, so they require less oxygen than most fishes. They have only three pairs of gills and a small area of gill surface relative to the weight of the body. One result of their slow-moving ways is that they can live in water poorly supplied with oxygen; they can, if necessary, draw upon the oxygen in their swimbladder as a temporary measure.

Foghorn sounds

One species especially, the oyster toadfish, which lives in shallow waters along the eastern coast of the United States, is famous for the sounds it makes. Other members of the family make sounds but the oyster fish has been singled out for study into the mechanisms. It has a heart-shaped swimbladder divided internally by a horizontal membrane and surrounded by a band of muscle. The inflated bladder is twanged by movements of the surrounding muscle, the membrane dividing its cavity probably acting like the velum of a drum. Sounds like grunts and growls as well as the louder foghorn noises are produced. Water damps sound, so although a toadfish can be heard by anyone at the surface the sound reaching his ear is more like that from a distant fog horn. The grunts and growls seem to be used in territorial aggression and they often precede an attack, in which the toadfish uses its teeth. The foghorn sounds are less easy to explain but they are probably used to advertise, like bird song, the possession of a territory. They may also be used in breeding, perhaps to bring the male and female together.

Experiments have shown that if the muscle surrounding the swimbladder or the nerve supplying it are stimulated electrically, a swimbladder will emit grunts and growls after it is removed from the toadfish.

Omnivorous eater

Lethargic, bottom living fishes with wide mouths, toadfishes snap up anything edible, including worms, shrimps, crabs, sea snails, small bivalves, squid and any fish that can be taken in at one gulp. They also eat any carrion, or offal, thrown overboard by ships, benefiting from man's waste as they do from his litter, for in coastal water toadfishes use tin cans and other such receptacles dumped in the sea as shelters from which to make their feeding sorties.

Zealous fathers

During June and July, the male oyster toadfish establishes a nest among rocks or stones, or in an old can, boot or other object lying on the seabed. Several females lay their eggs in it, to a total of 7–800. The eggs are $\frac{3}{16}$ in. diameter, amber-coloured, and sticky, and are laid in a single layer, carpeting the floor or the ceiling of the nest. During the 10–26 days before they hatch, the length of time needed depending on the temperature of the water, the male guards the nest, and he is unusually belligerent during this period. He also aerates the eggs by fanning them with his pectoral fins, and he keeps the nest clean. After hatching, the baby toadfishes stay in the nest for a while, until they are about 1 in. long. Then they leave the nest and cling to rock surfaces or to pebbles, by a sucker on their underside, but this disappears as they grow. They reach a length of $3\frac{1}{2}$ in. after one year.

class	**Pisces**
order	**Batrachoidiformes**
family	**Batrachidae**
genera & species	**Opsanus beta** *Gulf of Mexico toadfish* **O. tau** *oyster toadfish* **Porichthys notatus** *Northern midshipman* **P. porosissimus** *Atlantic midshipman others*

The Arrival of the Amphibians

In order to arrive at a typical amphibian from a fish-like ancestor, one more change is needed in addition to the modification of the limbs and the development of air-breathing respiration. This is the loss of scales in the skin.

Although most fishes have a very obvious covering of scales, many have a smooth skin with tiny, vestigial scales embedded in it or else are quite scaleless. This reduction in the size and number of scales has taken place independently in the course of the evolution of fishes and is found in several unrelated families. The evidence that members of the Amphibia may have had scaly ancestors is fairly clear, and at least one group, the caecilians, still have vestigial scales.

Although several different groups of fishes show a tendency towards air-breathing and emergence on land (see page 54), there is only one that, in addition, has internal features that link it with the Amphibia. This is the Crossopterygii. They are freshwater fishes and their fossils are found from the Devonian period onwards. One group of crossopterygians in particular, the extinct Rhipidistia, had all the characters needed in an amphibian ancestor. The fins had fleshy lobes in which the skeleton had basically the same arrangement of bones as in a land-living quadruped.

The oldest amphibian fossil, Ichthyostegia, nearly 400 million years old and 3 ft long, had a large fish-like tail and its limbs, although short, were capable of supporting the body.

The rest of the Amphibia, other than the caecilians, can be divided into two distinct orders, the Caudata or Urodela, often referred to as the tailed amphibians, and the Anura or Salientia, known as tailless amphibians.

The Caudata include salamanders and newts. Typically, these have an elongated cylindrical body, a long tail and two pairs of feebly developed legs. They tend to spend more time in water than the Anura and a number of species live wholly in water, retaining gills throughout life. A few of these are dealt with here, including the olm, siren and mudpuppy. The last is a special case for, like the axolotl, it can under certain circumstances lose its gills and develop lungs. The other two never do and cannot be induced to do so.

The olm was once described as a 'doubtful amphibian' or a fish-lizard. The doubts may have been resolved, since it is now accepted as a true amphibian, but the problem remains. Presumably its wholly aquatic state is secondary and its ancestors were partly land-living, like other salamanders. Yet it draws attention to the evolutionary twists and turns that can occur and the ease with which organisms can, in the course of generations, turn from wholly terrestrial to wholly aquatic, or vice versa, or to an intermediate condition as in most salamanders and newts.

Frogs and toads, that together make up the second group of amphibians, have lost the tail although this is present in the larval or tadpole stage. Their group name, Anura, means tailless. The alternative group name, Salientia, is from the Latin meaning to leap and their skeleton is well-adapted to their jumping habits. A tail would be in the way for this. The backbone, with only nine vertebrae, is short and rigid. The hip girdle is firmly fixed to the backbone. The hindlegs are usually much longer than the forelegs and the shoulder girdle is strengthened to withstand the shock of landing after a leap.

As in other vertebrates, the skin of amphibians is composed of two layers, an outer epidermis and an inner dermis. The outer layer is composed of dead cells which helps to prevent the loss of too much water when the animal is on land. Nevertheless, amphibians as a whole must seek out damp places. This is the more necessary since respiration is largely through the skin. The lungs are not filled and emptied by movements of the ribs but by movements of the mouth. The floor of the mouth moves up and down and air is inhaled and exhaled through the nostrils, which are closed and opened alternately forcing air into the lungs and then allowing it to escape, driven out by contraction of elastic lungs.

The skin contains two kinds of glands. The mucus glands, found all over the body, give out a clear fluid which helps keep the skin moist for breathing. In tree frogs the mucus glands on the toes exudes a sticky liquid that helps them to cling to vertical surfaces. The second kind of gland is distributed mainly in patches and contains a poison, a milky liquid given out when the animal is alarmed.

Caecilian

The caecilian is a limbless amphibian with a long cylindrical body marked with rings, living wholly underground. The 158 species are worm-like or snake-like according to size, the smallest caecilian being only $4\frac{1}{2}$ in. long, the largest, $4\frac{1}{2}$ ft. Their colour is usually blackish but may be pale flesh-colour. The skin is smooth and slimy, but unlike that of other amphibians, it has small scales embedded in it, in most species. The eyes are small, sometimes covered with skin, and usually useless. There is a peculiar sensory organ; a tentacle on each side of the head lies in a groove running from eyes to tip of snout.

As in snakes, one lung is large and long, the other is reduced to a small lobe.

Caecilians live in warm regions, in America from Mexico to northern Argentina, in southern and south-east Asia and in the Seychelles and parts of Africa. They live from sea-level to about $6\,000$ ft.

Ancient burrower

Caecilians are the sole surviving relatives of the earliest land animals, large fossil amphibians which roamed the earth 400 million years ago. Burrows are made in soft earth, and caecilians seldom come above ground except when heavy rain floods the burrows. One species, at least, is aquatic, and a few species live in leaf litter which is found on the floor of rain forests.

Feeding

Little is known for certain but earthworms are probably the main diet for most species, and a few may eat termites. The sticky caecilian, of southeast Asia, the best-known species, also eats small burrowing snakes.

They themselves are eaten by certain large burrowing snakes.

Life history

There is no difference between male and female externally. Fertilisation is internal and some species lays eggs, others bear live young.

More is known of the life history of the 15 in. sticky caecilian, the female of which lays some two dozen eggs, each about $\frac{1}{4}$ in. in diameter, connected in a jelly-like string. They are laid in a burrow near water, the female coiling her body around the egg-mass until they hatch. The larvae, which escape to water, have a breathing pore on either side of the head. This leads into internal gills, connected with the throat, as in fishes. External gills, present in the embryo, are lost before hatching. They have normal eyes, a flattened tail for swimming, and a head like a newt. At the end of its larval life the breathing pores close, lungs are developed and the young caecilian lives permanently on land, burrowing underground.

The aquatic species of caecilian has sometimes been observed swimming in an eel-like fashion.

Three-way links

The first mention of a caecilian was by Seba, in 1735, when he described it as a snake. Linnaeus, in 1754, also included it among the snakes. In 1811, Oppel put caecilians with frogs, toads and salamanders as amphibians, but these were generally regarded as reptiles as late as 1859. Then came a change, and the caecilians were thought to be degenerate salamanders. From 1900 on there followed studies of the anatomy, and it gradually became clear that caecilians provided an interesting link with the past.

Even now our knowledge of the caecilians is not extensive. They have always been regarded as rare animals, although it is now known that they are plentiful enough in suitable habitats. Yet, as with all animals living wholly underground, it is hard to find out anything about their way of life. What we can do, however, is study how they are made, and this is important, because it tells us that caecilians are a link with the large extinct amphibians that lived nearly 400 million years ago. Their large footprints are known from the Devonian rocks and their skeletons from the rocks of the next geological period, the Carboniferous (Coal Age). After that there is no trace of them, so they seem to have died out 300 million years ago. Some were crocodile-like, lived on land in the marshes where the coal measures were laid down, and they started life as aquatic larvae. They seemed to have been the first backboned animals to live permanently on land, and they almost certainly evolved from air-breathing fishes, the lobe-finned fishes which were the ancestors of the amphibians.

These ancient amphibians gave rise not only to the present-day amphibians but also to the reptiles. They link, therefore, the fishes, amphibians and reptiles, and the caecilians seem to be their direct surviving descendants. This relationship is seen not only in the degenerate scales found in the caecilian skin but also in the caecilian skull being so like that of these giant amphibians of 400 million years ago. It will be interesting to see if any fossil caecilians are found in the future and to compare them with the present day order. As yet no fossil caecilians have been found.

class	**Amphibia**
order	**Apoda or Gymnophiona**
family	**Caeciliidae**
genera	***Caecilia, Typhlonectes, Ichthyophis,*** *others*

*Feeding habits of many caecilians are still unknown, but earthworms are probably important in their diet, as in this species **Siphonops annulatus.***

Axolotl

The axolotl is the Peter Pan of the amphibian world, being able to reproduce its own kind while still in its aquatic larval stage. This is unlike the usual development of amphibians such as the common frog, toads and newts, which as larvae, or tadpoles, are confined to fresh water. In the adult form they can live in water and on land, reproducing in water in the breeding season. Certain amphibians, the Mexican axolotl being the most famous, are able to complete their life cycle without ever leaving the water, as sexual maturity is reached in the larval stage.

The axolotl is a newt-like creature, 4—7 in. long, usually black, or dark brown with black spots, but albinos are quite common. The legs and feet are small and weak, while the tail is long, with a fin running from the back of the head to the tail and along the underside of the tail. It breathes through the three pairs of feathery gills on the sides of the head.

Habits and habitat

Axolotls are quite often kept in aquaria, especially in schools. This is rather surprising as they are rather dull animals, spending most of their time at the bottom of the tank, occasionally swimming about lazily for a few seconds before sinking again. A probable reason is that the axolotl can reproduce its own kind without ever leaving the water. Newts and most salamanders, kept in captivity, need water, land and very careful keeping if they are to survive and breed successfully.

Axolotls cannot be kept together with complete safety as they are liable to bite off each other's gills and feet, and bite pieces out of the tail. If this does happen, however, and they are then separated, the missing pieces will regenerate.

In the wild, axolotls are confined to certain lakes around Mexico City, where they are regarded as delicacies when roasted. The name axolotl is Mexican for 'water sport'.

Zoologists were unable to decide where to place axolotls in the classification of amphibians, until 1865 when, at the Jardin des Plantes in Paris, the problem was solved. Several specimens had bred successfully, when one day it was noticed that the young of one brood had lost their gills and tails, and had quite a different coloration. They had, in fact, turned into salamanders. This was the secret of the axolotl. It is one of several species of salamander, an amphibian which normally has an aquatic tadpole resembling the axolotl, that normally changes straight into the adult. The axolotl, however, usually becomes sexually mature while still a larva. This is because the axolotl fails to metamorphose.

Sperm capsule

In most frogs and toads, fertilisation of the eggs takes place externally. In other words, the female sheds the eggs into the water and the male simply releases his sperm near them, to make their own way to the eggs. The axolotls, related salamanders, and newts have a system of internal fertilisation but it is different from the normal method in which the male introduces the sperm into the female's body to meet the eggs waiting there. Instead, the male axolotl sheds his sperm in a packet called a spermatophore. It sinks to the bottom and the female settles over it and picks it up with her cloaca.

*Albino axolotl **Ambystoma mexicanum**. Externally it seems to be juvenile, but internally it is a sexually mature adult. For years zoologists were unable to decide where axolotls fitted into the classification, until they were observed changing into adult salamanders.*

The male attracts the female by a courtship dance, secreting a chemical from glands in his abdomen and swishing his tail, presumably to spread the chemical until a female detects it and swims towards him.

About a week later, 200—600 eggs are laid, in April or May. They are sticky, and the female attaches them to plants with her back legs. The young axolotls hatch out a fortnight to three weeks later, depending on the temperature of the water. At this stage they are only about ½ in. long and remain on the plant where the eggs are laid. After a week they start swimming in search of food and, if the water is warm and food plentiful, they will be 5—7 in. long by winter. They will then hibernate, taking no food, if the water temperature drops below 10°C/50°F.

Carnivorous feeders

The youngest axolotls feed on plankton, minute organisms that float in water. Later they eat water fleas such as daphnia, and when fully grown they hunt for worms, tadpoles, insect larvae, crustaceans and wounded fish. Their prey has to move, however, and axolotls will ignore still, dead food given to them but will snap up a piece of food that is waved about in the water.

Precocious amphibians

The axolotl's habit of breeding while in the larval stage is known as neoteny, or the retention of juvenile characteristics in the adult form. By 'adult' is meant a sexually mature animal. This habit is not restricted to the axolotl. Other amphibians, including some salamanders, sometimes exhibit neoteny, failing to emerge onto land, but continuing to grow in the larval form.

The basic cause of neoteny seems to be a lack of thyroxine, the hormone secreted by the thyroid gland, which controls metabolism. If the secretion is upset in humans, several bodily disorders occur, including the formation of goitres, swellings in the neck caused by the thyroid gland enlarging. Administration of thyroid gland extracted from cattle, for instance, can often cure the goitre, and axolotls will change into adult salamanders if given thyroid gland.

It would seem, then, that there is something lacking in the diet of both axolotls and humans with goitres. In Wyoming and the Rocky Mountain area the tiger salamander regularly exhibits neoteny and humans are liable to get goitres. This has been traced to a lack of iodine in the water, for iodine is an essential component of thyroxine. In these cases the administration of iodine, rather than thyroxine, is all that is needed either to effect the metamorphosis of an amphibian or cure a goitre. However, iodine treatment is not the only way of making axolotls metamorphose. Sometimes a consignment sent to a dealer or a laboratory will change into adults shortly after being received. Apparently, the jolting during travel has been sufficient to start the change.

When faced with an odd occurrence like this, a zoologist asks whether it confers any advantage on the animal. The freshwater animal has an advantage over a land animal because it does not have to conserve its body water. This could well be the reason

△ *It is now known that several species of salamanders are able to breed while still in the gilled stage. The eastern mud salamander* **Pseudotriton montanus** *is one such amphibian.*

for the axolotl's neoteny. The lakes where it lives do not dry up and there is an abundance of water, so it is an advantage to live and breed there, rather than risk life on the dry, barren land around. If the lakes dry up, then it can still change into a salamander, having the best of both worlds.

class:	**Amphibia**
order:	**Caudata**
family	**Ambystomatidae**
genus & species	***Ambystoma mexicanum***

▽ *Adult of* **Ambystoma mexicanum**. *The axolotl in juvenile form can be made to change into an adult salamander by giving it extract of thyroid, or sometimes when given a physical jolt.*

△ *Striking colours are the mark of the fire salamander, as shown by this black-and-yellow candy-striped version.*

Fire salamander

No hard and fast line can be drawn between salamanders and newts, although salamanders are generally the larger amphibians and spend less time in the water. They are sometimes mistaken for lizards of the reptile class, but the salamanders' heads are rounded and they have smooth scaleless skins compared with the more pointed heads and scaly skins of the lizards.

The habitat of the fire or spotted salamander ranges from France and Spain across to central and southern Europe and through to Asia Minor. It grows to 7½ in., of which 3½ in. is tail. It is strikingly coloured, glossy black with brilliant yellow, orange or sometimes red blotches that on some individuals join up to form lines running down the body.

Sluggish creatures

Fire salamanders are sluggish, spending the warmer parts of the year under stones or in crevices in logs, among rocks or under dense vegetation in damp woods and slopes. They very rarely enter the water and can only remain submerged for a few minutes at a time. At night, or after heavy rain, fire salamanders come out to feed, catching slow-moving creatures such as worms,

snails, large insects and small crustaceans.

From October to March (depending on the climate in different parts of their range), they hibernate under stones and logs or in crevices, where two or more may be found together.

Strange courtship

The courtship and mating of salamanders resembles that of newts except that newts retire to ponds during the breeding season. Salamanders stay on land and when male and female meet there is a very strange courtship, found only in a few of the tailed amphibians. The male tries to climb on the female's back and to grasp her with his front legs. The female usually rejects these advances and struggles, sometimes so violently as to throw the male off. The climax of the mating is not the usual joining of the male and female openings, but the male depositing a gelatinous capsule containing the sperm cells on the ground. The female then presses it into her body with her hind legs. This part is similar to the mating of newts except that with them it takes place in water.

After mating, most amphibians lay their eggs in the water where they are left to develop and eventually hatch into tadpoles. The female fire salamander retains the eggs inside her body until they are ready to hatch. This takes a relatively long time; after a mating in the summer the tadpoles are born the next spring. She then goes to a stretch

of shallow water and immerses only the hind end of her body to bring forth her 30–40 young, two at a time over a fairly lengthy period. The 1 in.-long tadpoles swim away from their mother and immediately live an independent existence. After 10 weeks, when 2 in. long, they lose the feathery gills they had from birth, develop lungs and come onto land, usually not to return to water except to give birth to a new generation.

Its poison is part bluff

Like other conspicuously coloured animals such as wasps, the black and yellow of the fire salamander advertises the fact that it is poisonous. It has no sting or poison fangs but a venom called salamandrin is secreted from pores just behind the eyes. If the salamander is molested the poison is secreted as a milky fluid which can be very unpleasant if it gets into the mouth or eyes. The poison that common toads secrete from their parotid glands (page 86) has the same effect. A dog or any animal that picks the amphibian up in its mouth very quickly drops it again and salivates copiously, in order to rid itself of the unpleasant effects. Unlike burnet moths fire salamanders are not immune to their own poison.

This poison has certainly had the effect of deterring attacks by man. From early times the fire salamander has had the reputation of being a fatally dangerous animal. Edward Topsell in his *Historie of Four-*

Footed Beastes, written in 1607, said 'If a salamander bite you, then betake you to the coffin and winding sheet'—a poetic way of stating that the bite is fatal, but showing how strong was the idea then that death inevitably followed from a salamander's bite. Even now, this legend persists. Yet salamanders do not bite and no harm can come from handling them unless the poison gets into a cut or is rubbed into the eyes.

Ancient legends

In the same passage Edward Topsell wrote 'Some do affirm that it is as cold as ice, and that it therefore quencheth heat or fire.' This was a legend as old as that of the supposed fatal bite. It was said that if a salamander was thrown into fire, it not only remained unharmed but it even put the fire out. The rational explanation usually offered for this legend is that fire salamanders often hibernate in logs. If then a wet or green log was put on a fire it might well quench it, yet get sufficiently hot in the process to arouse any salamander inside. The sudden appearance of so striking an animal as a fire salamander in the middle of a fire could hardly be overlooked and it is perhaps not so surprising that the legend should have arisen. When asbestos was discovered, at least as long ago as the time of the Ancient Greeks, it was thought to be the hair or wool of salamanders because it was fire-proof.

As often with the ancient legends, original observations were distorted and misquoted by later writers and legends grew despite their being obviously wrong. It was Pliny, the Roman naturalist, who popularised the story about the fire-extinguishing salamander—despite the fact that he describes a medicine made from the ashes of a salamander!

class	**Amphibia**
order	**Caudata**
family	**Salamandridae**
genus & species	***Salamandra salamandra***

◁ *Living poison gland; when handled gently the fire salamander is quite harmless, but it reacts to any rough treatment by secreting a burning, poisonous fluid which can cause death in a small mammal.*
▽ *Fire salamander emblem on the chimney piece in the Guard Room of Henri III of France at the Château de Blois.*

Lungless salamander

The name 'lungless salamander' covers 200 species of salamanders living in Tropical and North America that have neither lungs nor gills but breathe through their skin and the lining of the mouth. A further peculiarity is that some of them cannot open their lower jaw to the normal gape. There is only one species outside America, represented by three subspecies in France, Italy and Sardinia.

Lungless salamanders range in size from 1½ to 8½ in. A few live permanently in water but most of them spend their lives on land. They are mainly sombrely coloured—black, grey or brown—but some have patches of red and the redbacked salamander occurs in 2 colour phases: red and grey with the belly of each spotted black and white. Varying proportions of red and grey individuals are found in any batch of larvae. Most lungless salamanders have the usual salamander shape, a long rounded body, tail about the same length, and short legs, the front legs with 4 toes, the back legs with 5. The four-toed lungless salamander has 4 toes on each foot. The longtailed salamander is so called because its 7 in. tail dwarfs a 4 in. body. The California slender salamander is snakelike, with vestigial legs, and lies under fallen logs, coiled up tightly like a watch-spring.

Some species are widespread. The dusky salamander ranges over the eastern United States from New Brunswick southwards to Georgia and Alabama and westwards to Oklahoma and Texas. Other species are very localised. The Ocoee salamander lives in damp crevices in rocks or on the water-fall-splashed faces of rocks in Ocoee Gorge, southeast Tennessee. One of the European subspecies lives in southeast France and north Italy, the second lives in Tuscany, the third in Sardinia.

From deep wells to tall trees

Lungless salamanders mostly live in damp places, under stones or logs, among moss, under leaf litter, near streams or seepages or even in surface burrows in damp soil. The shovel-nosed salamander lives in mountain streams all its life, hiding under stones by day. Others live on land but go into water to escape enemies. The pygmy salamander, 2 in. long, living in the mountains of Virginia and North Carolina, can climb the rough bark of trees to a height of several feet. The arboreal salamander does even better, climbing trees to a height of 60 ft, sometimes making its home in old birds' nests. The Californian flatheaded salamander uses webbed feet to walk over slippery rocks and swings its tail from side to side as it walks, to help itself up a slope. On descent its curled tail acts as a brake.

Several species live in caves or artesian and natural wells as much as 200 ft deep. All are blind, one retains its larval gills throughout life and one cave species spends its larval life in mountain streams but migrates to underground waters before metamorphosis. It then loses its sight.

Creeping, crawling food

All lungless salamanders eat small invertebrates. Those living in water feed mainly on aquatic insect larvae. Those on land hunt slugs, worms, woodlice and insect larvae. One group of lungless salamanders *Plethodon* are known as woodland salamanders. They live in rocky crevices or in holes underground and eat worms, beetles and ants. The slimy salamander also eats worms, hard-shelled beetles, ants and centipedes as well as shieldbugs, despite their obnoxious odour and unpalatable flavour. The European species catches food with a sticky tongue which it can push out 1 inch.

Different breeding habits

There is as much diversity in their breeding as in the way they live. Some lay their eggs in water and the larvae are fully aquatic;

△ *Mountain salamander,* **Desmognathus ochrophaeus** *lives near springs and streams where the ground is saturated.*
▷ *Red-backed salamander, occupant of old garden plots where there are tree stumps, rotting logs and moisture-conserving debris.*

others lay them on land, and among this second group are species in which the females curl themselves round their batches of 2–3 dozen eggs as if incubating. In a few species the female stays near her eggs until they hatch, but without incubating them or giving them any special care. The woodland salamanders lay their eggs in patches of moss or under logs and the larvae metamorphose before leaving the eggs. A typical species is the dusky salamander. The male deposits his sperm in a capsule or spermatophore. He then rubs noses with the female. A gland on his chin gives out a scent that stimulates the female to pick up the spermatophore with her cloaca. Her eggs are laid in clusters of two dozen in spring or early summer under logs or stones. Each egg is $\frac{3}{16}$ in. diameter and the larva on hatching is $\frac{5}{8}$ in. long. It has external gills and goes into water, where it lives until the following spring, when it metamorphoses. The adults, $5\frac{1}{4}$ in. long, are dark brown or grey. When it first metamorphoses the young salamander is brick-red and light cream in patches. Later it takes on the colours of the fully grown adult but has a light band down the back and a light line from the eye to the angle of the jaw.

Not so defenceless

Lungless salamanders, like other salamanders and newts, seldom have defensive weapons, a possible exception being the arboreal salamander with its fang-like teeth in the lower jaw. It is known to bite a finger when handled. The slimy salamander gives

out a very sticky, glutinous secretion from its skin when handled and this possibly deters predators. The enemies are small snakes and frogs, which take their toll of the larvae and the young salamanders. It may be in an attempt to evade such enemies that the dusky salamander sometimes leaps about, several inches at a jump. The yellow blotched salamander, of California, has a curious behaviour that may be defensive. It raises itself on the tips of its toes, rocks its body backwards and forwards, arches its tail and swings it from side to side. It also gives out a milky astringent fluid from the tail. And it squeaks like a mouse.

Peculiar features

Peculiar features of these salamanders are that they lose their larval gills as they grow and they do not grow lungs. Instead, their skin has become the breathing organ with the skin lining the mouth acting the part of a lung by having a network of fine blood vessels in it, like the lining of a lung.

The arboreal salamander has a similar network of fine blood vessels in the skin of its toes, which may play the part of lungs (or should they be called terrestrial gills?). Another extraordinary feature is that others, like the yellow-blotched salamander, squeak, although they have neither lungs nor voice box. They do this by contracting the throat to force air through the lips or nose.

The loss of lungs in the lungless salamanders must be seen as a secondary condition. That is, the ancestral salamander had lungs and these had been lost in the later evolution. The most reasonable explanation for this would be that the losses correlated with the brook-dwelling habits. In the normal salamander the lungs function not only as respiratory organs, but also as hydrostatic organs, decreasing the total specific gravity of the animal, so bringing the salamander very near to having neutral buoyancy. The salamander needs then only a flick of its tail or slight movement of the limbs to propel itself through water and, more especially, to make it rise towards the surface. When it then becomes immobile again it does not immediately sink, as it would do if its specific gravity was greater, but slowly sinks. With the loss of lungs the lungless salamanders have increased their specific gravity and are therefore able the more readily to keep near the bottom in fast moving water.

The loss of lungs is compensated by the greater oxygen content of moving water and so has made their respiratory function also less important. The loss of lungs could be a disadvantage in another respect and a special adaptation has been needed to counteract this. Lungless salamanders have a nasolabial groove running from each nostril to the lips. It is believed that these act as gutters carrying from the nostrils water that has collected there when the head has been submerged.

class	**Amphibia**
order	**Caudata**
family	**Plethodontidae**
genera & species	***Aneides lugubris*** *arboreal salamander* ***Batrachoseps attenuatus*** *California slender salamander* ***Desmognathus fuscus*** *dusky salamander* ***D. ocoee*** *Ocoee salamander* ***D. wrighti*** *pygmy salamander* ***Ensatina croceator*** *yellow-blotched salamander* ***Eurycea longicauda*** *long-tailed salamander* ***Hemidactylium scutatum*** *four-toed salamander* ***Leurognathus marmoratus*** *shovel-nosed salamander* ***Plethodon cinereus*** *red-backed salamander* ***P. glutinosus*** *slimy salamander*

Mudpuppy

The mudpuppy is a kind of salamander living in the weedy streams, ponds and rivers of parts of North America. In the southern part of its range it is called water dog. Both names depend on a belief that it makes a barking sound.

It grows up to 20 in. long, although it is usually about 1 ft long, and is grey to rusty or dark brown with indistinct bluish-black spots and mottlings. There is a conspicuous dark mark on the side of the head running through the eye. Its short, weak legs are suitable only for crawling over mud and are held against the sides when swimming. Each foot has four fairly long toes. Just behind the head are three pairs of conspicuous, bushy and velvety red, plume-like gills. The head is flat and squarish with small eyes.

The mudpuppy ranges from southern Canada to the Gulf of Mexico, from the Mississippi and Missouri basins to New Jersey, and eight subspecies or forms are recognized. A dwarf mudpuppy lives in the Neuse River in North Carolina and the largest form lives in the rice field ditches of both North and South Carolina.

Asking to be caught

Mudpuppies, slow and sluggish salamanders, often take bait, getting themselves hooked, to the annoyance of fishermen. As well as losing his bait the fisherman finds the mudpuppy a slippery customer to handle, due to the slime-covered body. Inevitably this has led to the idea that the mudpuppy is poisonous, which is partly true. It has poison glands in its skin but the poison is not strong enough to affect human beings. Some people claim mudpuppies are good to eat, and one writer speaks of their fine quality and white flesh, rivalling frogs' legs in flavour,

The mudpuppy (above and below) is neotenous, it keeps its gills throughout its life.

Mudpuppies are mainly nocturnal, hiding during the day under stones or buried in the mud, but among dense weed they sometimes move about by day. They feed on worms, insect larvae, fish eggs, crayfishes, small fishes and frogs' eggs.

Never grow up

These salamanders are neotenous (see page 69); they never become fully adult but keep their gills throughout life. They do, however, become sexually mature. The size of the gills can vary. In cold, fresh water with plenty of oxygen the gills contract, but in warmer, more stagnant water low in oxygen they expand, becoming larger and more bushy so as to take up as much oxygen as possible. It is said that if the filaments of the plume-like gills become tangled the mudpuppy will rearrange them with its forefoot.

Delayed spawning

Before going into a dormant state in winter, the mudpuppies mate, and a male and female may share the same hole in the bank. In the following spring the female lays 18–880 yellowish eggs, according to her size, each in its jelly envelope and ¼ in.

across. She sticks them one by one in a crowded group on the underside of a log or large stone or boulder in about 5 ft of water. Sometimes they are laid in a sandy hollow on the riverbed. She stays beside them until they hatch in 38–63 days according to the temperature of the water. As in all such instances, the warmer the water, to some extent, the less time the eggs take to hatch. It is usual to say that the female guards the eggs. Whether this is so or not has never been investigated, but despite their defenceless appearance mudpuppies can give a sharp nip when handled. When first hatched, they still have the yolk sac hanging from their underside. This lasts them until they are 1½ in. long and about 2 months old, and able to find their own food. They mature in 5–7 years, at about 8 in. long and may live for 20 years.

Whining like a puppy

Newts do have a larynx and European newts can make faint squeaks like the sound made by drawing a wet finger over glass. As these newts have lungs the sound is probably made by air driven from the lungs across the vocal cords. The lungless salamanders of California (page 72) make a mouse-like squeak by contracting the throat and driving air either between the half-open jaws or through the nostrils. There is a legend that mudpuppies can bark like a dog. Perhaps this has arisen because when a mudpuppy is taken out of water it sometimes makes a sound like the whine of a puppy. If so, it would not be long before the story had grown to 'barking like a dog'.

class	**Amphibia**
order	**Caudata**
family	**Proteidae**
genus & species	***Necturus maculosus***

Newt

Newts are amphibians of the salamander family. They have a life history very similar to that of frogs and toads in that the adults spend most of their life on land but return to water to breed. They are different in form, however, having long, slender bodies like those of lizards with a tail that is flattened laterally. The name comes from the Anglo-Saxon **evete** which became **ewt** and finally a newt from the transcription of the 'n' in an **ewt**. In Britain, newt refers solely to the genus **Triturus** but in North America it has been applied to related animals which are sometimes, confusingly, called salamanders.

Newts of the genus **Triturus** are found in Europe, Asia, North Africa and North America. There are three species native to Britain. The most common is the smooth newt which is found all over Europe and is the only newt found in Ireland. The maximum length of smooth newts is 4 in. The colour of the body varies, but is mainly olive-brown with darker spots on the upper side and streaks on the head. The vermilion or orange underside has round black spots and the throat is yellow or white. The female is generally paler on the underside than the male and sometimes is unspotted. In the breeding season the male develops a wavy crest running along the back and tail. The palmate newt is very similar to the smooth newt, but about 1 in. shorter and with a square-sided body. In the breeding season the males of the two species can be told apart because black webs link the toes of the hindfeet of the palmate newts, and its crest is not wavy. In addition, the tail ends abruptly and a short thread, about $\frac{1}{8}-\frac{1}{4}$ in. long protrudes from the tip. The largest European newt is the crested or warty newt. It grows up to 6 in. long. The dark grey skin of the upperparts is covered with warts, while the underparts are yellow or orange and spotted with black. The distinguishing feature apart from its size is the crest of the male. From the head to the hips runs a tall, 'toothed' frill —its crest, which becomes the tail fin.

▽ A male smooth newt with its spotted front, as seen from below.

Hibernating on land

When they come out of hibernation in spring, newts make their way to ponds and other stretches of still water where water plants grow. They swim by lashing with their tails, but they spend much of their time resting on the mud or among the stems of plants. They can breathe through their skins but every now and then they rise to the surface to gulp air. Adult newts do not leave the water immediately breeding has finished but remain aquatic until July or August. When they come on land the crest is reabsorbed and the skin becomes rougher. The crested newt keeps its skin moist from the numerous mucus glands scattered over the surface of its body. A few individuals stay in the water all the year round, retaining their smooth skins and crests.

Hibernation begins in the autumn, when the newts crawl into crevices in the ground or under logs and stones. They cannot burrow but are very adept at squeezing themselves into cracks. Occasionally several will gather together in one place and hibernate in a tight mass.

Two rows of teeth

The jaws of newts are lined with tiny teeth and there are two rows of teeth on the roof of the mouth. These are not used for cutting food or for chewing but merely to hold slippery, often wriggling, prey. They feed on a variety of small animals such as worms, snails and insects when on land, and crustaceans, tadpoles and insect larvae while living in water. Unlike frogs and toads, newts do not use their hands to push the food into their mouths, but gulp it down with convulsive swallows. Snails are swallowed whole, caddis flies are eaten in their cases and crested newts eat smooth newts.

Internal fertilisation

The mating habits of newts are quite different from those of common frogs and common toads. Fertilisation is internal and is effected in a most unusual way. The male stimulates the female into breeding condition by nudging her with his snout and lashing the water with his tail. He positions himself in front of or beside her, bends his tail double and vibrates it rapidly, setting up vibrations in the water. The female is also stimulated by secretions from glands in the male's skin. At the end of the courtship the male emits a spermatophore which sinks to the bottom. The female newt positions herself over it, then picks it up with her cloaca by pressing her body onto it.

After fertilisation the 200–300 eggs are usually laid singly on the leaves of water plants, although some American newts lay their eggs in spherical clusters. The female newt tests the leaves by smell and touch. When she has chosen a suitable one she holds it with her hindfeet, then folds the leaf over to form a tube and lays an egg in it. The jelly surrounding the egg glues the leaf firmly in place to protect it.

The eggs hatch in about 3 weeks and a more streamlined tadpole than that of a frog or toad emerges. It is not very different from the adult newt except that it has a frill of gills and no legs. Development takes longer than in frog tadpoles but the young newts are ready to emerge by the end of summer. A few spend the winter as tadpoles, remaining in the pond until spring, even surviving being frozen into the ice.

Unpleasant secretion

Newts have many enemies: the young are eaten by aquatic insects and the adults by fishes, water birds, weasels, rats, hedgehogs and many other animals. The crested newt has an unpleasant secretion that is produced in the glands on the back and tail and is exuded when they are squeezed. Grass snakes are known to be dissuaded from eating crested newts because of this.

Newt's nerve poison

The poison of the crested newt is not only unpleasant, but men who have tasted it have found it to be burning. A far more potent poison is that of the California newt. The poison is found mainly in the skin, muscles and blood of the newt, as well as in its eggs. Analysis showed that the poison is a substance called tetrodotoxin, which is also found in puffer fish. Tetrodotoxin extracted from newts' eggs is so powerful that $\frac{1}{3000}$ oz. can kill 7 000 mice. It acts on the nerves, preventing impulses from being transmitted to the muscles. Somehow, in a manner that is not understood, California newts are not affected by their own poison. Their nerves still function when treated with a solution of tetrodotoxin 25 000 times stronger than that which will completely deaden a frog's nerves.

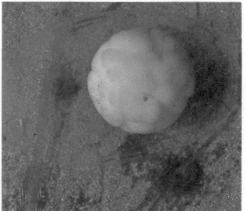

△ Left: Segmenting embryo of a crested newt. Right: The legless tadpole of the crested newt.
▽ Alpine newt **Triturus alpestris**.

class	**Amphibia**	
order	**Caudata**	
family	**Salamandridae**	
genera & species	**Taricha torosa** California newt	
	Triturus cristatus crested newt	
	T. helveticus palmate newt	
	T. vulgaris smooth newt	
	others	

Olm

Since it was first made known to science in 1689 the olm has presented many problems to scientists. Olms (the 'l' is pronounced) belong to the same family of amphibians as the mudpuppy. They live in underground rivers and pools and like many other cave-dwelling animals they are blind and lack pigment in the skin. Olms grow to a length of about 1 ft. The eel-like body has a laterally flattened tail and the head is broad with a blunt snout. The legs are very short, with 3 toes on the front legs and 2 on the hind-legs. The eyes are minute and buried in the skin; they cannot be seen in the adult. The body is a translucent white, becoming pinker when the olm is active and blood is flowing through the skin. The three pairs of feathery gills are red.

The olm is the only cave-dwelling amphibian in Europe and is restricted to limestone caverns in southeast Europe. It is found in parts of Yugoslavia such as Dalmatia, Herzegovina, Bosnia and Croatia, and in a small area of Italy. It is most common in caverns that form part of the underground course of the River Pivka in Slovenia.

Cave-dwellers

The first record of the olm is in a book by the 17th-century Baron Valvasor who recorded that some Yugoslavian peasants ascribed the periodic flooding of the River Bella to a dragon that lived inside a mountain and opened sluice gates when its hideaway was threatened with floods. In the floodwaters the villagers often found lizard-like animals which they took to be the dragon's babies. These animals were olms, and it is only during floods that they are found outside their underground caverns.

It seems the olm retains some sensitivity to light. If, in captivity, it is exposed to light it turns black.

Inside the caverns, olms live in still pools or in the foaming cascades of the underground rivers where they spend most of their time concealed under boulders. They can, however, swim with great agility and are very difficult to catch. Like newts, olms absorb oxygen through their skin but they also rise to the surface to gulp air. Olms feed on small aquatic animals such as crustaceans and small fish. They are known to be very sensitive to vibrations so they probably detect their prey by the movements they make in the water.

Losing colour

It is usually impossible to distinguish the sexes of olms but in the breeding season the females become plump and pink. Courtship and mating are similar to that of newts (page 75), the female picking up a spermatophore deposited by the male. A little later the female lays 30–40 eggs, $\frac{1}{3}$ in. across, over a period of 3 weeks. She coils her body round them, gently waving her tail for aeration and to prevent silt settling on them. After 3 months the larvae, nearly 1 in. long, hatch out. They lack limbs and gills and spend most of their time lying on their sides. Later they become more active and feed on minute algae and crustaceans.

When olms have been kept in water warmer than that of their native caves, they occasionally give birth to live young, the eggs being retained in the female's body until they hatch.

When they hatch young olms are almost black, but as they develop the pigment is gradually lost. Their eyes are also well-developed but they gradually degenerate and sink into the skin, becoming invisible, although the eye muscles and nerves remain. If they are kept in the light from the beginning the colour is retained.

Olms mature at about 10 years and live for at least 25 years.

△ *Agile swimmers. Olms are the only cave-dwelling amphibians in Europe. They are blind and lack any pigment in their skin.*

Refusing to change

When olms were first discovered our knowledge of the relationships of animals was very imperfect and great difficulty was experienced in fitting the olm into its right place in the animal kingdom. It was once described as a 'doubtful' amphibian, as it had features of both amphibians and fish, and Linnaeus left it out of his *Systema Naturae*. Sir Everard Home, who studied the first fossil *Ichthyosaurus*, even related these two, considering them both to be a kind of fish-lizard or fish-newt. About the same time it was realised that the olm was very like an axolotl (page 68). It was an amphibian that retained its gills throughout life and reproduced in the larval stage — a process known as neoteny.

When it was found that an axolotl could, under certain circumstances, change into a salamander, experiments were carried out on olms to see if they could be induced to change. They all failed, so it seems likely that the olm is not the neotenous larva of another amphibian, as an axolotl is a neotenous salamander, but that it is a wholly aquatic amphibian that has never lived on land. In this case, the olm is a primitive member of the order of amphibians, the Caudata or tailed amphibians. Originally the caudates kept their gills all their lives, then modern types, who spent part of their lives on land, like the newts and salamanders, arose. The olm is, therefore, an evolutionary relic, or 'missing link'.

class	**Amphibia**
order	**Caudata**
family	**Proteidae**
genus & species	***Proteus anguinus***

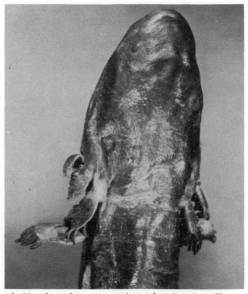

△ *An amphibious Peter Pan, the siren retains its larval characteristics throughout its life.*

△ *Head of the greater siren showing its gills.*

Siren

Sirens are North American amphibians named after mythical beings, and are almost beyond belief. They are related to salamanders but look like eels—they are sometimes called mud eels—and they have never properly grown up.

The greater siren is up to 2½ ft long and is slimy to the touch. It is dark green with its underside flecked with green or yellow. The body is long and slender, tapering more or less evenly to the tip of the tail. Behind the small head, on either side, are bunches of feathery external gills. The siren has no hindlegs—it has even lost all trace of the bones of the hip girdle—and its front legs are small and weak and have four small toes. The greater siren ranges from Washington DC to Florida. The lesser siren ranges over the southeastern United States, the lower Mississippi valley, parts of Texas and into Mexico. It measures 7—20 in. and is dark brown or bluish-black. There is also a dwarf siren with five well marked subspecies ranging from South Carolina to Florida. Each is up to 8 in. long, brown, grey, green or greyish-black, with three toes on each forefoot, the forelegs being even smaller than in the larger species. The subspecies differ in details, such as the distinctiveness of the stripes running along the body and are called the narrow-striped, broad-striped, slender, Everglades and Gulf hummock dwarf sirens.

Surviving the drought

The greater and lesser sirens live in shallow streams and ditches, hiding by day among water plants and coming out at night to feed. They swim by wriggling their bodies in an eel-like way. If they find themselves stranded on mud, they may use their legs to drag themselves along. The dwarf sirens have similar habits except that they keep more to the marshes, swamps and bogs, burrowing in mud or hiding among submerged vegetation. Sirens are toothless except for teeth in the front part of the roof of the mouth. The jaws have horny plates instead of teeth. They eat both plant and animal food. The two larger sirens take mainly animal food such as worms, water snails, freshwater shrimps and crayfish but also eat green filamentous algae. The dwarf sirens eat especially the leaves of the water hyacinth.

Sirens keep their gills throughout life. In periods of drought they burrow into the mud, to as much as a foot down. Their skin loses its sliminess, their gills get smaller, sometimes almost disappearing, and when conditions have become very dry, they go into a state of dormancy or suspended animation. This total dryness may last for up to two months without much harm to the sirens. Then when the rains come again and the streams and swamps fill up with water, the sirens' gills return to their normal size, sometimes hanging like curtains over the front legs. The body becomes slimy again and the sirens resume their usual activities.

Another peculiarity of sirens is that they have very few ribs and because the body is so long in relation to its girth, the pumping capacity of the heart must be increased. This is done by the auricles having finger-like extensions from their sides which provide this capacity. Sirens have no poison glands in the skin to protect them, as so many amphibians have, and their chief enemy is the red and black rainbow snake *Abastor erythrogrammus*.

Evolutionary failures

The female sirens lay their eggs, singly or in batches, on the leaves of water plants. The development of the larva follows the usual lines of salamander and newt larvae except that there is no metamorphosis to the adult. The larva remains a larva, keeps its external gills and becomes sexually mature while still retaining the physical characteristics of a larva, a process known as neoteny (see axolotl page 68). So the sirens have not grown up; they are physically degenerate. In a sense they are evolutionary failures yet they have survived.

Confusion confounded

Sirens passed unnoticed until 1795 when Dr Garden, a Scottish naturalist and physician, found one and sent it to Linnaeus, the Swedish botanist who nearly 40 years before had re-classified the animal kingdom. He, however, was misled by it and it was Cuvier, the French zoologist, who finally recognised that the siren is an amphibian. Why these animals should be called sirens is hard to say. The sirens of Greek mythology were water nymphs who lived on the rocks by the shore and sang sweetly to lure mariners to their doom. The sirens of the streams and marshes of North America make no more than a faint whistle or a tiny yelp. The choice of name is unfortunate because the sea cows, known as manatees, have also been called sirens. They are large marine mammals, totally unlike the American amphibians, and are placed in the order Sirenia. The amphibians are in the family Sirenidae.

class	**Amphibia**
order	**Caudata**
family	**Sirenidae**
genera & species	*Pseudobranchus striatus* dwarf siren *Siren intermedia* lesser siren *S. lacertina* greater siren

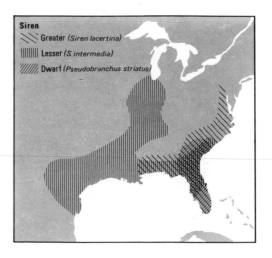

Siren
\\\\ Greater *(Siren lacertina)*
||||| Lesser *(S. intermedia)*
///// Dwarf *(Pseudobranchus striatus)*

Arrow-poison frog

Arrow-poison frogs are found only in Central and South America where the Indians have long extracted poison from their bodies for use on arrow-heads. Many amphibians have at least a trace of poison in their bodies or secrete poison from glands in the skin, and quite a few can cause a good deal of pain to any human that handles them. Only the arrow-poison frogs and one or two others secrete such a strong poison as to cause rapid death.

Most arrow-poison frogs can be distinguished by the nail-like plate on each toe. Many species are brilliantly coloured. The two-toned arrow-poison frog is brick red with patches of blue-black on its legs. More brilliant is the three-striped arrow-poison frog, which is yellow with stripes of black running lengthways down the head and body and around the limbs. Some species have 'flash colours' which are suddenly exposed as the frog jumps. It is thought that the bright colours, especially the 'flash colours' are warnings to other animals that they are not fit to eat.

A Cuban member of the family, **Sminthillus limbatus** *is the smallest frog in the world, measuring less than ½ in.*

Each female lays only one egg. The egg is large in comparison with the size of the mother's body and is laid in a moist spot on land, the larva completing its development and undergoing metamorphosis before hatching. This particular frog is by no means uncommon and its slow rate of breeding is in striking contrast to most frogs that ensure the perpetuation of the species by laying large numbers of eggs.

Habits

The various species of arrow-poison frogs are found in forests of different parts of Central and South America, some living in trees, others living on the forest floor.

Feeding

Arrow-poison frogs conform to the usual amphibian diet. As adults all amphibians are carnivorous. They take insects or other small invertebrates which are full of protein to restore worn-out tissue, and salts, fats, vitamins, and water needed for their metabolism. They also need carbohydrates which can be rebuilt from surplus protein.

Male carries the tadpoles

There are several peculiar features about the breeding habits of arrow-poison frogs. Courtship or courtship rituals are rare amongst frogs and toads, but the golden arrow-poison frogs, and probably other species, 'play' together for as much as two or three hours. They repeatedly jump at each other, sometimes landing on one another's backs, as if fighting. Following the 'play', the eggs are laid, but there is no 'amplexus', the process in which the male, as in the common frog, perches on the female's back and fertilises the eggs as they

are laid. The female arrow-poison frog lays her eggs on the ground and the male, who has been waiting nearby, comes over and fertilises them.

The absence of amplexus may be linked with the occurrence of the courtship play, because in frogs using amplexus it is often the pressure of the male hugging the female that causes the eggs to be extruded. When there is no amplexus, it may be necessary for another stimulus, in this case leaping about with the male, to initiate egg-laying. Both methods ensure that there is a male present to fertilise the eggs which is the primary purpose of animal courtship.

When the eggs have been fertilised, the male carries them on his back where they become attached to his skin although how this is done remains to be discovered. After they hatch, the tadpoles remain on their father's back, getting no moisture except from rain. Up to twenty tadpoles can be found on one arrow-poison frog, and, as they grow, their father has to seek larger and larger holes in which to rest. Eventually he takes them down to the water and they swim away to lead an independent life.

Predator deterrent

Snakes, predatory birds and some carnivorous mammals will often prey on the majority of frogs. The arrow-poison frogs, however, possess the ultimate deterrent of the animal world—their flash colours give a warning to the predator, not to attempt to eat them because of their poisonous nature, giving the frogs a much safer life in their hazardous jungle existence.

It is very usual for an animal that carries a venom, or is in some other way unpleasant or unpalatable, to be brilliantly coloured in red, yellow or black or in some combination of these colours. Among arrow-poison frogs which are so highly poisonous these colours tend to predominate and are accentuated by the use of flash colours, as we have seen. This makes it even more puzzling that one species, *Dendrobates pumilio* should be dark blue and very difficult to see in the dark forests which are its home. The warning colours, red, yellow and black are very conspicuous, and it is their purpose to be conspicuous, because they are advertising a warning to predators. Yet *Dendrobates pumilio* seems to be doing its best to efface itself although it has eight times more poison in its skin than those arrow-poison frogs that are bright red and very conspicuous.

Self-effacing relative

Although it is usual to speak of the Dendrobatidae as the family of arrow-poison frogs, not all its members are poisonous. It is of interest to compare the case of a Brazilian species *Dendrophryniscus brevipollicatus* with other members of the family being discussed here. Apparently this particular species has no venom or very little of it. It is coloured brown, tan and buff, it lives among the leaf litter of the forest floor, and when molested its flattish body becomes stiff and the front part of the body bends upwards and backwards so that it looks like a dried leaf.

Poison arrows

The Indians of South America are renowned for their use of poisoned-tipped arrows,

△ *Golden arrow-poison frog (* **Dendrobates auratus** *).*
Overleaf: Arrow-poison frog **Dendrobates leucomelas.** *The poison secreted by these amphibians is so strong it kills very rapidly. Their bright colours give other animals warning of their poisonous nature so they are not eaten.*

which are reputed to cause death if they do no more than scratch the skin of their target. The best known of the poisons is curare, which is extracted from certain plants, but even this is a mild poison compared with that of the arrow-poison frogs.

The Indians collect the poison by piercing the frog with a sharp stick, and holding it over a fire. The heat of the fire forces the poison through the skin where it collects in droplets. These are scraped off into a jar. The amount collected from each frog, and its potency, varies with the species. The kokoi frog of Colombia secretes the most powerful poison known. This is a substance called batrachotoxin which has recently been shown to be ten times more powerful than tetrodotoxin, the poison of the Japanese puffer fish which had previously held the record as the most powerful known animal venom. 1/100,000 oz. of batrachotoxin is sufficient to kill a man.

One kokoi frog, only 1 in. long, can supply enough venom to make 50 lethal arrows. But the arrow-poison frogs are now being sought for more peaceful purposes. In the same way as curare has become an important drug because of its muscle-relaxing properties, so the venom of arrow-poison frogs is now being used in the laboratory for studies on the nervous system. It has been found that it acts in the same way as the hormones secreted by the adrenal gland, blocking the transmission of messages between nerves and muscles. Large amounts rapidly cause death, but in tiny doses it could well have medicinal value.

class	**Amphibia**
order	**Salientia**
family	**Dendrobatidae**
genera	***Sminthillus***
	Dendrobates, Phyllobates

△ *African bullfrog,* **Pyxicephalus adspersus,** *can puff out its vocal sacs to bellow like a calf.*

△ *With its powerful back legs, the bullfrog can leap over 3 ft. This ability helps in catching its prey; it lies in wait and leaps out on passing prey, catching it while it is in the air.*

Bullfrog

The bullfrog is a large species of North American frog. The adult grows to be about 8 in. long. Its skin is usually smooth like that of a common frog but sometimes it is covered with small tubercles. The colour varies; on the upper parts it is usually greenish to black, sometimes with dark spots, the underparts are whitish with tinges of yellow. The females are browner and more spotted than the males. The best way of telling them apart is by comparing the size of the eye and the eardrum. In females they are equal, but in males the eardrum is larger than the eye.

The natural home of the bullfrog is in the United States, east of the Rockies, and on the northern borders of Mexico. They have also been introduced to the western states of America, as well as to Cuba, Hawaii, British Columbia, Canada.

The bullfrog's damp world

Bullfrogs are rarely found out of the water, except during very wet weather. They like to live near ponds and marshes or slow-flowing streams, lying idly along the water's edge under the shade of shrubs and reeds. In winter they hibernate, near the water, under logs and stones or in holes on the banks. How long they hibernate depends upon the climate. Usually they are the first amphibians in an area to retire and, in the spring, they are the last to emerge. In the northern parts of their range they usually emerge about the middle of May, but in Texas, for example, they may come out in February if the weather is mild enough. In the southern areas of their range they may not bother to hibernate at all.

A voracious appetite

The bullfrog gets most of its food from insects, earthworms, spiders, crayfish and snails. Many kinds of insects are caught including grasshoppers, beetles, flies, wasps and bees. The slow-moving larvae and immobile pupae, as well as the active adults, are taken. The unfortunate dragonfly is usually caught when it is in the middle of laying its eggs.

The bullfrog captures small, active prey like this by lying in wait and then leaping forward as the prey passes. Its tongue flies out by muscular contraction and wraps around the prey like a whiplash wrapping itself around a post. The frog then submerges to swallow its victim.

Its diet of insects, however, is usually supplemented by bigger prey. This can include other frogs and tadpoles and small terrapins and alligators. The bullfrog even eats snakes, including small garter and coral snakes. The fact that it eats these snakes is a measure of its voracity. Garter snakes themselves feed largely on amphibians and coral snakes are venomous. There is one case on record of a 17 in. coral snake being taken by a bullfrog. It can even capture small animals like mice and birds and especially ducklings. Even swallows, flying low over the water, are not safe from its voracious appetite and leaping ability.

Unusual mating call

When the water temperature reaches about 21°C/70°F mating takes place. This can be about February in the south of its range, to June or July in the northern parts. At night the males move out from the banks to call, while the females stay inshore. They join the male only when their eggs are ripe.

Find an empty barrel somewhere and shout into it, as deeply as possible, the word 'rum' and, according to Clifford Pope, the American herpetologist, the hollow, booming sound which will emerge is very like the mating call of the bullfrog. The call has also been described as sounding some-

thing like 'jug o' rum' or 'more rum' and the alcoholic allusion is carried a bit further in some parts by referring to the bullfrog as 'the jug o' rum'.

The bullfrog makes this extraordinary sound 3 or 4 times in a few seconds. Then, after an interval of about 5 minutes, it repeats it. The sound is made by air being passed back and forth along the bullfrog's windpipe, from lungs to mouth, with the nostrils closed. Some of the air enters the airsacs in the floor of the mouth and they swell out like balloons and act as resonators, amplifying the sound so that the noise can be heard half a mile away.

After the mating the female bullfrog lays 10—25 thousand eggs which float in a sheet on the surface of the water, in among the water plants. With its envelope of jelly, each egg is just over ½ in. It is black above and white below. The eggs usually hatch within a week of being laid. If the temperature is low, however, they may take 2 years, sometimes more, to change into an adult frog, by which time they are 2—3 in. long. They feed on algae and decaying vegetation with occasional meals of small pond animals. After about another 2 years the young bullfrogs are almost fully grown and are ready to breed.

Many enemies

Both the tadpole bullfrog and the adult have a lot of enemies. Fish, snakes, birds and mammals, such as skunks and raccoons, all take their toll. A particular enemy of the tadpoles is the backswimmer, which grapples with a tadpole, inserts its 'beak' and sucks out the body fluids. All the bullfrog can do to protect itself from any enemy, apart from hiding at the bottom of the pool or stream, is to use its tremendous jumping powers to leap several feet clear.

Man is another enemy of the bullfrog. Men hunt them for their legs which are considered as much of a delicacy as those of

the edible frog. In California, where they multiplied rapidly after their introduction half a century ago, limits had to be set on the numbers that could be collected in an attempt to prevent them being wiped out altogether. The usual method of killing them is to search for them after dark, dazzle them with a flashlight and then shoot before they can leap clear.

The jumping-frog

There are many ancient legends about 'jumping-frogs' and how their owners have been double-crossed. Mark Twain tells one of the best versions in a short story about one Jim Smiley of Angel's Camp, Calveras County, California. In the story Jim Smiley catches a frog. He calls it Dan'l Webster. The frog is a terrific jumper and Jim makes a lot of money betting on it in contests with other frogs. Then a stranger arrives in the camp and says that he does not think that Dan'l, the frog, is that good a jumper. He's quite prepared to back his word with 40 dollars. The trouble is that, being a stranger, he does not have a frog. Unwilling to let 40 dollars slip by so easily Jim Smiley goes off to find a frog. He leaves his frog with the stranger.

Eventually the new frog is lined up alongside Dan'l Webster. The starting signal is given and both frogs are prodded. The new frog leaps away. Dan'l Webster doesn't move an inch. The stranger collects his 40 dollars and smugly takes his leave. Jim Smiley is baffled and furious.

He can't imagine what's happened to his champion frog. Maybe it's ill. So he picks it up to have a look.

'Why, bless my oats,' he exclaims, 'if he don't weigh a double handful of shot!' So he turns Dan'l Webster, the champion frog, upside down and out pours a couple of pounds of lead shot.

Mark Twain's story was a roaring success. In 1928 when a celebration was held in Angel's Camp, to mark the paving of the streets, the ceremonies included, naturally, a frog-jumping contest. The winner was an entrant called 'Jumping Frog of the San Joaquin' with a leap of 3 ft 4 in.

The contest became very popular and it is now held every year. Allowances are even made for the unpredictable natures of the frogs. Because the first jump might be short and the second record-breaking the contest is judged on the distance travelled by the frog in three consecutive leaps. The record now stands at over 16 ft. So many entries are attracted every year that a stringent set of rules is enforced. One can surely presume that all entries are weighed before jumping so that competitors are spared the embarrassing experience of Jim Smiley—whose tortured ghost is said still to haunt the arena.

class	**Amphibia**
order	**Salientia**
family	**Ranidae**
genus & species	*Rana catesbeiana* *bullfrog*

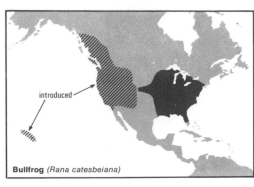

Bullfrog (Rana catesbeiana)

◁◁ Bullfrog, **Rana catesbeiana**. It will take quite large prey including other frogs, small terrapins and alligators, and even coral and garter snakes.
◁ Australian bullfrogs, **Limnodynastes dorsalis**. The female lays eggs in a mass of jelly which she beats up as the eggs are extruded so the eggs are coated and given protection.
▽ The bullfrog rarely leaves the water except during very wet weather. It lives in ponds, marshes or slow-flowing streams, and is often seen lying idly along the water's edge under the shade of reeds and shrubs.

Clawed frog

Although sometimes called a toad, the clawed frog belongs to the Aglossa, a group of tongueless frogs. It is larger than a common European frog, usually around 4 in. long, with large females reaching 5 in. The front legs are short and weak, each having 4 long, straight fingers. The back legs, however, are long and very muscular, with large webs between the toes. A clawed frog 3 in. long may have webbed feet 2 in. across. The South African name 'platanna' is derived from 'plathander' meaning flat hands. The three inner toes on each back foot have sharp black claws.

Clawed frogs can change colour to match their background. When this is a contrasting mixture of light and shade, the frogs are mottled, but they can become almost black or a pale buff if placed against uniformly dark or light areas.

A fully aquatic amphibian

Clawed frogs live in tropical and southern Africa, in swamps, streams and ponds. Unlike most other frogs which spend a large part of adult life on land, hiding in damp places and returning to water only to breed, the clawed frog lives in water the whole time. When it does come on land it is clumsy, but in water the strong legs and large webs make it a powerful swimmer. The front legs are also used as paddles, and not held in to the sides as in typical frogs. To escape from enemies, the clawed frogs give a violent forward thrust of the back legs, shooting themselves backwards. The sharp claws are probably used for gripping boulders or plants in fast running streams but they can also be used, by accident or design, as weapons, for a struggling frog can give some nasty scratches with its claws.

When many of the swamps and ponds dry up in summer, the frogs burrow into the mud to remain cool and moist. If the bed, too, dries out, however, the frogs will hop overland in search of permanent water. Otherwise, clawed frogs leave their home waters and move overland only during heavy rain.

Although so wedded to an aquatic life, clawed frogs still need to come to the surface to breathe. Even when inactive, a large frog surfaces every 10 minutes, although it will survive much longer than this if prevented from surfacing. Even common frogs can stay underwater for a long time, getting most of their oxygen through the skin. It is only to be expected, therefore, that the more completely aquatic clawed frog with its very large areas of particularly permeable skin, on the large webs to the feet, can absorb a far greater proportion of dissolved oxygen from the water.

Feeding

Clawed frogs and their relatives do not have the extensible tongue that is used as a kind of sticky harpoon by other frogs. Instead they catch their prey with their hands, digging their thin, pointed fingers in to prevent escape. The food, which consists of carrion, crustaceans, aquatic larvae and small fish, is then crammed into the mouth.

Clawed frogs are full-time amphibians, preferring not to leave the water at all unless forced by summer droughts to move overland. Their muscular hind legs have very large webbed feet, which provide the main drive for powerful swimming.

Small particles of food are swept into the mouth by a fanning action of the front feet. Mosquito eggs and larvae are eaten in vast numbers, so that where abundant, clawed frogs benefit men by reducing malaria and other mosquito-borne diseases.

Breeding

At the end of the summer, when the ponds fill and the streams start to run again, the clawed frogs begin to breed. During the breeding season, the males croak morning and evening. Eggs are laid and fertilised after amplexus (the characteristic pick-a-back mating of frogs) the eggs being laid singly on the stems of water plants or on stones. Each egg, and there may be 500 – 2 000 of them, is 1 mm across and sticky so that it adheres where the female places it.

The tadpoles hatch after about a week, depending on the water temperature, and for another week they hang motionless at the surface of the water. During this time their mouths are closed and they live off the remains of the egg yolk, which has become enclosed in their body. Then they begin to feed on microscopic plants, but instead of scraping these off rocks and the surfaces of larger plants like most tadpoles, they suck water into their mouths and strain off the minute organisms. On each side of the mouth, just under the eyes, the tadpoles have a small tentacle that appears to be sensitive to touch. Quite how it functions is not known. It has been suggested that it helps keep the tadpole out of the mud as it feeds, hanging vertically downwards a short distance from the bottom.

The tadpoles take 2 months or more to turn into adult frogs, during which time they grow legs and lose their tail. They reach sexual maturity in 3 – 4 years.

Pregnancy testing

The first test for confirming pregnancy at an early stage was devised in 1928. Samples of urine were injected into mice, which were killed and examined 5 days later. If the urine came from a pregnant woman, changes would be found in the ovaries of the mouse, caused by substances called gonadotrophins that are excreted in quantity by pregnant women only. These tests were extremely reliable, but slow, and a year later it was found that tests on rabbits could be completed in a day or two.

Then in 1931 there came a breakthrough. A scientist working in Cape Town found that urine of pregnant women injected into a female clawed frog would cause it to discharge its eggs 5 – 18 hours later. Here was a test that was not only twice as quick as any other, but it left the animal alive. Each frog could be used many times, so the process of confirming pregnancy became rapid and reliable and, consequently, clawed frogs were exported all over the world.

class	**Amphibia**
order	**Salientia**
family	**Pipidae**
genus & species	***Xenopus laevis***

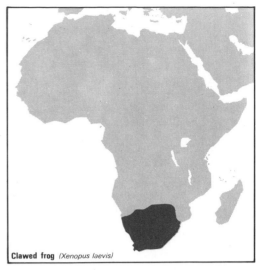

Clawed frog (Xenopus laevis)

△ *A closer look at a clawed frog's right foot shows the sharp black claws on the three inner toes. Also visible is the pattern of blood vessels which the frog uses to breathe through the large skin area created by its wide webbed feet.*

▽ *Clawed frogs mating in the characteristic pick-a-back way. Larger than the European frog, female clawed frogs can grow to 5 in.*

Common toad

Despite a superficial resemblance to the common frog, few people have difficulty in recognising a common toad, even if they recoil in horror on seeing it. It has a flatter back and relatively shorter legs. Instead of the moist, bright skin of the frog, the toad has a dull, wrinkled, pimply skin. Its movements are slow and grovelling, and, although it can jump a short distance on all fours, it usually walks laboriously over the ground.

The rough skin blends well with the earth, so a toad can easily be over-looked as a clod of earth. This impression is heightened by the dark

Common toads mating.

brown or grey colouring which can change, although only a little and slowly, to match the surroundings, becoming almost red in a sand pit, for instance. Its jewel-like eyes are golden or coppery-red, and behind them lie the bulges of the parotid glands that contain an acrid, poisonous fluid.

Male toads measure about 2½ in. and the females 1 in. longer.

The common toad ranges over Europe, north and temperate Asia and North Africa.

Hibernating toads

The common toad, like the common frog, hibernates from October to February, but in drier places. Dry banks and disused burrows of small mammals are chosen, and hibernating toads are sometimes found in cellars and outhouses. In the spring they migrate to breeding pools, preferring deeper water than frogs. Where the two are found in the same ponds, the frogs will be in the shallows and the toads in the middle.

The migrations of these toads are more spectacular. Toads give the impression of being slower movers and the migration route becomes littered with the remains of toads that have fallen foul of enemies. The route is especially well marked where it crosses a road and passing cars have run over the toads.

Although the migration may be long and arduous, perhaps covering 2 or 3 miles at

a rate of ¾ mile in 24 hours, the toads are very persistent, and laboriously climb stone walls and banks.

Outside the breeding season toads live in hollows scooped out by the hindlegs. In soft earth they bury themselves completely, otherwise the hole is made under a log or stone. These homes are usually permanent, the toad returning to the same place day after day. One toad was recorded as living under a front-door step for 36 years until it was attacked by a raven. Occasionally the retreats may be in places that must cost the toad some effort to reach. One is known to have made its home in a privet hedge, 4 ft above the ground, and others have been found in birds' nests.

Every now and then there are stories of toads being found in even odder places. Quarrymen and miners tell of splitting open a rock or lump of coal revealing a cavity in which lies a toad that leaps out hale and

with glass plates. The toads in the compact sandstone soon died but the ones in the porous limestone lived for a year or more. These rather macabre experiments suggest that the toads found in rocks and tree trunks could not have been there for long. It is most likely that either they had crawled into a crack or cavity which had later been filled in, or perhaps the miner or quarryman had hit a rock that happened to have a cavity in, thereby causing a toad hidden nearby to leap out suddenly, so creating the impression that it had come out of the hole.

Prey must be moving
At night and during wet weather, toads come out to feed on many kinds of small animals, but they must be moving because toads' eyes are adapted to react to moving objects. Any insect or other small invertebrate is taken, ants being especially favoured, and the stomach of one toad was found to

Spawn in strings
There is little to distinguish the breeding habits of common frogs and common toads. Both breed at roughly the same time of year and may be seen in the same pools. Male toads start arriving before the females but later the males may arrive already in amplexus on the females' backs. There is no external vocal sac and, unlike many of its relatives, a male common toad has a very weak croak.

The spawn is laid in strings rather than in a mass. The eggs are embedded three or four deep in threads of jelly that may be up to 15 ft long. Each female lays 3—4 thousand eggs, which are smaller than those of a frog, being less than $\frac{1}{16}$ in. in diameter. The jelly swells up but the spawn does not float, because it is wrapped round the stems of water plants.

The eggs hatch in 10–12 days and the tadpoles develop in the same manner as

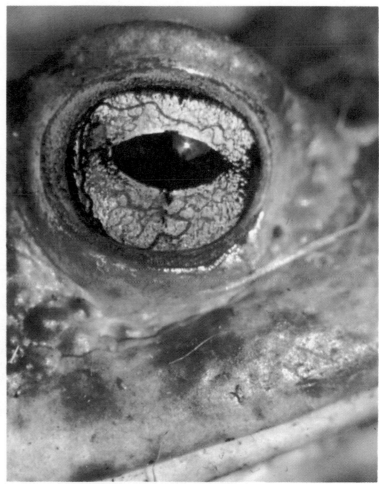

The coppery-golden eye of the toad, its most attractive feature, shown with pupil expanded (left) and contracted (right).

hearty. Another story is told of two sawyers working in a saw pit, some 90 years ago. They were sawing the trunk of an oak into planks when they noticed blood dripping out of the wood. Examination revealed the now grisly remains of a toad in a cavity in the trunk. In every story there is speculation as to how the toads came to be imprisoned. It is hardly likely that they were trapped when the coal or rock was first formed millions of years ago, as was once believed. They could not have lived that long, as was shown by the following experiments performed over a century ago. Holes were drilled in blocks of sandstone and limestone, toads put in and the holes sealed

contain 363 ants. Some distasteful animals such as burnet moth caterpillars or caterpillars covered with stiff hairs are left well alone, but toads are known to sit outside beehives in the evening and catch the workers as they come back home. Snails are crunched up and earthworms are pushed into the mouth by the forefeet which also scrape excess earth off them. Young newts, frogs, toads and even slowworms and grass snakes are eaten. One toad had five newly-hatched grass snakes in its stomach, while another had the head of an adder in its mouth. Toads will often return to a favourite retreat after hunting and will use the same home for years.

frog tadpoles, becoming shiny, black, ½ in. toadlets in about 3 months. Sexual maturity is reached in 4 years, before the toads are fully grown.

Poisonous toads
Toads suffer from all the enemies to which frogs fall prey, despite the poisonous secretions of the parotid glands. The poison is certainly effective against dogs, that salivate copiously after mouthing a toad, and show all the signs of distress.

Toads react more strongly to danger signals than frogs do, possibly because, not being leapers, they are more vulnerable and need added protection from enemies. One

Strings of spawn rope through the water during mating, to be wrapped around the stems of water plants and convenient pebbles.

reaction is to inflate the lungs more than usual, so increasing the volume of the body by as much as 50%. Snakes, their chief enemies, know fairly accurately when an object is more than they can swallow, but how far the inflated body of the toad deceives them has never been tested.

Unless the snake is only small, the swelling of the toad will make little difference to the outcome if attacked by a constricting or a poisonous snake.

The defence mechanism of the toad of inflating itself against enemies is instinctive. This is seen by the following experiment. Any long cylindrical object, such as a length of thin rubber tubing, moved across its field of vision, will cause it to blow itself up. This reaction becomes progressively weaker when the experiment is repeated, and in a short time no reaction is produced.

In old age, toads fall victim to flesh-eating greenbottle flies, which lay their eggs on them. The larvae then crawl into the nostrils, hampering breathing, and eat their way into the toad's body, eventually killing it.

Many superstitions

Toads are often regarded with horror, and in folklore they generally play an unpleasant role. Their mere presence was said to pollute the soil, but one method of preventing this from happening was to plant rue, which toads could not abide. Without it, tragedies could occur of the kind that befell a mediaeval couple strolling in the garden. The young man plucked some leaves of sage, rubbed his teeth with them and promptly fell dead. His young woman was charged with murder and, to prove her innocence, took the judge and court to the garden to demonstrate what had happened, and fell dead too. The judge suspected the cause and had the sage dug up. There was a toad living in the ground beside it.

By contrast, 'the foule Toad has a faire stone in his heade', as the 16th-century writer John Lyly declared. To obtain this jewel the toad was placed on a scarlet cloth which pleased the toad so much that it cast the stone out. The toadstone was then set in a ring, for it had the valuable property of changing colour in the presence of any poison that an enemy might put in food and drink. It was also effective as a cure for snakebite and wasp-stings.

class	**Amphibia**
order	**Salientia**
family	**Bufonidae**
genus & species	*Bufo bufo*

Edible frog

Edible frogs are rather larger than common frogs, 2½−4 in. when full grown and with darker and bolder markings, especially the marbling of bright yellow and black on the hinder parts. The head is more slender than that of the common frog and lacks the dark patch running back from the eye. The marbling on the upper surface of the thigh and pale stripe down the back also distinguish the edible frog. The general colour varies from one to another; an edible frog is usually green when exposed to the sun and brown at the end of hibernation.

The most distinctive feature is found in males only. Just below the ear, there are external vocal sacs that swell to the size of large peas when the frog is croaking. They act as resonators, the volume of sound depending on the amount of air in the sacs.

The ranges of the edible and marsh frog, which is nearly related to the edible frog, overlap in central Europe, where the marsh frog breeds some two weeks earlier. If, however, bad weather causes it to breed late, interbreeding with the edible frog may take place, but it is not known whether the offspring are fertile. Despite this interbreeding, opinion is now strongly in favour of regarding the two as separate species.

Newcomers to England

The native home of the edible frog is in continental Europe and northern Asia, but it has been introduced into England on several occasions. The first recorded introduction was in 1837, when 200 were set free in Norfolk. During the next 5 years some 1 700 were brought over by a Mr Berney. His motive is not known, but he seems to have gone to some trouble, making special hampers, each having a series of movable shelves with water lily leaves stitched to them 'so that the frogs might be comfortable and feel at home'. Initially these colonists flourished, but land drainage has destroyed many of their homes and only a few scattered colonies are left. Since then more colonies have become established from frogs brought over from the Continent, in Surrey, Hampshire, Oxfordshire and Bedfordshire, but the colonies usually die out after a time. It would seem that conditions in England are, for some reason, not very favourable for edible frogs.

Edible frogs spend more time in the water than common frogs. If their ponds dry up, the frogs will migrate to other stretches of water, and they will sometimes come on land to feed at night; but young edible frogs do not wander like young common frogs.

Adult edible frogs hibernate in the mud at the bottom of ponds or by the water's edge, but young will come ashore and crawl into crevices or under logs and stones. They emerge from hibernation in April, the exact date depending on the weather.

Leaping on its prey

The prey, especially of young frogs, is mainly insects, including ants, wasps, flies, beetles, butterflies and moths. The frog lies in wait, hidden by water weed, and jumps at its prey, sometimes bringing down flying insects. The extensible tongue is used to capture small insects, but large ones such as dragonflies, or even larger prey such as newts, small fish, small mammals and birds, are caught in the jaws and crammed into the mouth by the forelegs.

▽ Edible frogs mating. The male is showing a distinctive feature of edible frogs which is found only in the male: the vocal sacs just below the ears, which swell to the size of peas when the frog croaks, amplifying his call.

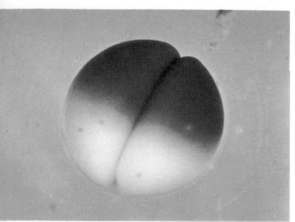

△ *Start of a life: a frog's egg divides for the first time after fertilisation.*
▽ *Edible frog tadpoles often grow fast, turning into froglets in as little as 3—4 months.*

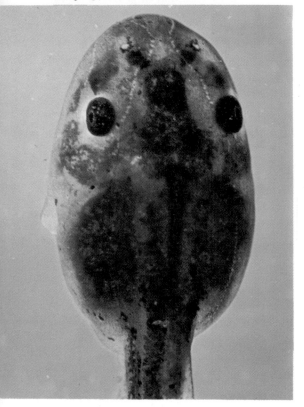

Giant tadpoles

The life history of the edible frog resembles that of the common frog. Mating takes place a month or more after emerging from hibernation. Croaking is heard most at this time although it continues all through the summer. A chorus of several hundred male frogs can be heard over a mile, sounding like the quacking of many ducks.

At the spawning pond males outnumber the females by 8 or 10 to 1. There is, however, no fighting or jostling between the males as one might expect from the breeding behaviour of most other animals. A mated pair can continue spawning in the middle of a crowd of unattached males without interference. Yet, should a pair in process of spawning become separated the female will immediately be seized by another male. Since the male's grasp during amplexus is not tenacious as in most other frogs such separation is not uncommon and the separate parts of the spawn from a single female may have been fertilized by two or more males.

Spawning takes place in shallow water at the edges of pools. Each female can produce up to 10 000 eggs, but in the British Isles they have never been found to lay more than 2 000. The spawn is laid in groups of 250, rather than in large masses as in the common frog. It does not float to the surface because it is laid among water weeds. The tadpoles leave the eggs in 10 days and develop in a similar fashion to the tadpoles of the common frog, but the rate of development varies considerably. Some tadpoles develop rapidly and turn into froglets, about 1 in. long, 3—4 months after hatching, but others will fail to complete their development before winter. Most will die, but some survive and grow to perhaps 2½ in. before changing into froglets. Sometimes they fail to metamorphose and continue to live as tadpoles. This is an instance of neoteny (see axolotl, page 68) and one

Edible frogs reach sexual maturity at 2 for 11 months in captivity, dying when 4¾ in. long.

Edible frogs reach sexual maturity at 2 years but are not fully grown until their fourth or fifth year.

Fishing for frogs

Edible frogs have all the enemies that afflict common frogs, but they have the added disadvantage of being prized as food by man. Edible frogs are by no means the only frogs that are eaten; common frogs are caught before the edible frogs have emerged from hibernation, and in other parts of the world various species are eaten—the bullfrog in the United States, for instance. The edible frog, however, provides the traditional dish of frogs' legs, which may be fried crisp like whitebait, or served with sauce or in a risotto.

The usual way of catching frogs is by rod and line. No hook is used, instead a brightly coloured lure is dangled in front of the frogs. This must be kept on the move for the frogs to strike at it. They are then flipped out of the water before they can let go of the lure.

The lure is traditionally a piece of red flannel or a skein of thread formed by winding a few yards of thread around the finger. The colour is immaterial and the important factor is that the lure must be on the move. A frog's vision is such that it reacts only to moving prey. Since the normal feeding habits of the edible frog include leaping upwards from the water to capture insects flying just above the surface, almost any small dancing lure will bring this reaction. The frog leaps, grips the lure with its jaw and must be immediately pulled up to be caught.

Frog fishing is best done on warm summer days because, like all cold-blooded animals, the edible frog is most active and will the more readily bite in proportion as the temperature rises. The experienced frog fisher will then be able to capture one frog after another as rapidly as he can raise and lower his line slipping each expertly into his hand.

It has been estimated that 15 to 20 frogs are needed to make a meal for one person and a single fisherman may take hundreds a day in favourable weather.

Frogs and electricity

The story goes that in 1786 Galvani, an

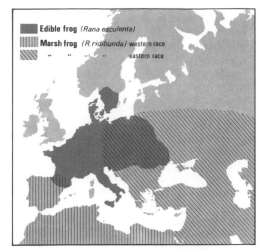

Edible frog *(Rana esculenta)*
Marsh frog *(R. ridibunda)* western race
" " eastern race

In the east and west of the edible frog's range, it overlaps the territory of the marsh frog. The marsh frog, however is isolated in that it breeds two weeks earlier than the edible frog. If bad weather brings the breeding seasons together, interbreeding may take place.

Italian physiologist, noticed that the skinned legs of an edible frog twitched when they were touched with a scalpel that had been charged with electricity. Sometimes this story is elaborated, and one can read that it was Signora Galvani who first noticed this when she was using a scalpel, accidently charged by one of her husband's electrical gadgets, to prepare frogs' leg soup. The truth is that Galvani had known of this effect for some years; ever since he had suspended some edible frogs, on copper hooks from an iron railing, and they had started to dance. According to Galvani, the muscle contractions were due to 'animal electricity' which was conducted from nerve to muscle by the two metals. Convinced of this, Galvani continued to investigate this strange source of power for the rest of his life, although other experimenters showed that the linking of these two different metals was the basis of an electric charge that stimulated the muscles to contract. The only contribution made by the frog's legs was that they provided a ready conductor for the electricity. The edible frog, however, had had its moment of glory in the advancement of science, even if its actions had been misunderstood.

class	**Amphibia**
order	**Salientia**
family	**Ranidae**
genus & species	***Rana esculenta***

△ **Bombina variegata** *peers at the camera, showing its brightly-coloured throat and waistcoat. When faced with imminent attack, it throws itself on its back to show its yellow patches to better advantage, eyes closed and covered with its forepaws, and holds its breath until danger passes. If pressed, however, it exudes a corrosive white fluid.*

Firebelly

The firebelly is a toad with an unusual way of scaring its enemies. Less than 2 in. long, the males smaller than the females and sometimes only 1 in. long, the firebelly is dark grey over its back with black flecks. Its underside is blue-grey to blue-black with white spots and patches of orange or red. When disturbed or alarmed it throws its head up, arches its back and rises on stiff legs to expose its vivid fire-coloured belly. Faced with more immediate danger—for example, if someone goes to pick it up—the toad throws itself on its back displaying its vivid patches; at the same time glands in its skin give out a white poison fluid with caustic properties and a strong smell. So it remains motionless, its eyes closed and breathing suspended, until the danger is past. As in some other amphibians, including the common frog of Europe, the firebelly holds its paws over

its eyes as if it cannot bear to look at its tormentor.

Close relatives are the yellow-bellied toad of Europe, sometimes called the variegated fire-toad, the firebelly of China and Korea, and another Asiatic species, the largest of all—but still not more than 3 in. long.

The firebelly is distributed from southern Sweden and Denmark, through Germany and the Balkans, east to the Ural mountains. The yellow-bellied toad, of similar size, habits and colour except that yellow replaces the red patches, extends from the Low Countries through France, Germany and Switzerland to northern Italy, but lives at higher altitudes, in ponds, on hills and mountains.

Toad with a musical voice

Both the firebelly and the yellow-bellied toad have melodious voices, the firebelly uttering a musical 'unk-unk'—it is known in Germany as the Unke—which often goes on all night. The yellow-belly sounds like soft

bells which are ringing in the distance.

The firebelly feeds on insects, snails and worms. It belongs to the family Discoglossidae, or round-tongued toads, in which the rounded tongue is joined throughout to the floor of the mouth, so it must snap up its prey instead of shooting out its tongue. Feeding is mainly at night when the toad comes out on land. The firebelly is inactive for much of the day, floating among water plants in ponds and ditches. It is a good runner, as well as a good swimmer. It leaves the water to hibernate in soft ground.

Modest spawning output

In the breeding season black pads appear on the forearm and the first two fingers of the male. Then his 'unk-unk' call begins, made the louder by an internal vocal sac which acts as a resonator. Spawning is from May to June, during which time each female lays two or three times at well-spaced intervals. Each session lasts about 3 days. When the male embraces the female he holds her around the loins, to fertilise her eggs that are laid one at a time, or in small groups.

91

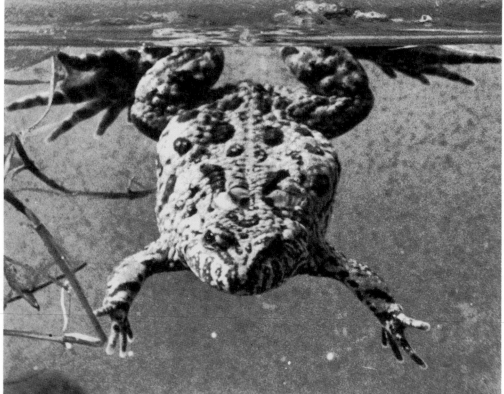

◁ *Tensed for take-off, a firebelly shows its full underside pattern through the glass of an aquarium wall.*
▽◁ *Top view. A submerging firebelly heads for the bottom with powerful strokes.*

She lays only a few dozen in all, certainly not more than 100, in contrast with the thousands of the common toad. The eggs stick to water plants or to vegetable rubbish on the bottom.

The eggs are $\frac{1}{3}$ in. diameter. They hatch in 7 days and the tadpoles grow to a length of 2 in. by autumn, then begin to shrink to toadlets $\frac{2}{3}$ in. long. The baby toads do not have warning colours at first; these appear gradually and are complete by the time the toad is mature, in its third year.

Safe from enemies

The firebelly probably has no serious enemies, and this seems borne out by the very large numbers living in some localities. These are not obvious to the casual eye partly because this toad will, if possible, escape, at the first disturbance, diving to the bottom and burying itself in the mud. Even if it only remains still its back looks so like a piece of mud that the toad is extremely difficult to see. Indeed, the firebelly, so long as it is the right way up, enjoys extraordinarily good camouflage protection. It is the more odd that it should have in addition, on its underside, the striking warning colours. Perhaps camouflage is its first line of defence, with warning coloration as a second.

No bluffing

These colours are no bluff. The white fluid given out by the firebelly at the same time as it shows its warning colours is caustic and corrosive. Naturalists collecting frogs and toads have found that to put a tree frog into a container with a firebelly half its size is to sentence it to death. Freshly caught firebellies soon become covered with a white froth when handled and merely the vapours from this quickly cause bouts of sneezing and running at the eyes.

class	**Amphibia**
order	**Salientia**
family	**Discoglossidae**
genus & species	*Bombina bombina* *B. variegata* *B. orientalis* *B. maxima*

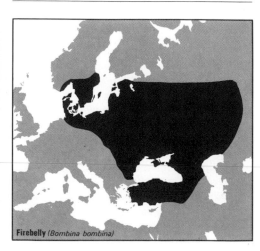

Firebelly (*Bombina bombina*)

Ghost frog

The ghost frog of South Africa gets its name from the white skin of its underside, which is so thin that the digestive organs are visible through it. Its back is green, marked with a reddish network. Compared with other frogs, its body is small relative to the head and unusually long legs, and there is almost a suggestion of a neck. The head is flattish with the eyes more prominent than is usual in frogs, and the toes of all four feet end in discs. When an animal species is placed first in one family, then in another, it usually means that its relationship with other animals is not clear. Some scientists put the ghost frogs in a family of their own, the Heleophrynidae, others put them in the Leptodactylidae, but all leading authorities now agree on the latter. The animals normally end up in a genus of their own. This is true of the ghost frogs, of which there are three species. One species **Heleophryne rosei** *lives on Table Mountain, another* **H. purcelli** *is found in Cape Province, and the third* **H. natalensis** *is in the Transvaal and Natal. The frogs are elusive in another way: they are very hard to find, but the real reason for their name is that you can almost see through them.*

The ghost frog gets its name from the white skin of its underside. It is very difficult to track down and as a result is rarely seen. This may be partially explained by the fact that it is nocturnal— as shown by its diamond-shaped pupils formed during daylight to keep out bright light.

Equipped for climbing

Ghost frogs have toes shaped like those of tree frogs, although they climb little. Instead, they tend to spend the day crouching in holes in the ground, under stones or in caves, and they also spend much of their time in water. At night they come out and clamber over large rocks or into trees. Another unusual feature is that the skin of the undersides of the forelimbs and the tops of the fingers has groups of small hooks, and similar hooks form a double row on either side along the lower jaw with scattered hooks on the upper jaw and the snout. It has been suggested that these help the frog to cling to the surfaces of slippery rocks. This description applies to the best known of the ghost frogs, *Heleophryne rosei*. Another species also has spines on the skin, and this one climbs into bushes.

Mainly insect-eaters

Frogs shed their skins periodically and in most species the frog eats the cast skin, which is sloughed more or less in one piece. Ghost frogs shed their skins in pieces and make no attempt to eat them. It should be emphasized, however, that in this as in everything else concerned with their biology we have only a small amount of information. Ghost frogs are difficult to track down and are rarely seen. Possibly part of the explanation is seen in their eyes, diamond-shaped with the long axis of the diamond vertical—an unusual eye, showing nocturnal habits.

Ghost frogs probably eat insects, and one species *H. purcelli* has been seen capturing flies by leaping up at them.

Holding onto food

By dissecting the dead female ghost frog it is known that she lays about 30 large eggs. Where she does this is not known, and the guess is that she lays them in a hole in a river bank just above water level. More is known about the tadpoles which are somewhat flattened, especially in the head. Seen from above they are wedge-shaped except for the tail. Around the mouth is a large sucker by which the tadpole can cling to submerged rocks and browse the small algae on their surfaces.

Difficult to research

Those not versed in field natural history may wonder why, once a species is known to exist, somebody does not set to work to learn all about it. To illustrate the difficulties we cannot do better than tell the story of the mountain chicken of the West Indies. This is a frog *Leptodactylus fallax* which belongs to the same family as the ghost frogs if we accept the majority view. It is nearly 6 in. long, weighs up to 2 lb and lives on the islands of Dominica, Montserrat and Martinique. The frog lives in the steep-sided valleys which are heavily forested and difficult of access. During the day, so far as anyone can tell, it rests in burrows in the ground or in cavities among boulders. The females have never been seen and nothing is known of the way they breed. They do not live near streams, so possibly they make foam nests in the trees like related species living in South America are known to do. The males come out at night and call with a musical, bird-like 'song', but the reason why they are called mountain chicken is that the flesh of their legs cooked with egg and bread crumbs is delicious, like the best chicken. The frog has been almost eliminated from Martinique, partly because introduced mongooses have preyed on them and partly because they are much prized for the table.

An English zoologist visiting Dominica tried to find the females in the hope of studying the life history of the species. He found some of the males, but even this entailed climbing the steep slopes at night in rain, negotiating tangles of tree roots, creepers and boulders, finding his way by electric torch and guided by the somewhat ventriloquial musical calls of the males, which go on singing all night. Even to find a few males was a small reward for all the effort and discomfort he expended. The males themselves do not help because they tend to sit near the mouth of a burrow or cavity among the boulders into which they can readily retreat.

After all, if you can only find males your knowledge of a species must be very incomplete. And if you eat those males it cannot be long before a population of spinster frogs is created—and that means the end of the species.

class	**Amphibia**
order	**Salientia**
family	**Leptodactylidae**
genus	*Heleophryne natalensis* *H. purcelli* *H. rosei*

Gliding frog

There are a few species of frogs which are also referred to as 'the so-called flying frogs', or else they are called 'flying' frogs. The writer then goes on to say that of course they do not fly, they only glide. It is high time, therefore, that we stopped calling them flying frogs and followed the lead given, for example, by Doris B Cochran, of the United States National Museum, and called them gliding frogs, which is what they are.

The gliding frogs are members of a family of tree frogs, Rhacophoridae, which will be dealt with later. The most common are the Malayan and Wallace's gliding frogs which are 4 in. long in the head and body, shining green above, yellow on flanks and white underneath. They range from Malaya to Borneo. As with other tree frogs of this family the ends of the toes on all four feet have sucker discs at the tips, for clinging to trees. Gliding frogs differ in having the toes of all four feet longer than usual and fully webbed.

Jumping and gliding

Gliding frogs spend the day in trees and tall bushes holding on by the discs on their toes. In strong sunlight they are a greenish-blue, turning to green in the evening and finally to black, the change taking place more rapidly in the males than the females. They become active at night, leaping from branch to branch and taking gliding leaps from tree to tree. The leaps may be up to 6 ft but the glide may cover 40–50 ft to the base of the next tree. In a glide the toes are fully stretched and held rigid and the underside of the body is drawn up, giving a concave surface that increases the lift. The direction and length of a glide can be controlled to some extent.

Foam nests

Gliding frogs feed mainly on grasshoppers but take other insects as well, and when breeding they do not take to water but make foam nests among large leaves. While mating the male clings on the female's back, as is usual in frogs. As the eggs are laid quantities of albumen are given out with them and both female and male beat this into a frothy mass with a paddling action of the hindlegs. The outside of the mass hardens while the inside of it becomes more and more fluid. The eggs float in this until rain washes either the eggs, or the tadpoles, out of the nest, to fall into pools below. If no rain falls the outer crust eventually liquefies to release eggs or tadpoles.

Flying frogs

The first Europeans to learn about these frogs heard the story from Chinese labourers in southeast Asia who spoke of the frogs flying down from the trees. The story that there were frogs that flew was accepted at first. Then came disbelief and this was reinforced by a curious accident. Alfred Russel Wallace, the distinguished naturalist, who worked so much in the southeast Asian region, calculated that the area of the spread feet with their webs was sufficient to enable the frogs to glide. He made an error in his calculations and when this was detected the story of flying frogs became further discredited. Few zoologists had ever seen the gliding frog alive so it was difficult to check Wallace's statement or those of the Chinese in Malaya. In 1926, however, HB Cott carried out experiments with the Brazilian tree frog *Hyla venulosa* which showed that even tree frogs with less webbing than gliding frogs could fall from considerable heights and land safely on their feet. He dropped the frogs from a tower 140 ft high and the frogs landed on the ground 90 ft out from the base of the tower. They reached the ground at such a slow speed that they were quite unhurt. Almost any small tree-living animal will do the same and the reason is that they spread their legs and keep their body the right way up, as a cat does when it falls from a height, and this acts as a brake. By contrast, the ordinary common frog, although the webs on its feet are larger than those of a tree frog, simply tumbles head over heels when it falls and plummets straight down. It only needs that little extra webbing on the feet, which gliding frogs have, to keep them gliding.

class	**Amphibia**
order	**Salientia**
family	**Rhacophoridae**
genus & species	***Rhacophorus nigropalmatus*** *Wallace's gliding frog* ***R. reinwardtii*** *Malayan gliding frog*

▽ *Ready to go: a Siamese gliding frog* **Rhacophorus prominanus** *takes aim for the leap which will start its long glide towards the base of the next tree—perhaps 50 ft away.*

▽ *Airborne amphibian: Bornean gliding frog on the way down, each webbed foot a tiny parachute. Even the body is held concave to add to the gliding surface and so increase lift.*

Hochstetter's frog is a New Zealander, living near mountain tops where the air is always moist and cool. It is small—never growing larger than 2 in.—and its toes are only partly webbed.

Hochstetter's frog

Hochstetter's frog is here chosen as a representative of the primitive frog family Leiopelmidae of which three species live in New Zealand, with the only other species in northwest America—the opposite corner of the Pacific. Although none of the four species has a tail they still have two tail-wagging muscles. The toes are only slightly webbed. Each vertebra is concave on both faces, a condition known as amphicoelous. The vertebrae of nearly all fishes are amphicoelous, those of all other frogs are not. Hochstetter's frog and its relatives seem therefore to be very near the early fish-like ancestors of amphibians and it is tempting to think that they have found sanctuary in mountains, as many animals have done. The Leiopelmidae are not only the most primitive frogs, but are very rare. They are protected in New Zealand.

No tadpole stage

Hochstetter's frog and its relatives are less than 2 in. long. They live mainly near mountain tops where the air is moist and cold and the temperature of any water there may be is usually not above 4°C/40°F. They are chiefly interesting for the way they breed. The eggs of Hochstetter's frog were found in November and December of 1949 in the seepage from a mountain stream, in tunnels in the wet clay. The tunnels were probably made by dragonfly larvae. On the floors of the tunnels the eggs, $\frac{3}{16}$ in. diameter when laid and strung together like beads in groups of 2—8, lie on the mud washed by slow trickles of water. Near the mouths of the tunnels the males sit as if guarding the eggs. There is no tadpole; the embryo develops and grows through the tadpole stages within the egg. All the fluid necessary for development is inside the eggs. The first froglets appear 41 days after being laid but not all eggs in one clutch hatch at the same time. Those in large clusters take several days to hatch, some being as much as 9 days after the first hatch. For the first month after hatching the froglet lives on the remains of yolk from the egg. It breaks out of the egg by lashing with its long tail, and this then becomes an important breathing organ. The lungs do not develop fully for some weeks after hatching, and in the meantime the froglet breathes through the skin of the belly and tail, both of which are richly supplied with fine surface blood vessels.

Archey's frog, also on the New Zealand mountains, lays its eggs under stones, but otherwise behaves like Hochstetter's frog. Its food is insects and larvae, spiders and woodlice or sowbugs. These frogs have a large tongue, rounded or pearshaped, almost completely fastened to the floor of the mouth, so it cannot be shot out to capture prey.

Tailed frogs

The American relative has been variously called tailed frog and American bell toad.

It lives in the Rockies from southern British Columbia through Washington to Oregon, on the western side, and in Idaho and western Montana, on the eastern side. It lives in the swift, icy mountain streams and at breeding time from May to September the males, which are voiceless, creep about the bed of the stream to find the females. The females lay their eggs in strings of 30—50 fastened to the undersides of rocks. The eggs hatch a month later and within an hour the black or blackish tadpoles, up to 2 in. long, grow a triangular adhesive disc on the head. Using this they cling to rocks, so avoiding being swept away by the current. They often use it to climb above water onto the wet rock, and during rain will travel overland for distances of up to 100 ft.

The tadpole is peculiar in having funnel-like nostrils that it can close when the rush of water is too great. They can also be closed to regulate the flow of water through the mouth and across the gills for breathing. The tadpoles scrape small algae from the rocks for food while holding on with the sucker, and turn into froglets the following year, between July and September.

Tailed frogs are so completely adapted to low temperatures that if trees around their home are felled, so more sunlight gets through to raise the temperature of the water, they move into more sheltered spots. The name has nothing to do with the way the froglet retains its tail longer than is usual in the commoner frogs. It is from an apparent tail seen in the male. This is an extension of the cloaca which is used in mating, to give internal fertilization. External fertilization, more usual in frogs, would be impossible in the fast-flowing streams, as the sperm would be washed away. This organ looks slightly like a tail and presumably has given rise to the name.

No voice, no ears?

The males of typical frogs croak and all frogs have ears, apart from Hochstetter's frog and its relatives. They have what appear to be degenerate ears. They lack both eardrum and Eustachian tube (the tube that connects the inner ear with the throat). It has been suggested that tailed frogs are voiceless and at least semi-deaf because of the turbulent streams in which they live. Presumably the reasoning is like this. The females would not hear the males calling because of the noise made by the gushing, tinkling mountain streams. So males have lost their voices because they are useless. Since the frogs are voiceless, there is no use for ears, and these have degenerated. Those who propounded this theory cannot be aware of the 'cocktail party' effect, when the ear ignores the heavy babble and chatter all around and picks out one particular voice or sound.

class	**Amphibia**
order	**Salientia**
family	**Leiopelmidae**
genera & species	*Ascaphus truei* American tailed frog *Leiopelma archeyi* Archey's frog *L. hochstetteri* Hochstetter's frog *L. hamiltoni* Hamilton's frog

Horned frog

Some horned frogs are hornless, some are armoured, but they all have a reputation for pugnacity. Their numbers seem to be controlled largely by cannibalism.

The horned frog is a large amphibian up to 10 in. long and unusually wide. It has a big, bulky head with a wide mouth. The body is handsomely, even garishly, ornamented with geometrical patterns of green and yellow or rusty red and yellow on a blackish ground colour. The skin is covered with warts on the upper parts and is finely granular on the underside. In some species the eyelids are drawn out into what look like small horns. These are, however, only flaps of skin, neither hard nor sharp. Nevertheless, they add to the grotesque and somewhat forbidding appearance of these frogs.

The dozen or so species all live in Central and South America, as far south as Argentina. There are also several horned frogs in southeast Asia.

Puzzle over their colours

Horned frogs are, in places, abundant near rivers and swamps and after rain are seen crawling through the grass in large numbers. At other times they lie buried in soft ground or among leaf litter with only the back and head exposed. In spite of their striking colours they are hard to see so long as they remain still. They give an example of how difficult it is sometimes to decide the value of an animal's colours. Lifted from its natural surroundings the horned frog's colours are conspicuous, yet their disruptive pattern is one we always associate with camouflage. Moreover, some people claim that their bright colours are warning colours, and we know from experience with other animals that a warning coloration is something flaunted to warn off would-be attackers—the reverse of camouflage.

Ferocious frogs

Whatever the meaning of its colours the fact remains that a horned frog, in marked contrast with most other frogs, is highly belligerent. People have told of having horned frogs in captivity that leaped at them when they went to feed them, biting their fingers and hanging on like a bulldog. This is probably no more than the frogs' normal way of feeding, for the adults do not go in search of food but lie half-buried waiting for prey to come near. They then seize their victims, even jumping out from their hiding place to do so. Their prey is almost anything moving they can swallow: insects, frogs, lizards, even snakes, small birds and small mammals. They are thought to be strongly cannibalistic and this may control their numbers, for they have few enemies.

Horned frogs are said not to be venomous but it would be surprising if the many warts on their bodies were not able to give out a poison of the kind found in toads. Their aggressive actions help no doubt to deter some enemies. In addition, the Wied's horned frog of Brazil has a dense bony shield covering the head and part of the back, which might make it hard to deal with.

More ferocious frogs

In southeast Asia there are other species known as horned frogs, but they belong to a separate family. This means they differ from the South American horned frogs in their anatomy but resemble them in outward appearance. They have a 'horn' on each eyelid and have wide mouths and strong jaws like the South American species. They are also strongly cannibalistic and have a bony shield covering the head and part of the back. So the horned frogs of America and southeast Asia give us yet another good example of convergent evolution in which unrelated animals having the same way of life are superficially alike.

Two contrasting tadpoles

The two groups of horned frogs differ, however, in the behaviour of the tadpole. Those of the South American horned frogs are predatory from the start, feeding on other small animals. The tadpoles of the southeast Asia horned frogs are vegetarians. Some of them have large funnel-like mouths by which they hang vertically from the surface film of the water. Their mouths are armed with rows of minute horny teeth which act as rasps to scrape algae and other small growths from the leaves of waterplants.

Horse-killers?

The horned frogs of southeast Asia look as grotesque as those of South America. One addition they have is a spine—a pointed flap of skin—on the snout, which makes them look more formidable than they are. Guenther's horned frog, of South America, also has a 'spine' of skin on its snout that looks like a sting. Even those that lack these nasal ornaments look fearsome enough to have earned them a bad reputation. When their pugnacity is added to this the way is open for exaggerated ideas. One of these, from the Argentine, is that the *escucrzo*, as it is called there, may bite the lip of a grazing horse and that the horse will die from the bite. From what we know of horned frogs it is easy to believe that it would not hesitate to snap at a horse. Even a young horned frog, less than an inch across, will make quite a show at attacking. And even if the horned frog's mouth contains no venom, it is not impossible that its teeth might leave a wound that becomes septic, so causing the death of a horse.

△*Cold-blooded power:* **Ceratophrys calcarata.**

△ *Camouflaged but pugnacious:* **Megophrys**
▽ *That hungry look:* **Ceratophrys ornata.**

class	**Amphibia**		
order	**Salientia**		
family	**Leptodactylidae (S America)**		
genus & species	***Ceratophrys appendicula*** Guenther's horned frog *C. stolzmanni* escucrzo *C. varia* Wied's horned frog others		
family	**Pelobatidae (SE Asia)**		
genus	*Megophrys*		

Marine toad

Sugar cane has been spread, from an unknown native home in the Far East, to warm countries round the world, including tropical America. With it went the grey cane beetle, the larvae of which live on the roots and can destroy the canes. In tropical America lived the marine toad which feeds on cane beetles. In an effort to control the beetle the marine toad has been taken round the world, wherever sugar is grown. On the whole it has failed to control the beetle, but for the toad itself this is a success story.

The marine toad does not normally live in the sea. It was presumably so named because one was first seen by the sea. Its habits are similar to those of more familiar toads, like the common European toad, and at first sight its main claim to fame is its size; it is sometimes called the giant toad. Usually it is 5 in. long and weighs ¾ lb, but females, which are larger than males, may be up to 10 in. long and weigh 3 lb. It is mottled yellow and brown in colour and has numerous dark reddish-brown warts on its body.

Its native home is from southeastern Texas, through Mexico and Central America to South America as far south as Patagonia. It has been introduced into Florida, many of the islands of the Caribbean, Bermuda, Hawaii, New Guinea and Australia, and to a few other places where sugar cane is grown.

Nocturnal toad

During hot weather the marine toad, also known as the cane toad in Australia, remains under cover of vegetation or burrows in the ground, coming out at night, or in wet or cool weather, to feed. It will take anything that moves which is small enough to swallow, especially insects and beetles, and also smaller toads and frogs, small snakes and even mice.

Rapid growth

One of the more unusual features of this toad is that some males change sex later in life and become females. Mating, however, is normal, by amplexus in water. Each female lays several batches of eggs, up to a total of 35 000 in a year. The young toads, after completing the tadpole stage, grow rapidly and are said to reach a length of 5 in. after a year.

Toxic toad

When it is attacked, the marine toad is said to be the most poisonous of all toads; its poison may cause closed eyes and a swollen face, with other unpleasant symptoms such as nausea and vomiting. In extreme cases

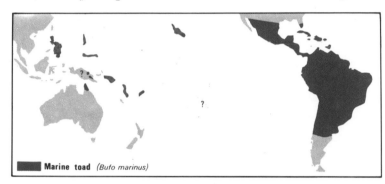

Marine toad *(Bufo marinus)*

Haughty stare from a disgruntled marine toad. Contrary to its name this toad does not live in the sea but stays hidden under vegetation or burrows in the ground on hot days, coming out at night to feed. With a large appetite to satisfy the marine toad eats all sorts of insects and anything that moves and is small enough to swallow. The characteristic warts on the skin of toads are the sites of swollen poison glands. In the marine toad there are two large glands on the back of the neck which produce a milky, poisonous secretion. So when the toad is attacked it is not its bite that is fatal but the white fluid exuded from its warts. This toad has few enemies probably because of the bad taste of this exudate but predators such as dogs and snakes are often killed by mouthing these toads. If swallowed, the toad blows itself up inside the throat of the predator, so suffocating it.

it may result in death as the poison acts like digitalis and slows the heart beat, so leading to heart failure. The poison is a whitish fluid exuded in small doses from a patch of glands on each side of the head. The toad blows itself up when disturbed, as so many toads do. Although it has no warning colours, in its native home it has few, if any, enemies. In countries where it has been introduced the native predators have not the instinct to leave it alone, largely because it has no warning colours, and those that try to eat it either suffer from its poison or are suffocated when, having quickly gulped down the toad alive and whole, it blows itself up and blocks the throat or the gullet of the unfortunate predator.

Murderous intruders

In 1863 sugar cane was planted in Queensland, Australia, near the town of Brisbane, and the first processing mill was set up. Because of the success of this venture more land was cleared for sugar, with losses among some of the native animals robbed of their habitat. Others benefited because cultivated land suited them. After 90 years the marine toad was imported from Hawaii,

where it had been introduced in the hope it would clear the cane beetle. This was the hope also in Queensland, but now after 20 years, the cane beetle is still there, the toad has greatly multiplied and is spreading rapidly. Already it is widespread over a 1 000-mile coastal strip.

Toads do more good than harm, as a rule, but this is not the case with the marine toad. It is having a drastic effect on the native fauna. The smaller species have suffered in numbers from being eaten by the toad, while snakes and birds like the ibis were killed off when they tried to eat the toad, either by being poisoned or by having the toad impacted in the throat. An unexpected damage has been caused by the toad in dry summers when ponds and water-holes dry up. Such water as was left became so packed with breeding toads and with their spawn that it became undrinkable. Finally, as the cane beetle was still rampant, insecticides were used, especially benzene hexachloride, with the inevitable result that more of the native animals were killed off.

Already Australians see in the millions of marine toads now living in Australia a parallel story to that of the rabbit. Because in their original range the toads extend from

Gathering of marine toads — a typical scene in the Queensland bush. These large toads are becoming a problem in Australia because of the rate at which they are spreading throughout the country and the effect they are having on the other fauna. The cane beetle, which it was hoped the toad would clear, still abounds!

the tropical to the temperate zone of South America there is reason to fear that in time they may spread throughout Australia. In addition, the marine toad is fast becoming a favourite laboratory animal. It is easy to keep and each year now more and more is being published on their physiology than on their habits in the wild. With such an adaptable animal, capable among other things of going without food for 6 months, it needs only a few to escape from laboratory animal houses for the toad to become established in unexpected places.

class	**Amphibia**
order	**Salientia**
family	**Bufonidae**
genus & species	***Bufo marinus***

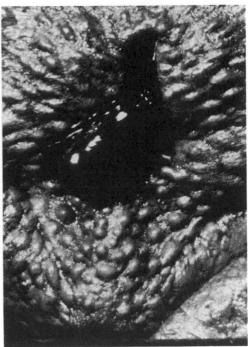

Marsupial frog

There are several species of South American tree frogs the females of which, instead of staying with the spawn to guard it, like some frogs, carry the spawn about with them in pouches. The first scientists to discover this, in 1843, merely saw that the female had a pouch and gave the frogs the scientific name **Gastrotheca**. *Translated literally this means 'stomach pouch', but in fact the pouch is on the female's back.*

Marsupial frogs are fairly ordinary tree frogs except that some are very small, ¾–1¼ in. long. The largest are only 4 in. long. They have sucker pads on the tips of the toes, usual in tree frogs, and some have stouter legs than most tree frogs. Their colours are mainly green with brown spots, blotches or stripes.

The tadpole-pocket

Marsupial frogs have an unusual way of taking care of their young, which varies from one species to another. In the smallest of them each female lays only 4–7 eggs, rich in yolk. The larger species may lay 50 or more. In these the eggs remain in the pouch until they hatch and the tadpoles stay there also, leaving the pouch only when they have changed into froglets.

When these frogs are pairing the male clasps the female as usual but he is slightly farther forward on her back. Just as she is about to lay, the female raises herself on her hindlegs so her back tilts steeply downwards towards her head. Her cloaca, the opening through which the eggs are laid, is directed upwards. As a result the eggs roll down her back and into the pouch, the male fertilising them as they go. Once the eggs are all safely inside, the mouth of the pouch closes and the surface of the female's back looks lumpy. How the froglets get out was discovered some 15 years ago; the female lifts a hind toe over her back and

pulls apart the edges of the slit-like opening to the pouch.

As adults the frogs live in trees, eating insects. Because of their unusual baby care, they do not have to go to water to spawn.

Launching the tadpoles

Several species of marsupial frogs let their young go as tadpoles; the female goes to water and lowers herself into it. Then she brings her hindlegs over her back and puts the first toe of each foot into the opening of the pouch and pulls, so the mouth of the pouch opens wide to let the tadpoles out. They come out one at a time, at short intervals. These species also have a different way of putting eggs in the pouch. They lay up to 200 eggs and as the spawn is being given out by the female the male fertilises it as usual. At the same time he uses his hind feet to push the spawn into the pouch.

Inside the pouch the tadpoles are enclosed in the egg membrane. Their external gills are much enlarged to form a sort of placenta for breathing. The details of how this works during the 100–110 days inside the pouch are not yet known, but soon after the tadpoles leave the pouch the gills are quickly absorbed. The hindlegs appear 26 days after the tadpoles enter water, the forelegs grow out 19 days later and at the end of 56 days from the time of release, they have changed into froglets.

The incredible frog

The discovery of a frog that brooded her eggs in a pouch was remarkable but over 100 years passed before it was known how the eggs got into the pouch. Then in 1957 Professor EC Amoroso of the Royal Veterinary College in London, having some marsupial frogs sent over from South America, filmed the whole process, giving zoologists everywhere a chance to see a quirk of nature which might have been scorned by the scientific world if presented in another way. But there is more to come; the discovery of how the tadpoles got out of the pouch. Even this is not the end because apparently the female marsupial frog can

◁ △ *Tadpoles-in-waiting: female marsupial frog* **Gastrotheca mertensi** *with young in back pouch to which eggs were transferred on laying. As tadpoles they escape from the pouch singly into the surrounding water (above).*
▽ **Gastrotheca marsupiatum** *– the generic name means 'stomach pouch'.*

feel when an egg is about to burst and release the tadpole. She has been seen to flex one hindleg over her back to let a tadpole out of the left side of the pouch, then flex her right leg over her back to release a tadpole from the other side.

class	**Amphibia**
order	**Salientia**
family	**Hylidae**
genus & species	*Gastrotheca marsupiatum others*

Meadow frog

One of the commonest frogs in North America, the meadow frog has a variety of common names, including grass, leopard, or shad frog and 'herring hopper'. Its body is slender, its head pointed, and it measures 2¼—4 in. overall. Its colour varies but most commonly the meadow frog is brown or greenish-brown with rows of green, brown or black spots, each ringed with a lighter colour. The legs are bright green and the belly white. Meadow frogs are found from Labrador and Mackenzie in southern Canada through the United States and Mexico to Nicaragua. They are not so common along the Pacific coast as in the central and eastern parts of the United States.

Lives near water

The meadow frog usually lives near streams, lakes or marshes, or even along irrigation streams running through deserts. It is found both up mountains and on plains, its range being limited apparently only by its ability to reach water. Adult frogs may wander a mile or more from open water but the younger ones tend to stay near the banks. In wet places meadow frogs live in crevices or holes to which they return year after year, while in drier areas they make small 'forms' by clearing away a patch of leaf litter. In winter meadow frogs hibernate underwater, in mud or beneath stones.

Varied diet

The food of the meadow frog includes leeches, snails, spiders and many kinds of insects, both terrestrial and aquatic. These include crickets, grasshoppers, houseflies, beetles, backswimmers, caddis flies—even bees and wasps. Meadow frogs also take larger prey such as small fish, tadpoles and smaller frogs, small snakes and, most surprisingly, they have been known to catch small birds such as the ruby-throated hummingbird.

Mating songs

As soon as the meadow frogs come out of hibernation they breed, in April in the more northerly part of their range. The male has three distinct calls or songs. The main song is a low, long, grunting note followed by several short notes and does not carry very far. This is to attract other males and females to the breeding pools. The males indiscriminately grasp any other frog, recog-

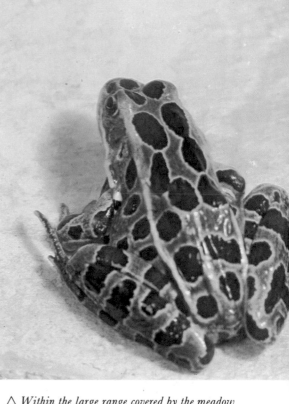

△ *Within the large range covered by the meadow frog there are many colour variations; enough,*

▽ *Portrait of a meadow frog. The bulge made by the top of the pelvis – the long hip bone that makes a platform for frogs' leaping – shows above the head in this unusual view.*

nising them as male or female by touch—the females are swollen with eggs—and by voice. If a male is clasped it utters the warning call to deter the clasping male. The male also calls to tell the female that he intends to clasp her, so preparing her for mating. If she is not ready for mating she warns him off by grunting. The male grasps the female around the shoulders and executes a series of 'backward shuffles', swimming backwards for a short distance then resting.

About 3 000—6 000 eggs are laid in spherical masses of up to 6 in. diameter and fertilised immediately. The masses are usually attached to water plants but may float free in the water. Depending on the water temperature the eggs hatch in 2—3 weeks, liberating tadpoles about $\frac{1}{3}$ in. long. The tadpoles change into froglets when they are about 1 in. long, after 8—11 weeks' growth. The small frogs live in marshes and begin breeding when 3 years old. A meadow frog lived in the London Zoo for 9 years.

Leaping to safety
Meadow frogs are very good jumpers. They can leap 6 ft, which is 15 times their body length, compared with the bullfrog's jumps of nine times its body length. Most meadow frogs live near enough to water for them to be able to reach the safety of the mud

with a few leaps. Experiments have shown that meadow frogs have a simple mechanism that guides them towards water. Their eyes are particularly sensitive to blue light and, if placed in a box with two windows, behind which different coloured screens are stood, a meadow frog jumps towards a blue screen more often than it jumps towards any other colour. By contrast the frogs very rarely jumped towards green.

Putting oneself in the place of a frog in its home in the plants near a lake or stream, all will be green except for the water which reflects blue light. Even on an overcast day when a lake or stream appears grey, the water is still reflecting blue light. When an enemy appears a frog jumps out of the way, but which way is it to jump? The obvious place of safety is in the water where it can hide in the mud or among the weed. The frog's sensitivity to blue light gives it automatic and very rapid guidance.

class	**Amphibia**
order	**Salientia**
family	**Ranidae**
genus & species	*Rana pipiens*

in fact, to make some scientists believe that several separate races are represented.

▽ *Leaper extraordinary: for most meadow frogs safety is seldom far away; if disturbed they can reach water in a series of 6ft bounds—a startling performance for their size.*

Midwife toad

The midwife toad is named after its most peculiar mating habits, in which the male apparently helps the female in laying her eggs. Its total length is $1\frac{1}{2}-2\frac{1}{2}$ in., the female being a little larger than the male. The head is relatively small, the snout pointed and the back is covered with small round warts. The feet are partly webbed, the webs extending only about $\frac{1}{3}$ of the way along the toes. The upperparts are greyish or light brown with a darker patch between the eyes. The underside is dirty white with spots of dark grey on the throat and breast. Females have rows of reddish warts down the sides of the body.

Midwife toads are found in western Europe from Belgium and Germany as far north as Hameln, near Hanover, and southwards to Spain and Portugal, and as far east as Switzerland. They live at heights of 5–6 000 ft in the Pyrenees where snow lies for most of the year.

Seldom seen

Towards evening these shy, nocturnal toads give away their presence by a whistling call that sounds like a chime of bells when several toads call together. This sound gives them the alternative name of bell toad. Although very abundant in some places, they are seldom seen as they spend the day in holes which they dig with their forelegs and snout, or in crevices between stones and the deserted burrows of small mammals. Midwife toads are quite common in towns, where they hide in cellars or under woodpiles.

When they come out at night midwife toads crawl slowly, rather than hop, in search of insects, slugs and snails. Even when disturbed they can hop only clumsily. They are protected from enemies by the poison in their skin which is secreted from the warts. There is sufficient poison in one midwife toad to kill an adder in a few hours, so any predator that takes a fancy to a midwife toad is unlikely to last long enough to kill another.

Father carries the eggs

The breeding habits of midwife-toads are notable for two unusual features; the male stimulates egg-laying by manipulating the female's cloaca, and after the eggs are laid, he carries them wrapped around his hindlegs until they hatch. These habits were not described until 1876 when a Frenchman spent 3 years studying midwife toads.

Breeding starts in April and continues throughout spring and summer. The females are attracted to the males' burrows by their calls. Mating is difficult to watch because it takes place under cover at night, and does not last long. Other frogs and toads stay in amplexus for as much as one day, but in midwife toads amplexus lasts for less than one hour.

The male midwife toad seizes the female around the waist and strokes her cloaca with his hindfeet, even pushing his toes into the cloaca. After a period of up to 20 minutes these movements suddenly stop, the female stretches her hindlegs and the eggs are extruded onto them. The male moves forward, transferring his grip to the female's neck, and fertilises the eggs. At the same time he urinates, soaking the jelly surrounding the eggs, making it swell up.

After fertilisation, the male wraps the string of 20–100 yellowish eggs around his hindlegs and walks off with them. For the next 3 weeks he carries the eggs, resting in his burrow by day and feeding by night. The eggs are kept moist by the dew, but on dry nights he goes to water and immerses them. He may mate again with another female, so carrying two or more strings of eggs. The females also mate again and may produce three or four lots of eggs in one season. When the eggs are ready to hatch, the male enters water and the tadpoles force their way out of the jelly and swim away. How he is aware the eggs are ready to hatch is not known.

The tadpoles are quite advanced when they hatch, being just over $\frac{1}{2}$ in. long and having one gill on each side. Most of them change into frogs before the autumn but some spend the winter as tadpoles and emerge the following spring.

◁△ *Male midwife carrying the developing eggs. This behaviour is one of the most peculiar types of breeding yet to be seen in amphibians. The male, after fertilising eggs as the female lays them, walks through them so they are wrapped round his hind legs. After about 3 weeks they are ready to hatch and the male enters water so the tadpoles can swim away.*
△ *Eggs with visible tadpoles about to hatch.*

Melting their way out

In early descriptions of the life history of frogs and toads it was assumed that tadpoles bit their way out of the egg capsule. Closer examination revealed that during hatching tadpoles of the midwife toad kept their mouths shut. A hole appears in the egg apparently by the capsule being dissolved away. The whole process of hatching takes about $\frac{1}{2}$ hour. First the tadpole moves so its snout pushes against the capsule which then becomes pointed. After 15–20 minutes the capsule softens, then liquefies completely where the tadpole's snout is pressing against it. Then the tadpole forces its way out.

Between the nostrils of the tadpole is a gland which secretes an enzyme that dissolves the egg capsule. A similar gland had been found in the tadpoles of other frogs and toads whose eggs hatch in water. Those that hatch on land, such as the greenhouse frog, bite their way out of the egg.

class	**Amphibia**
order	**Salientia**
family	**Discoglossidae**
genus & species	***Alytes obstetricans***

Mouth-breeding frog

Also known as the vaquero, in Argentina, and as Darwin's frog and Darwin's toad, the mouth-breeding frog is probably the most remarkable of all the amphibians. First discovered by Darwin, it is only 1 in. long and its tadpoles mature to tiny froglets inside the father's vocal sacs.

This midget frog is an inconspicuous greenish brown with darker stripes and patches and a dark line running from behind each eye to the hind end of the body. There are many warts arranged in irregular rows on the body and legs. In front of the large eyes the snout rapidly narrows to a pointed, false nose, the nostrils lying halfway between the eyes and the tip of this 'proboscis'. The front legs are fairly short with long, slender toes, the hindlegs being long as in a normal frog.

The mouth-breeding frog was found by Darwin in the Argentine during his famous **Beagle** voyage, and has since been found to range through southern Chile as well as southern Argentina.

Weak voice

The home of this frog is in the beech woods where it hops around in a lively manner, rising well up on its hindlegs before making a short hop forward. The male has a small bell-like voice—weak for the size of the

vocal sacs which, as we shall see, have a more important function. These form a large pouch under the throat which extends backwards under the belly to the groin and upwards on each side, almost to the backbone. Inside the mouth is a pair of slits, one on each side, that lead into the vocal sacs, which lie between the skin and the muscles of the body.

Strange nursery

In the breeding season the females lay 20–30 eggs over which the males stand guard for 10–20 days. As the eggs are about to hatch the males pick them up with their tongues, several at a time, and they slide through the slits into the vocal sacs which have now become much swollen. Each male may have anything up to 17 large eggs in his vocal sacs, and quite naturally he now becomes silent. The males do not have to fast while the tadpoles develop. The tadpoles can take no food, however, except for the yolk contained in the eggs which becomes enclosed in their intestines. When about ½ in. long, and with just a stump of a tail left, they leave the vocal sacs. Everything now goes back to normal in the male parent's body. The vocal sacs shrink and his shoulder girdle and internal organs, which had become distorted to make room for the growing tadpoles, go back to their former shape.

The males do not necessarily tend their own offspring; the females lay their eggs in masses and the males take whichever eggs are nearest at the time.

The earliest voice

The first voice in the history of the earth was probably that of a frog, and it may have sounded some 200 million years ago. Plenty of other animals made sounds, the crickets and grasshoppers, for example, as well as many fishes, but a voice-box in the throat came first in the tailless amphibians. Even the tailed amphibians, the salamanders and newts, who can hear, although they were once thought to be deaf, use only a very weak voice, though they have a larynx. By recording the calls of frogs and toads and playing these back to the animals during the breeding season and at other times the value of the voice was discovered. First and foremost, it seems, the voice is used as a mating call. The frogs and toads react most to calls when they are ready to breed. Males move towards any source of calls as a potential breeding site. Once the females have spawned, the voices of the males have no charms for them. So the mouth-breeding males suffer little from having to fall silent, as the females have already spawned. When the voice is used outside the breeding season it is to keep individuals spaced out.

class	**Amphibia**
order	**Salientia**
family	**Rhinodermatidae**
genus & species	***Rhinoderma darwinii***

The mouth-breeding frog was first found by Darwin and so is named after him. It is just over 1 in. long and has a peculiar false nose.

The colouring and patterning of the skin of this tiny frog varies tremendously from one frog to another as pictures 1, 2 and 3 show.

The tadpoles, picture 4, develop in the swollen vocal sac of the male. This sac is opened, picture 5, showing the tadpoles inside.

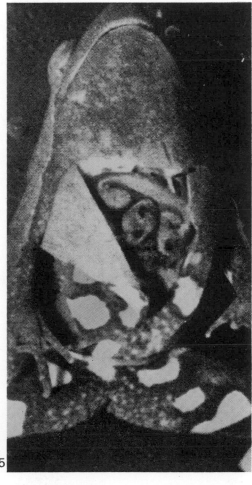

Natterjack

The most distinctive feature of the natterjack toad is a yellow line running down the head and back from the snout to the vent. This has given rise to one of the local names of 'goldenback'. It is very similar to the common toad in appearance but rather smaller, the maximum length being just over 3 in. There is no marked difference in size between the sexes. The legs are proportionately shorter than those of the common toad. The body is greyish or pale yellowish-brown, sometimes with distinct spots of brown, reddish, yellow or green. The underside is yellowish-white with dark spots, and the legs are barred with black. The skin of the upperparts is covered with wart-like glands as in the common toad but the two large parotid glands behind the eyes are smaller than in the common toad. The male can be distinguished by its stronger forelimbs and, during the breeding season, by the blackish patches of horny skin on the hands, the so-called nuptial pads, and a bluish patch of skin on the throat. The green toad **Bufo viridis** which is very closely related to the natterjack, lives in Europe. It lacks the stripe running down the back except in the parts of its range where the natterjack is absent.

Natterjacks are confined to Europe, being common in France and Spain, but ranging from southern Sweden in the north to the Gulf of Riga and Poland in the east. In the British Isles they are restricted to certain localities in England and Scotland, and to Co. Kerry in Ireland.

△ An extremely fat female natterjack spreads herself on a rock while a younger one crawls around her. Secretions from the mucous glands prevent the sun drying the skin out.

▽ A squatter by nature. A natterjack toad sits squarely on its short plump legs, which are so short that it cannot jump like other toads, but runs instead, sometimes quite fast.

Running toad

Because of their short hind legs natterjacks do not jump but move at a fast run, and in some places they are called running toads. They run down their prey which consists of small animals, such as spiders, insects, worms and snails.

Natterjacks are nearly always found in sandy places where they can burrow easily, such as in the sand dunes along the coast, but because of the increasing development of seaside areas, natterjacks are becoming scarce. In England, their last strongholds are the counties of Dorset, Hampshire, Surrey and Lancashire. It is difficult to ascertain the exact distribution of natterjacks because they will suddenly appear in an area where they have never been seen before, then disappear, moving to a new breeding ground.

In loose sand a natterjack can dig itself out of sight within a few seconds, using its hindlegs to push itself in. In firmer soil it scrapes a hole with its forelegs, shooting the loosened soil back under its belly. Deserted burrows of other animals may be used by a group of natterjacks. In the winter natterjacks hibernate in burrows 1 ft or more deep and have been known to climb walls of sand, wintering in sand martin burrows.

Natterjacks usually emerge at night but they are sometimes active during the day when they may be seen sunning themselves. Their skin is not as dry as that of common toads, being kept moist by secretions from mucous glands, which allows them to come out in quite strong daylight.

Breeding in salt water

The breeding season is lengthy and in exceptional years it may start in late March and continue to August. Natterjacks are not good swimmers and during breeding they are usually found among reeds, not far from the banks of the breeding pools. They are able to breed in brackish pools near the sea because both eggs and tadpoles can survive quite strong salt concentrations. They also breed in ditches and puddles devoid of water plants. Mating usually takes place at night, the males attracting females with a loud croak of *ra, ra, ra* that, in chorus, can be heard for a mile or more. The vocal sac under the chin is three times the size of the head when it is extended and the forelegs have to be straightened to allow it to expand. The eggs are laid in a few hours. The strings are shorter than those of the common toad, measuring 5−6 ft long and containing up to 4 000 eggs. When first laid, the eggs, each $\frac{1}{18}$ in. in diameter, lie in two rows within the jelly string, but as they grow they push each other aside to form a single row. The tadpoles emerge within 5−10 days of the eggs being laid. They are the smallest tadpoles of any European amphibian, rarely more than an inch long, and greyish black with bronzy spots. The young toads, which measure only $\frac{1}{3}$ in. after the tail has been lost, leave the water 5−8 weeks after hatching. By autumn they are twice as large but they do not become fully grown until 4−5 years old.

Nasty smells

When alarmed a natterjack blows itself up in the same way as a common toad. It is also said to 'feign death' by spreading itself flat on the ground. When handled, natterjacks exude a white liquid from the skin which has been described as smelling like burnt gunpowder or boiling rubber.

Trained to live in water

Natterjacks are mainly land animals, living on dry sandy soil and only taking to water for the few hours necessary for mating and egg-laying. It has been found, however, that they can be trained to take up an aquatic way of life. They can be conditioned to gradually spending more and more time in water until they are living permanently in water. So profound is the conditioning that if a trained natterjack is liberated it voluntarily continues its aquatic life. Furthermore, such toads change their basic behaviour patterns and perform frog-like actions that they never use normally. The implication of such experiments are that the behaviour of amphibians cannot be assumed to be rigid and that they are capable of learning or adapting their habits.

class	**Amphibia**
order	**Salientia**
family	**Bufonidae**
genus & species	***Bufo calamita***

△ *Dead or alive? Two natterjacks pose together as dead wood.*

▽ *Natterjacks are not good swimmers by nature although they can be trained.*

Paradoxical frog

These frogs are quite the reverse of other frogs: at metamorphosis they are several times smaller than their tadpoles.

In outward appearance the paradoxical frog looks like any ordinary frog. It is up to 3 in. long. Its hindfeet are webbed but the toes project beyond the webbing more than usual. Its colour varies among the usual greens and browns with darker spots and blotches but the hindlegs have a harlequin colouring of yellow and black.

There are several sub-species, the best known living on the island of Trinidad and in the northeastern area of South America and in part of the Amazon basin. Others are found in other parts of South America as far south as northern Argentina.

Stirring up mud

Paradoxical frogs are usually heard and not seen. They seldom come onto land and whenever they come to the surface of the water, they usually expose just their eyes or nostrils, and these are usually hidden among small water plants crowding the surface. The moment they are disturbed they dive. They have an added protection: their skin is unusually slippery so they are extremely hard to hold. They often make coughing grunts, however, almost like pigs.

Another peculiarity is that the toes have an extra joint, which gives them greater length, and this is linked with the method of feeding. They stir up the mud at the bottom of shallow lakes to find the small mud-dwelling invertebrates which they feed on. The first toe on each forefoot is opposable to the others, and it is used as a thumb for grasping food.

From giant to dwarf

The outstanding feature of this frog is the size of the tadpole, which may be 10½ in. long. When it changes into a froglet it shrinks to 1½ in. This is so unusual that the first scientists to study these frogs could not believe they belonged to the same species. When the tadpole shrinks by this tremendous amount all the internal organs must shrink proportionately, which was quite unheard of, so the adult frog was given one scientific name and the tadpole was given another. Only when the actual change from one to another had been observed was it realized that only one species was involved. In fact, the whole process was so puzzling that for a time there were several different scientific names for the different stages in the life-history. This is not the only time such a thing has happened, but it is very rare for there to be such a great reduction in size from the young or larval animal to the adult. It raises all manner of questions to which we do not yet know the answers; for example, how large the eggs are and whether they contain large quantities of yolk to feed the growing tadpole in its early stages. Another question to which we would like the answer is what advantage there can be in a tadpole growing so large then shrinking so much as it turns into a froglet.

Tadpoles as food

One reason why information on these frogs is so scanty is that they are difficult to find and therefore to keep in sufficient numbers in captivity to study them. Three individuals of one species were collected 100 years ago but there is no record of its having been seen since. Within the last few years, however, South American zoologists have been finding more of other species in areas south of the Amazon Basin, so more information may soon begin to trickle through. The tadpoles are easier to catch as they can be netted but even this apparently is not simple. The local Indians catch the tadpoles, as well as the adults, on hooks baited with grasshoppers, then sell them in the markets, and the tadpoles are particularly relished.

class	**Amphibia**
order	**Salientia**
family	**Pseudidae**
genus & species	*Pseudis paradoxa*

*Peculiar puzzling pseudid—the paradoxical frog has long been a zoological problem as it has no close relatives and so is difficult to classify. It is now put in its own family Pseudidae. This species, **Pseudis paradoxa** is the largest and best known paradoxical frog so called because of the disproportion in size between the tadpole and adult. It seems unbelievable that a 10½in. tadpole could metamorphose into a 1½in. froglet, but this is what happens.*

*Frog that shrinks as it grows, the paradoxical frog **Pseudis paradoxa**. An entirely aquatic frog, it lives in remote swamps and marshes where it is nearly invisible among the water weeds.*

Recorded distribution, although the frog probably has a wider unrecorded distribution.

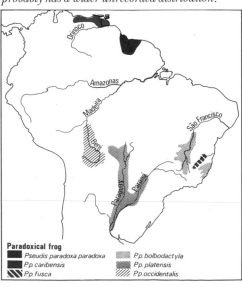

Paradoxical frog
- Pseudis paradoxa paradoxa
- P.p.caribensis
- P.p.fusca
- P.p.bolbodactyla
- P.p.platensis
- P.p.occidentalis

Rain frog

The rain frog is so-called because it appears in large numbers at the onset of rain. It is a most peculiar member of the Microhylidae or narrow-mouthed frogs. It has a round, bladder-like body which it inflates when disturbed, and a very short head, the two together measuring about $1\frac{1}{2}$ in. The male is slightly smaller than the female. The rain frog and others belonging to the genus **Breviceps** are often called shortheads, for when the body is inflated the head appears to be just a continuation of the rounded body, except for a pair of protruding eyes. Its skin is warty like that of the common toad, mottled brown and black above and white below. The rain frog lives in South Africa, southwest Africa and Rhodesia where it is also known as blaasop.

△ A frog respected by many Africans because of its supposed power of being able to bring or withhold rain that is much needed for crops. This rain frog, away from the safety of its burrow, has inflated its round body like a puffball. Characteristic of this peculiar frog is the straight up and down front of its small head and its large eyes. Although this frog is named after its habit of emerging from the ground after heavy rain it cannot in fact swim and never takes to water voluntarily.

Frog that does not swim

Unlike most amphibians the rain frog and its relatives live well away from water. They have been found 50 miles from the nearest standing water and some relatives live in coastal sand dunes and in deserts. They do not even resort to water to breed but lay their eggs in the ground. Rain frogs that fall into water are likely to drown unless they inflate their bodies and float to the side and safety.

Apart from the 3 months when they are breeding and feeding, rain frogs live underground in a state of torpor. They have spadelike horny projections on their hindfeet with which they loosen soil, throwing it sideways so they sink backwards out of sight. Rain frogs are very rarely found during their underground phase but two dozen comatose rain frogs were once found tucked together in a hollow in moist earth.

Termites as favourites

During their 3 months of activity from October to December rain frogs live in shallow burrows from which they come out to feed on earthworms and insects building up a store of fat to tide them over the 9 months of fasting. A favourite food is flying termites which emerge in large numbers after rain. When they have settled on the ground and cast their wings the rain frogs give chase, running after them in a surprisingly nimble way, rather than hopping like most frogs.

Subterranean mating

Throughout their period of activity rain frogs can be heard calling all night, and throughout the day if it is misty or overcast. The call is a monotonous 'oink' repeated at fairly long intervals by the frogs sitting in their tunnels with only their snouts exposed, but where rain frogs are abundant they combine in a loud chorus. Mating takes place in a burrow. The small male clings to the back of the female and is fastened securely by some unknown adhesive substance. It would be impossible to detach the male without tearing his arms off. This seems a very necessary device as the pair dig down backwards, the male's hindlimbs being free to excavate, while his forelimbs are far too short to obtain a secure grip on the female.

The pair make their tunnel under a log, boulder or bush where the ground is likely to stay damp for some time. They dig down 1 ft or so then hollow out a chamber, 2–3 in. across. They stay together for 3 days during which time 20–40 eggs are laid, stuck together in a solid mass. Each egg is $\frac{1}{2}$ in. across, of which over half is transparent jelly. Development takes 6–8 weeks. First a tiny tadpole is formed, then the legs appear, front pair first, and the tail is absorbed. Finally a small frog, $\frac{1}{4}$ in. long, breaks out, metamorphosis having taken place in the egg, the tadpole never being free swimming.

Sticky repellant

Apart from blowing itself up, a rain frog can defend itself by exuding droplets of a white substance from pores scattered over the body. This substance is extremely sticky and very difficult to remove if it gets on the skin. It is also irritating if it gets into the mouth or eyes. Presumably it is a good deterrent but a tame glossy ibis has been known to feed on rain frogs. beating them to a pulp before swallowing them. The sticky white substance may also be the means by which the male is fixed to the female during mating.

Weather prophet

Although any number of frogs could be called rain frogs because they appear and call during wet weather, the rain frog deserves its name because it is a weather prophet. It begins to call just before the spring rains start. The calls are often in chorus, thousands of rain frogs 'oinking' at once. Then the chorus dies down to silence and suddenly starts up again. At other times the chorus splits up, calls coming from one area dying down as another area starts.

Animals regarded as weather prophets usually fall short in practice as they do no more than indicate current weather conditions, for instance appearing or calling when it is actually raining. Imagination then embroiders fact to credit them with foreknowledge. The rain frogs, however, live up to their reputation, except that they are sometimes credited with being able to bring or hold back rain. Because of this they are treated kindly by some African farmers who replace them in their burrows if disturbed, together with a little food.

class	**Amphibia**
order	**Salientia**
family	**Microhylidae**
genus & species	*Breviceps adspersus*

Large bulging eyes, body blown up out of all proportion; a rather disdainful rain frog just manages to prop itself up on its straddling legs.

Reed frog

There are over 200 species of reed or sedge frogs, all living in Africa. Many are beautifully patterned and coloured, and can change colour in response to temperature or background. They are small, about 1 in. long. The five-lined reed frog, from Angola to Tanzania, is pale, almost golden brown with five mauve-brown stripes running down its back. These stripes are more distinct in the male than in the female. The painted or marbled reed frog has intricate patterns on its back. The patterns and their colours vary from frog to frog and with the background. Painted reed frogs may be black and white, black and green, black and yellow, brown and

△ A tiny painted reed frog clings onto a twig by the sucker-like discs on its fingers and toes. The beautiful pinky-red belly and markings on the head and arms are typical of this frog, which often proves difficult to identify because its colour and patterning varies so widely in different parts of its range.

yellow as well as several other variations. The painted reed frog ranges from the Cape to Rhodesia and Angola. At the

their new background. The arum frog basks with its legs drawn under it but it may suddenly stretch its legs and leap away. If only slightly disturbed, however, it swings around and disappears behind the lily.

class	**Amphibia**
order	**Salientia**
family	**Rhacophoridae**
genera & species	*Afrixalus* *small golden spiny reed frog* *A. fornasinii* *brown and white spiny reed frog* *Hyperolius horstocki* *arum frog* *H. marmoratus* *painted reed frog* *H. tuberilinguis* *green reed frog* *H. quinquevittatus* *five-lined reed frog*

southern end of its range it is green or brown with light green spots, each spot ringed with a narrow black line. By contrast, the rare green reed frog is a plain brilliant green with no markings but is white on the belly and pink on the hindlegs.

The two spiny reed frogs live up to their name, for with the aid of a magnifying lens minute spines can be seen on their heads and backs. They differ from the other reed frogs in that the pupil of the eye is vertical instead of horizontal.

Sun-loving frogs

Apart from the spiny reed frogs, which hide during the day, reed frogs like to sunbathe, and can be found clinging to reeds or other plants even in hot sun. They are, however, always ready to leap to safety. Usually this means that they leap back into the pond but the painted reed frog that often lives miles from water escapes by long bounding leaps. During the dry season reed frogs disappear into cracks and crevices in the ground or bury themselves in the earth. Reed frogs feed on flying insects such as mosquitoes.

Varied breeding habits

The life histories of reed frogs have been largely made known through the studies of Vincent Wager, the South African expert on frogs. While the majority probably have life histories similar to other frogs such as the common, edible or bullfrogs, some reed frogs have unusual habits. The life history of the arum frog appears straightforward. Clusters of about 30 eggs

are laid among water plants and the surrounding jelly is sticky so the eggs become camouflaged with mud. The tadpoles feed on minute floating organisms rather than scraping at the slime of algae on stones.

The giant reed frog lays its eggs above water. About 300–400 are laid in a sticky mass on floating plants or on the leaves of plants overhanging water. At first the jelly is stiff, then it softens and hangs down. The tadpoles develop within this mass and wriggle about until the jelly liquefies, when they break out and fall into the water. The painted reed frog lays its eggs in clusters on stones or plants underwater, but the southern spotted form, called the pondo reed frog, sometimes loses its eggs through an unusual habit. The mated pair jump onto an erect stalk and bend it over with their weight until its tip hangs into the water. Some eggs are laid on the submerged part which sometimes springs up again after the frogs have let go. The eggs dry out in the sun and die. The egg-laying habits of the spiny reed frogs recall those of newts (page 75). The eggs are stuck to a leaf which is folded over to make a protective tube. The golden spiny reed frog lays its eggs under water, the brown and white spiny reed frog on plants up to 3 ft above the water.

Flower frog

The arum frog lives in flowers of the arum lily, where its ivory colour makes it inconspicuous as it basks in the sun. It is also overlooked by insects that are attracted by the scent of the arum lily and so fall prey to the frog. When arum lilies are not in flower the frogs move to other plants and change their colour to dark brown to fit

Spadefoot

The spadefoot toads are named after the spade-like horny projection on the side of each hindfoot, with which they dig their burrows. The family of spadefoots is widely distributed over Europe, North Africa, southern Asia and North America. They are usually 3–4 in. long with a soft skin which is moist like that of a common frog rather than dry and warty like that of a common toad. The colour of the skin varies greatly between species. It may be grey, brown or green with red, white or black markings. There is also some variation in markings between the individuals of one species.

The European spadefoot is found over much of Europe south of southern Sweden and extends into Asia as far as Iran. Another European species is the mud-diver of southwestern Europe. In Asia there are the horned frogs which have three pointed projections of skin on the head, one on the snout and one above each eye. The best known spadefoots live in North America. They are related to the European spadefoot.

Burrowing habits

Spadefoots are nocturnal, spending the day in burrows which they excavate by digging themselves in backwards with their spade-like hind legs. As they disappear beneath the surface the entrance of the burrow caves in so concealing it. The burrowing and nocturnal habits of spadefoots mean that they are often overlooked when they may be quite abundant, except during the breeding season when the males can be

▽ *Backward bulldozer: American spadefoot toad* **Scaphiopus intermontanus** *from the Great Basin of Nevada. The horny 'blade' used to burrow in reverse shows clearly on the hindfoot.*

△ *The tadpoles of the striped pixie toad* **Pyxicephalus delalandii** *of east Africa, are fast growers. They hatch from eggs laid in rain puddles which may or may not dry up before the tadpoles reach the stage when they can change into small toads.*

heard calling. Spadefoots are mainly found in sandy areas where burrows are easy to dig. In dry weather they may burrow 6–7 ft down to find moist soil.

Some spadefoots give a shrill cry when handled, which may be a means of deterring predators. They may also give off secretions from glands in the skin. In certain species such as the Mexican spadefoot small glands give off an unpleasant tasting secretion that also irritates the lining of the nose and mouth. The European spadefoot is called the *Knoblauchskrote,* or garlic toad, in Germany because the secretions from its skin smell rather like garlic.

The food of spadefoots is insects and other small invertebrates.

Growing up together

The general breeding pattern of the spadefoot is not very different from that of the common toad. In spring the males of the European spadefoot, for example, resort to ponds where they call, attracting the females to them. Their eggs are laid in gelatinous strings among the stems of water plants. The tadpoles hatch out about 5 days later and, at first, lack both gills and tail, and measure only ⅛ in. External gills and tail grow within a day or so and development continues normally, with the external gills being replaced by internal gills and the legs growing, until the tadpoles are 4 in. long. The tail is then resorbed and the resulting toadlets leave the pond.

A variation of this pattern is seen in an Asian species in which courtship takes place on land and the pairs then go to a stream for egg-laying. Among the North American spadefoots there are, however, some very remarkable habits. These toads live in the dry parts of the southwestern United States

and breed when shallow ponds are temporarily filled with rainwater. They have, therefore, to start breeding as soon as the ponds fill and their offspring have to be independent before they dry up again.

A brief adolescence

Shortly after a storm the males of these spadefoots search for water and when they have found a suitable stretch of standing water they start to call. Their calls attract other males so a chorus builds up that eventually attracts the females and pairs form for mating. The louder the chorus from any pond, the more females are attracted to it, which is an efficient way of ensuring rapid pairing. The eggs hatch in 2 days, a much shorter time than that known for any other frog or toad. The tadpoles grow very rapidly but sometimes the temporary pools dry up before they can change into toadlets. In some species the tadpoles gather in compact groups if the water level is dangerously low and wriggle together to form a depression in the mud where the remaining water can collect. The tadpoles change into toadlets by the resorption of the tail in half an hour. They gather at the water's edge in masses and they all leave together, so overnight the pond loses all its tadpoles.

When there is a shortage of food in a pool the tadpoles band together and move over the bottom, stirring it with their tails to expose food. The tadpoles also eat the bodies of other tadpoles that have died from starvation. This means that in bad conditions a few survive instead of all of them dying. It has also been found that when a pond is drying up tadpoles which have fed on other tadpoles complete their development more rapidly, so increasing the chances of the strongest youngsters' survival.

Occasional interbreeding

In the western United States there are four species of spadefoot which are very similar but only rarely interbreed. Where two or more live in the same place, interbreeding is prevented by females only responding to the calls of males of their own species and by the slightly different habits of different spadefoot species. Thus Hunter's and Couch's spadefoots breed in the shallows while the plains and Hammond's spadefoots prefer deeper water.

There is also a great difference in the kinds of soil in which the American spadefoots prefer to live and this also results in the species being kept apart. In Texas Hunter's spadefoot likes sandy areas whereas Couch's spadefoot prefers soil which is not sandy. This is a sufficient barrier to keep them apart, except where man has disturbed the soil. At one place disturbed ground supports both species, and they interbreed occasionally.

class	**Amphibia**
order	**Salientia**
family	**Pelobatidae**
genera & species	**Megophrys nasuta** *horned frog* **Pelobates fuscus** *European spadefoot* **Pelodytes punctatus** *mud-diver* **Scaphiopus bombifrons** *plains spadefoot* **S. couchi** *Couch's spadefoot* **S. hammondii** *Hammond's spadefoot* **S. holbrookii** *Hunter's or eastern spadefoot* **S. multiplicatus** *Mexican spadefoot*

Surinam toad

The Surinam toad is very flat, has remarkable breeding habits and has long been kept in aquaria as a pet. It is about 4 in. long, the male being smaller than the female. Its flattened body is rather like a square pancake, its head is small and triangular and on the upper lip near the eyes are flaps of skin or short tentacles. Its skin is slippery and covered with small warts. Like all members of its family, the Surinam toad has neither tongue nor teeth and with them it is sometimes referred to as a tongueless frog. Although it has very small eyes it can see in all directions, an advantage for any animal in detecting its enemies. The toad's feet have long fingers and toes but only the hindfeet are webbed; it uses its front feet mainly to capture food and to push it into its mouth. It is a blackish-brown colour above, which makes it almost invisible in the black mud of the streams and pools where it lives. Its underparts are paler brown spotted with white or sometimes whitish with a dark brown stripe along the belly. The whole effect makes for a well-camouflaged toad.

The Surinam toad is found in Brazil and the Guianas.

Skilful scavenger

The Surinam toad's flat, flabby body looks most ungainly if it is taken out of water but in water the toad swims strongly and gracefully using its powerful hindlegs. It lives its life almost entirely in the water, scavenging in the mud for any small aquatic animal, dead or alive, that its long slender fingers can sweep up. At the tip of each finger is a cluster of glandular filaments, sensitive organs of touch, that help the animal to find its food even in black mud or when the stream or river is thick and silty.

The Surinam toad does not hibernate but during dry weather it will bury itself in the mud sometimes in large numbers.

Surinam toads live quite well in captivity but they do not often breed under the artificial conditions of an aquarium.

Carrying her eggs on her back

The Surinam toad is noted chiefly for its remarkable breeding habits. Mating takes place soon after the start of the rainy season. After uttering a series of strange metallic ticking calls the male grasps the body of the female with his arms. Just before he does this the female's oviduct grows out and, in amplexus, the male presses it beneath his body and over the female's back. This helps to squeeze out the eggs onto the thick, spongy skin on her back. In all, about 60 eggs are laid in this way and pressed into her skin by the male.

A Surinam toad follows its fingers when searching for food. The filamentous tips (above) are tactile organs which find food in its normally opaque home.

113

When the last has been laid the male swims away but the female stays quietly resting while her oviduct goes back to normal and disappears into her body. The skin of her back slowly swells, a hole forms round each egg and, most astonishing of all, a lid forms over the top, so that each egg lies in its own pocket, the whole of the female's back looking rather like part of a honeycomb. Although the female now looks fat and clumsy she does not seem to be inconvenienced in her movements.

As with other frogs and toads the eggs hatch into tadpoles but all this takes place inside each small pocket, where the larva remains until the whole of the metamorphosis is completed. Then, 3—4 months later the lids of the pouches open and the young toads emerge and swim around freely.

▽ *Last egg trailing from her extraordinarily extensible oviduct, a female Surinam toad rests after amplexus, with the majority of the eggs firmly placed in the thick, spongy skin of her back by the pressure of the male.*

Birth of legends
The Surinam toad used to be called the pipa in the 18th century, when it was already well known in western Europe. The people of that time were puzzled to know how the toadlets got into the mother's back. A Mr Ferman who claimed to have been an eyewitness of the event, told them that 'the eggs are generated within the female, who, when they have attained the proper degree of maturity, deposits them on the ground. The male amasses together the heap, and deposits them with great care, on the back of the female, where after impregnation they are pressed into the cellules, which are at that period open for their reception, and afterwards close over them.' That, indeed, was the accepted explanation until about 55 years ago. Mr Ferman added: 'In this singular production of young, the pipa seems to bear considerable analogy to the different species of opossum.' This was almost prophetic for it was from this same part of the world that an even worse piece of misinformation came and was perpetu-ated even more firmly Moreover it concerned the opossum Mr Ferman mentioned.

Madame Maria Sibylla Merian who went to Surinam or Dutch Guiana in 1699 to paint tropical butterflies found she had a vacant space at the end of her book so she included a fanciful picture, based on the local legend, of a mother opossum *Didelphis dorsigera* carrying her young ones on her back while they wrapped their tails around her tail for support. There was no scientific foundation for this picture but it has been copied in textbook after textbook until Dr Carl G Hartman exposed the truth of it in 1952 in his book *Possums*.

class	**Amphibia**
order	**Salientia**
family	**Pipidae**
genus & species	***Pipa pipa***

Water-holding frog

Any frog or toad is likely to discharge a fluid from its bladder when gently squeezed, and this fluid is mainly water. Frogs and toads living in deserts hold more water in their bladders and are therefore termed water-carrying or water-holding. One more especially has been singled out for this name: the water-holding frog of the deserts of Australia.

It is squat-bodied, 2½ in. long, with fairly short, stout front legs and plump hindlegs with webbed toes. It is greenish-grey, often with a dark line down the middle of the back, and its skin is warty. The head seems small for the bloated body; the animal looks more like the European common toad than the common frog. This may be why this and other similar species in Australia have at times been called water-holding or water-carrying toads.

The range of the water-holding frog covers the dry areas of New South Wales and Queensland, northern South Australia and Central Australia.

Water holders

Frogs and toads can lose water rapidly through their skin, but they can also rapidly absorb water through it, which is why they never drink. Most of this water is stored in the lymph spaces under the skin and between the muscles. Much of it is stored in the bladder and can be taken back into the rest of the body if needed. What this means can best be appreciated by comparing the clawed frog (page 84) of Africa with the water-holding frog. The clawed frog continually lives in water and has a small bladder capable of holding only 1% of its body weight. The bladder of the water-holding frog can hold up to 50% of its body weight in water.

Cocooned for the dry spell

The climate map of Australia shows that over half the surface of the continent has 10 in. or less of rain each year. The driest places are in the heart of the continent, where the annual rainfall is less than 5 in. a year. In this area, however, the rain falls as heavy but infrequent showers, and in a given district there may be a lapse of several years between one rainstorm and the next. During periods of drought the water-holding frog lies buried, as much as 3 ft down in the ground, where the soil is permanently moist. It also lays down a skin-bag or 'cocoon' around itself, by casting off the cell-deep outer layer of its skin. This is separated from it except at the nostrils, and water accumulates between the skin and the skin-bag, which inhibits evaporation. The frog remains so, in a torpid state, eating nothing, until the next rainstorm. Then it casts off the skin-bag and comes to the surface to feed rapidly on insects that become abundant during the wet spell. At the same time the frog replenishes its water supply and breeds.

△ *Fat frog:* **Cyclorana australis** *is adapted to living in the more arid regions of Australia.*

Brief infancy

The frogs breed in the temporary pools caused by the heavy rains, in the same way as pond-breeding frogs and toads everywhere (see page 86). The main difference is that the eggs hatch in much less than the usual time and the tadpoles develop much more quickly. They become froglets in less than a fortnight, compared with, for example, the 10 weeks taken by the European common frog to reach the same stage. The young frogs feed heavily and rapidly and also fill up with water, then they bury themselves in the ground before the hot sun dispels the moisture remaining from the heavy rainfall.

Speed kills

It is hardly surprising that little precise information is available on many aspects of the biology of animals living under such rigorous conditions. It is only within recent years that a few of the animals in deserts near the more densely populated regions of the world, where biologists are more numerous, have been subjected to close scrutiny. It seems reasonable to suppose, however, that the main hazards in the life of water-holding frogs are connected with the very brief period of infancy. When so much development, feeding and water storage must be carried through in so short a space of time there must be many tadpoles and froglets that fail to make the grade. It may also be shown in due course that there is predation, by birds and reptiles principally, while the frogs are above ground. That such enemies are few may, however, be inferred from the large populations of this and other desert amphibians known to exist, not only in Australia but in other deserts, as in the southwest United States.

Food and drink in one

In fact, some water-holding frogs and toads occur outside Australia but these have received less notice than their Australian relatives. This is partly because their adaptations are less extreme, but it is due more to the link between the amphibians and the aborigines of Australia. We are told that when the aborigine feels thirsty he digs a water-holding amphibian out of the ground, holds it over his open mouth and squeezes it to quench his thirst. This is, it seems, an over-simplification. Harry Frauca, in his *Book of Australian Wild Life*, tells us that water-holding frogs are 'said to be found in large numbers in the claypans of Centralia and to provide some aborigines with food and drink. There are reports to the effect that some tribes will dig up Water-holding Frogs from the claypans, squash them and drink the liquid contained inside the bodies and later on throw the frogs into the cookpot'.

Amphibians re-defined

Frogs and toads belong to the class Amphibia, the name meaning loosely 'animals leading double lives'. We tend, therefore, to think of them as spending half their time in water and half on land. In fact, some like the clawed toad spend all their time in water. At the other extreme there are many which never go into water, including the Stephen Island frog of New Zealand, 80 different kinds in New Guinea and adjacent islands and four in Australia. All of them, when not in water, must live in moist places, where evaporation from the skin can be counterbalanced by intake of water through the skin, or else must take their water supply around with them. Amphibians are therefore not so much animals spending half their time in water and half out, but animals adapted to ensuring to themselves a supply of water whether they are immersed in it or outside it. When outside it, however, the desert-living amphibians can lose water equal to a third of their body weight without necessarily dying.

class	**Amphibia**
order	**Salientia**
family	**Leptodactylidae**
genus & species	*Cyclorana platycephalus others*

The Reptiles

Although reptiles appear above the amphibians in the classification of the vertebrates, it would be wrong to suppose they have been evolved from any of the amphibians living today. To trace the link between them it is necessary to go well back in time, to the earliest-known fossils from the Carboniferous period, which succeeded the Devonian, and which are a hundred million years more recent than the earliest known amphibian.

The earliest known reptiles are the cotylosaurs, or 'stem-reptiles', and when the remains of their bones are compared with those of the earliest known amphibians the differences are not great. Unfortunately, too little is known or can be deduced from fossils to know how their soft parts compared. Nevertheless, it can be reasonably assumed that the two types of animals arose from a common stock. And it is clear that reptiles also gave rise later to birds and mammals.

Reptiles were the first wholly terrestrial vertebrates and in the present-day forms the combination of characters sharply distinguishes them from the amphibians. The skin is scaly, giving protection from drying through loss of moisture to the air. Also, the kidneys excrete insoluble uric acid rather than urea or ammonia and the water filtered from it returns to the body, thus preventing further loss of body fluid.

Since amphibians breathe so much through the skin they must preserve a large surface area in relation to the volume of the body. They cannot therefore grow to large size. Reptiles have no such limitations and consequently have produced giants.

The reptiles of today are poor in numbers compared with the past when, as in the Cretaceous period, the Age of Reptiles, 135–70 000 000 years ago, they were the dominant land animals.

Another important step towards living totally on land was the production of shelled eggs, with a large yolk protected by a leathery or limy shell, porous so that the contained embryo could breathe but resistant to drying out. Internal fertilisation was needed in reproduction, because fertilization must precede the laying down of the shell, and embryo membranes, including an amnion, needed to be developed. There is therefore no

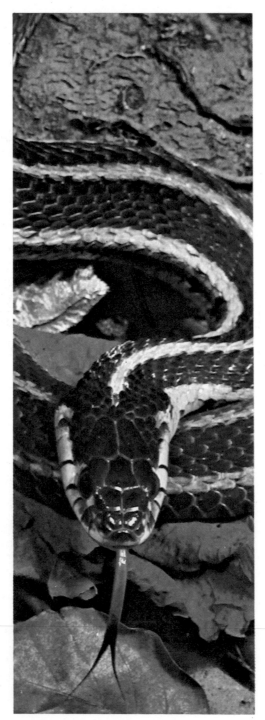

larval stage in reptiles, the young being hatched as miniatures of the adult.

Because they are cold-blooded both amphibians and reptiles are most numerous in the tropics, the numbers of species decreasing sharply in the temperate regions, with very few reaching the Arctic.

There are five orders of living reptiles but many more than this number became extinct at the close of the Cretaceous period. Each of the orders is well-defined but the way they are arranged is a matter of opinion because their evolutionary relationships are complicated. It is usual to start with the Rhynchocephalia, with its single species the tuatara. This one species has persisted relatively unchanged since the Triassic period over a period of 200 000 000 years, during which the rest of the order has died out.

The tuatara is always described as primitive, but so are the turtles and tortoises, of the order Testudines, and the crocodilians, order Crocodilia. Both can claim an ancestry as old as that of tuatara. Indeed, recognisable crocodiles are represented by fossils as old as the oldest known rhynchocephalian.

The last two orders contain the lizards and snakes. They are the Sauria and Serpentes respectively, sometimes combined in a single order, the Squamata, divided into two suborders Sauria and Serpentes. Their ancestry can be traced back to the Triassic but their representatives living today are more diversified in terms of appearance and habitats. These are the truly modern reptiles.

Three stages can be traced in the evolution of the reptiles. Beginning in the Carboniferous, 300 million years ago, and lasting 100 million years, there was a variety of terrestrial reptiles. The most numerous were the mammal-type reptiles from which the mammals evolved. The second stage, which lasted 130 000 000 years, until the close of the Cretaceous period, the dinosaurs on land, some of which gave rise to birds, the pterodactyls in the air and the crocodilians in the sea and fresh waters, were the dominant forms, and there were also the plesiosaurs and ichthyosaurs in the seas.

For reasons not yet clear, about 70 million years ago, most of these became extinct, leaving those that have given us our modern reptiles.

Tuatara

The tuatara is the sole survivor of the beak-heads, a group of very ancient reptiles that flourished during the Age of Reptiles, which lasted from 250 to 70 million years ago. It is the only species of reptile in an order and family of its own. Outwardly it looks like a fairly large lizard but internally it has many fundamental differences from modern lizards. With a length of 2 ft or more, it has a large head with teeth set along the edges of the jaws and a pair of enlarged front upper teeth. The nostrils are double and there is no external opening to the ear. The body and limbs are strongly built and there are powerful sharp claws on the partially webbed, five-toed feet. There is a crest of enlarged spines along the neck, back and tail and the back and sides are covered with small granular scales interspersed with tubercles. The scales of the underparts are larger and more regularly arranged. Like many of the modern lizards the tuatara is able to regenerate its long compressed tail, but not so efficiently. The tuatara's ground colour varies from blackish-brown to olive green or grey with a small yellow spot on each scale, which is brightest after the skin is shed and fades as the animal gets older. The scales of the crest are green.

It is only when the tuatara's anatomy is examined that the distinctions are found that cause it to be placed in a separate order and which make it so interesting to zoologists. In particular the skull is much stronger and firmer than that of other lizards, being more like the skull of a crocodile, with its parts joined together by bony arches. The backbone is primitive in structure, the vertebrae being concave at both ends. The ribs have hook-like processes about halfway along their length for attachment to the muscles. These are found also in birds and some fossil reptiles. The so-called abdominal ribs are well developed, forming a shield made up of several segments. Another unusual feature of the tuatara is the absence of an organ of copulation in the male.

Up to the middle of the 19th century the tuatara was common on the New Zealand mainland but today it is confined to a few rocky islands off the northeast coast of North Island and in Cook Strait between

▷ Of the many 'beak-heads' – reptiles that flourished 100 million years ago – only the tuatara survives, on a few islands around New Zealand.

△ *A tuatara on guard outside its burrow, which it shares with various species of shearwaters.*
△▷ *Looking seaward – a tuatara and its young.*

North and South Island. On some of these islands it is now plentiful owing to the New Zealand Government's policy of strict protection.

Three-eyed lizards

Perhaps the tuatara's most interesting feature to zoologists is the presence of the third or parietal eye, which is a feature of so many fossil vertebrates. This parietal eye is not, however, peculiar to the beak-heads; it is shared with many other species of lizards but it is better developed in the adult tuatara than in any other animal. Its presence in many embryos confused early ideas on evolution's relation to embryology. It is situated on the top of the brain, with a hole in the skull just above it, and has the vestiges of a lens and retina but no iris. It connects with a glandular body in the brain, but in adults the skin thickens over the opening in the skull and it is unlikely that any light from outside is conducted to the brain. The parietal eye was probably an important sense organ in some of the earlier reptiles but it is not known for sure what function it serves in the tuatara.

One breath an hour

The tuatara may dig its own burrow or share one with a petrel. As far as is known the tuatara lives only on islands where the top soil has been so manured and worked over by these birds' numerous burrows that there is a layer of loose upper soil 18–24 in. deep. The tuatara can often be seen basking in the sun in the morning or evening but spends most of the day in its burrow, coming out to hunt for food only at night. It is active at quite low temperatures, sometimes as low as 7°C/45°F, the lowest temperature recorded for any reptile activity. Its rate of metabolism is very low; the normal rate of breathing even when it is moving about is only one breath per seven seconds, but it can go for at least an hour without a breath.

Although good-tempered when handled gently, a tuatara will scratch and bite in self-defence. Its voice is a harsh croak, and it

118

resembles the well-known croak of a frog.

The tuatara's diet consists largely of spiders, crickets, beetles and other insects, although snails and earthworms are also taken. Contrary to the popular image of bird and reptile living amicably together, the tuatara sometimes eats petrel eggs and chicks, even an occasional adult bird.

Unusually long gestation

Nothing is known of the courtship habits of the tuatara. Pairing occurs during January but the sperm are stored in the female's body until the following October or December when 5–15 white, oval, soft-shelled eggs are laid in a shallow depression in the ground which has been scooped out by the female, and covered over with earth. The

eggs receive no attention from either parent and do not hatch out until 12–15 months later, the longest incubation period known for any reptile. The young tuataras, which are brownish pink in colour, break the shells of their eggs and dig their way to the surface. They are about 4½ in. long at this stage but their growth rate is very slow and they do not breed until they are over 20 years old, and they continue to grow until they are 50.

The tuatara has been kept in captivity on a number of occasions, one specimen in New Zealand having been kept for over 50 years. In the wild it lives to well over 50 years, and some claim that it may live to be 100 to 300.

Island sanctuaries

The tuatara probably became extinct on the

mainland of New Zealand because it was preyed upon by the many rodents, feral cats and pigs introduced by the English immigrants to New Zealand and which now inhabit the bush. These predators are not present on the islands to which the tuatara is now confined and it can consequently live and breed freely with little disturbance.

Dinosaur contemporary

The beak-heads flourished during the Age of Reptiles, along with the earliest turtles and long before the great dinosaurs trod the earth. They evolved into a remarkable variety of forms which are known from fossils found in many parts of the world. Some of these were larger than the tuatara as we know it today but none reached a length of more than 5–6 ft. After the Jurassic period most of the beak-heads became extinct, the tuatara being the only member of the group to survive until today. It was first named by Dr John Edward Gray, an English zoologist who was on the staff of the British Museum, from a specimen received there in 1831, who thought it was merely a new species of lizard. It was not until 1867 that his successor at the Museum, Dr Albert Günter, realised that the animal was no ordinary lizard but was related to the ancient beak-heads, and was truly a living fossil.

class	**Reptilia**
order	**Rhynchocephalia**
family	**Sphenodontidae**
genus & species	*Sphenodon punctatus*

▽ *The islands on which the tuatara lives have a remarkable soil and vegetation. Beneath a canopy of low trees of the genus* **Coprosoma** *is a deep layer of soft humus. This is largely maintained by the burrowing activities of the shearwaters which mix leaves, twigs and excreta into an even composition. The islands' vegetation has suffered due to the introduction of goats, but fortunately their numbers have now been checked.*

Bigheaded turtle

This, the only species of the family Platysternidae is probably the most extraordinary turtle alive. Its nearest relatives are the river turtles of America. The bighead is up to 14 in. long, olive or reddish-brown above, yellowish below, with soft parts black. It is unlike the usual freshwater turtles in many ways. Its shell is flat and broad. Its head is large relative to the size of the body and cannot be withdrawn into the shell, and it is armoured on all sides with thick horny plates. The jaws are powerful, the upper jaw ending in front in a curved beak. The tail is almost as long as the shell and covered with large scales. The legs are short and strong, covered with unusually large scales. The toes, five on the front feet, and four on the hind feet, have sharp claws. Male and female are very similar, the female having a slightly longer tail and a narrower head. The male's head is as broad as it is long.

Tree-climbing turtle

The bigheaded turtle lives in the clear swiftly-flowing mountain streams at altitudes of 6 000 ft or more, where the temperature of the water seldom exceeds 15°C/59°F. Essentially aquatic, it leaves the water mainly to lay its eggs or to sunbathe. Several writers have testified to its ability to climb astonishingly well, even to climbing trees. It probably does this with its strong sharp claws and with the long strong tail being used, woodpecker-like, to support the body.

Its colour is a dark grey-green, and the shell is usually overgrown with algae, further increasing its camouflage. In addition, because of its flat shell, and using its strong legs and tail, it can quickly push itself under stones and into crevices, from which it can be removed only with difficulty. This ability to hide, added to its camouflage and its inaccessible habitat, has meant that the bigheaded turtle is rarely captured.

Water-snail feeders

Its food seems to be mainly water snails, which it cracks with its macaw-like horny beak. In captivity a pair thrived on the flesh of freshwater fishes, so it is possible that other aquatic animals than molluscs are eaten.

Aggressive display to enemy

Nothing is known of its enemies, and it can be assumed that these are few because of the turtle's ability to hide. Moreover, it has an aggressive display unusual in turtles and tortoises. With its mouth agape, the third eyelid (nictitating membrane) drawn up over the eye, it hisses and snorts and presents a truly menacing appearance likely to deter all but the more powerful or well-armed predators.

Life history

Little is known except that the few pairs so far kept in captivity have occasionally reproduced, the female laying two eggs only, each oval and about 1½ by ¾ in.

Probably the most extraordinary turtle. Its head cannot be withdrawn but is heavily armoured and its scaly tail is nearly as long as the shell.

Tortoise-turtle babel

When the Pilgrim Fathers sailed from Plymouth in 1620, tortoises of any kind must have been practically unknown in England except to the scholars, who would have read about them in the classical literature. These Pilgrim Fathers, the 102 Separatists from the Church of England, who founded the New England States in North America, did more than colonise a new land —they caused confusion in words that is troubling us more and more as books written in Britain and in America are exchanged between the two countries.

In Britain today the Testudines (the zoological order to which tortoises belong) is subdivided into tortoises, terrapins and turtles. The first of these groups includes the chelonians that live on land and also the European pond tortoise that spends its time partly in the water and partly on land. The terrapins are relatively small fresh-water chelonians, while the turtles are exclusively marine. In the United States and Canada there is a tendency for some writers to group all chelonians under the single heading 'turtle', although other more informed writers recognize land tortoises, freshwater turtles, terrapins (but using the word in a restricted sense) and sea-turtles. Even this is a simplification because the usage varies among American writers.

Once we start to ask why there should be this divergence between British English and American English we uncover a complicated but interesting history. The word 'tortoise' came to us from the Latin *tortus*, meaning twisted, and from 1398 onwards it appears in a number of spellings: tortuce, tortose, tortuca, totuge. These were applied to land-living and water-living chelonians alike and there was, in fact, one word for both tortoise and turtle. Our present word 'turtle' is a corruption handed down by English mariners from the French word *tortue*, itself derived from the Latin *tortus*.

The Pilgrim Fathers, we may be fairly certain, were more occupied with religious matters than with natural history. They may have read about turtles in the Bible, the Authorized Version in English having been published in 1611, but these were turtle doves (from the Latin *turtur*, meaning a dove). The Pilgrims were more likely to have heard about turtles—the marine chelonians—during their voyage across the Atlantic. When they arrived in America, with its numerous chelonians on land and in fresh water, it would have been natural for them to call them all turtles, while their kinsmen left behind in England were learning to speak of marine chelonians as turtles and the rest as tortoises.

class	**Reptilia**
order	**Testudines**
family	**Platysternidae**
genus & species	***Platysternon megacephalum***

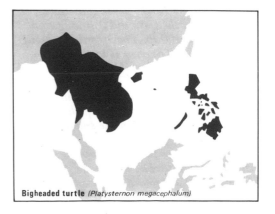

Bigheaded turtle *(Platysternon megacephalum)*

121

A distrustful-looking Amazon river turtle pulls its head in with a sideways bend of its neck. Compared with the cryptodire turtles' method – withdrawal in the orthodox vertical fashion – hidden-necked turtles' technique is far more primitive.

Hidden-necked turtle

When a tortoise or terrapin pulls its head into the shelter of its shell its neck usually bends vertically. The hidden-necked (or side-necked) turtles, however, bend their necks horizontally. Apart from this they are of interest because of the way they are distributed, and there is a special interest in the history of the South American species.

There are three kinds of hidden-necked turtles: two in Africa and one in South America that turns up again in distant Madagascar. The half-a-dozen or so African species are usually grouped under two names: pelomedusas and box turtles. After that the species themselves are apt to be given different names in different places. For example, the pelomedusa is also called helmeted terrapin and water tortoise. The box turtles of Africa have the front part of the underside of the shell (plastron) hinged so it can be drawn up to shut the head in once it is withdrawn.

Here we will be concentrating on two species: the Amazon river turtle, also living in the Orinoco, and the African water tortoise.

Breeding will tell

Known in the Orinoco basin of Venezuela as the *arrau*, the female Amazon turtle reaches 3 ft long, while the smaller, almost circular male grows to a diameter of 1½ ft. Most females weigh about 50 lb, but weights of up to 130 lb have been recorded. These turtles live on a variety of animal food, taking also some plant food, but little is known of their habits. They behave generally as other turtles do, apart from their breeding. This is remarkably like that of some marine turtles, such as the green turtle. In early February, as the dry season begins, the waters drop, exposing sandbanks and islands in mid-river. The turtles gather in the water around the sandbanks in their thousands, and they mate in the water. Some have travelled 100 miles to a suitable sandbank area. After mating, the males leave, while the females land at night to lay.

Millions of sand-packed eggs

Each of the thousands of females fairly closely packed on the sand digs a pit, 3 ft wide and 2 ft deep, with a smaller pit at its base in which the eggs are deposited. The larger pit is dug with all four legs, the smaller one with hindlegs only. Into it up to 150 eggs (average 80), nearly 2 in. diameter and soft-shelled, are laid. After this the female fills in the pit, disturbs the sand all around masking the actual site, and leaves. Night after night thousands more females arrive to lay. Six weeks later the 2 in. hatchlings dig their way up out of the sand, to run the gauntlet of vultures, storks and ibis. Those that reach the water face another hazard from crocodiles and predatory fishes.

Unwanted tortoise

The African water tortoise is up to 13 in. long and nearly 10 in. across. Its back is a mottled greenish-brown. The turtle, found over Africa, south of the Sahara, has earned a bad reputation in South Africa, and possibly in other parts, for its repulsive smell and its attacks on ducklings. It also steals bait from anglers' hooks. The odour comes from four glands, one under each leg, which give out an evil-smelling liquid, said to be especially objectionable to horses as well as humans. The tortoise's food is almost entirely animal, although it readily feeds on plants. It runs fast on land and it swims even faster, so that ducklings are highly vulnerable, being seized by a leg, dragged underwater and consumed when drowned.

There is nothing spectacular in its breeding. The female about to lay comes on land, selects a site, releases a quantity of urine on the ground and puddles the mud with her feet. She repeats this ejection of urine several times until a stiff mud is formed, making digging easier. Then, using the leading edge of her plastron as a bulldozer, and pushing with her hindlegs, she digs a hole 4 in. across at the bottom of which she excavates a smaller chamber. Into this she lays about a score of oval, soft-shelled eggs, 1½ in. long by ¾ in. across. The shell membrane later hardens. When the hatchlings burrow up to the surface, they also have to face the threat posed by hammerheads, herons and other birds waiting for them.

A mixed family?

Although the African and the South American species are placed in the same family it is tempting to think they cannot be closely related. The African water tortoise makes the same kind of nest as a land tortoise, and behaves in the same way. The South American river turtle behaves in every way like the marine turtles, so one could imagine its ancestors living in the sea and gradually moving to large rivers.

Give and take

As far back as records go, the local people in the Amazon and Orinoco basins have used the turtle eggs as food. When Henry Bates wrote his *Naturalist on the Amazons* a century ago he described how the eggs were collected. The people were forbidden by law to take eggs before all the female turtles had left the islands. Then, at a given signal, all began digging in the sand. Bates estimated that 48 million eggs were gathered each year. The local people also killed and ate the adults as well as large numbers of hatchlings. The result was that even then the numbers seemed to be dwindling. Recently Dr Janis Arose, Venezuelan zoologist, has described similar scenes on the Orinoco and expressed fears for the survival of the

turtles. But it is interesting to note that the crocodiles which formerly preyed on the hatchling turtles have been much reduced in numbers because of the market for crocodile skins for leather. Moreover, jaguars, which eat the adults, are less numerous than they were. These two things may perhaps go some way to counterbalancing the slaughter of the turtles by human beings.

class	**Reptilia**
order	**Testudines**
family	**Pelomedusidae**
genera & species	**Pelomedusa subrufa** *African water tortoise* **Podocnemis expansa** *Amazon river turtle*

△ *In the swim: a South American hidden-necked turtle under way. This genus, **Podocnemis**, is based in tropical South America—but it also crops up in faraway Madagascar. The most probable reason for this puzzling distribution is that the ancestral marine turtles were widely dispersed through the shallow coastal seas; some of them entered the rivers to become the ancestors of modern freshwater turtles, leaving the sea to other families. These freshwater types grow quite large: the biggest of the Amazon river turtles can reach a shell length of 30 in.*

▽ *African water tortoise sunning itself on a log. Unlike the Amazon river turtles, these rarely have a shell length bigger than 12 in. Although mostly aquatic they take readily to land, and are found all over central and southern Africa wherever they can be near to water. Mainly carnivorous, they take some plant food.*

Early morning and the leathery turtle completes her task of egg-laying by filling in the nest hole. This rare sea turtle spends more time in deep water than any other turtle, coming onto land only to nest and lay eggs. Each female comes ashore, usually late at night, about four times a season.

Leathery turtle

The leathery or leatherback turtle or luth is the largest sea turtle, and also differs from the others in the structure of its shell. The upper shell or carapace is made up of hundreds of irregular bony plates covered with a leathery skin instead of the characteristic plates of other turtles. There are seven ridges, which may be notched, running down the back, and five on the lower shell, or plastron.
Leathery turtles are dark brown or black with spots of yellow or white on the throat and flippers of young specimens. They grow to a maximum of 9 ft, the shell being up to 6 ft, and may weigh up to 1 800 lb. The foreflippers are very large; leathery turtles 7 ft long may have flippers spanning 9 ft.

Rare wanderer

The leathery turtle is the rarest sea turtle and lives in tropical waters, probably spending more time in deeper water than other turtles. Little is known about its habits and even its breeding haunts are not well known. Leathery turtles are known to breed in the West Indies, Florida, the north-eastern coasts of South America, Senegal, Natal, Madagascar, Sri Lanka and Malaya. The breeding populations are quite small and predation of eggs by men and dogs endangers the populations of some beaches. Although generally restricted to warm waters, leathery turtles are occasionally found swimming in cooler waters or washed up on beaches, especially when carried by adverse winds or currents. They have been seen off Newfoundland and Norway in the north, occasionally straggling as far south as New Zealand.

Unlike some other turtles leathery turtles

do not carry encrustations of barnacles and seaweeds. This may be due to the very oily skin. The oil has been found to have anti-biotic properties but it is not known whether this prevents other organisms settling on the skin. Also, like the other turtles without barnacles, they are fast swimmers. Leathery turtles are regularly escorted by pilot fish, which are more commonly associated with other fishes, such as sharks.

Although the leathery turtle is described here as the rarest of the turtles, it is of interest to note that it has been increasingly reported in recent years, especially in the North Atlantic. One reason for this, possibly the main reason, is that fishermen have switched to faster, motorized vessels.

A soft diet

The stomach contents of leathery turtles show that they feed on jellyfish, salps, pteropods (planktonic sea snails) and other soft bodied, slow-moving animals, including the amphipods and other animals that live in the bodies of jellyfish and salps. Leathery turtles have been seen congregating in shoals of jellyfish and the 2—3in. horny spines in the mouth and throat are probably a great help in holding slippery food.

Breeding in bands
Female leathery turtles come ashore in small bands to lay their eggs, usually late at night. They come straight up the shore to dry sand, stop, then start to dig the nest. They do not select the nest site, by digging exploratory pits and testing the sand, as in green turtles. A hollow is excavated with all four flippers working rhythmically until the turtle is hidden. She then digs the egg pit, scooping out sand with her hindflippers until she has dug as deep as she can reach. About 60—100 eggs, 2—2¼ in. diameter, are laid, then she fills the nest with sand and packs it down. Finally she masks the position of the nest by ploughing about and scattering sand, then makes her way back to the sea. Each female comes ashore to lay about four times in one season. The eggs hatch in 7 weeks and the babies emerge together and rush down the shore to the water.

The Soay beast
In September 1959 a large animal was seen in the sea off Soay, a small island off the Isle of Skye, western Scotland. There was much speculation at the time about what it could be. The two men who saw it gave a description and each made a rough sketch of it. The interest was increased by the fact that on at least one occasion many years previously a similar animal had been reported from these same waters. So the Soay Beast, as it came to be called, passed into history as an unsolved mystery, possibly a sea monster, probably one of the several different kinds of sea-serpent reported at various times. All these things seemed possible when one looked at an artist's impression published at the time. In due course Professor LD Brongersma had little difficulty in showing that, beyond reasonable doubt, the animal was nothing more than a large leathery turtle. In this he confirmed the opinion of Dr JH Fraser of Aberdeen, expressed in May 1960, a few months after the sighting was reported.

If the artist's impression was misleading we cannot blame him. He had only the verbal statements to go upon, together with two crude sketches. The real moral is that one should pay more attention to Occam's Razor. William of Occam (now Ockham) was a 14th century English scholar and philosopher who expounded the principle that if there are two or more theories to account for something, choose the simplest.

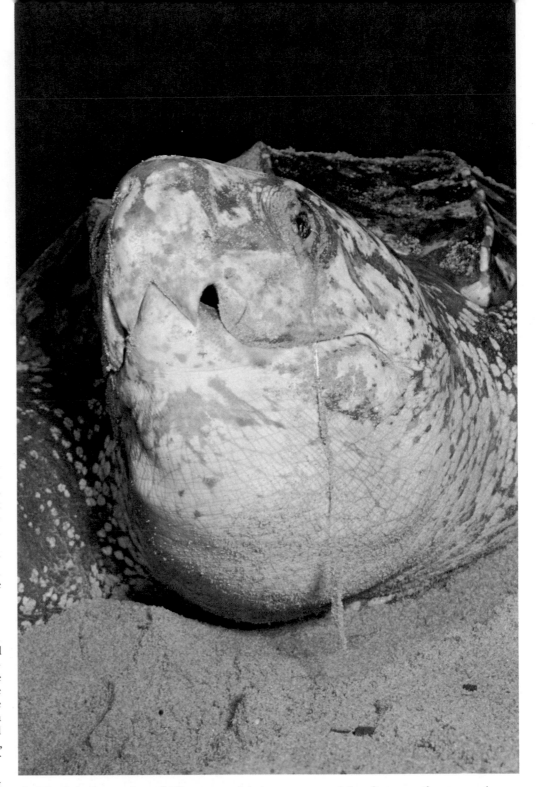

△ Why do leathery turtles cry? The answer might be to remove sand from its eyes on the rare occasions when the turtle comes ashore to nest and lay eggs. The accepted theory is that the tears a turtle sheds get rid of the excess salt that has been swallowed with gulps of sea water.
▽ The leathery turtle ranges into cooler waters than the green turtle, as this map shows.

Leathery turtle (Dermochelys coriacea)

class	**Reptilia**
order	**Testudines**
family	**Dermochelidae**
genus & species	*Dermochelys coriacea*

With a shell length of little more than 4 in. this tiny turtle, the common mud turtle, is one of the smallest water turtles of North America.

The common musk turtle has a much reduced plastron without hinges. The shields of the plastron are separated along the mid-line by soft skin.

Mud turtle

The mud turtles and musk turtles of the family Trionychidae are some of the smallest North American turtles: the adult eastern mud turtle has a brown or olive shell which is little more than 4 in. long. The young of this species has three ridges on the carapace, the upper part of the shell, but these disappear as it grows up. The plastron, or underpart of the shell, is light brown or yellow and the turtles have yellowish green spots on the head. The central part of the plastron is joined to the carapace while its front and rear portions are hinged to this central portion by strong connective tissues forming movable lobes. When the turtle withdraws its head, limbs and tail it draws these lobes over the openings, completely sealing itself in. Musk turtles are similar to mud turtles except that the plastron is very much smaller in proportion to the carapace and is without hinges, but the two kinds of turtles are alike in having musk glands along the sides of the body. The musk is much stronger in the musk turtles which are often called stinkpots as a result. Male mud turtles differ from females in having larger heads and longer tails and, when adult, their plastrons are concave. They also have patches of horny scales on the hindlegs, which are used to hold the female in mating.

There are about 17 species of mud turtle, 4 or 5 in the United States, and the rest in Central and South America. One large South American mud turtle has enlarged lobes on the plastron that make a perfect fit with the edges of the carapace, so the turtle inside is fully protected. The musk turtles live in the United States.

Quiet life

Mud and musk turtles live in pools and sluggish streams where there are plenty of water plants. They crawl over the bottom and occasionally wander out over the land or bask on banks and tree stumps. The

Stinkpot—a three day old common musk turtle.

common musk turtle is rarely seen out of water but the keel-backed musk turtle of the southeastern United States often comes out to bask in the sun. The mud turtles are more likely to be found on land and they often live in very small pools and roadside ditches.

An unpleasant catch

Mud turtles and musk turtles feed on tadpoles, snails, worms, water insects and fish. They also eat a large amount of carrion and are unpopular with anglers because they often take their bait. After giving an angler the impression that he has hooked a large fish the turtle adds insult to injury by discharging its foul-smelling musk when lifted from the water.

Leisurely courtship

The courtship of mud turtles usually takes place in the water but the female comes on land to lay her eggs. To mate the male approaches the female from behind and noses her tail to confirm her sex. He then swims beside her, nudging her just behind her eye. She swims with him for some distance then stops suddenly. This is a signal for the male to climb onto her back, grasp the edges of her carapace with his toes and hold her tail to one side with the scaly patches on one of his hindlegs. Several fertile clutches may result from one mating and females isolated for 3–4 years have laid fertile eggs.

The eggs are laid under rotten logs and stumps or in nests dug in the earth. The musk turtles sometimes lay their eggs in muskrat nests. Up to 7 eggs with hard, brittle shells are laid in each clutch. They hatch in 60–90 days, depending on the heat provided by the sun and the decaying vegetation around them. The newly-hatched turtles have shells about 1 in. long. Males mature in 4–7 years and the females in 5–8 years. In captivity mud turtles have lived for 40 years but in the wild they fall prey to several predators; crows attack the adults, while king snakes, raccoons and skunks eat the eggs.

The turtle frame

It is natural to assume that the plastron is no more than a breast plate to protect the underside of a turtle or tortoise, but in some species it is so small that it can offer very little protection. Even so, it still has an important part to play. In all turtles and tortoises the ribs are incorporated into the carapace and the plastron takes over to some extent the work of the ribs in bracing the body and in providing an anchoring surface for the muscles of the shoulders and hips. In the snapping turtle, for instance, in which the plastron is very much reduced, scientists have calculated that this small plastron is just sufficient to give the necessary strength and support to the body. It is much the same in the mud and musk turtles when they are young; they have a soft carapace and a rigid plastron which braces the carapace. As the turtles grow older and the carapace hardens the plastron is freed from this duty. Then, in mud turtles, it develops the hinges which, acting like lids, close over the turtle when it withdraws into its shell so giving it maximum protection from its enemies.

class	**Reptilia**
order	**Testudines**
family	**Trionychidae**

genera & species	***Kinosternon subrubrum*** common mud turtle ***Sternotherus carinatus*** keel-backed musk turtle ***S. odoratus*** common musk turtle others

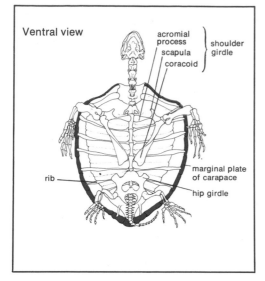

Ventral view

acromial process
scapula
coracoid
} shoulder girdle

marginal plate of carapace

rib

hip girdle

Diagrams of a turtle skeleton showing the bony plates forming a box into which the head and limbs can be withdrawn. To support the box the limb girdles are modified and lie inside the encircling ribs. The shoulder girdle has three prongs, a scapula that meets the carapace dorsally, and a long acromial process and a backwardly directed coracoid. These two are fixed with ligaments to the plastron which is removed in the drawing above.

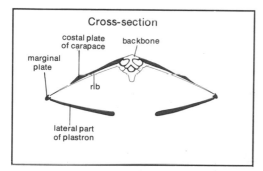

Cross-section

costal plate of carapace
backbone
marginal plate
rib
lateral part of plastron

Painted turtle

The painted turtle, also known as the pond turtle or painted terrapin, is the most widely distributed, and in many places the commonest, small turtle in North America. Its smooth, flat carapace is 4–6 in. long. The markings are particularly handsome and the name of painted turtle is well deserved. The carapace is olive-green to black with yellow transverse bands and bright red markings around the edge. The red markings are less conspicuous in older turtles. The legs are marked with red lines and the head and neck with horizontal yellow lines. The plastron is bright yellow and looks as if it has been freshly scrubbed. The single species of painted turtle has four subspecies living in different regions of the United States and southern Canada. **Chrysemys picta picta** is found on the Atlantic coastal plain and **C. picta dorsalis** in the Mississippi valley. These two have a plain yellow plastron. **C. picta marginata** lives in the strip of country between the Allegheny mountains and the Great Lakes. Its plastron has black markings confined to the centre. The most widely distributed subspecies is **C. picta belli** which has black markings around the edges of all the plates of the plastron. It is found in the plains of northern United States and southern Canada and along the east of the Rockies to New Mexico.

Closely related to the painted turtle are

▽ *Dazzled by the photographer's light, a male* **Chrysemys picta** *shuts his eyes and holds on tight with his long claws.*

the small turtles of the genus **Pseudemys**, known as cooters and sliders. The habits of the two genera are similar.

A slow life
When food is plentiful painted turtles do not move far, each having a home range of about 100 yd. When they are taken away from their home water, they can find their way back from distances of only about 100 yd, probably by landmarks. Such poor navigation is only to be expected in an animal that does not travel much. When painted turtles set off in search of food they move apparently at random, although they may be able to tell where water is from the brightness of the light which is reflected from the water.

Painted turtles live in ponds, shallow parts of lakes and other quiet stretches of water. They may be found in the sluggish, well vegetated parts of streams. Their distribution is determined by the abundance of water plants, their chief food. They are particularly fond of long, trailing plants that float on the surface. Aquatic insects, including beetles and dragonfly larvae, snails, tadpoles and fishes are also eaten. If food runs low, as in a drought, painted turtles migrate to other stretches of water.

Apart from journeys in search of fresh food supplies, painted turtles rarely come on land. Like all turtles, however, they lay their eggs on land, and they also climb onto banks or logs to bask, during the morning and afternoon, but they avoid the midday sun. It has been suggested that one benefit of basking is that it dries the skin of parasitic leeches, causing them to drop off.

Fast swimming suitors
In the spring and early summer the male painted turtle, which is distinguished by his

△ *Red-eared turtle,* **Pseudemys scripta** *(see also page 139), a close relative of the painted turtles, turns on its side to reveal the beautiful markings on its plastron.*

longer tail and claws on his forefeet, seeks out and courts the female. He swims after her, overtakes, and turns to face her head on. The female continues swimming and the male has to swim backwards, but as he goes he brushes the long claws of his forefeet against the female's cheeks. If a female is receptive she sinks to the bottom of the pond and allows the male to mate with her.

Eggs are laid in May—July. The females crawl onto land and dig their nests up to 100 yds or more from the water's edge. They dig the nest with the hindfeet and sometimes soften the soil with urine. Each egg is carefully positioned in the nest by the hindfeet. The clutch averages 7—10 eggs and after it is completed the female turtle fills in the hole and stamps the soil down. The eggs hatch in the autumn, except in the most northerly part of the range where

they may not hatch until the following spring. The newly-hatched turtles are about 1 in. long. They try to make their way to the water almost immediately, in an effort to avoid being caught by their numerous enemies. They are mature at 4 years, when they are 3½ in. long.

Seeking warmth
In the northern parts of their range, painted turtles hibernate, burrowing into mud or sheltering in a muskrat hole from November to March. When they emerge in the spring their pond may still be covered with ice and it has been found that they will sometimes move some distance from their 'home' pond at these times, and travel up the streams that flow in or out. To find what, if anything, guided the turtles, they were placed in Y-shaped tubes. The turtles could choose which arm of the Y to swim up

and it was found that they responded to the temperature of the water in the arms. Turtles do not become active until 10°C/50°F. If the water in which they had been living was too cool they swam up the warmer arm, but if used to warm water they followed the cool current. In the spring, then, the turtles sometimes leave their ponds if they are still too cold, and swim up the slightly warmer streams; as their bodies warm up, the turtles become more active and start feeding.

class	**Reptilia**
order	**Testudines**
family	**Emydidae**
genus & species	*Chrysemys picta*

Snake-necked turtle

The 30 species of snake-necked turtles are found in South America, Australia and New Guinea. Together with the side-necked turtles of South America, Africa and Madagascar, they make up the sub-order Pleurodira. They differ from the other turtles, suborder Cryptodira, in withdrawing the head and neck sideways into the shell instead of vertically. They bend the neck sideways and tuck the snout under loose skin on the shoulder. A pleurodire turtle cannot withdraw its head completely into its shell, unlike the cryptodires which can withdraw their heads out of sight.

The common feature of the snake-necked turtles is their long necks. The neck is longest in an Australian snake-necked turtle, or tortoise, in which an individual with a 15in. shell may have an 11in. neck. A close relative of snake-necked turtles is called the 'stinker' because when alarmed it gives off a pungent odour from a gland at the base of each leg. The carapace of this turtle is dark brown above, dark yellow below. The neck is covered with warts and the eyes are yellow. The average length of the shell is 6 in. Another very long-necked turtle is the otter turtle or Cope's terrapin of Argentina, Brazil and Paraguay. It is generally blackish with a 7—8in. shell. The matamata of Brazil and the Guianas,

▽ *The Australian snake-necked turtle* **Chelodina longicollis**, *its extended neck taking up nearly half of its total length of 10 in.*

Fully extended (above) a snake-necked turtle's neck is vulnerable. Retracted (below) it shows the unorthodox withdrawal which gave rise to the name.

is the strangest-looking turtle. Its shell, which may grow to 18 in. long, has three ridges, covered with small knobs. The neck is covered with folds of skin and the head is flattened with a very large mouth and a stalk-like proboscis.

Built-in schnorkels

Snake-necked turtles live in fresh water. The long, pointed snout allows several of the snake-necked turtles to breathe without showing their heads, and the long necks enable them to breathe in shallow water while resting on the bottom. The matamata lives in stagnant pools and the rare western swamp tortoise of Australia lives in flooded pot-holes near Perth. Other snake-necked turtles live in permanent, fresher water. Most snake-necked turtles spend the greater part of their time in the water. *Mesoclemmys gibba* of Trinidad, the Guianas and Brazil rarely leaves the water but the *carranchina* of Colombia can run quite quickly on land.

Eats almost anything

Snake-necked turtles eat small animals, carrion, and some plant food. The snapping turtle of northern Australian rivers feeds on fruit and berries that fall into the water from overhanging trees, as well as other plants and animals such as crayfish and frogs. Whereas most snake-necked turtles catch their prey by suddenly throwing

out their long necks, the matamata sucks in passing animals. It lies in wait almost invisible with algae obscuring the already broken outline of the body and opens its mouth wide so that small animals are engulfed as water rushes in. Unlike other turtles, the matamata has very weak jaws, but the mouth is very large and can be opened suddenly, while the neck is expanded to increase its volume.

Pile-driver female

The life history of the snake-necked turtles is not at all well known, especially of those that live in South America and New Guinea. Breeding habits have been observed among some of the Australian species. The best known is the Murray River turtle of south and west Australia. Egg-laying is carried out in much the same way as in the marine turtles. The female crawls anything up to 200 yd from the water's edge and digs a conical hole about 8 in. deep with her hind-feet. As each egg is laid a hindleg is inserted into the hole to arrange the egg on the growing pile. She lays between 10 and 20 eggs and when the clutch is complete the hindlegs are used to scrape soil into the hole. The soil is tamped down by the body of the turtle which is raised and dropped like a pile driver. When the turtle has finished the nest is almost impossible to find and in 3 months the young hatch and push their way to the surface.

Strange rare turtle

The western swamp turtle of Western Australia is very likely the rarest turtle. It is also one of the most interesting as it appears to be closely related to ancestral turtles. Unlike other snake-necked turtles, the swamp turtle has a short neck.

The first specimen of the swamp turtle was found in 1839 but the next did not come to light until 1907. Then a third appeared in 1953 in an area of clay swamps, called 'crabhole country' near Perth. The swamps dry out in summer and the turtles burrow into the clay to aestivate until the rains. After the discovery of the 1953 specimen a detailed search was made for this rare turtle. Some were found in neighbouring swamps and the land was made into a nature reserve. Since then a few more swamps have been found to harbour swamp turtles.

class	**Reptilia**
order	**Testudines**
family	**Chelidae**
genera & species	***Chelys fimbriata*** matamata
	Emydura macquarriae *Murray River turtle*
	Hydromedusa tectifera *otter turtle*
	Pseudemydura umbrina *swamp turtle, others*

Snapping turtle

The snapping turtles of America are well named and they need to be handled with caution. A full-grown snapping turtle can easily break a pencil in two or severely maul a man's hand. Snapping turtles are heavily built with large heads and limbs which cannot be retracted into the shell. The common snapping turtle, usually known as 'the' snapping turtle, has a shell length of up to 15 in. but it is proportionately very heavy and can weigh up to 50 lb. The tail is half the length of the shell and bears a row of scales like a crest on the upper surface. The feet are partly webbed and bear strong claws. The skin is greenish and

the shell is often covered with green algae. The plastron, the underside of the shell, is reduced in size and forms a cross with the turtle's limbs fitting between the arms of the cross.

The common snapping turtle is found in the eastern half of the United States. The other snapping turtle, the alligator turtle, is restricted to the United States, from Illinois to Texas and east to Florida. The alligator turtle is one of the largest freshwater turtles and can grow up to 200 lb, larger weights of up to 400 lb being unconfirmed. The shells of the alligator turtles grow up to nearly 3 ft long and bear three ridged keels. Unlike the common snapping turtle the eyes are set on the side of the head and cannot be seen from above.

Aggressive on land

Snapping turtles are more aquatic than most freshwater turtles and spend most of their lives in muddy ponds, lakes and rivers. Alligator turtles in particular are very lethargic, walking on the bottom rather than swimming and, when disturbed in the water, their one idea is to escape. It is only when snapping turtles are found on land that they are aggressive and common snapping turtles are quite likely to advance on their foes. Snapping turtles hibernate, but can sometimes be seen swimming in lakes under ice during the winter months.

Contrasts in turtles

The common snapping turtle actively hunts for its food, which consists of plants, carrion, insects, fish, frogs, ducklings and young muskrats. Live prey is caught with a quick thrust of the head and snap of the jaws and

▽ Not fast enough to evade a speedy head thrust, a water snake writhes its last in the gin-trap jaws of a snapping turtle.

is then pulled apart by the mouth and claws. The fish-eating habits of snapping turtles often bring them into conflict with anglers or the owners of fish farms. Too many snapping turtles in a fish pond can lead to too few fish but some studies have shown that the harmful effect of snapping turtles on fish populations is often over-exaggerated. In many places, however, snapping turtles are trapped either because of their supposed depredations or to be turned into 'snapper soup'.

Unlike the common snapping turtle, the alligator turtle lies in wait for its prey, half buried in the mud and camouflaged by the algae growing on its shell. From this concealed position the alligator turtle lures small fishes into its mouth by a most remarkable piece of deception. The tongue is forked and the two branches are fat and wormlike. The turtle moves its tongue, making the wormlike tips wriggle and this attracts small fishes which are then promptly snapped up. Larger prey, including ducklings, are also caught, but by more active hunting, not by means of the lure.

Over-wintering eggs

The common snapping turtle may crawl some distance from water to find a suitable place to make a nest. It seems to prefer open areas, and even cultivated land. The nest is dug with the hind feet and about 20 eggs are laid in each clutch. Hatching takes place in late summer, and eggs that are laid late may not hatch until the following spring. Breeding habits of the alligator snapper are similar but it lays its eggs, which may number from 17 to 44, near the water.

'Bloodhound' turtle

The carrion-eating habits of snapping turtles once led one of them to be used as an efficient, but gruesome, bloodhound. There was an occasion in the 1920s when a murderer hid the bodies of his victims by sinking them in the muddy waters of a lake. Although the police had a very good idea which lake had been used, they were hard put to find the bodies until an elderly Indian offered his services. It only took him a few hours to find each corpse yet his method was very simple. He released a large snapping turtle with a long line attached to its shell. When the line stopped playing out the Indian followed and, if he was in luck, the turtle would be found feeding on one of the murdered bodies.

class	**Reptilia**
order	**Testudines**
family	**Chelydridae**
genera & species	***Chelydra serpentina*** *common snapping turtle* ***Macrochelys temmincki*** *alligator snapper*

▷ *Turtles in suspension. Common snapping turtles are poor swimmers and usually prefer to walk over the bottom. Although aggressive on land, they are quite the opposite in water, and often lie in wait for their prey.*

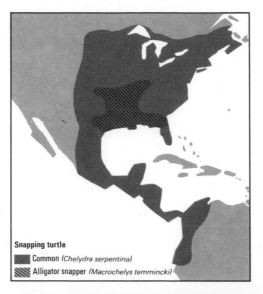

Snapping turtle
■ Common *(Chelydra serpentina)*
▨ Alligator snapper *(Macrochelys temmincki)*

▷ *An alligator turtle opens its mouth to display its wriggling, worm-like tongue, which acts as a successful lure for many small fishes. The turtle's tongue is forked into two fat, pink branches which stand out against the dark background of the inside of the mouth. The turtle lies half buried in the mud, well camouflaged by its dull brown colour and rough, often algae-covered, shell. There it lies in wait for small fishes, opening its mouth as they pass, and luring them in. Only small prey is caught in this way; larger prey is hunted actively in the same way as the common snapping turtle.*

▽ *An alligator snapping turtle, showing its rough, three-keeled, mud-coloured shell which protects it and camouflages it as it lies in the mud. The eyes of this turtle, which is one of the largest freshwater turtles in the world, are on the side of its head, unlike those of the common snapping turtle.*

Soft-shelled turtle

The soft-shelled turtles are unlike other turtles because their shells are covered by a layer of leathery skin instead of horny plates. The shell is flat and almost circular which gives some of them the alternative name of 'flapjack turtle'. The jaws are hidden under fleshy lips and the snout is drawn out into a tube-like proboscis. The fourth and fifth toes are elongated, clawless and are webbed to form paddles.

Soft-shelled turtles are found in many parts of Africa, Asia and America and fossils of one genus, **Trionyx**, have been found in many parts of Europe. Modern members of **Trionyx** are still spread over three continents. The spiny soft-shelled turtle is widespread in North America, from the St Lawrence to the Rocky Mountains. The front edge of its shell is lined with soft spiny tubercles. The upperside of the shell, which reaches 16 in. in length, is greyish-green with many small dark spots, often arranged in small circles. The Nile soft-shelled turtle ranges from

△ *A retiring* **Pelochelys bibroni**. *Like other 'soft-shells', it has fleshy lips and an elongated snout.*
▽ **Trionyx** *paddling along with periscoped head. Apparently it can swim at 10 mph.*

Palestine to Zaire and has a shell up to 2 ft long. Some of the Asian soft-shelled turtles have hinged flaps at each end of the plastron, the underside of the shell, which completely close up the shell when the head and limbs are withdrawn. The largest species is the long-headed soft-shelled turtle that ranges from North India to Malaya. Its shell reaches over 4 ft in length.

Supplementary breathing

Soft-shelled turtles usually live in freshwater but the long-headed is apparently able to live on the shore. They are extremely active, perhaps as a result of their lightweight shells. They have been reported to swim at 10 mph and to be able to outrun a man on level ground. These turtles must be handled with care, as they can strike very rapidly, sometimes causing nasty wounds, but the long-headed soft-shell, which strikes like a snake, does no more than butt its adversary with its snout.

Although capable of bursts of great activity, soft-shelled turtles spend much of their time lying almost submerged in the muddy bottoms of lakes and rivers. They

△ *A soft-shelled turtle breaks the surface as it stretches out its long neck to breathe in air through its long, tubular nostrils.* ▽ *Front view of a* **Trionyx**.

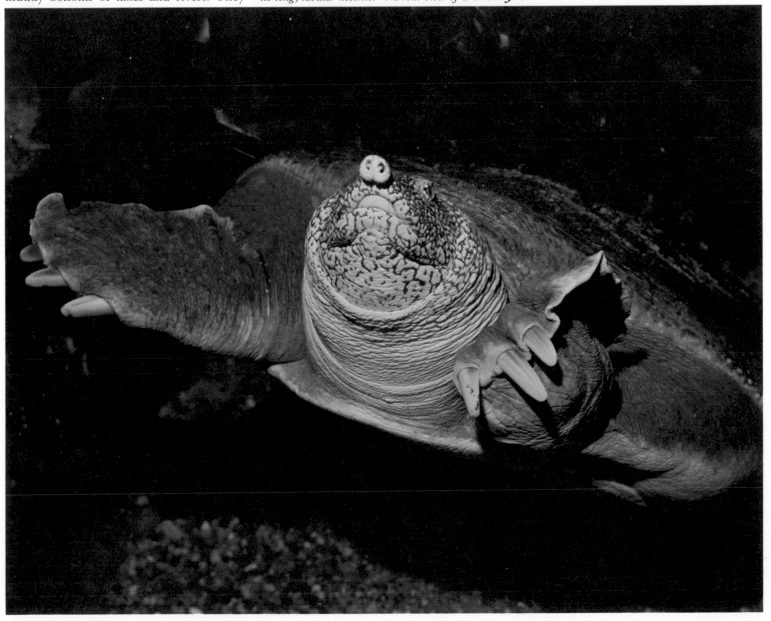

A turtle with a matching head and shell: **Lissemys punctata.** ▽ Its underside shows the plastron and the pair of strong, hinged flaps which close over the hind limbs when they are withdrawn.

can stay underwater for long periods by stretching their long necks until the tube-like nostrils break the surface of the water, rather like a submarine's snorkel. They can also stay under by using a supplementary method of breathing: using both mouth and rectum as gills they extract oxygen from the water that is circulated through them.

Cutting or crushing

Like other freshwater turtles, such as the snapping turtles, the soft-shelled turtles live on a variety of food including plants, carrion and live animals. The main food of the spiny soft-shelled turtle is crayfish and aquatic insects and it is doubtful whether it ever harms angling interests as is sometimes asserted. The jaws of these turtles appear deceptively soft as they are hidden by fleshy lips. They are, in fact, very strong. In some species the jaws have a sharp cutting edge suitable for dealing with fish, while others have jaws with surfaces better suited for crushing the shells of molluscs.

Breeding mysteries

Very little is known about the breeding habits of soft-shelled turtles. Nesting takes place in spring or early summer in North America. The females leave the water to dig nests on land. These nests are similar to those of many other turtles: they are flask-shaped holes dug as far as the hind legs reach, which is up to 1 ft deep. Ten to twenty-five round white eggs are deposited in the nest and covered over. The length of the incubation period is not known, but some eggs do not hatch until the following spring.

Sacred turtles

Some of the soft-shelled turtles are greatly esteemed as food but others have been rigorously protected for religious reasons in Asia. For several centuries Mohammedans have kept a pond of *Trionyx gangeticus* at Orissa in India and there is a pond of *T. formosus* at Mandalay. A third collection of sacred turtles is held at Chittagong in Bangladesh. These are *T. nigricans* and are the only known examples of this species. These turtles are often very tame and will come to be fed by hand when called. In parts of Africa the Senegal soft-shelled turtle is kept for a more practical purpose. It is placed in wells to eat any refuse that falls in.

class	**Reptilia**
order	**Testudines**
family	**Trionychidae**
genera & species	***Chitra indica*** *long-headed soft-shelled turtle* ***Cyclanorbis senegalensis*** *Senegal soft-shelled turtle* ***Pelochelys bibroni*** *Malayan soft-shelled mud turtle* ***Trionyx spinifera*** *spiny soft-shelled turtle* *others*

Terrapin

The name terrapin is derived from an American Indian word for 'little turtle' and is one of those common words about which there is confusion as to the precise meaning, in the same way as there is confusion about 'turtle' and 'tortoise' (see bigheaded turtle page 121). In Britain 'terrapin' is often used as the name for any small freshwater member of the order Testudines, particularly those kept as pets in aquaria. West of the Atlantic, however, the word has a more restricted meaning and some writers insist that terrapin should refer only to the diamondback terrapin **Malaclemys terrapin**. This is a very sensible idea and will certainly save the confusion that occurs when American natural history books are published in British editions with no explanation of the terms 'turtle', 'tortoise' and 'terrapin', and vice versa. The diamondback terrapin is well known

gastronomically as the basic ingredient of 'Terrapin à la Maryland', and because of its economic importance as food, its biology has been studied in detail. It is so named because of the bold, rhomboidal or whorled markings etched in each plate of the carapace. The small plates that border the carapace like the scalloping on a pie crust, are hollowed and lighter in colour. The plastron is yellow and is speckled and lined with small black dots, as is the skin of the head and limbs. Female diamondback terrapins grow up to 8 in., the males to 6 in. and they weigh up to 2 lb. They range from Cape Cod, Massachusetts to Florida, Texas and Mexico.

Other freshwater turtles or tortoises sometimes known as terrapins, are the red-eared terrapin or pond terrapin **Pseudemys scripta** (see page 130), the Spanish terrapin **Clemmys leprosa** of Spain, Portugal and North Africa and the geographic or map terrapin **Graptemys geographica** of the St

Lawrence, the Great Lakes and the Missouri. Confusingly, the box turtles of North America are in the genus **Terrapene**.

Salt essential for health

The diamondback terrapin is never found far from the coast and is restricted to brackish waters, such as tidal estuaries and salt marshes, or the sea, where it may be found in bays. It is found up rivers only as far as the tide penetrates. It seems strange that diamondbacks should be restricted to brackish water but if captive terrapins are kept in fresh water they develop a fungus on the skin, which is cured by adding some salt to the water.

Terrapins come onto rocks to bask in the sun but they spend most of their time swimming with their webbed feet. They have the habit of floating with their shells hanging vertically with only the snout showing above water and with the hindfeet slowly moving to keep them steady. During the winter months terrapins hibernate under the mud of their habitat.

The diamondback terrapin, so called from the bold sculpturing of the plates of the carapace, is famous as a delicacy in the southern USA.

Crushed food

Apart from a few water plants, terrapins feed mainly on small animals such as fiddler crabs, periwinkles, insects and worms, which are crushed in the powerful jaws.

Males not always needed

Most of our knowledge of the breeding habits of diamondbacks comes from observations at terrapin farms where they are bred commercially for their flesh. In the wild, however, they lay their eggs in nests not far above the high water mark. The females, and probably the males as well, mature when about 7 years old. They may lay 1—5 clutches a year, younger terrapins laying fewer, and each clutch consists of 7—24 elliptical white eggs, 1½ by ¾ in. The laying season depends on the climate, being from early May to late July in North Carolina. The young hatch in about 90 days.

Observations at terrapin farms showed that female terrapins can lay fertile eggs although they have been separated from males for several years. In one test 10 females laid 124 eggs one year after being separated from males. Only one failed to hatch. After 3 years they laid 130 eggs and 91 failed to hatch but in the fourth year only 4 out of 108 hatched. It seems that the live sperms are stored in the ovaries and it is now known that this also occurs in other turtles and in snakes.

Gourmet's turtle

The diamondback terrapin has had a varied career as human food. During the 18th century it formed a cheap source of food for slaves, then over the course of the 19th century its fortunes changed as some whim of fashion decided its taste was superior to any other turtle. 'Terrapin à la Maryland' is a rich dish of terrapin meat cooked with vegetables, wine and eggs, with sherry added before serving. By 1920 diamondbacks were fetching $90 a dozen. As a result their numbers decreased so protection laws were passed and they were reared artificially. In recent years, however, there has been a decrease both in demand and price for terrapins.

class	**Reptilia**
order	**Testudines**
family	**Emydidae**
genus & species	***Malaclemys terrapin*** *diamondback terrapin*

▽ *Horny lips, goggle eyes and spotted wrinkled chin and throat – close-up of the diamondback terrapin.*

Tortoise

Tortoises are well known for their slowness of movement and for their long life span. They live longer than any other animal today; and they are about the most heavily armoured. There is a difference between American and British usage. In the United States the name 'tortoise' is used only for land-living chelonians belonging to the family Testudinidae. In British usage some water-living chelonians, such as the European pond tortoise, are also given the common name of tortoise.

There are about 40 land tortoises, the best known of which are the so-called garden tortoises and the giant tortoises. Since the way of life of all of them is much the same, most attention will be given here to the Iberian or Algerian tortoise and the Greek or Hermann's tortoise, both garden tortoises. They have high domed shells, up to 1 ft long. The legs are covered with hard scales which often have bony cores and the five toes on the forefoot and the four on the hindfoot all have stout claws. When disturbed a tortoise pulls its head and limbs into the shelter of the bony box covered with horn which is usually spoken of as its shell. The head is completely withdrawn. The front legs are pulled back to make the elbows meet in the middle, protecting the entrance with their scaly skin. The hindlegs and tail are similarly withdrawn, the soles of the hindfeet sealing the entrance.

Tortoises live in tropical and subtropical regions. The Iberian or Algerian tortoise is found in northwest Africa and Spain, the Balkans, Iraq and Iran. The Greek tortoise ranges from southern France through parts of Italy to the Balkans. The star tortoise of southern Asia has pale star-shaped markings on its shell. The gopher tortoises of the southern United States get their name from the French gaufre, a honeycomb, an allusion to their burrowing. There are other land tortoises in southern Asia, Africa, Madagascar and other islands of the Indian Ocean, South America and the Galapagos Islands.

△ *A leopard tortoise* **Testudo pardalis** *about to enjoy a refreshing mouthful of cactus.*

The warmer, the faster

Tortoises live in sandy places or among rocks or in woodlands. They are active by day and generally slow in their movements, yet they can at times reach a speed of 2 mph over short distances. This may be slow compared with the speed of most quadrupeds but it is nearly the walking speed of a man and is faster than we normally consider tortoises' speed. The behaviour of a tortoise is geared to the temperature of the surrounding air. Its movements are faster in warmer temperatures but like other reptiles it is intolerant of the higher air temperatures. Tortoises spend some time every day basking. In temperate latitudes garden tortoises hibernate from October to March, fasting for a while prior to digging themselves into soft earth or under dead vegetation.

Seedlings a favourite meal

It was once widely believed that the smaller tortoises fed on insects and slugs and for this reason people, in England at least, bought tortoises to keep in their gardens. The idea is not yet wholly dead. It may be that a garden tortoise will sometimes eat the smaller garden vermin, but anyone who has seen a tortoise travel along a row of seedlings just showing through the ground will need little convincing that tortoises are wholly or almost exclusively vegetarian, eating low growing vegetation such as seedlings, succulent leaves, flowers and fallen fruits, and only occasionally insects.

Battering ram courtship

Males and females look alike but in most species there is some small difference in shape. In Hermann's tortoise, for example, the plastron, or underside of the shell, is flat in the female, concave in the male. In the Iberian tortoise the tail shield is flat in the female, curved in the male. Another sign is that a male in breeding condition butts the female in the flank, at the same time hissing slightly. Male garden tortoises, when there is no female around, will butt the shoes of people sitting in the garden or the legs of garden chairs. The female lays 4–12 whitish spherical eggs, each 1½ in. diameter, in a hole which she digs in soft ground. The eggs hatch 3–4 months later.

Man the enemy today . . .

The solid box of bone with its horny covering and the tortoise's habit of withdrawing into this fortress at the slightest disturbance, seem the best possible protection against enemies. The Bearded Vulture is a traditional enemy, flying to some height with a tortoise and then letting it drop to the ground to crack its shell. Rats attack and eat tortoises. Apart from these the natural enemies must be limited. On the other hand, tortoises are probably very vulnerable to the elements, especially to such catastrophes as grass and woodland fires. After a grass fire the number of dead tortoises of all sizes, and especially the small ones, gives an indication of how numerous these animals can be in places where normally little is seen of them. The greatest danger today is the trade in tortoises for pets. Once a tortoise has been bought and installed in a garden it will be treated with the greatest care. The method of packing them for transport has meant, however, that in recent years there has been a hideously high mortality between their being collected, mainly in North Africa, and their reaching the dealers.

. . . and in the past

The four species of gopher tortoises, which may be up to 13 in. long, have also suffered from the pet trade. Two, the Texas tortoise and the desert tortoise, are now protected by law but the Mexican is very rare and may be extinct. The giant tortoises which live on the islands of the Galapagos and on islands in the Indian Ocean have also suffered in numbers, but in a different way. The largest of them have reached nearly 5 ft long, stood 2½ ft high and weighed 200—300 lb. Those of the Galapagos especially were taken by the crews of whalers, sealers and buccaneers for fresh meat. Between 1811 and 1844, a mere 105 whalers took 15 000. The giant tortoises of the Indian Ocean suffered even more, and in recent years a population on Aldabra Island was threatened through a proposal by the British Ministry of Defence to make the island an air staging post.

A ripe old age

Keeping tortoises as pets has been the only reliable way of estimating how long they can live.

The longest authentic record we have is for one of the giant tortoises, Marion's tortoise. It was taken to Mauritius, when full grown, by Marion de Fresne in 1766. In 1810 the British captured the island and the tortoise continued to live in the artillery barracks until 1918. It was, therefore, at least 152 years old, and probably 180 years or even more. Another famous giant was the Tonga tortoise, presented by Captain James Cook in 1774, when it was already 'a considerable age'. There is some doubt about this tortoise, largely because in Tonga the records are oral, not written, but there seems no reason why the present tortoise should not be the same as the one Captain Cook handed over.

class	**Reptilia**
order	**Testudines**
family	**Testudinidae**
genera & species	***Gopherus agassizi*** *desert gopher tortoise* ***G. berlandieri*** *Texas* ***G. flavomarginatus*** *Mexican* ***Geochelone elephantopus*** *Galapagos giant* ***G. gigantea*** *Indian Ocean giant* ***Testudo graeca*** *Iberian or Algerian* ***T. hermanni*** *Greek, others*

▷ *Galapagos giant tortoises: some of the few remaining members of a species once numerous enough to give its name to the islands but numbers are now greatly diminished. In the 19th century they were easy prey for the crews of passing ships, and their hardiness enabled them to be kept on board as a live source of meat.*

When annoyed, alligators open their vast jaws and roar. Male alligators also roar during their quarrels in the breeding season and to attract females.

Alligator

*Two species of reptiles which, with the caimans, belong to a family closely related to the crocodiles. Alligators and crocodiles look extremely alike: the main distinguishing feature is the teeth.
In a crocodile the teeth in the upper and lower jaws are in line, but in the alligator, when its mouth is shut, the upper teeth lie outside the lower. In both animals the fourth lower tooth on each side is perceptibly larger than the rest: in the crocodile this tooth fits into a notch in the upper jaw and is visible when the mouth is closed, whereas in the alligator, with the lower teeth inside the upper, it fits into a pit in the upper jaw and is lost to sight when the mouth is shut. In addition, the alligator's head is broader and shorter and the snout consequently blunter. Otherwise, especially in their adaptations to an aquatic life, alligators are very similar to crocodiles.*

*One of the two species is found in North America, the other in China. The Chinese alligator averages a little over 4 ft in length and has no webs between the toes. The American alligator is much larger, with a maximum recorded length of 19 ft 2 in.
This length, however, is seldom attained nowadays because the American alligator has been killed off for the sake of its skin; whenever there is intense persecution of an animal the larger ones are quickly*

eliminated and the average size of the remainder drops slowly as persecution proceeds.

*It is sheer accident that two such similar reptiles as the alligator and the crocodile should so early have been given different common names. The reason is that when the Spanish seamen, who had presumably no knowledge of crocodiles, first saw large reptiles in the Central American rivers, they spoke of them as lizards—**el largato** in Spanish. The English sailors who followed later adopted the Spanish name but ran the two into one to make 'allagarter'—which was later further corrupted to 'alligator'.*

Long lazy life

Alligators are more sluggish than crocodiles; this may possibly have an effect on their longevity. There is a record of an American alligator living for 56 years. They spend most of their time basking on river banks.

The American alligator is restricted to the south-eastern United States and does not penetrate further north than latitude 35. The Chinese alligator is found only in the Yangtse River basin.

Meat eaters

Alligators' food changes with age. The young feed on insects and on those crustaceans generally known as freshwater shrimps. As they grow older they eat frogs, snakes and fish; mature adults live mainly on fish but will catch muskrats and small mammals that go down to the water's edge to drink. They also take a certain amount of waterfowl. Very large alligators may

occasionally pull large mammals such as deer or cows down into the water and drown them.

Alligator builds a nest

It seems that the female alligator plays the more active role in courtship and territorial defence. The males apparently spend much of the breeding season quarrelling among themselves, roaring and fighting and injuring each other. The roaring attracts the females to the males, as does a musky secretion from glands in the male's throat and cloaca. Courtship takes place usually at night, the pair swimming round faster and faster and finally mating in the water with jaws interlocked and the male's body arched over the female's.

A large nest-mound is made for the reception of the eggs. The female scoops up mud in her jaws and mixes it with decaying vegetation; the mixture is then deposited on the nest site until a mound 3 ft high is made. The eggs are hard-shelled and number 15—80; they are laid in a depression in the top of the mound and covered with more vegetation. The female remains by the eggs until they hatch 2—3 months later, incubated by the heat of the nest's rotting vegetation.

The hatchling alligators peep loudly and the female removes the layer of vegetation over the nest to help them escape. Baby alligators are 8 in. long when first hatched and grow 1 ft a year, reaching maturity at 6 years.

The biter bitten

Young alligators fall an easy prey to carnivorous fish, birds and mammals, and at all stages of growth they are attacked and eaten

△ *A female alligator builds a nest of rotting vegetation for her clutch of 15—80 eggs. She stays for 2—3 months by the nest until they hatch.*

▽ *Alligators spend much of their time basking on the banks of jungle rivers. Here they have made a lagoon by their thrashing about.*

by larger alligators. This natural predation was, in the past, just sufficient to keep the numbers of alligator populations steady. Then came the fashion for making women's shoes, handbags and other ornamental goods of alligator skin. So long as these articles remain in fashion and command a high price, men will be prepared to risk both the imprisonment consequent on the laws passed to protect alligators and the attacks of the alligators themselves.

There is also another commercial interest, detrimental both to the alligator and to the fashion industry. For, while the fashion for skins from larger individuals shows no sign of abating, a fashion for alligator pets also persists—though it may have dropped in intensity since its inception. Baby alligators are still being netted in large numbers for the pet shops, but—as so commonly happens with pets taken from the wild—not all those caught are eventually sold. Of a consignment of 1,000 hatchlings that reached New York City in 1967, 200 were already dead and putrefying, and many others were in a sorry condition and unlikely to survive.

In addition to persecution, land drainage has seriously affected the numbers of the American alligator. The Chinese alligator is an even worse case. Its flesh is eaten and the various parts of its body are used as charms, aphrodisiacs and for their supposed medicinal properties. The New York Zoological Park has recently announced plans to try and breed the Chinese alligator and so protect it from complete extermination.

Unwanted pets

The fashion for alligator pets has its disadvantages for owners as well as the alligator populations. Even setting aside the largest recorded lengths for the American species of 19 ft upwards, it still achieves too large a size to be convenient in the modern flat, and people who invest in an alligator often find it necessary to dispose of it. Zoos have proved unable to deal with the quantity offered them—Brookfield Zoo near Chicago has built up an enormous herd from unwanted pets—and it is widely said that unfortunate alligators are disposed of in such a way that they end up in the sewers. One result of this is that every now and then, despite official denials, reports have appeared in the press to the effect that the sewers of New York are teeming with alligators that prey on the rats and terrorise the sewermen.

class	**Reptilia**
order	**Crocodilia**
family	**Alligatoridae**
genus	***Alligator mississipiensis***
& species	*American alligator*
	A. sinensis *Chinese alligator*

Young caiman showing its many, pointed teeth.

Caiman

The several species of caiman are confined to the northern part of South America, mainly in the Amazon basin, and one of the species extends into the southern part of Mexico. They are closely related to alligators, differing mainly in having the skin of the underside reinforced with bony plates. This makes them useless for the leather market, for which crocodiles and alligators have been killed in large numbers, because it is the skin of the belly that is tanned, as well as the sides. Otherwise, in appearance and in habits, caimans and alligators are very much alike. The smallest is the dwarf caiman, up to 4 ft long, the largest is the black caiman, up to 15 ft long.

The five species can be grouped as the spectacled caiman, plus the broad snouted caiman, two smooth-fronted caimans and the black caiman (one species only). Spectacled and broad snouted caimans have a ridge across the nose, between the eyes, like the bridge of a pair of spectacles. Smooth-fronted species lack this. The black caiman also has a smooth forehead but is glossy black in colour, contrasting with the sombre browns and olive of other species.

Belligerent and agile

Caimans can often be seen sunning themselves in great numbers on river banks or in muddy streams in dense jungle. They move with surprising speed over a short distance on land, and are even more agile in water, being quicker and more active than alligators. Those who have kept caimans in captivity claim they are more vicious and ready to bite than alligators or crocodiles, and there are many reports of attacks on human beings. Apart from the possibility of

accidental encounters there are no substantiated reports of deliberate attacks. They are said, however, to kill many domestic animals and when, in some parts of their range, they congregate in small pools during the dry season (November—December) they are killed in great numbers by cowboys.

Caimans readily show fight. Young caimans will blow themselves up, leap about and hiss, with the mouth open ready to bite. Older ones also hiss, and in the breeding season they bellow loudly.

Kills its prey by drowning

Prey is sometimes seized on land and carried back to water to be held under until drowned. A stratagem used for catching a water bird or a mammal coming down to drink is for the caiman to turn and move away, submerge and then swim round to capture it. When swallowing, a caiman stretches its neck out of water, manoeuvring its victim to a head foremost position in the mouth. The hind foot is used for scratching, for rubbing the eyes and to tear the food.

As with most crocodilians, they feed on freshwater crustaceans when small, graduating to amphibians, fish, reptiles, birds and mammals as they mature. An exception is the Paraguayan caiman which seems to live largely on giant snails.

Enemies

Little is known about enemies of the caiman. The jaguar is said to kill young or half-grown caimans, and they have been found in the stomachs of anacondas. Man often kills them.

Fifty eggs in a nest

After mating, the female builds near water, a nest of vegetation and mud scraped together in a mound, which she consolidates by crawling over it. Then she digs a hole in the top and may lay up to 50 eggs in it, the size of a hen's or a goose's egg, according to the species and size. These are hard-shelled and the baby caiman must break the shell, with the egg-tooth on its snout, in order to emerge, the egg-tooth then being shed. Just before hatching, the babies start to croak. The mother, who has remained near the nest, on hearing this, begins to scrape the top from the nest to help their escape. The young caimans are like the parents except for having relatively larger eyes and shorter snouts. In most species they are coloured like the adults; dark or olive brown on the back, lighter on the flanks and dull white on the belly, with various dark blotches and patches, but the black caiman is a glossy

black when adult, with the underside white or yellow, but the young are black with yellow bands.

Baby caimans are nearly 1 ft long but may grow rapidly to 2 ft at the end of the first year, and possibly reaching 5 ft at the age of 5 years.

Caimans hunt by taste

It is usually said that caimans, like crocodiles and alligators, find their prey by smell. This is not borne out by tests made on a variety of crocodilians kept in captivity. These tests suggest that sight and taste are the important senses in the search for food. First of all a crocodilian closes both its nostrils and its ears when submerged, so smell and hearing are out of action, at least when it is under water. Then, we know the eyes are adapted to night vision because they show a slit pupil by day and a wide-open rounded pupil at night, and presumably sight is used both underwater and on land. More refined details about sight have been given by Zdenek Vogel, the Czech zoologist, who found that caimans appear to be able to recognize colours, can distinguish the outlines of large objects up to 33 ft away, and can detect sharp movements made 100 ft or more away.

His tests on the way they detect their food were even more decisive. Dried blood put into a tank where they were swimming produced no reaction, nor did washed meat hung in the water on a string or placed on a rock. Even hungry caimans ignored these but swallowed food eagerly when it was placed in their mouths. They seemed not to be affected by paraffin poured into the water until they opened their mouths and got it on their tongues. Similarly, meat that tinged the water red produced no reaction until the water touched their tongues.

The conclusion seems to be, therefore, that the main sense-organs used in hunting are the taste-buds on the tongue, used when in the water, and sight, used when the caiman is above or out of water.

class	**Reptilia**	
order	**Crocodilia**	
family	**Alligatoridae**	
genera & species	***Caiman crocodilus*** *spectacled*	
	C. latirostris *broad snouted*	
	Melanosuchus niger *black*	
	Paleosuchus palpebrosus	*smooth*
	P. trigonatus	*fronted*

Caimans differ from crocodiles and alligators in having very large overlapping bony plates on their bellies. They move with surprising speed over a short distance on land, and are even more agile in water, being quicker than alligators.

Crocodile

The crocodiles and their close relatives alligators, caimans and gharials are the sole survivors of the great group of reptiles, the Archosauria, that included the well-known and awe-inspiring dinosaurs. The crocodile family itself includes the dwarf crocodiles and the false gharial as well as the dozen or so species of true crocodiles.

Crocodiles are often distinguished by the shape of the snout. This is long and broad in the Nile crocodile, the best-known species, short in the Indian marsh crocodile or mugger, and long and narrow in the false gharial. The differences between crocodiles and alligators are set out under alligator, page 144.

As with many large, fearsome animals, the size of crocodiles has been exaggerated. There is reliable evidence for the Nile crocodile reaching 20 ft and American and Orinoco crocodiles have measured 23 ft. At the other extreme the Congo dwarf crocodile has never been found to exceed 3 ft 9 in. Now that crocodiles have been hunted too intensively, large ones have become extremely rare.

Cold-blooded lover of warmth

Crocodiles are found in the warmer parts of the world, in Africa, Asia, Australia and America. Unlike alligators, they are often found in brackish water and sometimes they even swim out to sea. Estuarine crocodiles swim between the islands of the Malay Archipelago and stray ones have been found in the Fijis and other remote islands.

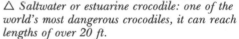

▽ *Smaller relative, different jaw structure: the broad-fronted crocodile of West Africa only grows to 5–6 ft and does not attack man.*

△ *Saltwater or estuarine crocodile: one of the world's most dangerous crocodiles, it can reach lengths of over 20 ft.*

Reptiles are said to be cold-blooded because they cannot maintain their body temperatures within fine limits, as can mammals and birds. A reptile's body temperature is usually within a few degrees of that of its surroundings. It cannot shiver to keep warm or sweat to keep cool. Many reptiles, however, can keep their body temperatures from varying too much by following a daily routine to avoid extremes of temperature. Crocodiles do this. They come out of the water at sunrise and lie on the banks basking in the sun. When their bodies have warmed up, they either move into the shade or back into the water, escaping the full strength of the midday sun. Then in the late afternoon they bask again, and return to the water by nightfall. By staying underwater at night they conserve heat, because water holds its heat better than air.

Stones in their stomachs

When crocodiles come out of the water they generally stay near the bank, although occasionally they wander some distance in search of water, and can cause great consternation by appearing in towns. They are generally sluggish, but, considering their bulky bodies and relatively short legs, they are capable of unexpected bursts of speed. They have three distinct gaits. There is a normal walk, with the body

lifted well off the ground with the legs under the body – a gait most unlike the popular conception of a crocodile walking. More familiar is the tobogganing used when dashing into the water. The crocodile slides on its belly, using its legs as paddles. The third method is used by a young crocodile which will occasionally gallop along with the front and back legs working together, like a bounding squirrel.

In the water, crocodiles float very low, with little more than eyes and nostrils showing. They habitually carry several pounds of stones in their stomachs, which help to stabilise their bodies. The stones lie in the stomach, below the centre of gravity and work as a counterpoise to the buoyant lungs. This is particularly useful when the crocodiles are fairly young. At that age they are top heavy and cannot float easily at the surface.

Maneaters: myth and fact

For the first year of their lives, young crocodiles feed on small animals, frogs, dragonflies, crabs and even mosquito larvae. Young crocodiles have been seen cornering the larvae by curving their bodies and tails around them. Larger animals are stalked. The baby crocodile swims stealthily towards its prey then pounces, snapping at it with a sideways movement of the jaws, necessary because the crocodile's eyes are at the side of its head.

As a crocodile grows the amount of insects in its diet falls, and it turns to eating snails and fish. The adult crocodiles continue to catch fish but turn increasingly to trapping mammals and birds. They capture their prey by lying in wait near game trails or waterholes. When a victim approaches the crocodile will seize it and drag it underwater or knock it over with a blow from its tail or head. Once the victim is pulled into the water the crocodile has a definite advantage. Drowning soon stills the victim's struggles, and, grasping a limb in its jaws, the crocodile may roll over and over so that the victim is dismembered.

Crocodiles are well-known as maneaters – but how true is this reputation? The maneating habit varies and it may be that only certain individuals will attack man. In parts of Africa, crocodiles are not regarded as a menace at all, while elsewhere palisades have to be erected at the water's edge to allow the women to fetch water in safety. It seems that crocodiles are likely to be more aggressive when their streams and pools dry up so they cannot escape, or when they are guarding their young.

In the crocodile's nest

The Nile crocodile breeds when 5 – 10 years old. By this time it is 7 – 10 ft long. The full-grown males stake out their territories along the banks and share them with younger males and females. They defend the territories by fighting, which may sometimes end in one contestant being killed.

A male crocodile approaches a female

Like an extra for a film on the first amphibious reptiles, a small saltwater crocodile comes ashore in Queensland, Australia. Unlike alligators, crocodiles can be found in brackish waters, estuaries, and swimming out at sea.

149

△ *Hatching out: while still in the egg, baby Nile crocodiles grunt a signal to the mother to uncover the nest.*

▽ *Prelude to feeding: prey trapped in its vice-like jaws, a crocodile returns to the water where it will take its meal at leisure.*

crocodile and displays to her by thrashing the water with his snout and tail. They swim in circles with the male on the outside trying to get near her so he can put a forelimb over her body and mate.

Up to 90 eggs are laid during the dry season. They hatch 4 months later, during the rainy season when there are plenty of insects about for the babies to feed on.

The Nile crocodile and the marsh crocodile dig pits 2 ft deep for their nests, but the estuarine crocodile of northern Australia and southeast Asia makes a mound of leaves. The nests are built near water and shade, where the female can guard her brood and keep herself cool. During the incubation period she stays by the nest defending it against enemies, including other crocodiles, although in colonies they sometimes nest only a few yards apart.

The baby crocodiles begin to grunt before hatching. This is the signal for the mother to uncover the nest. The babies climb out and stay near her, yapping if they get lost. They follow her about like ducklings and forage for insects, even climbing trees, and grunting and snapping at one another. They disperse after a few days.

The young Nile crocodiles are about 1 ft long at hatching and for their first 7 years they grow at a rate of about 10 in. a year.

Cannibals

The mother crocodile has to be on her guard all the time as many animals will wait for their chance to eat the eggs or the baby crocodiles. Their main enemy is the monitor lizard. They are bold enough to dig underneath the crocodile as she lies over her nest, and once a male monitor was seen to decoy a crocodile away from the nest while the female stole the eggs. Other crocodiles, herons, mongooses, turtles, eagles and predatory fish all eat baby crocodiles. Adult crocodiles have been killed by lions, elephants, and leopards, and hippopotamuses will attack crocodiles in defence of their young.

Crocodiles are cannibals, so basking groups are always sorted out into parties of equal size and the smaller crocodiles keep well away from the bigger ones.

Crocodile tears

If we say that someone is shedding crocodile tears it means that they are showing grief or sympathy that they do not really mean. The idea that crocodiles are hypocrites is an ancient one, and is described in TH White's translation of a 12th century bestiary: 'Crocodiles lie by night in the water, by day on land, because hypocrites, however luxuriously they live by night, delight to be said to live holily and justly by day.' The hypocrisy seems to be manifested in the form of tears, and malicious or misunderstanding comparisons are made with women's tears. Thus when Desdemona weeps, Othello complains:

'O devil, devil!
If that the earth could teem with woman's tears,
Each drop she falls would prove a crocodile.'

John Hawkins explains crocodile's tears as meaning 'that as the Crocodile when he crieth, goeth then about most to deceive, so doth a woman commonly when she weepeth'. The deception practised by the 'cruell craftie crocodile' is that it lures unwary travellers into drawing near to find out what is the matter.

The story, like many myths and legends, may have a basis of truth. It could have sprung from the plaintive howling that crocodiles make. Crocodiles, however, do have tear glands to keep their eyes moist and tears, or water trapped in their lids, may run from the corners of their eyes. This, with the permanent grin of their jaws, could have led to their legendary reputation as hypocrites.

class	**Reptilia**
order	**Crocodilia**
family	**Crocodylidae**
genera & species	***Crocodylus niloticus*** *Nile crocodile*
	C. porosus *estuarine crocodile*
	C. palustris *marsh crocodile*
	Osteolaemus *dwarf crocodiles*
	Tomistoma schlegeli *false gharial*

▷ *'African crocodiles at home': a romanticized print shows waterfowl scattering in panic from the threat of an evil-looking flock of crocodiles.*

▽ *Although in parts of Africa crocodiles are not regarded as maneaters, the Nile crocodile has a very bad reputation. One crocodile (15ft 3ins long) shot in the Kihange River, Central Africa, was reported to have killed 400 people over the years.*

Gharial

The gharial is a long, slender-snouted crocodile living in the rivers Indus, Ganges and Brahmaputra and in a few other rivers of this same region. The alternative name of gavial, although Latinized to give its scientific name, was originally due to a misspelling.

The Indian gharial can grow to 20 ft in length. The eyes are set well up on the head and the nostrils are at the tip of the long slender snout. The jaws are armed with small sharp teeth of nearly uniform size. The upper surface of the neck and the back have an armour of bony plates. The legs are longer proportionately than in most other crocodiles and the toes, especially those of the hindfeet, are webbed.

A crocodile very similar to the gharial lives in the rivers and marshes of Malaya, Borneo and Sumatra. Its snout is long but proportionately shorter than that of the gharial, and the two are similar in habits. It is, however, known as the false gharial and is one of the crocodile family (see page 147) or **Crocodylidae**, *while the gharials have a family of their own, the* **Gavialidae**.

Inoffensive crocodiles

Gharials keep to the water more than other crocodiles. They tend to lie just under the surface with only the eyes and nostrils exposed. When anyone approaches, the eyes sink slowly out of sight, leaving only the nostrils breaking surface. With the closer approach of an intruder the tip of the snout is then submerged. Both gharial and false gharial are little danger to people although there are rare records of fatal encounters. The gharial is sacred to the Hindus, and although its stomach is sometimes found to contain articles of personal adornment, such as bracelets, these have come almost certainly from human corpses committed to the sacred River Ganges.

Useful snout for feeding

The food of the gharial and false gharial is almost entirely small fishes, seized with a sideways snap of the jaws. The slenderness of the snout allows quick movement sideways; it is easier to wave a stick from side to side in water than a plank.

Two-tier incubator

The male gharial has a hollow hump on the tip of the snout with the nostrils at the centre of it. Otherwise there is little outward difference between the sexes. In the breeding season the female lays about 40 eggs in sand on a river bank, each $3\frac{1}{2}$ in. by $2\frac{3}{4}$ in.

These are in 2 layers, probably laid on separate days, and each layer is covered with a fairly deep covering of sand. The newly-hatched young, 14 in. long, have absurdly long snouts and they are coloured greyish-brown with five irregular dark oblique bands on the body and nine on the tail. The adults are mainly dark olive.

Same head, same feeding

Crocodiles in general and their immediately recognisable ancestors have a very long history going back over 200 million years. The crocodiles proper, living today, which must include also the caimans (see page 146) and alligators (see page 144), do not differ much from their earliest ancestors, except that some of the extinct crocodiles are larger than the largest living today. There was, however, a separate group of crocodilians whose fossils also date from those very early times, known as the Mesosuchia. They also had 'frying-pan' heads like the gharials, but they lived in the sea and they died out 120 million years ago. The gharials came into existence much later, less than 70 million years ago, and one of them was 54 ft long, the largest crocodilian we know of, living or extinct.

The Mesosuchia and the gharials are,

▽ *Gharial siesta, slumped on a warm bank to make the most of the midday sun.*

apart from being members of the order Crocodilia, not related. But they both had the long slender snout and both had many small sharp teeth. They both had the same feeding habits, seizing fast-moving slippery prey with a sideways slash of the head. We know gharials do this because people have watched the living animals feeding. We know false gharials do also, for the same reason, and we can deduce the Mesosuchia did this from the finer details of their bones. So we have three kinds of crocodilians with the same shape of head, feeding in the same way but all three unrelated. We know the gharials snatch fish; we can deduce the Mesosuchia snatched squid.

Many animals have pebbles in their stomachs. Living crocodiles are one example. Extinct crocodiles are another, and

we know this because when their skeletons are dug out of the ground groups of pebbles are found lying where the stomach would have been.

How do we know the Mesosuchia ate squid? Because the stomach stones found where their stomachs would have been are stained with the ink contained in the bodies of squids.

class	**Reptilia**
order	**Crocodilia**
family	**Gavialidae**
genus & species	*Gavialis gangeticus*

△ *Fish trap: once caught in this array of vicious teeth by a sideways slash of the gharial's head, few fish, slimy or not, can escape.*

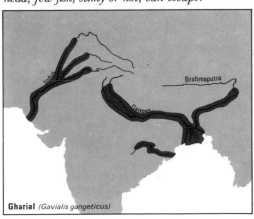

Gharial *(Gavialis gangeticus)*

153

Agama

*A genus of about 50 lizards belonging to the family Agamidae, which is related to the iguanas and includes in its 300 species such types as the Australian moloch or thorny devil, the frilled lizard and the flying dragons. The best known agama is the foot-long common agama of Africa, **Agama agama**. The male agama's head is bright terracotta, the colour of the African earth; his body and legs are dark blue; his tail banded pale blue, white, orange and black. His skin is rough to the touch, like sandpaper, and he has a dewlap of loose skin under his chin and a row of small spines on his neck like the comb of a young cock.*

*Other members of the genus include the starred agama (**A. stellio**) of the eastern Mediterranean region, and the desert agama (**A. mutabilis**) of North Africa. Among other genera of agamids not separately treated in this work are: **Phrynocephalus** (about 40 species, the toad-headed agamids), **Calotes** (about 25 species), **Uromastix** (spiny-tailed lizards), **Hydrosaurus** (water lizard).*

△ *Green crested lizard (**Calotes cristatellus**) of south-east Asia, one of the Agamid family.*

African distribution and habits

Agamas are the commonest reptiles in West Africa. Anyone who sets foot there cannot fail to notice them within the first few minutes. They are seen wherever the forest and bush have been cleared. In villages they run up and down hut walls, scamper across compounds and clatter over corrugated iron roofs, while in the main streets of the big towns thronged with people and traffic, they sunbathe in decorative groups on walls of modern stores or on ruins of houses—an urban rabble in their rubble slums.

At first sight there seems to be a confusing variety of other lizards as well. They can be seen in all sizes from five inches to a foot—some sandy, some chocolate, some with green-spotted heads, some with orange blotches on their sides. But it soon becomes clear that they are all the same species, the smallest being hatchlings, the middle-sizes females, and the largest of all, males. Only mature males that are dominant—that is, strong enough to boss other males—maintain the bright orange-and-blue colouring. Weak or subordinate males, or any that have had a bad fright, are dull brown. The mature male agama with his red face and ferocious mien looks extraordinarily like the traditional picture of a peppery colonel about to explode in an apoplectic fit.

The common agama has adapted its ways to become a companion of man, living in the thatch of huts, emerging to feed on scraps and insects, but always ready to race back to shelter if disturbed. If caught in the open it is able to run on its hind legs.

During the day the lizards are extremely active, hurtling across open spaces from one heap of stones to another, darting out to snap up ants, even leaping into the air after flying insects. Only in the afternoon, when the temperature reaches around 37·8°C/100°F in the shade, do they try to find a cool spot in which to lie down. As soon as it becomes a little cooler they begin to chase about again.

They seem to be always quarrelling. Fights are constantly breaking out between the colourful males. When two rivals catch sight of one another, both will repeatedly raise and lower the front part of the body in an extremely comical bobbing action, as if they were doing jerky press-ups. If the contestants are equally matched they will quickly come to blows, lashing out at each other with their strong tails and threatening with open jaws. Many of the large males have shortened or broken tails, the result of such fights. Even the females chase and fight each other, and sometimes the tiny hatchling lizards play at fighting, as kittens and puppies do.

Towards dusk the agamas congregate in communal roosts, often in the eaves of houses, and at night all the males, regardless of their social standing, go a dull brown colour all over, like the subordinate males. But the next morning, when out in the early sun, their brilliant colours return.

The desert agama lives in the dry areas of North Africa, avoiding bare sand. After the cold night an agama will be literally stiff with cold, but with the sunrise it absorbs energy and its temperature rises so that it can start hunting, courting and so on. As the sun's power increases the desert agama must be careful not to overheat—although it can tolerate greater temperatures than most reptiles. The sparse scrub of the desert gives sufficient shelter to the agamas, who dash from one bush to another as they go about their daily business.

Insectivorous feeders

Agamas are mainly insectivorous, chasing their prey at speed and catching small insects with the tongue or snapping up larger ones directly with the mouth. The incisor-like front teeth are pointed like those of insectivorous mammals. Agamas may also eat grass, berries, seeds and the eggs of smaller lizards.

Polygamous breeder

The common agama is polygamous. The brilliantly coloured male may be seen with half a dozen or more females, in a territory which he defends vigorously.

In courtship the male comes alongside the female, bobbing his head, and then, if she allows him, grips her neck with his jaws. If she is out of breeding condition and does not allow this, he will continue bobbing until exhausted. If he is successful, he puts one hind leg over her back, grasps her hind leg with his foot, and twists the hind end of his body under her. The female then raises her tail away from the male and the vents are brought together.

Sometimes the female initiates the courtship by running up to the male and raising her tail in front of him. He then chases her until she lets him catch up.

Even common agamas living near the Equator have a very definite breeding season, which occurs after the 'long rains' of March-May. The males have ripe spermatozoa all the year, but the females can only lay eggs from June to September, some months after the rains. At this time the vegetation becomes lush and the insect population rises, providing the female agamas with an ample supply of protein for the formation of eggs, which are then laid in clutches of up to twelve.

The peppery colonel

The reference to peppery colonels is not without point, for agamas have their little empires to defend. In rural districts they are well spaced out, each male owning his country estate. By watching the different males it is easy to pick out each one's stronghold: a tree, a log or a rock near the middle of his territory. Fairly accurate lines marking the boundaries of these territories can then be drawn, and along these lines the owners battle to maintain or extend their properties.

In the towns, where agamas are thicker on the ground, the territorial instinct can lead to more frequent fighting and to situations which appear somewhat comic.

An illustration of this is an actual situation observed in Akure in West Africa. Close to a bungalow lived a fine male agama, readily recognisable because he had a clubbed tail, having lost an inch of tip. He was nicknamed Old Apoplexy—Apo for short—by an English family occupying the bungalow. His territory included a strip of grass with four trees and a hedge to one side. He basked much of his time beside his three 'wives', but was often engaged in fights with a neighbouring agama, 'Rival', who had five wives.

Rival had to patrol the other boundaries of his territory, and while he was absent Apo would rush in and grab one of his females, beating a speedy retreat when Rival returned. One day he failed to make a quick enough getaway. Rival drove him up a tree, higher and higher, until he lost sight of Apo, who faded to a dull grey as his fighting spirit ebbed. But Rival, after descending the tree, waited at the base for Apo.

By the following day a third male had taken over Apo's territory, and two mornings later he was still in possession. In the afternoon a club-tailed male agama, chocolate in colour, entered this territory. It was Apo, who had at last escaped. Suddenly there was a muddle of flailing feet and tails. The third lizard, caught off balance, retreated as fast as he could. Gradually, Apo, back victorious on his own territory and lord once more of three wives, changed from chocolate to grey flecked with green, and his head resumed its orange tint.

△ *A male African common agama, bobbing his head in boundary threat display. The bright red head is a sign of his aggressiveness.*

▽ *Agama bibroni grows to about 10 in. from nose to tip of tail. Here the dull brownish colour suggests it is of inferior rank.*

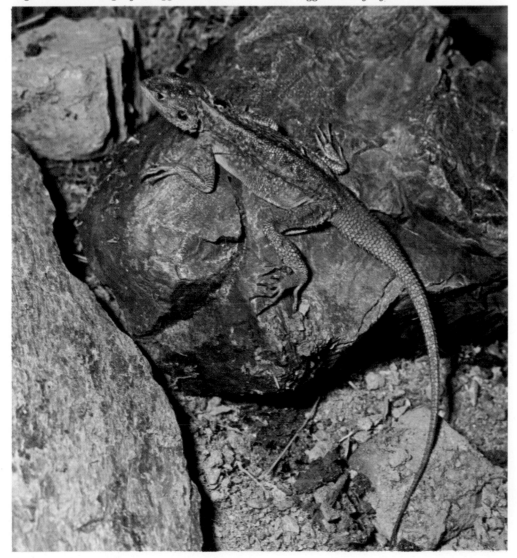

class	**Reptilia**
order	**Squamata**
suborder	**Sauria**
family	**Agamidae**
genera	***Agama*** *and others*

Anole

There are 165 species in the genus **Anolis**, that is, one quarter of the total number of species in the iguana family of lizards. Unfortunately for the scientist, the species of the anoles show little variety in form and so are difficult to identify. Their heads are triangular with elongated jaws. The body is slender, ending in a long, whip-like tail. The toes have sharp claws as well as adhesive pads, in the form of grooves on one of the joints, that enable the anoles to climb sheer walls. Males have a flat throat sac which can be extended by muscular action when they are excited. This expands the folds of skin to reveal a remarkable pattern of colours between the scales – green, red, white, yellow and black in many combinations.

Anoles are small lizards ranging in total length from 5 in. to the 18 in. knight anole of Cuba. Of this, two thirds is tail, so that the knight anole is by no means a large lizard. It is, however, a handsome animal, pale green with white markings on the body; on the head there is a braided pattern in yellow with patches of blue around the eyes. The male's throat sac is pale pink.

The best-known anole is the green anole from the southeast of the United States. This is a medium-sized lizard 6–7 in. long, with a beautiful pale green body marked with brown spots, the throat sac being spotted with red and white. The leaf-nosed anole of Brazil is so-called from the peculiar sideways flattened structure that projects beyond its snout for a distance equal to the length of the head.

Habits and colour change

Anoles are found only in the Americas where they range from North Carolina to southern Brazil and are abundant in the West Indies. Most of them live in trees, running around the branches with the aid of their long delicate toes and adhesive pads. A few species have enlarged toe pads which give some parachute effect, enabling the anoles to descend from considerable heights with safety. Other anoles have become associated with man, living in houses and gardens where they can take advantage of fruit in the gardens and insects that infest houses. Such anoles become very tame and some disturbance is necessary to send them scurrying. In this way they resemble the agamas and geckos of the Old World.

One of the more unusual anoles, the water anole of Cuba, lives along the banks of streams, diving into the water and hiding under stones when frightened. Also living in Cuba are two cave-dwelling anoles. One of these, a pale, translucent lizard with brick-red stripes running across the body, lives in limestone caves frequented by bats.

△ Male Jamaican anole. The long, specialised toes enable it to climb sheer walls.

▽ Anoles asleep on poinsettia. To escape, a lizard will often forfeit its tail as seen here.

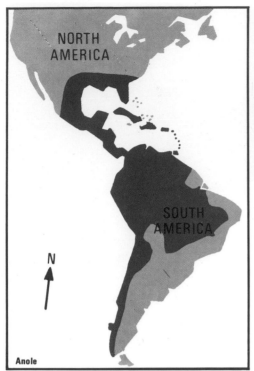

Anole

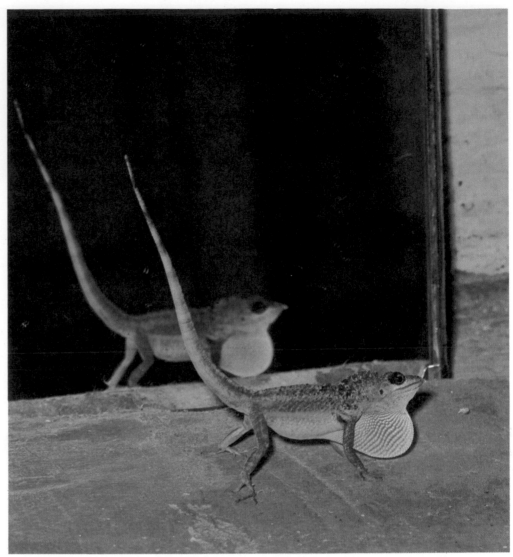

▷ *A mirror placed in this anole's territory caused regular displays by the lizard at its own reflection. Displays often lasted 3 hours completely exhausting the lizard. This anole is at the climax of an aggressive display.*

It can be found clinging to the walls of the caves in the twilight zone near the entrances, and, unlike most cave dwellers, it will come out into broad daylight.

The green anole is commonly called the 'American chameleon' because, excluding the cave dwellers, most anoles are adept at changing colour. This ability is often exaggerated and the anoles are sometimes said to be able to alter their colour and blend completely with their background, turning green when placed on a leaf and dark brown when moved to a tree trunk. Experiments and observations in natural conditions show that the anoles change colour in response to temperature, light intensity and emotional state. Background colour will affect the colour of an anole to some extent, but if it is kept cool, at about 10°C/50°F it will go brown whatever the background. If the temperature is raised to 21°C/70°F it turns green, but only so long as the light is dim. If the light is bright it stays brown. Then, if the temperature is raised another 30 or 40 Fahrenheit degrees the lizard becomes pale green and stays that colour whatever light there is. In normal conditions the green anole tends to be green at night and brown by day.

The mechanism of colour change varies in different kinds of reptiles. The pigment-containing cells in the skin, responsible for colour changes, are controlled by nerves in chameleons, so chameleons can change colour quite rapidly. In anoles, on the other hand, the cells are controlled by a hormone, a chemical messenger called intermedin which is secreted into the blood by the pituitary gland, which lies at the underside of the brain. It is carried by the blood stream to the colour cells where it causes them to alter the concentrations of pigment within. This is a slow process compared with

the action of the nervous system, and anoles will take up to 10 minutes to change colour.

The pituitary gland, which controls colour change, is close to that part of the brain responsible for emotions, so it is not surprising that the colour of males is influenced by their aggressiveness. The green anole male becomes bright green if he wins a fight but brown if he loses.

Fruit and insect eaters

Anoles are fruit and insect eaters, taking whichever is available, according to the time of year.

Breeding behaviour

The male anole is larger and more brightly coloured than the female. He holds a territory which he defends against other males by displaying the colours of his throat sac and, at times, by fighting. Apart from territorial fights, there is also a peck-order system (so called as such a system of hierarchies was first studied in flocks of hens) in which the big males bully the medium ones, who in turn worry the small ones. Such encounters are short-lived, as the inferior male knows his place and retreats immediately. When two equals meet, perhaps on the boundary of their territories, the outcome is more spectacular, although in the end perhaps less decisive. The two sidle round each other with bodies puffed up, then one, followed by the other, raises its body off the ground and stretches out its

brilliant throat sac. At the same time the tail wags up and down. After holding this pose for a few minutes they subside and start parading again. Many bouts of displaying may take place before the two lose interest in each other and wander away, having decided nothing. Only rarely will a fight break out, the contestants grappling with their jaws and thrashing around until one breaks away and retreats at speed. The displaying and such contests as there are constitute threat and a test of strength rather than actual combat.

The throat sac is also used to attract the female, who if willing coyly turns her head to one side. The male approaches her from the rear, grabs her neck with his jaws, puts one hind foot over her body to clasp her leg, slips his tail under hers and mates. It is not uncommon in animal life that an action which a male interprets as threatening behaviour and to which he responds aggressively, will to a female indicate courtship so she will respond submissively.

The eggs are nearly always laid in the ground, the female coming down the tree to dig a hole with her snout. The eggs are laid into the hole, or pushed in if they miss, and the hole is filled in. The cave anoles have a different habit. They lay their eggs in the caves, where they may be found in narrow crevices in the walls or between stalactites in groups of two to seven. As anoles regularly lay only one or two eggs at a time, it is likely that the clusters of eggs

△ *Male anole in aggressive display, showing the throat sac fully extended by muscular action to reveal the throat colours. The anole raises itself off the ground at the same time wagging its tail up and down. Display is the usual form of aggression, fights only taking place as last resort.*

are laid by several females.

The eggs, which are not guarded, hatch after 6—10 weeks when the ground appears to swarm with baby anoles.

Many enemies

Hawks, cats, mongooses, and many other predators take their toll of anoles. In one experiment 200 were marked and released. A year later four had survived and they had gone in another 6 months. Like many abundant animals, there is a very rapid turnover of population, very few even reaching maturity although the maximum age an anole can reach if protected in a vivarium is over 6 years.

Aggression in a mirror

The territorial instinct is as strong in the male lizard as in any other animal and much of his time is devoted to making threatening displays at other males encroaching on his pitch.

A few years ago, in a house in Barbados where an anole had taken up residence, the owners experimented by propping a mirror against the wall to see how the

lizard might react to his own image. Three days later he was seen in front of the mirror displaying at his image. He continued to do this for 1¼ hours, and after this he returned almost daily to the mirror to display at the supposed rival. Between these displays the lizard would parade backwards and forwards in front of the mirror with much animation, or would try to bite his image. Several times he went behind the mirror as if looking for his opponent.

Some of these displays would last for as much as 3 hours on end, by which time the lizard seemed completely exhausted. It was almost as if once he had stationed himself in front of the mirror he was unable to tear himself away, as if, fascinated by his own image, he was under a spell that could only be broken when somebody went into the room and disturbed him. Then he would go out to the back door, rest on the step, occasionally blowing out his throat at lizards on a pawpaw tree nearby or on a wall across the yard. Usually he would return to the mirror within an hour, but sometimes, after an initial bout of aggressive display, he would go away and stay away all day.

By the end of 6 weeks the lizard still seemed attracted by his own reflection. He had stopped actively displaying in front of it although he still paraded up and down and occasionally tried to bite his own image, and at very long intervals would display by blowing out his throat, but no more.

This was an artificial situation for the

lizard and in a natural state he would not display for so long at a time, nor so vigorously because either he or his opponent would drive the other away. The importance of the experiment lies in this: while the image in the mirror represented for him another male intruding on his territory there was every indication that the lizard remembered this 'other male' and this supposed rival was seldom 'far from his mind'. For example, the lizard might be in another part of the house or on the back step, feeding or sunning himself, when he would suddenly drop everything he was doing, make a bee-line for the room in which the mirror was standing, go straight across to it and start to display. This is important in helping to interpret one aspect of the behaviour of birds that bang themselves against windows. It was not merely a case that the lizard on seeing his own image in the mirror treated it as a rival male. Again and again, he behaved as if he had suddenly remembered that in the other room was a rival demanding his attention.

class	**Reptilia**
order	**Squamata**
suborder	**Sauria**
family	**Iguanidae**
genus & species	***Anolis spp.***

Basilisk

There are several species of basilisks, all living in tropical America. They are iguana lizards of peculiar habits. The common basilisk is typical. The male is 2 ft long, including its long tapering tail, and has a crest of skin on the head reminiscent of a cock's comb. The crest continues down the mid-line of the back and onto the first half of the tail. The female is slightly smaller than the male and lacks the crest, which is not present in the young basilisk either. Alternative names are **paso-rios**, *the river-crosser, in Mexico, and the Jesûs Christo lizard, in South America, because it can walk or run, on water. The basilisk of mythology, after which the lizard is named, was said to be deadly, but there is nothing dangerous about its modern namesake. An outstanding feature of this iguana lizard is its long hind legs ending in long toes fringed with scales. The hind limbs have some similarity to those of frogs and, although not webbed, the feet resemble those of a frog in having a large sole. The front legs, by contrast, are small.*

Runs on the water

Basilisks always live among shrubs and trees near water onto which they drop the moment they are disturbed. The animal may either go straight to the bottom of the water and stay there for a while, surfacing when the intruder has had time to move away, or it may run over the surface with the body semi-erect. It will run over the ground or along branches of trees in the same way, the long tail held out behind and curving slightly upwards, the long hind legs moving in strides recalling those of an ostrich or emu running. There are other lizards that can run like this but it seems that all must gather speed by running on all fours, later lifting the front part of the body and the forelegs from the ground. The basilisk seems able to go straight into the semi-erect position from a standing start.

The usual explanation of the basilisk's ability to run over the water is that it travels so fast that it has not time to sink. Whether such an explanation will wholly or partially satisfy those better versed in the laws of mechanics is an open question. There can be little doubt, however, that the basilisk's lightweight body, as well as the spread of the long-fringed toes, is important in this act of scuttering across water. There is at least one species of frog that uses a similar scuttering as a means of escape, and its action is more to be compared with the flight of a flat pebble over water in the game of ducks-and-drakes. Provided the basilisk is moving quickly over water, the soles of the feet do not break through the surface film, but as the pace slackens, the lizard drops on to all-fours, becomes partially submerged and finishes the journey swimming.

A curious habit of the basilisk, one as yet unexplained, and one it shares with the zebra-tailed lizard of the deserts of the

The crested male basilisk clinging to tree trunk with its long clawed toes. It is named after the fabled basilisk, whose glance was said to be fatal to man or any living thing.

south-western United States, is that of curling its tail while at rest, and then wagging it. The basilisk eats plants and insects.

Breeding

The common basilisk lays eggs, the female digging a cavity in the ground about 3 inches deep. Having done this she stations herself with her cloaca over the hole and tail curled to one side, to lay about 20 eggs. These she covers with soil and leaves. They hatch 18–30 days later. The young basilisk inside cuts criss-cross slits in the parchment-like shell, using the egg-tooth on its snout. It takes 30 to 40 minutes to climb out of the shell, or even as much as 3 hours. When hatched it is about 3 in. long.

Convergent evolution

It is interesting that the East Indian water lizard *Hydrosaurus* has developed similar habits to the basilisk, including the feat of running on water. This is an example of evolutionary change in different families, in similar but separate environments, producing similarly designed creatures to fit a vacant niche in nature. This is known as convergent evolution.

The fatal look

This iguana has been named basilisk because of its crest. Incidentally, the tiny bird

known as the goldcrest or kinglet has been given this name also, and for the same reason. The original basilisk, of mediaeval times, also had a crest, but there the comparison ends. It was the king of serpents, and people who saw it, according to the ancient chroniclers, ran for their lives. The earliest drawings we have of the basilisk show it in the form of barnyard chanticleer with a serpent's tail. It was said to have been hatched from an egg laid by an elderly cockerel which was then guarded and incubated by a toad. There was at least one occasion in the Middle Ages when a toad, found squatting near a hen's egg, was publicly tried and condemned to be burnt at the stake. The cause of all this was the belief that a basilisk had only to look at a man to destroy him. In fact, it was believed that the glance of a basilisk was fatal to any living thing, even to another basilisk.

class	**Reptilia**
order	**Squamata**
suborder	**Sauria**
family	**Iguanidae**
genus & species	***Basiliscus basiliscus***

Bearded lizard

The bearded lizard is also known as the bearded dragon or Jew lizard. Its whole surface is beset with small spines, and, forming a sort of shield around the snout, is a jaw pouch. This, when swollen, looks like a beard. The male is larger than the female and has a black throat. The beard is more strongly developed in the males than in the females and is also smaller in individuals living inland. It is a stout-bodied lizard of the agamid family, up to 2 ft long with a long head and a whip-like tail, living in Australia. The colour ranges from greyish to yellow, depending largely on its emotional state. When injured, sick or dying its back goes black and its legs pale yellow.

Dry, warm habitat

The bearded lizard lives in sparsely forested country, scrub, desert sands and also the shore. It is most abundant in eastern Australia and is absent from only the north-west of the continent. It is more numerous in dry than damp country, and the drier its habitat the richer its colours. The lizard is very active and hard to catch by hand. Its preferred temperature range is between 30° and 40°C/86° – 104°F; it hardly moves at all when the temperature is outside this range. It differs from lizards generally, in that its bulky body and its habit of basking allows it to store heat, so that it can operate at lower temperatures, where other lizards are likely to be inactive. Conversely, it can survive higher temperatures for several hours, where other lizards might get heat-stroke, because it can regulate its body temperature by evaporation and because its rate of water-loss is low. Both with lower tempera-

tures and higher, however, the margin is very small, and the lizard's behaviour is also adapted to keeping it comfortable.

To bask, it climbs onto a tree trunk, stump or termite mound, and flattens itself out in the sun, staying like this for several hours.

When cornered, or when facing a rival in dispute over territory, the bearded lizard goes into an aggressive display. It expands its body by raising its ribs, erects its beard by distending the jaw pouch, opens its mouth to show the golden yellow to yellowish-green inside of the mouth and tongue, and hisses like a snake. This is more a warning display since the lizard rarely bites. More often, it will attempt concealment by remaining still and changing colour.

Insectivorous feeder

Its food is mainly insects, supplemented with small lizards and snakes and some vegetation, especially ground blossoms.

Male bearded lizard's spiny throat pouch is blown up during the courtship display. He stretches his beard to its fullest extent and the female lizard is further impressed when the male opens his mouth to show its bright yellow inside.

Bearded lizard's threatening display used when cornered by an enemy or when disputing territory with a rival. He expands his body by raising the ribs, erects his beard by distending the jaw pouch and opens his mouth to show its bright yellow inside. He rarely bites, however.

Elaborate courtship

Breeding involves an elaborate courtship. The female develops a red patch at the base of her tail, the male shows a green patch in the same place. But he goes black on the underside, from belly to throat, whereas his back shows bright colours, mottled grey, yellow and bright green. The male also blows out his body and opens his mouth from time to time, showing the yellow interior. He stamps with his fore-feet, making a surprisingly loud sound, jerks his head up and down and stretches his beard to the full. Then he runs round in front of the female and positions himself at right angles, about 2 ft in front of her. Repetition of these actions, with variations, may continue for some time before mating occurs.

The female, after mating, scoops a hole in the ground and buries herself in it. After laying 8–24 eggs connected by a membrane, she comes out of the hole and carefully covers them with sand. The young hatch 3 months later.

Sprinting to keep cool

When the surrounding air warms up we keep cool by sweating. That is, we automatically control our body temperature. We can keep cool also by the things we do, such as removing clothing or stretching out full-length. This is behavioural control. Cold-blooded animals must rely almost wholly on behavioural controls. They have

no sweat glands, and few other physiological means of controlling temperature. The various lizards related to the bearded lizard have been closely studied to see what they do during the day, from sunrise to sunset. Each species differs slightly in its daily activities, but there is an overall pattern, and this follows a regular daily routine.

When the sun rises, the air is cool, so the lizard turns its back to the sun and exposes as much of its body surface to the warming rays as possible by flattening itself. As the surrounding air warms up, and also the lizard's body, the animal becomes active, mainly in hunting food. Meanwhile the sun gets higher and both air and ground heat up. When the temperature reaches a certain limit, 40°C/104°F in the case of the bearded lizard, the animal seeks shade, under a rock or bush, or in a burrow underground.

As the day wears on the air begins to cool, but the ground has warmed up and is holding its heat. The lizard, now emerged from its retreat, turns its head towards the sun, to take in the minimum heat from it, raises its tail to keep it off the hot ground and stands up on its legs with only the toes of the fore-feet and the heels of the hind-feet touching the scorching earth. Finally, at the end of the day, as both air and ground cool off and the sun is beginning to set, the lizard basks again, climbing onto some high point, turning its back full into the sun to make full use of any warmth reaching it

from the weakened rays.

Obviously, this is a brief sketch of events, and such an orderly account of the daily routine is somewhat idealized. There must be interruptions to it, as when an enemy draws near. Then, the bearded lizard and its relatives may make their escape by rising on their hind-legs and running bipedally. This looks as if they are trying to make a faster speed. But we know that a quadruped is usually faster than a biped.

It seems now that they do this only when the air temperatures are high. The reason why the Australian desert lizards run on their hind-legs is, therefore, largely a matter of temperature control. They are lifting their bodies up from the hot ground, so counter-balancing the heat they generate in running, by reducing the amount of heat they would otherwise take in from the ground and by increasing the cooling airflow over the bodies. Perhaps this was one factor which led to the evolution of birds from bipedal running lizards of the Jurassic, about 200 million years ago.

class	**Reptilia**
order	**Squamata**
suborder	**Sauria**
family	**Agamidae**
genus & species	***Amphibolurus barbatus***

Chameleon

The chameleons are a family of lizards renowned for several unusual features. The body is high in proportion to the length and is flattened from side to side. The tail in most species is prehensile, is often held in a tight coil, and can be wrapped round a twig for extra grip. The toes of each foot are joined, three on the inside of the front feet and on the outside of the hindfeet, resulting in feet like pairs of tongs that can give a tenacious grip on a perch. Above all, a chameleon is remembered for three things: its ability to change colour, its eyes set in turrets that can move independently of each other, and its highly extensible tongue which can be shot out at speed to a length greater than the chameleon's head and body. To add to their bizarre form, some species have rows of tubercles down the back or a 'helmet' or casque like the flap-necked chameleon or horns like Jackson's chameleon.

A few species grow to 2 ft long, while dwarf species measure less than 2 in.

There are about 80 species of chameleon most of which live in Africa south of the Sahara and including Madagascar. One species, the common chameleon, ranges from the Middle East along the coast of North Africa to southern Spain. Two others live in the southern end of the Arabian peninsula and a third in India and Sri Lanka.

Chameleons live in slow motion

Chameleons live mainly in forests, and seem to spend most of their time virtually rooted to the spot, the only movement being of the eyes, each independently sweeping from side to side searching for food or danger. When they move they creep slowly along a twig. Sloth-like, a fore foot is released on one side and the hind foot on the other, and both are slowly moved forward to renew their grip on the twig while, equally stealthily, the other two advance. Although most chameleons keep to the trees as much as possible, the stump-tailed chameleons can often be found on the ground.

Periodically chameleons shed their skins. Before it comes off the old skin comes away from the new skin under it, leaving an air-filled gap that gives the chameleon a pale, translucent appearance as if it were neatly wrapped in polythene. Then the old skin splits, first just behind the head, and chunks of it flake off exposing the brilliant new skin.

Extensible tongue

Chameleons eat the usual food of small reptiles, that is, insects and other small invertebrates, but the larger species will also catch small birds, lizards and mammals. The similarity with other reptiles ends here, for the method of capture is unique except in frogs and toads. Chameleons capture their prey by shooting out their long tongue, trapping the victim on the tip and carrying it back to the mouth. The whole

△ *Portrait of* **Chamaeleo bitaeniatus** *taken on Mt Elgon, Kenya. It lives above 9 000 ft.*

◁ *A chameleon in the later stages of shedding its skin. A new skin has first grown under the old. Notice that it even sheds the skin on its eyelids.*

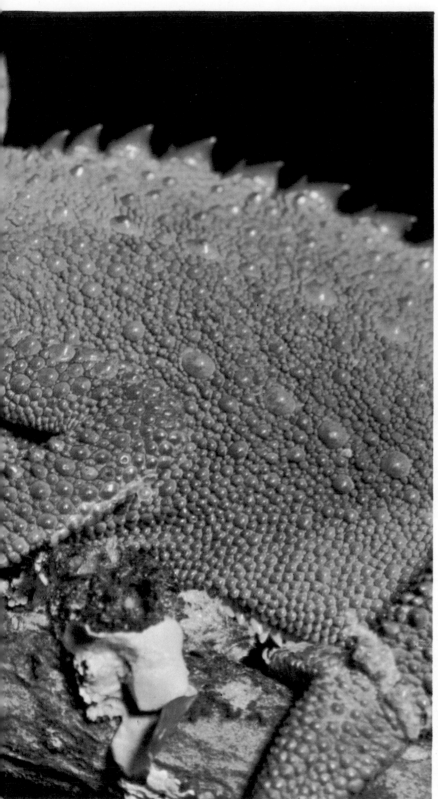

△ Stage one: lining up on the target with tongue protruding. Note the spider in the top right corner.
▽ Stage two: muscles shoot the tongue to its full extent.

▽ Stage three: muscles contract, withdrawing the tongue. Despite its speed, the spider was quicker!

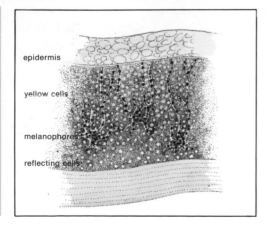

epidermis

yellow cells

melanophores

reflecting cells

◁ Simplified diagram of section through skin: colour change is mainly due to melanophores moving dark pigment into or out of upper layers.
▷ Catapult mechanism of the chameleon's tongue: special bone with its own muscles pushes tongue forward and circular muscles squeeze it out. Longitudinal muscles withdraw the tongue.

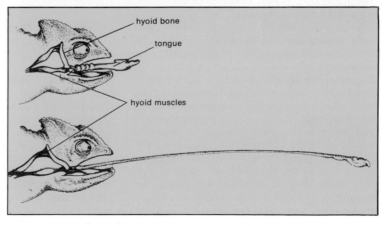

hyoid bone

tongue

hyoid muscles

action is so rapid that high-speed photography is needed to show the mechanism at work. By using a ciné camera it has been found that a 5½ in. tongue can be extended in $\frac{1}{16}$ second and retracted in $\frac{1}{4}$ second. Without such aids all one sees is the chameleon watching its prey from its perch, or slowly edging towards it, for chameleons only take sitting prey. When in range it directs both eyes at its victim and rocks from side to side, improving its stereoscopic vision and range-finding capacity by looking at the target from different angles. While doing this the tip of the tongue protrudes from the mouth like a wad of chewing gum, then suddenly the insect disappears from its perch and is seen to be crushed in the chameleon's jaws. Young ones begin eating insects when a day old, and with a little practice become expert.

How the chameleon shoots out its tongue has been deduced by a careful study of its anatomy. Two mechanisms throw the tongue forward, both of them activated by powerful muscles. At the back of the jaw lies a V-shaped bone with the point of the V pointing backwards. Attached to this bone by a flexible joint is the tongue bone, over which the tongue fits like a glove on a finger. When the chameleon is about to shoot the V-bone is moved forward slightly to push the tip of the tongue out of the mouth. Then, the circular muscles in the thick tip of the tongue contract violently so that the tongue is forced out in the same way as an orange pip squeezed between the fingers, and simultaneously the V-bone is thrust further forward, giving added impetus.

The end of the tongue is sticky with saliva but an insect can settle on a chameleon's head and walk across its protruding tongue with no difficulty. On the other hand some people who have kept chameleons as pets report that the end of the tongue does feel adhesive, but this may be due to the minute hooks or hairs or other roughenings of its surface. Finally, there are photographs that show the tongue apparently grasping an insect. It may be that a combination of all three may be operating as in toads.

Breeding poses problems

Male chameleons hold territories which they guard against other males, keeping them out by bluff. The lungs of chameleons have branches spreading through the body and by inflating its lungs a chameleon can blow itself to a most impressive size. Females, of course, are allowed to enter the territories and the males chase after them and mate with them, unless dissuaded by a female already pregnant.

Some chameleons lay eggs, others bear their young alive. The former course has some disadvantages for chameleons lay up to 50 eggs in a clutch, each has a diameter of perhaps ½ in. Places to hide such a large clutch must be rare in a tree and the chameleon, who is bulky and ungainly when carrying her eggs, has to climb down the tree and dig a hole in the ground. A common South African chameleon has been described as digging the hole with her head and front feet, pushing the loose soil away with her hind feet. It takes a long time but eventually she has a hole nearly the length of the body. She then backs into it and lays

Independently-swivelling eyes and palsied gait.

her eggs, pressing each one into place with her hind legs. When she has finished she fills in the hole, tamps it down, camouflages it with sticks and pieces of grass and leaves it. In due course the young hatch out and fight their way to the surface.

Other chameleons bear their young alive. Before the birth the female's body becomes greatly distended. The young are born in a translucent membrane. As each one is due the mother presses her cloaca against the twig on which she is perching and the membrane sticks to it. After a short interval the baby chameleon struggles out and walks off down the twig. The mother takes no more interest in her offspring, except that, if she is very hungry, she may eat them. The young start to feed when a day old, and with a little practice become expert at catching insects.

Quick colour change

Although other reptiles, as well as many fish and squid, can change colour, it is the chameleon that is renowned as a quick change artist. This is epitomised by the story of the chameleon put on a red cloth that changed to red, then when put on a green cloth turned to green, but had an apoplectic stroke when placed on a Scottish tartan. This greatly exaggerates the chameleon's power of colour change. The truth is that most species of chameleon have a basic colour and pattern that suits their particular habitat and do not really change colour to resemble the background but in response to

light intensity, temperature, or emotional state. Thus, colour change serves two purposes: to camouflage the chameleon and to act as a signal telling other chameleons its mood. An angry chameleon, for instance, goes black with rage. How the colour change is controlled is still not properly known. There is evidence for control by nerves and also by the secretion from the brain of chemicals which act on the colour cells; probably both act in different circumstances.

What is better known is the mechanics of colour change. The specialised colour cells lie under the transparent skin in four layers. The outermost is made up of xanthophores or yellow-bearers, together with erythrophores, the red-bearers. Under this layer are two reflecting layers, one reflecting blue light, the other white light. Beneath is the most important, and most complicated, layer of melanophores. These contain a dark brown pigment called melanin, the same substance that colours human skin brown or black. The main body of each melanophore lies under the reflecting layers but it sends tentacle-like arms up through the other layers.

To alter the colour of the skin, the colour cells alter in size, so that by variation of the amounts of yellow, red and dark brown, different colours are produced by mixing. The reflecting layers modify these effects. When the blue layer is under yellow cells, green is produced and where the blue layer is missing, light reflected from the white layer enhances the yellow or red coloration. The melanophores control the shading of the colours. When the colours are bright all the melanin is concentrated in the bodies of the melanophores. If the melanin spreads along the 'tentacles' to obscure the white layer, greens and reds become darker and if the melanin is dispersed completely, the chameleon becomes dark brown.

class	**Reptilia**
order	**Squamata**
suborder	**Sauria**
family	**Chamaeleontidae**
genera & species	***Chamaeleo chamaeleon*** common chameleon
	C. dilepis *flap necked chameleon* ***C. oweni*** *three horned chameleon* ***C. jacksoni*** *Jackson's chameleon* ***Brookesia spp.*** *stump tailed chameleons others*

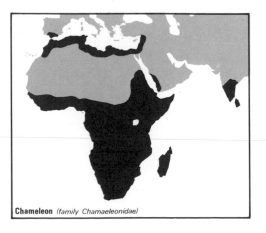
Chameleon *(family Chamaeleonidae)*

Earless monitor

Earless monitors are flesh-eating lizards, and up to 1961 less than 10 had been found, all in Sarawak. These had been enough to show that the lizard is sufficiently unusual to be of great interest to zoologists, although to the non-specialist it is undistinguished in appearance. It was not considered a true monitor and was placed in a family of its own. It even seemed to have some affinities with snakes.

Because of this interest and because so few had been found, the Sarawak Museum offered a reward of $50—2 weeks' wages for an unskilled labourer—but no earless monitors turned up until January 1961, when someone found one while hoeing his garden. It was 13 in. long, probably about average size, the largest ever found being about 17 in. Its legs were small and the body was brown and covered with pimples or nodules. Other features of the earless monitor, which are shared by various other lizards, are the forked tongue that can be flicked in and out like that of a snake and the transparent lower eyelid. The earless monitor is so called because the ears cannot be seen from the outside; in other words, the eardrums are covered.

Rare because it hides

Since a Sarawak gardener found a specimen while hoeing, at least 25 more earless monitors have been collected, all from the flat coastal plains of Sarawak, and some have been kept in captivity so their behaviour has been studied. The first to be collected lived for 3 months in captivity, but several times during that period it worried its captors by giving every appearance of being dead. It would spend several hours at a time, flopped down and breathing very slowly, but if touched it would react by flattening its body against the ground or twisting and moving away.

Further observations showed that earless monitors are active only at night, usually after midnight. Like other short-legged lizards, such as skinks, the earless monitors move like snakes, with a side-to-side swimming movement. The animal sometimes moves by pushing with its hindlimbs, while the forelimbs are dragged passively or are used for scrambling over obstacles. Earless monitors also swim well, apparently preferring shallow water where they lie on the bottom. The longest recorded time underwater is 36 minutes.

Together with what could be seen when catching them, these observations give us some idea of the earless monitors' life in the wild. They have been caught either in fish traps or by being dug up. The original 1961 specimen was found 6 in. underground, and in captivity they have been seen burrowing, forcing their heads into crevices. So it seems that earless monitors are nocturnal, living underground but coming to the surface where they apparently make for water. They seem to be able to go for a long time without food, perhaps because

of their ability to relax so completely, so they probably spend long periods underground. As they surface at night it is not surprising that so few have ever been found and that they are unknown to the local peoples. If this were not enough, their rough, brown skin makes them very easy to overlook.

As they live in flat, readily flooded areas, it may be that they deliberately wait for floods before coming out, or at least get washed out during floods. In January 1963, for instance, during serious floods, a dozen specimens were collected from one small river.

Before earless monitors became so relatively well known it was thought that they may have been venomous. This was largely because at one time they were thought to be related to the venomous Gila monsters. Captive specimens, however, have shown no inclination to bite when handled, and close examination shows no sign of poison apparatus.

Egg-suckers

In captivity the only food earless monitors have taken has been turtle or chicken eggs. They nibble and suck the yolk with the mouth hardly opened, so presumably do not eat large or hard food items in the wild.

A missing link?

The reason for the great interest in earless monitors is that they appear to be a missing link. Before 1961 an eminent authority on reptiles suggested that to see an earless monitor alive would be the fulfilment of a dream. In the event they seem to be remarkably uninspiring, but to the anatomist, they are of great importance.

After the first specimen had been described in 1878 the earless monitor was classed sometimes with the monitors and sometimes with the Gila monsters. Now it seems that it is also related closely to some extinct lizards and may be a link between the snakes and the lizards.

It has always been presumed that the snakes arose from lizards that gradually lost their legs. This is a trait that has developed in several types of lizard such as amphisbaenids and slowworms, although these lizards are not related to snakes. The lizards previously reckoned to be fairly closely related to snakes were the monitors, although they are not directly linked. The earless monitor now seems to be a more likely candidate, for it shares several features with snakes, and has fewer of the special features that separate other lizards from them. Among these characters are similarities of teeth and skull, the absence of the external ear and the long, forked tongue in which the forked end retracts into the root. The transparent lower eyelid may be the forerunner of the 'clear spectacle' covering a snake's eye.

class	**Reptilia**
order	**Squamata**
suborder	**Sauria**
family	**Lanthanotidae**
genus & species	***Lanthanotus borneensis***

Sluggish and dull-coloured, the earless monitor is not an exciting-looking animal—but it may well be a missing link, for no other lizard has so many of the features shared by snakes.

Fence lizard

The commonest lizard in the United States, it is also called swift lizard, pine lizard, eastern fence lizard, and common fence lizard. Often seen sunning itself on fences or fallen trees, it lives especially in pinewoods and is noted for its speed in fleeing when disturbed.

The fence lizard may measure nearly 10 in. of which one third is tail, but is commonly less than this. The males are bark-coloured, with grey wavy dark bands across the back. The females are more variable in colour, brownish grey to greenish. Although it looks and behaves like a true lizard (family Lacertidae) the fence lizard is an iguana (family Iguanidae) and belongs to the group known as spiny lizards. Its scales are keeled and pointed and the skin of its head is roughened and wrinkled. Its legs are slightly bowed. From the state of Maine in the northeast it ranges across the United States southwards to Florida and westwards to about Colorado, and thence southwards into Mexico.

Colours that come and go

Like most other lizards, the fence lizard spends much of its time basking. When not basking it is hunting or lying up in a crack or crevice, especially under logs. The males hold territories which are vigorously defended against other males. This territorial fighting includes showing the male markings, a longitudinal stripe of cobalt blue on either side of the belly. This is visible only when a male rises high on its legs and flattens its body from side to side. These are the preliminaries to the aggressive display which are supplemented by inflating the dewlap and bobbing up and down as two males face each other. Size is important in these encounters and the function of the cobalt blue stripes is best illustrated by saying that when these are experimentally painted over, a male is treated as a female by other fence lizards.

Other colour changes are linked with temperature and light. At low temperatures the fence lizard is dark, at high temperatures it becomes light. It darkens in bright light and becomes pale in darkness. The changes are due to microscopic grains of the black pigment, melanin. These are contained in chromatophores or pigment-carrying cells that can expand and contract to some extent. When fully expanded they send out long finger-shaped processes. This is a general description of chromatophores, which cause fluctuating colour changes in reptiles, fishes, some crustaceans and others. In the fence lizard the skin appears dark when the melanin grains are spread out, pallid when they are withdrawn and concentrated at the centres of the chromatophores.

Insectivores

The food is insects, especially the grubs of wood-boring beetles, but others such as grasshoppers are also taken. An interesting aside to the matter of feeding is the way

temperature affects it. A related species *Sceloporus magister*, it has been found, feeds most at a temperature of 30°C/83°F. This is one of the reasons why, in the northern parts of its range, the fence lizard must hibernate—the weather is too cold for it to be active in winter.

Hibernation brings another advantage. In Florida, where it is active throughout the year, the fence lizard never lives longer than 2 years. In fact, less than 6% survive for one year. In the northeastern United States, when it hibernates for about half the year, the lifespan is 4—8 years.

Vulnerable infancy

Breeding comes in springtime. A short while after mating, the female digs a hole in the ground and lays in it a dozen white, oval eggs, each ½ in. long, with a very thin shell. The eggs hatch 6—10 weeks later, the baby lizards being 2 in. long. They feed on very small insects. This infancy is a vulnerable stage when the lizards are picked up by different species of birds, and this continues as the lizards grow, with other lizard-eating animals. If the list were given in full it would include almost every animal in the fence lizard's range that lives wholly or partially on flesh.

Social hierarchy

The fighting between males is of importance in the species. It leads, in fence lizards and others, to a social hierarchy. Within a given area, there is a boss or dominant male, with others of increasingly subordinate rank, in which No 2 bosses all but No 1, and No 3 bosses all but No 1—2.

The individual may be endangered by the fighting, and as soon as his vigour begins to wane he is ousted from his dominating position, and so debarred from breeding. In general, however, it is the most virile and healthy male that mates with the majority of the females. This has little to do with the old idea of the survival of the fittest. It merely helps to ensure that the general level of vigour and health in a population does not suffer. The hierarchy is also a means whereby the individuals of a population are kept well spaced out, thus keeping to a minimum the ill effects of overcrowding.

class	**Reptilia**
order	**Squamata**
suborder	**Sauria**
family	**Iguanidae**
genus & species	***Sceloporus undulatus***

Fence lizard *(Sceloporus undulatus)*

△ *The egg-tooth breaks the leathery shell.*
▽ *A short rest, a wriggle, and the head is free.*

▽ *At the most difficult stage: after a long struggle, the baby forces out its front legs.*

▽ *Many frantic wriggles and rests later, a 2in. sand lizard faces the world: an adult replica.*

△ *Female above and male below, a fence lizard duo basks in the sun, showing distinctive colours.*

▽ *Living up to its name: a fence lizard rests on a fencepost, speculatively eyeing a mobile morsel wandering unawares round its perch. As well as spiders, it will eat insects and their grubs.*

△ *Defiance: a cornered lizard unfurls its frill.*

Frilled lizard

One of the so-called dragons of Australia, the frilled lizard grows to about 3 ft long, with a slender body and long tail. It is pale brown, either uniformly coloured or with patches of yellow and darker brown. Its most conspicuous feature is the frill around the throat, like the ruff fashionable in Europe in the Middle Ages.

Apart from its size the only remarkable thing about this lizard is its frill. Normally this lies folded over the shoulders like a cape. It is a large area of skin supported by cartilaginous rods from the tongue bone which act like the ribs of an umbrella. In moments of excitement, muscles pulling on these raise the frill to 8 in. or more across, about as wide as the length of the head and body together.

It lives mainly in sandy semi-dry areas of northern and northeastern Australia.

Hindleg sprinter

The frilled lizard lives in rough-barked trees, coming to the ground after rainstorms, to feed. When disturbed on the ground it runs on its hindlegs with the frill laid back over the shoulders, tail raised, and the forelegs held close into the body. It may sprint for a considerable distance, or it may seek safety by climbing a tree. When brought to bay it turns, opens its mouth wide and extends its frill. The best description of what happens next is given by Harry Frauca in *The Book of Australian Wild Life.* It does not raise its tail, as it has often been reported to do, and as some other similar lizards are known to do, but keeps it flat on the ground. It sways from side to side and with its open mouth, coloured dark blue inside edged by pinkish yellow, surrounded by the greenish-yellow frill splashed with red, brown, white and black, it looks like a large flower among broad leaves. The colours of the lizard vary from one region to another. In Queensland the general colour is a sombre grey, in the Northern Territory it is pinkish, often with a black chest and throat. The colours of the mouth and frill also vary.

The open mouth and spread frill are a warning display. If the warning is ignored it passes to an aggressive display. The lizard steps boldly towards the intruder, keeping its mouth open and frill fully extended, and from the mouth comes a low hiss. The remarkable thing is that people who know very well the lizard can do nothing to harm them, tend nevertheless to be intimidated by all this show. Even a dog used to attacking larger lizards will retreat before it.

Meals of ants and eggs

The frilled lizard eats insects, including large quantities of ants, as well as spiders and small mammals. It is also said to be an egg thief. One of the many difficulties found in keeping this animal in captivity is that of getting enough of the right kind of food. In 1893, when the time it took to travel from Australia to Great Britain was much longer than it is today, the naturalist W Saville Kent brought a frilled lizard to London, the first to reach Europe alive. When it was exhibited before an audience of learned gentlemen one eminent zoologist is said to have followed it, in his excitement, on hands and knees, to watch it careering round on its hind legs and displaying its frill. Unfortunately, there is no record of how Saville Kent managed to feed his pet, but, like many reptiles, the frilled lizard can probably go without food for months.

Umbrella trick

Neither does history record whether any of the learned gentlemen noticed a comparison between the lizard and a lady. At that time ladies carried parasols and it was not uncommon for a lady, confronted by a cow as she crossed a field, to frighten the cow away by suddenly opening her parasol in its face. Konrad Lorenz, in *King Solomon's Ring,* tells how his wife kept geese from devastating her newly-planted flower beds. She carried a large scarlet umbrella and this she would suddenly unfold at the geese, with a jerk, causing the geese to take to the air with a thundering of wings. It is almost instinctive for a woman carrying an umbrella to use it in this way against a powerful and persistent opponent. It is a matter of no small interest to find that this same effective defence should have been evolved by a lizard.

class	**Reptilia**
order	**Squamata**
suborder	**Sauria**
family	**Agamidae**
genus & species	***Chlamydosaurus kingii***

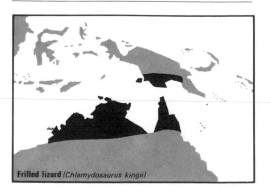

Frilled lizard *(Chlamydosaurus kingii)*

168

Gecko

Geckos form a family of lizards noted for the large number of species, the structure of their feet, their voices, the differences in the shape of their tails, and for the ease with which some of them will live in houses. The smallest is 1⅓ in. long; the largest—the tokay—may be 14 in. long.

Geckos are found in all warm countries: 41 species in Africa, 50 in Madagascar, about 50 in Australia, the same in the West Indies, with others in southern and southeast Asia, Indonesia, the Pacific islands and New Zealand, and South America. There are geckos in the desert regions of Mexico and southern California. Several have been introduced into Florida from the Caribbean islands. Spain and Dalmatia, in southern Europe, have the same wall gecko as North Africa.

A liking for houses

The majority of geckos live in trees, some live among rocks, others live on the sandy ground of deserts. Tree geckos find in human habitations conditions similar to, or better than, those of their natural habitat: natural crevices in which to rest or take refuge and plenty of insects, especially at night when insects are attracted to lights. Because geckos can cling to walls or hang upside-down from ceilings they can take full advantage of these common insect resting places, and so many of them are now known as house geckos.

Hooked to the ceiling

Most geckos can cling to smooth surfaces. Their toes may be broad or expanded at the tips with flaps of skin (lamellae) arranged transversely or fanwise. The undersides of the toes bear pads furnished with numerous microscopic hook-like bristles that catch in slight irregularities, even in the surface of glass, or have bristles ending in minute suckers. So a gecko can cling to all but the most highly polished surfaces. The hooks are directed backwards and downwards and to disengage them the toe must be lifted upwards from the tip. As a result, a gecko running up a tree or a wall or along a ceiling must curl and uncurl its toes at each step with a speed faster than the eye can follow. Some of the hooks are so small the high power of a microscope is needed to see them, yet a single toe armed with numbers of these incredibly small hooks can support several times the weight of a gecko's body. In addition to the bristles, most species have the usual claw at the tip of the toe which also can be used in clinging. In one species there are microscopic hooks on the tip of the tail which enable the animal to cling.

△ *Close pursuit. As firm as the flies it is hunting, a diurnal gecko* **Phelsuma vinsoni** *pauses on a vertical tree-trunk, unaware of the apparent impossibility of its position.*
▷ *Living crampons. Geckos get a grip from tiny hooks in the flaps of skin on their feet.*
▷▷ *After partial loss, regrowth and healing, the result is a three-tailed gecko.*

Leaf-like tail
The tail is long and tapering, rounded or slightly flattened and fringed with scales, according to the species, or it may be flattened and leaf-like. A South American gecko has a swollen turnip-shaped tail. It has been named *Thecadactylus rapicaudus* (*rapi* for turnip, *caudus* for tail). The flying gecko of southeast Asia has a leaf-like tail, a wide flap of skin along each flank, a narrow flap along each side of the head and flaps along the hind margins of the limbs. Should the gecko fall it spreads its limbs, the flaps spread and the reptile parachutes safely down.

Geckos can throw off their tails, like the more familiar lizards, and grow new ones. In some species 40% have re-grown tails.

Sometimes the tail is incompletely thrown and hangs by a strip of skin. As a new tail grows the old one heals and a 2-tailed gecko results. Even 3-tailed geckos have been seen. Temperature is important in growing a new tail. It has been found that when the wall gecko of southern Europe and North Africa grows a new tail with the air temperature at 28°C/82°F it is short and covered with large overlapping scales. With the temperature around 35°C/95°F the new tail is long and is covered with small scales.

Cat-like eyes
One difference between snakes and lizards is that the former have no eyelids. In most geckos the eyelids are permanently joined and there is a transparent window in the

△ *Pinhole sight: pupils shrunk to four tiny holes, to keep out excessive glare of the sun.*

lower lid. The few geckos that are active by day have rounded pupils to the eyes. The rest are active by night and have vertical slit-pupils like cats. In some species the sides of the pupils are lobed or notched in four places, and when the pupils contract they leave four apertures, the size of pinholes each one of which will focus the image onto the retina.

Surprisingly small clutches
All geckos except for a few species in New Zealand, which bear live young, lay eggs with a tough white shell. Usually there

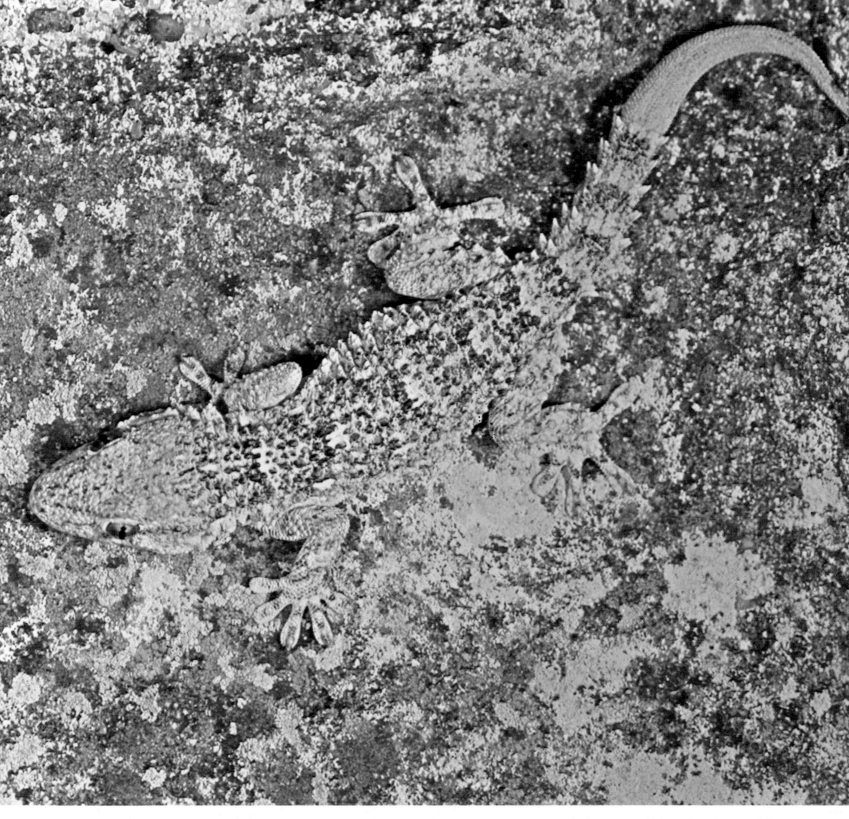

are two in a clutch, sometimes only one. The eggs are laid under bark or under stones and take several months to hatch.

Harmless creatures

Geckos eat only insects. They are harmless and wholly beneficial to man, yet among the people of Africa, South America, Malaysia and the aboriginals of Australia there are widespread beliefs that their bite makes them dangerous to handle. Possibly such beliefs spring from some of the more remarkable species, like the gecko that stalks insects as a cat does a mouse, even lashing its tail from side to side just before the final pounce. Then there are the web-footed geckos living on the sand dunes of Southwest Africa. They not only use the webbed feet

to run over loose sand but also to burrow. They scrape the sand away with the forefoot of one side and shovel it back with the hindfoot of the same side while balancing on the feet of the other side. Then they change over. They walk with the body raised high and the tail held up and arched.

One web-footed gecko has a delicate beauty. It is pinkish-brown with a lemon yellow stripe along its flank. Its eye has brilliant yellow lids, the iris is black, patterned with gold and coppery tints, while the edges of the vertical pupil are chalky white. Its skin is so transparent the spine and some internal organs can be seen clearly. In *African Wild Life*, GK Brain claims its two ear openings are almost in direct connection; by looking into one earhole light coming in

△ *A regrown tail shows that, despite excellent camouflage, only desperate measures saved this gecko's life.*

through the other can be seen.

class	**Reptilia**
order	**Squamata**
suborder	**Sauria**
family	**Gekkonidae**
genus & species	*Gekko gecko* *others*

171

△ *Massive-headed, belly-dragging, obese and ugly, the Gila monster is among the more repulsive of reptiles and one of the only two poisonous lizards. Surprisingly, many people have kept it as a pet; enough, in fact, to have made it rare. It is now protected by law to save it from extinction.*

Gila monster

Only two out of about 3 000 kinds of lizards are poisonous: the Gila monster (pronounced 'heela') and the beaded lizard. They look alike and live in deserts of the southwestern United States and adjacent parts of Mexico respectively. The first is named for the Gila basin in Arizona where it is plentiful, the second after the beaded nature of its scales.

The Gila monster is up to 23 in. long and weighs up to 3¼ lb. It is mainly pink and yellow with black shading. The beaded lizard, up to 32 in. long, is mainly black with pink and yellow patches. The Gila monster has 4–5 dark bands on the tail. The beaded lizard has 6–7 yellow bands. Both have a stout body, large blunt head, powerful lower jaw, small eyes, an unusually thick tail, short legs with 5 toes on each and remarkably strong claws.

Alternate gluttony and fasting

These lizards move about very slowly, although when captured they can move swiftly and struggle actively, hissing all the while. They spend long periods of time in their burrows in the sand, coming out at the rainy season and even then mainly at night. Being slow movers they must eat things that cannot run away. These are mainly eggs of birds and other reptiles, baby birds and baby mice and rats. They track them down partly by smell but more especially by taste, using the tongue to pick up scent particles on the sand from birds' nests or rodents' burrows. These are conveyed by the tongue to Jacobson's organ, a sort of taste-smell organ in the roof of the mouth. They eat insects and earthworms in captivity and from the behaviour of these captive animals it seems unlikely that venom is used to kill prey. Eggs are either seized, the head raised and the shell crushed so the contents flow into the mouth, or bitten in two and the tongue used to lap up the contents as the shell lies on the ground. The Gila monster drinks liquid food by lapping it up and holding its head back to let the liquid run down its tongue.

While active these lizards eat all they can find and store the surplus as fat in the body and especially in the tail. When well-fed their skeleton represents a small part of the total weight of the body and the lizards can then survive long periods of fasting. The fat tail will shrink to a fifth of its former girth, the rest of the body being little more than skin and bone. The lizard will quickly recover once it can find food. One that had survived three years drought, during which it took no food, was taken into captivity and in 6 months its tail had doubled in size and the body was as plump as usual.

Inefficient venom apparatus

The venom glands are in the lower jaw although teeth in both jaws are grooved. Each gland has several ducts that open into a groove between the lower lip and the gum, and the poison finds its way from this to the grooves in the teeth. Neither of the lizards can strike as a snake does but must hold with the teeth and hang on with a vice-like grip sometimes chewing to help conduct the venom. If bitten by a monster, the main problem is to free the tight-gripping jaws.

Nests in the sand

Mating takes place in July and eggs are laid a few weeks later. These are laid in a hole dug by the female with her front feet and covered with sand. There may be 3–15 in a clutch, each egg about 1½ by 2½ in. and oval, with a tough leathery shell. They hatch in about a month, the young lizards being 3½–4¾ in. long, and more vivid in colour than the parents.

Legally protected monster

Little is known of the natural enemies of the two poisonous lizards but by 1952 the Gila monster was becoming so rare it had to be protected by law to save it from extinction. It was being caught and sold in large numbers as a pet. Those who caught them were paid 25–50 cents an inch, and the lizards were then sold at 1–2 dollars an inch.

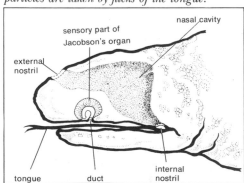

▽ *Section through Gila monster's head, showing Jacobson's organ in the roof of the mouth. This is specialised for taste and smell; scents are carried to it through the external nostrils (visible in both the pictures above), and particles are taken by flicks of the tongue.*

Diagram labels: nasal cavity; sensory part of Jacobson's organ; external nostril; tongue; duct; internal nostril

Map legend: **Gila monster** *(Heloderma suspectum)*; **Beaded lizard** *(H. horridum)*

Lizard with a bad name

In striking contrast with the popularity of the Gila monster as a pet are many erroneous beliefs that have gathered around it in the past. One is that it cannot eliminate body wastes, which is why it is so poisonous. For the same reason its breath is evil-smelling. Another is that it can spit venom, whereas at most, when hissing, it may spray a little venom. The lizard has been credited also with leaping on its victims, largely the result perhaps of the way it will lash out from side to side when held in the hand. Its tongue has been said to be poisonous, the lizard itself impossible to kill and possessed of magical powers. Lastly, it has been said to be a cross between a lizard and a crocodile.

More than 400 years ago, a Spaniard, Francisco Hernández, wrote that the bite of the lizard though harmful was not fatal, that it threatened no harm except when provoked and that its appearance was more to be dreaded than its bite. Although his writings had been overlooked the first scientists to study it seem to have taken much the same view when they named it *Heloderma suspectum*, because they were not sure whether it was poisonous, only suspected of being so. They were more certain about the beaded lizard which they named *H. horridum*. Now we know that the poison is a neurotoxin which causes swelling, loss of consciousness, vomiting, palpitations, laboured breathing, dizziness, a swollen tongue and swollen glands. Not all these symptoms appear in one person, however. The swelling and the

△ *Using tongue and 'nose' a Gila monster tests its surroundings.*

initial pain are due to the way the poison is injected. The lizard must hold on and chew with a sideways action of the teeth.

In 1956 Charles M Bogert and Rafael Martin del Campo published in America the results of their thoroughgoing investigation into the injuries suffered by human beings from the bite of the Gila monster. They found only 34 known cases of which 8 were said to have been fatal. Most of those who had died were either in poor health at the time or drunk. In several instances there were signs of repeated biting, as in the case of the man who carried the lizard inside his shirt, next to his skin. This may explain the drunks who fell victim. They teased the lizards in zoos and probably did not realise they were being repeatedly bitten.

class	**Reptilia**
order	**Squamata**
suborder	**Sauria**
family	**Helodermatidae**
genus & species	***Heloderma horridum*** beaded lizard ***H. suspectum*** *Gila monster*

Glass snake

Glass 'snakes' are, in fact, legless lizards that look like snakes. The Scheltopusik or Pallas' glass snake of southeast Europe and southwest Asia is nearly 4 ft long and about 2 in. across the body. It was first discovered by the naturalist Pallas on wooded slopes bordering the Volga. Since then it has been found as far west as Hungary and it is widespread throughout the Balkan peninsula. Another living in northeast India and Burma is 15 in. long and the glass snake of southern China is 2 ft long. There is another glass snake in Morocco and 3 others in North America, up to 3 ft long, ranging from Lake Michigan southwards through the eastern and southern states and into Mexico. One American species O. ventralis is brown, olive or black with green spots or stripes and greenish-white underneath.

Two-thirds of their length is made up of tail, whereas in snakes the tail makes up only a small fraction of the total length. Pallas' glass snake is bronze, yellow or chestnut-brown, often with tiny pale spots, and very old individuals are coppery-red. The glass snake of southern China has an
olive back and bright blue flanks. All glass snakes have a deep furrow running along each side of the body from the neck to the vent. There is no trace of the forelimbs and, in the European and North African species, there is a barely noticeable stump of a hindlimb at the rear end of the furrow.

Snake-like but not snakes

Glass snakes live in fields or copses, among heaps of stones or in bare rocky places. They avoid dense woods. They are not as agile as snakes but they can clamber over rocks easily. They do not climb trees, and they avoid water. Their habit is to hide under fallen leaves or burrow just beneath the surface where the soil is sandy and light. When they do come out they move over the ground like snakes but with a less graceful action. When chased they move with a rapid twisting of the body, stopping every 2—3 yards for a rest.

Glass snakes feed by day on insects, especially grasshoppers. They sometimes take mice, lizards, fledgling birds and the eggs of snakes and birds. Live prey is twisted rapidly round and round or beaten against the ground until stunned and then chewed with powerful jaws and swallowed whole. Glass snakes are said to eat snakes, including adders. When eating an egg they crack the shell with their jaws and ladle out the contents with their flat forked tongues. The American glass snake, also called glass lizard or joint snake, seems to spend more time burrowing than the European form. It has a similar diet but is said to eat earthworms as well as other underground animals.

The females lay their inch-long eggs under moss or dead leaves, 8—10 at a time. They take about a month to hatch, the female guarding them during that time in a half-hearted way. The newly-hatched glass snake is 5 in. long, ashen-grey with dark spots and bands along the back and dark vertical stripes on the sides of the head. They take several years to reach maturity and the glass snakes are said to live up to 60 years.

Two lines of defence

Little is known about the enemies of glass snakes. They would be likely to be taken by large birds of prey. They have, however, two lines of defence. Like other lizards they can shed their tails when attacked, and if held in the hand they twine round it in a most unpleasant manner, which would probably deter all but a large or a persistent predator.

Falling to bits

Glass snakes are named for their reputation of breaking into pieces when struck with a stick. The legend continues that the pieces later reassemble and that the lizard is none

△ *Brittle-tailed reptile: the 'glass' half of this animal's name is perhaps justified by the way its tail will fall off and break into several pieces in moments of alarm. 'Snake', however, does not apply; it is a legless lizard.*

▷ *Twisting sprinter—a European glass snake. Glass snakes do not move with the wriggling expertise of true snakes, especially when frightened; they use a twisting movement and have to stop for a rest every 2—3 yards.*

the worse for its adventure. As in other lizards the tail is shed in moments of alarm, but in glass snakes it also breaks into several pieces. Because the tail is so long, the body of a glass snake that has just cast its tail looks very small, little bigger than one of the portions of the shed tail, so it looks as if the whole animal is in pieces.

class	**Reptilia**
order	**Squamata**
suborder	**Sauria**
family	**Anguidae**
genus & species	***Ophisaurus apodus*** *European glass snake* ***O. ventralis*** *N. American glass snake* *others*

Green lizard

This is the second largest lizard in Europe; the male is 15 in. long, of which 10 in. is tail. Europe's largest lizard is the eyed lizard, 24 in. long of which 16 in. is tail, and there are records of 36 in. total length. The eyed lizard is often dark green spotted with yellow and black. There are blue spots forming rosettes on the flanks.

The head of the green lizard is large, its legs stout and the toes, especially on the hindfeet, long. The length of the toes is most marked in the males although the females are usually slightly larger than the males in total body size. The colour varies and while usually bright green in the male it may be yellowish-green or brown and yellow on the flanks of the female. Males are noticeably thick at the root of the tail.

Green lizards range across southern Europe from northern Spain and the south of France to southwest Russia and northwards to parts of Germany. They are also found in the Channel Islands, but attempts to acclimatize them a few degrees farther north, in southwest England, have failed.

Lovers of dampness

Green lizards live among rocks and on rough ground especially along the margins of woods, where the ground is not too dry. They are particularly found on river banks, but they may also occur in meadows, especially where there are damp ditches. They climb well and are reputed to be good swimmers and to take readily to water when disturbed and seek refuge on the bottom. They are active by day, hunting or basking, but seek the shade when the sun is hot. Hibernation is from October to March, in holes in the ground, under buttress roots of trees or under vegetation litter, the period of hibernation being shorter in the southern than in the northern parts of the range.

Shell-cracker jaws

Green lizards feed on insects, spiders, woodlice, earthworms and other small invertebrates but also eat smaller lizards and small rodents. They sometimes take birds' eggs, cracking the shells with their powerful jaws which can give a strong but non-venomous bite on the hand. They occasionally eat fruit.

Submissive females

The breeding season starts in late April and continues into May. The male's throat goes cobalt blue, and is used as a threat in the many contests that take place between males. He also uses the same intimidating displays towards females and it is the fact that she responds submissively, that is, she does not return his menacing attitude, which tells him she is a female. A short time after mating the female lays 5—21 dull white oval eggs, about ¾ in. long, in soft earth. She stays near her eggs and will come back to them even after being driven off. They hatch 2—3 months later, the newly-hatched young being 2—3½ in. long, brown with one or two rows of yellowish-white spots. They gradually turn

△ Green lizards fighting.
▽ The second largest lizard in Europe.

△ *A meal of a brimstone butterfly.*
▽ *A male in the mating season.*

green as they reach maturity. Green lizards may live for 10 years in captivity although their life in the wild is doubtless generally less than this.

Victims of pet-keepers

This lizard is attacked by the usual enemies of lizards, particularly the larger birds of prey, and it has the usual lizard defence of casting its tail and growing a new one. The chief danger to the green lizard, as with several other southern European reptiles, notably the Greek tortoise and the wall lizard, is their export for pet-keeping. Thousands each year find their way northwards to central and northern Europe to be kept in vivaria, to be used in laboratories, or to re-stock the many zoos.

Unsuccessful habitat

Some idea of the traffic in these attractive reptiles can be gained from the attempts to naturalize them in England. In 1899 an unspecified number of green lizards were liberated in the Isle of Wight and for a while they bred there. The last were seen in 1936. In 1931 some were introduced into Caernarvonshire, in North Wales. These did not breed and survived for only 4 years or so. In 1937, 100 green lizards were set free at Paignton, in south Devon. A few were still alive in 1952.

The wall lizard, a medium-sized European lizard, 8 in. long, was also introduced at Paignton in 1937, 200 being set free. They lasted only a few years, yet the wall lizard is a more northerly species than the green lizard, ranging from Jersey, in the Channel Isles, across Holland, Germany and Poland to the southern European mountain ranges.

South Devon is only a few degrees farther north than the Channel Islands, but it seems this is enough to make the difference between survival and extinction for the green lizard. Subtropical plants grow well in south Devon so, while temperature may be important, there must be other factors working against the lizards. An animal set down in a foreign environment must find suitable hiding places, suitable food and other necessities for successful living. Everything around is strange and, far more than for a plant, it is a gamble whether an animal will settle down. Nevertheless, we have the instances in which one group of green lizards survived in the Isle of Wight for at least 37 years and another group in South Devon continued for at least 15 years. The climate of the British Isles is said to be slowly getting warmer. It may well be that future attempts at acclimatization might prove more successful, provided there is then more sunshine than is usual now. Experience with captive green lizards shows that without sufficient sunlight they are prone to skin complaints that shorten their lives.

class	**Reptilia**
order	**Squamata**
suborder	**Sauria**
family	**Lacertidae**
genus & species	***Lacerta viridis*** *green lizard* ***L. lepida*** *eyed lizard*

*A horned toad **Phrynosoma coronatum** after a demonstration of its unsavoury but decidedly startling defence mechanism.*

Horned toad

The horned toad is not a toad as the name suggests but a lizard with the face of a toad. If it were larger it could be mistaken for a prehistoric reptile. As it is, its main claim to fame is its alleged ability to squirt blood out of its eyes.

It can measure up to 5 in. long, and has a squat, flattened, almost circular body, short legs and short tail. The head is ornamented with backwardly directed spines, the so-called horns, and the back is covered with smaller spines. Some have been called short-horned, because the head spines are not prominent, others are called long-horned. In both types the body is covered in small scales, as is usual in lizards, but there are larger thornlike scales as well. Usually the edges of the body are ornamented with large flat scales.

There are a dozen species of horned toads or horned lizards ranging from just over the Canadian border southwards through the western United States to Mexico. The most widely distributed is the Texas horned toad, from Nebraska in the north to Chihuahua and Sonora in Mexico.

Toad-like behaviour

These lizards live in deserts and semi-desert sandy country, from low-lying ground to 10 000 ft altitude. They drink dew and hunt insects, particularly ants. A horned toad moves slowly forward towards its prey and, when close enough, stops and bends its head slightly towards it. Then it shoots out a thick tongue and in a flash carries the insect back into its mouth. As the day wanes the horned toad buries itself in the warm sand. It pushes its blunt snout into the sand and by wriggling strenuously makes a fur-row in which it lies half buried, or with only the top of the head showing. As autumn approaches, the horned toad spends more and more time buried and in winter it buries itself deeper and goes into a torpid state.

Egg-layers and live-bearers

Most horned lizards are egg-layers. Between April and July the female digs a hole 6 in. deep in the sand. She does this with her forefeet, pushing the sand back with her hindfeet. She lays up to 30 yellowish-white, oval, tough-shelled eggs each ½ in. long, in the hole. These she covers with sand and leaves. The eggs hatch up to 90 days later, the time varying with the species. A few horned lizards bear live young, up to 30 at a time. These are from eggs that hatch just before being laid. The young measure 1¼ in. at hatching.

A dangerous mouthful

Horned toads have few enemies because of their armour and the camouflage effect of their colours. Snakes sometimes eat them and often pay for this with their lives since the horns of the lizard may penetrate the wall of the snake's gullet. They are also well camouflaged, for not only do the lizards bury themselves in the sand, but the mottled colours on their bodies tend to take on the colour or pattern of the sand or gravel on which they are living.

Blood-squirters

Horned toads are said to squirt blood from their eyes when alarmed. Yet there are many who have kept the lizards as pets or are used to seeing them around who say this is untrue. It is clear from all the evidence that they do this but in a curiously erratic way. Raymond L Ditmars, American specialist in the study of reptiles, and author of *The Book of Living Reptiles* (1936), handled several hundred horned toads before he saw one squirt blood from its eyes. Another American specialist, Winton, writing in 1914, tells how one of his students stooped to pick up a horned toad and received a splash of blood on his hand which spread in a fan-shaped smear from the second joint of the index finger to the wrist. Winton saw three toads do this. All were males and all were sloughing their skins at the time. In each, the eye from which the blood was ejected showed a small quantity of clotted blood in the back of the cornea, in which the blood vessels were swollen although the cornea itself remained intact. So it seems one person may handle three of the lizards and see the blood-letting three times, while another may handle hundreds over a period of years and never see it.

The usual explanation is that this action is defensive, and that the blood is an irritant to the eyes of small mammals. Another suggestion is that it may be connected with the breeding season, although nobody is very clear how. A third suggestion is that it may be due to a parasite, and a fourth is that it may be a secondary use acquired by relatively few individuals.

This habit is not unique, however, only particularly spectacular. It is like the 'blood-spitting' of the dwarf boas of the West Indies. And few authors, even specialist authors in books devoted to snakes, ever mention this.

class	**Reptilia**
order	**Squamata**
suborder	**Sauria**
family	**Iguanidae**
genus & species	***Phrynosoma douglassi*** **P. m'calli** *others*

Iguana

The iguana family contains lizards such as the anole, the basilisk, the horned toad and many others, some of which are called iguanas in everyday English. The marine iguana is discussed under a separate heading; here we are dealing with the green iguana, the ground iguana, the land iguanas and the desert iguana or crested lizard.

The ground iguana is one of the most primitive members of the family. It has a crest like the teeth in a comb running down its back starting behind the head and petering out in the middle of the heavy tail.

One kind, the rhinoceros iguana, has two or three hornlike scales on its head and a large swelling on either side of the chin. Ground iguanas reach a length of 4 ft, 2 ft shorter than the green iguana which has been introduced to the Virgin Isles and the Lesser Antilles where it has driven out the ground iguana. The native home of the green iguana is Central and northern South America. It is pale green in colour, has a crest similar to that of the ground iguana and an erectable sac under the throat. The males are larger than the females, their crests are longer and their bodies are more orange or yellow compared with the females' light green. The males

△ Flowers on the menu: although it eats mainly insects when young, this green iguana seems to be interested in the more adult diet of tender young buds. They often clamber in trees.

also have a row of pores on the underside of each thigh, whose function is unknown.

The desert iguana lives in the deserts of North America. It measures 1 ft and is cream coloured with brown or black lines and spots. The land iguana of the Gala-pagos islands grows up to 5 ft. It is yellow with brown spots on the sides and legs.

High diver

The green iguana is an agile climber and adults are rarely found far from the trees of the tropical forests in which they live. It can scramble from one tree to another providing the twigs are interlaced to give reasonable support for iguanas cannot leap far. Green iguanas will, however, throw themselves from a branch 40–50 ft up and land on the ground unhurt, sprinting away to the undergrowth with barely a pause for breath. For an animal that appears so clumsy, with a heavy tail and legs splayed sideways, an iguana is remarkably fast and is extremely difficult to catch. Its reflexes are very rapid and unless one has nets the only way to catch an iguana is to throw oneself at it and even then a fullgrown iguana will be very hard to hold, as it can inflict nasty bites and scratches. Iguanas often take refuge in water and their favourite haunts are in trees overhanging pools and rivers. If disturbed they leap from the branch where they were lying and dive into the water. They swim underwater, propelling themselves with their tails, and surface under cover of vegetation along the bank.

The green iguana comes down to the ground in cold weather and hides under logs or in holes, but the other iguanas are usually ground-living and only occasionally climb trees. The desert iguana is a very fast runner and races about on its hindlegs.

Vegetarian lizards

As adults green iguanas eat a variety of plant foods, including young shoots, fruits, flowers and leaves, but the young ones also eat insects. Other iguanas are also vegetarian. The desert iguana prefers the yellow-flowered creosote bush but also eats other flowers, and after the flowering season is over it eats insects and carrion. Land iguanas feed on cactus and the larger species eat small rodents.

Eggs need constant temperature

Male land iguanas of the Galapagos form territories which they defend against other males. Each keeps watch from a rock and if another male intrudes he climbs down from his vantage point, walks slowly over to his rival and displays at him, pointing his snout at the sky and jerking his head up and down. If this does not scare the intruder into running away a fight breaks out, each trying to grab the loose skin on the other's flanks.

The female land iguanas live in the same burrows as their mates or in separate burrows alongside. Iguanas generally lay their eggs in nests well separated from each other but on a small island in Panama green iguanas were found nesting in great numbers close together on a sandy beach. Each female spent up to 2 weeks on the shore. For the first few days she probed the sand and dug small holes seeking a suitable site. Then she dug a large burrow 1–2 yd long and 2–3 ft deep. Because the beach was so crowded some were seen digging up other nests and scattering the eggs. Eggs were laid at the bottom of the burrow which was

▷ *The Barrington Island iguana of the Galapagos* **Conolophus pallidus**. *Local people prize its flesh, goats destroy its home.*

◁◁ *The aptly named rhinoceros iguana, with two horn-like scales on the top of its nose.*
◁ *A green iguana pauses, throat sac down and crest erect, to fight or flee an intruder, its partly missing tail witness of a past escape.*

filled in afterwards. The females spent some time filling the hole and at the same time filling in adjacent holes. Sometimes this meant filling in the burrows of other females who might be trapped and buried.

The green iguana lays 20—70 eggs in a clutch. The eggs are spherical, white and about 1½ in. diameter. They hatch in 3 months and it has been found that an almost constant temperature is needed for their development. A few degrees too high or too low and they fail to hatch. Although the female abandons her eggs after they are laid she ensures their survival by burying them in a suitable part of the beach. She chooses a spot where the temperature fluctuates only 1°—2° either side of 30°C/86°F. The young iguanas measure about 10 in. when they hatch and grow to 3 ft in one year.

Fooling the iguanas

Man and his domestic animals are the iguanas' worst enemies. Their flesh is relished in many parts of the world. Hawks are also serious enemies, for they catch iguanas as they lie basking in trees. In parts of South America iguanas are hunted by men imitating the screams of hawks. The iguanas' reaction to the cries is to 'freeze' and they are then easily caught. Snakes also hunt iguanas; a 6 ft boa constrictor has been found with an adult green iguana in its stomach.

Vanishing iguanas

When Charles Darwin visited the Galapagos islands in 1835 land iguanas were extremely abundant. Darwin wrote 'I cannot give a more forcible proof of their numbers than by stating that when we were left at James Island, we could not for some time find a spot free from their burrows to pitch our single tent.' Since then man has settled on the island, bringing with him dogs, cats, pigs, rats, goats and other animals and the iguana population is now a fraction of its former size. On some islands, however, where there are no goats, there are still large numbers of iguanas. The link between goats and iguanas is that goats strip the vegetation, depriving iguanas of cover. Some islands seem to be populated by adult iguanas only. They can survive in the open but young iguanas need cover to protect them from the Galapagos hawk. Without this cover they are killed off, and when the old lizards die there will be none left.

class	**Reptilia**
order	**Squamata**
suborder	**Sauria**
family	**Iguanidae**
genera & species	***Conolophus subcristatus*** *land iguana* ***Cyclura cornuta*** *rhinoceros iguana* ***Dipsosaurus dorsalis*** *desert iguana* ***Iguana iguana*** *green iguana*

Lizard giant: a Komodo dragon takes a stroll, forked tongue flicking out to taste its way along.

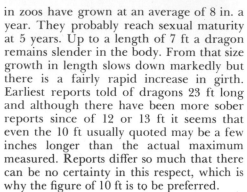

Gluttons enjoy photographer's bait.

Komodo dragon

Belonging to the monitor lizards—which will be dealt with later—the Komodo dragon deserves special mention. It is not only the largest living lizard—the males grow up to 10 ft long and 300 lb weight—but also the largest lizard of all time, except for the extinct marine mosasaurs which reached 50 ft. The only known rival to the Komodo dragon is an extinct monitor in Australia of about the same size. This lived during the Miocene period, 20—11 million years ago. Although the Komodo dragon is so large, it was unknown outside its native home until 1912. Its native home is a few small Indonesian islands: Komodo, Rintja, Flores and Padar. The first is the largest and this is only 20 by 12 miles, the others being even smaller.

The Komodo dragon has a stout, somewhat flattened body, long thick neck and longish head. Its legs are short and stout and the toes have long claws. Its tail is powerful and about the same length as the head and body combined. The tongue, which is constantly flicked out of the mouth, is long, narrow and deeply cleft. Young ones are dark in colour with red circles all over the body and vertical bands of black and yellowish green on the neck. These neck markings disappear with age but the red circles remain on the grey-brown bodies of adults.

Feats of gluttony

The islands where the Komodo dragon lives are hilly, their river beds filled only in the rainy season. The hills are covered in places with rain forest and the lowlands with tall grasses. The dragons spend the night in holes among rocks, between the buttress roots of trees or in caves. They come out at about 8.30 am to look for food—chiefly carrion, which is located by smell. The tongue seems also to be used as a taste-smell organ as in other lizards and snakes. The larger lizards monopolise any food, keeping the younger ones away by intimidating them, or beating them off with sideways sweeps of the powerful tail. Only when the bigger ones are full are the smaller able to feed. The dragons probably kill deer and pigs as well as monkeys. They eat heavy meals which last for days. An 8 ft dragon was seen to eat most of a deer, after which it rested for a week to complete the digestion. In eating flesh the dragon is helped by its back teeth being finely serrated, like small saws.

Young dragons feed on insects, lizards, rodents and ground-nesting birds and their eggs. Large individuals, feeding on carcases, tear the meat apart with claws and teeth and swallow lumps whole. One was seen to gulp the complete hindquarters of a deer, another to swallow a whole monkey.

Middle-age spread

Mating takes place in July and the female lays her eggs about a month later. The eggs are oval, 4 in. long with a parchment shell, and they hatch the following April. Dragons in zoos have grown at an average of 8 in. a year. They probably reach sexual maturity at 5 years. Up to a length of 7 ft a dragon remains slender in the body. From that size growth in length slows down markedly but there is a fairly rapid increase in girth. Earliest reports told of dragons 23 ft long and although there have been more sober reports since of 12 or 13 ft it seems that even the 10 ft usually quoted may be a few inches longer than the actual maximum measured. Reports differ so much that there can be no certainty in this respect, which is why the figure of 10 ft is to be preferred.

'Land crocodiles'

Komodo was an uninhabited island visited occasionally by pearl fishers and people hunting turtles. Then the sultan of the neighbouring island of Sumbawa used it to deport criminals and other 'undesirables'. Reports began to circulate early in the 19th century of a *boeaya-darat* or land crocodile, 23 ft long and alarmingly ferocious. In 1910 the reports became so insistent that Major PA Ouwens, director of the Botanical Gardens at Buitenzorg in Java, asked the Governor of Flores to look into the reports with the result that in 1912 Ouwens was able to publish a scientific description of this giant lizard. Then the First World War broke out and the giant was forgotten in Europe, but in 1923 Duke Adolf Friedrich von Mecklenburg, a keen explorer, went to the island of Komodo and came back with four skins of this lizard.

There are several reasons why the lizards were ignored for so long. One was that the islands were uninhabited until undesirable or doubtful characters were sent there. The stories they told were coloured by their own fears and superstitions and were so exaggerated that they were disbelieved. The other reason was that it was called a crocodile, and nobody in those days, before the crocodile leather craze, wanted to go all that way to look for crocodiles.

Unique photograph of a Komodo dragon swimming off Lesser Sundra Island, Indonesia.

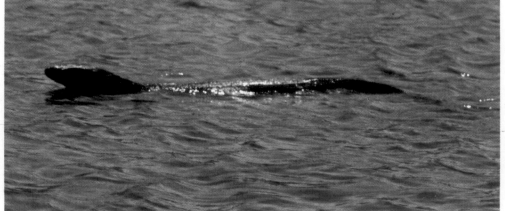

class	**Reptilia**
order	**Squamata**
suborder	**Sauria**
family	**Varanidae**
genus & species	*Varanus komodoensis*

△ Snake or lizard? In fact a silvery legless lizard, a reptile highly adapted to a subterranean existence. Loss of limbs, no external ears and small eyes ease its tunnelling in sand.
◁ Burton's legless lizard **Lialis burtonis** from Australia belongs to the family Pygopodidae.

Legless lizard

There are only two species of legless lizard in a family related to the slowworm, and both live in a restricted habitat in California. They are more specialized for burrowing than even the slowworm. Up to 10 in. long, the legless lizards have no limbs, the body is covered with smooth scales and the lower jaw is countersunk to improve the soil-moving efficiency of the head. The eye is very small with moveable eyelids to protect it, and there is no external ear. This not only means one less obstacle to a smooth passage through soil but an animal living so completely underground has no need to pick up soundwaves; vibrations through the soil are enough to guide it.

One species, living in a coastal strip, 600 miles long by 150 miles wide, from San Francisco southwards, is divided into two subspecies. The better known of the two is called worm lizard or silvery footless lizard. This lives up to 3 000 ft above sea-level. It is silvery grey, 7½ in. long, with a dark line down the centre of the back and one along each side. The other, the black legless lizard, blind worm or blind snake, about the same size, is black, and it is found only in the neighbourhood of Pacific Grove, whereas the other is found along the coast from Contra Costa County to Baja, California. A second species lives along the coast of Lower California and on the adjacent island of Geronimo, after which it is named.

Burrows to avoid heat

Legless lizards spend much of their time burrowing. They feed on insects and other arthropods in the soil, such as woodlice and mites, centipedes and millipedes, which they find by smell and touch. The depth at which the lizards are found varies with the time of year. In winter and spring they are 6–12 in. down when the soil is not heated to any great depth. As summer progresses they go deeper, to 3 ft in early summer and to 4–5 ft in midsummer. Several American zoologists have looked into this. They have taken the temperature of the lizard immediately on capturing it, the temperature of the soil at the depth of the lizard's burrow, and also the air temperature. There is a fairly steady correlation between these, with the lizard's body temperature about 1°C above that of the soil and the temperature of the soil about 2°C above that of the air. So we know that the lizards follow a 'temperature gradient', moving down as the soil heats up in summer and up as the soil cools in winter (in subtropical California).

Under logs and boulders the temperatures will be more constant and legless lizards are sometimes found there. They will come to the surface at night and there are at least two records of legless lizards crawling across streets, in Bakersfield, Kern County, moving from a piece of uncultivated ground. One had travelled 500 yards when it was picked up.

Young are born alive

As with many other legless lizards, the Californian species bear live young, the eggs hatching just before or at the moment of leaving the female's body. The baby lizards are 2½ in. long of which nearly a third is tail. They reach maturity at the age of 3 years, at a length of 8–10 in.

Snake-like lizards

It is interesting to compare the American legless lizards with the legless lizards of the family Pygopodidae found in Australia. One of them, found over much of that continent and known as Burton's legless lizard, *Lialis burtoni,* is 30 in. long, of which 20 in. is tail and only 10 in. head and body. This, to start with, is in striking contrast with the proportions of a snake, in which the tail is usually about an eighth of the total length. Burton's legless lizard has two tiny flaps—all that is left of its limbs—near the vent. It feeds on other lizards known as skinks, does not burrow but worms its way through grass, and is sometimes locally called a grass snake. This is excusable since, like the Californian legless lizards, it moves like a snake.

Long-bodied lizards with short legs walk at times with considerable sideways movements of the body. That is, they waggle their bodies. As the legs grow shorter and the body, including the tail, grows longer and more slender, the reptiles crawl rather than walk. With the total loss of the legs the way of moving over the ground becomes serpentine. This is an advantage, as in the Australian legless lizards, for moving through grass. It has its limitations for one living underground, as in the Californian legless lizards, because it restricts them to soft soil or loose sand.

class	**Reptilia**
order	**Squamata**
suborder	**Sauria**
family	**Anniellidae**
genus & species	***Anniella pulchra pulchra*** silvery legless lizard ***A. pulchra nigra*** black legless lizard ***A. geronimensis*** Geronimo legless lizard

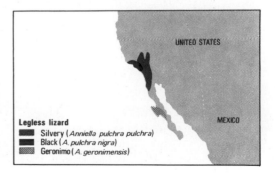

Legless lizard
▮ Silvery (*Anniella pulchra pulchra*)
▮ Black (*A. pulchra nigra*)
▨ Geronimo (*A. geronimensis*)

Marine iguana

The marine iguana is unique in its way of life, being the only truly marine lizard. It is found only in the Galapagos Islands, some 600 miles west of Ecuador. Because of its exceptional home, it is of great interest, but physically it is not so exciting. The accounts of early visitors to the Galapagos testify to the marine iguana's ugly appearance. One account describes them as having the most hideous appearance imaginable, and the same author, a captain of the Royal Navy, says that 'so disgusting is their appearance that no one on board could be prevailed on, to take them as food'. Marine iguanas grow up to 4 ft long. They have blunt snouts, heavy bodies, clumsy-looking legs with long toes and a crest that runs from the neck to the tail. The tail is flattened sideways and is used for swimming. Most marine iguanas are black or very dark grey, but on Hood Island at the south of the Galapagos Archipelago their bodies are mottled with black, orange and red and their front legs and crests are green.

Lizard heaps

Outside the breeding season, when they are not feeding at sea, marine iguanas gather in tight bunches, sometimes even piling on top of each other. They lie on the lava fields that are prominent but unpleasant features of the Galapagos. In the heat of the day they seek shelter under boulders, in crevices or in the shade of mangroves. At the beginning of the breeding season, the males establish small territories, so small that one iguana may be on top of a boulder while another lies at the foot. Fights occasionally break out but disputes are generally settled by displays. A male marine iguana threatens an intruder by raising itself on stiff legs and bobbing its head with mouth agape, showing a red lining. If this does not deter an intruder, the owner of the territory advances and a butting match takes place. The two push with their bony heads until one gives way and retreats.

While marine iguanas are basking, large red crabs will walk over them, pausing every now and then to pull at the iguanas' skin. The lizards do not resent this pulling and pinching and with good reason, because the crabs are removing ticks from their skin. Darwin's finches (named after Charles Darwin) perform the same service.

▽ 'It's a hideous looking creature of a dirty black colour, stupid and sluggish in its movements. The usual length of a fullgrown one is about a yard, some even 4 ft long.' Voyage of HMS Beagle, Charles Darwin 1890.

Diving for a living

As the tide goes down the marine iguanas take to the water and eat the algae exposed on the reefs and shores. They cling to the rocks with their sharp claws, so as not to be dislodged by the surf, and slowly work their way over the rocks tearing strands of algae by gripping them in the sides of their mouths and twisting to wrench them off. At intervals they pause to swallow and rest. Some marine iguanas swim out beyond the surf and dive to feed on the seabed. They have been recorded as feeding at depths of 35 ft but usually they stay at about 15 ft. The length of each dive is about 15—20 minutes but they can stay under for much longer. When Darwin visited the Galapagos in HMS *Beagle* he noted that a sailor tried to drown one by sinking it with a heavy weight. An hour later it was drawn back to the surface and found to be quite active.

Marine iguanas normally eat nothing but marine algae. Unusual exceptions are the marine iguanas that haunt the home of Carl Angermeyer. He has trained them to come at his whistle to be fed on raw goat meat, rice and oatmeal.

Easy courtship

When the males have formed their territories, the females join them. They are free to move from one territory to another but the males soon gather harems of females around them and mating takes place without interference from other males. Courtship is simple: a male walks up behind a female, bobbing his head, then grabs her by the neck and clasps her with his legs.

When the males leave their territories, the females gather at the nesting beaches. There is competition for nest sites and fighting breaks out. Each female digs a 2ft tunnel in the sand, scraping with all four feet. Sometimes they are trapped and killed when the roof falls in or when a neighbour scrapes sand into the hole.

Only 2 or 3 white eggs, $3\frac{1}{4}$ by $1\frac{3}{4}$ in., are

△ *Like a lichen encrusted monument—the marine iguana presents his best side to the camera and shows off his metallic colours. In profile his snout is seen to be blunt and the clumsiness of his legs and heavy body is apparent. But against the blue sky the red and green mottling of this otherwise rather grotesque reptile is given full due.*

▽ *The marine iguana is the only modern lizard that uses the sea as a source of food. It is herbivorous, and feeds exclusively on seaweeds.*

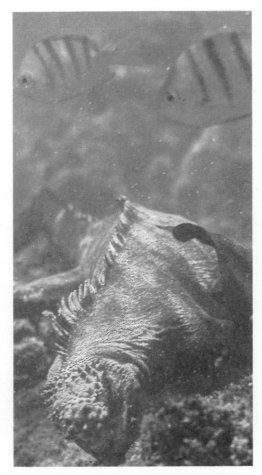

laid. Then the female iguana fills up and camouflages the tunnel. When the eggs hatch in about 110 days, 9in. iguanas emerge.

Apart from man the main enemies of full grown marine iguanas are sharks, but the iguanas usually stay inshore where sharks are not likely to venture. Young iguanas are caught by herons, gulls and Galapagos hawks, as well as introduced cats.

Warmer on land

While he was on the Galapagos, Darwin found that it was impossible to drive marine iguanas into the sea. They would rather let themselves be caught than pushed in and if thrown into the sea they would hurriedly make for the edge and clamber out. This is a surprising habit for an aquatic animal as most animals that habitually swim, such as turtles and seals, make for the safety of the sea when frightened. Darwin assumed that the marine iguana behaved in this strange way because it had no natural enemies on land but that the sharks were waiting for it in the sea. If this were so, it would mean that marine iguanas would have to be pretty hungry before setting out to feed. Recently another explanation has been put forward. While basking, marine iguanas regulate their body temperatures to within a range of 35—37°C/95—99°F (see Bearded lizard page 160 for a discussion on temperature regulation in lizards). The sea temperature around the Galapagos is 10°C/50°F less, so the marine iguanas are reluctant to escape into the sea, as this makes them too cool.

class	**Reptilia**
order	**Squamata**
suborder	**Sauria**
family	**Iguanidae**
genus & species	***Amblyrhynchus cristatus***

185

Moloch

Moloch was a Canaanite god to whom children were sacrificed and was also one of Milton's devils. It is therefore not surprising that the name should have been given to this uncouth Australian relative of the pretty agama lizards (page 154). The moloch is, however, much maligned by its name as it is a most inoffensive lizard, yet the Australian aborigines treat it with care as they believe it is harmful. The alternative names of the moloch are mountain devil or thorny devil. The latter is the most descriptive. The moloch is covered with thorn-like spikes over its head, body, tail and legs. They are triangular in section and as pointed as any rose thorn. The lizard's total length is 6 in. and the body is round, so a moloch looks like a walking horse chestnut burr.

Molochs are found in many parts of South and Western Australia and in Northern Territory.

Lizard with a hump

Molochs are prickly lizards that move slowly even when in a hurry. When frightened they tuck their heads between their front legs, presenting a thorny hump that stands on the back of the neck. It is, however, difficult to see how this can enhance the general prickly reception a predator gets. Another suggested function for the hump was that it is a food store, but as it does not shrink when a moloch goes hungry this seems unlikely.

Molochs live in deserts and semi-desert regions and, as with so many other desert animals, although they are active by day their behaviour is adapted to avoid the worst of the sun's heat. They can also change colour but this ability is often exaggerated. When transferred from one background to another they change colour slowly, taking several minutes. Against a sandy background a moloch may be a dull light grey but against other backgrounds it is sometimes prettily coloured with orange, chestnut and black markings.

Painstaking ant eaters

A favoured method of feeding is for a moloch to sit by a trail of ants, flicking them up with its tongue as they run past. It has been estimated that they pick up 30—45 ants a minute, and that a moloch eats 1—5 thousand ants at one sitting, each one being picked up separately, so one meal takes a long time. Molochs eat little else but ants, taking only those without stings. Their jaws are weak but their teeth have complex serrated crowns which are well suited for crushing the hard outer skeletons of ants so their soft interiors can be digested.

△ *An advancing moloch looms up over a fallen tree trunk.*
▽ *A walking thorn bush. The moloch, harmless in itself, is a mass of spikes to any aggressor.*

Outsize eggs

The breeding habits of molochs are known from those that have laid eggs while being kept in captivity. Mating takes place in October and November, and eggs are laid in January. The maximum recorded clutch was 10 eggs, each about 1 in. long and ½ in. wide—enormous eggs to be produced by a fairly small lizard like the moloch.

Before laying eggs the female moloch spends 2—3 days digging a nest in soft sandy soil. She does this according to a set pattern. Having started a hole and thrown out a small pile she removes the surplus by scraping earth backwards from the top, and gradually digs her way forwards into the hole. When she has reached the 'pit face' and dug out more soil she turns and goes back to the pile outside and starts again. In this way she continually throws the soil backwards, so the entrance and the tunnel are kept clear. The finished tunnel is 2 ft long, running downwards and ending 10 in. below the surface. It takes a long time to dig be-

cause the moloch often stops to rest. Having completed her task she lays her eggs at the bottom of the tunnel and fills it up again, leaving an air cavity around the eggs so the developing molochs can breathe. When the tunnel has been completely filled, the surface is levelled and swept so the entrance is concealed. The moloch then leaves the eggs to develop and the young to emerge on their own. Hatching takes place 10—12 weeks later and the young molochs, 2¼ in. long, dig their way out and disperse.

Dew-trap skin

It has been said that molochs can absorb water through their skin, because a drop of water placed on the back of one of them rapidly disappears. If this were so, the skin would be most unusual, because at the same time it must prevent water from leaking out, otherwise molochs would not be able to live in deserts. It is now known that the drop disappears because it spreads rapidly by flowing along minute grooves in the skin.

△ *Tiny grooves spread any moisture all over its body extremely quickly.*
△ △ *A moloch spends a long time over its meal, picking each ant up singly. This meal may last it for several weeks.*

If the tip of the tail is dipped into water the whole of the skin becomes wet in a few seconds. When the water reaches its lips the moloch starts to sip it. No one has studied the use of this mechanism but it may be a way of collecting dew, forming on the moloch's body during the cold desert night.

class	**Reptilia**
order	**Squamata**
suborder	**Sauria**
family	**Agamidae**
genus & species	***Moloch horridus***

187

Monitor lizard

The family of monitor lizards includes the largest lizards now in existence; several species reach 5 ft or more. The largest is the Komodo dragon (page 182) at 10 ft long, and the smallest is the 8-in. short-tailed monitor of Australia. The word monitor originally meant 'one who admonishes others about their conduct'. It was applied to these lizards because of an error in translation. The Arabic name for the lizards is **waran** *which is very similar to the German* **warnen** *meaning 'warning'. As a result these lizards became known as 'warning lizards'. In Malaya and Australia monitors are called iguanas or 'goannas' although the iguanas form a separate family.*

Monitors live in the warmer parts of the Old World, including the whole of Africa excluding Madagascar, Asia from Arabia to southern China down through southeast Asia to the East Indies and Australia. Unlike other lizard families where some species carry ornate crests, spines and frills, the monitors show very little variation in form. The snout, neck, body and tail are all long and slender and their eyes are prominent, making the lizard seem long, sinuous and alert. Monitors have several features in common with snakes although they are not so closely related to them as the earless monitors (page 165). Both snakes and monitors have long, forked tongues and have lost the ability to shed their tails.

The largest monitor, excluding the Komodo dragon, is the two-banded or water monitor, at 8—9 ft. **Varanus giganteus,** *the perenty, reaches 7 ft, and the Nile monitor 6 ft. The Nile monitor ranges throughout Africa from the Upper Nile south to the Cape, and the water monitor lives in Malaya.*

The Nile monitor is brownish or greenish grey above with darker markings and yellowish spots which are lost with age. Underneath the skin is yellowish with dark bands. The Indian monitor is light to dark brown, sometimes with scattered light and dark scales on its back. Its underparts are dirty white with speckling. Young monitors, and adults just after they have shed their skins, are more brightly coloured. Young Indian monitors are orange to light brown with alternating yellow and black bands across the back.

Fast to escape

Monitors are large lizards which can get quite nasty if brought to bay. At first they inflate their bodies and hiss. Then they attempt to deter any attack by violently lashing the tail like a whip. Finally they may attack by grabbing their adversary with their powerful jaws and clawing with their feet. Dogs often come off worst in such an encounter and a large monitor is a formidable opponent for a man. They may spend much of their time, however, basking in the sun and when alarmed they can run very rapidly with the tail held in a characteristic curve with the tip just off the ground. The Nile monitor can outpace a man, especially in thick cover. Except during cold seasons monitors are extremely active animals.

Each species of monitor has a fairly restricted habitat. The perenty, the largest of the Australian monitors, lives among rocky outcrops in the deserts. The desert monitor lives in similar habitats in North Africa and western Asia. Most monitors can climb trees but some forest-dwelling species are completely at home in trees. The Nile monitor and water monitor have flattened tails that are used for swimming and the water monitor has nostrils near the tip of its snout which allows it to breathe when almost completely submerged. When disturbed, monitors make for their natural home. Nile monitors usually bask on a branch or rock from which they can drop straight into the water. When surprised away from water they usually head for the bank but will sometimes hide in a tree or hole. The Indian monitor and the desert monitor also hide in holes in the ground while the forest-living Bornean rough-necked monitor takes refuge in trees.

Egg thieves

Like snakes, monitors swallow their prey whole rather than chew it as do iguanas and other lizards. A water monitor, for instance, has been known to swallow a 6 in. turtle whole. Snakes and monitors have a strong bony roof to the mouth which protects the brain from being damaged by the passage of large mouthfuls.

Monitors are carnivorous, eating a wide variety of animals, as well as carrion. The Indian monitor eats palm squirrels, musk shrews, lizards, snakes and invertebrates and the water monitor feeds largely on fish. The Nile monitor eats mainly insects, snails, crabs and other invertebrates and also catches small birds and mammals. In South Africa, the Nile monitor digs rain frogs out of their burrows, ignoring the poisonous secretions that deter other predators. All monitors have a fondness for eggs and as a result are often persecuted by farmers for

△ *An inelegant sunbather,* **Varanus exanthematicus,** *clumsily sprawled across a palm frond. Most monitor lizards are sun worshippers, spending much of their time basking on any bare surfaces.*

▷ *Close up of a head of a monitor lizard, alert and wary.*

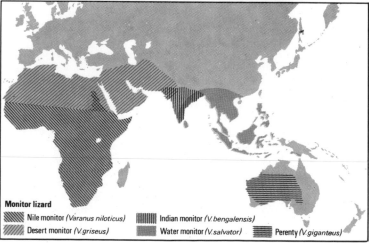

Monitor lizard
Nile monitor *(Varanus niloticus)* Indian monitor *(V. bengalensis)*
Desert monitor *(V. griseus)* Water monitor *(V. salvator)* Perenty *(V. giganteus)*

△ A monitor lizard **Varanus varius** with its voluminous food pouch. It often swallows its prey whole.

▽ Gould's goanna **Varanus gouldii** sticks its nose outside its front door; if alarmed, it can move with great rapidity.

△ A Nile monitor in its element. Although usually found in or near water, it can run rapidly and climb trees well.

▽ A lace monitor **Varanus varius** tastes the air with its flickering forked tongue, like that of a snake.

taking the eggs of poultry. The Nile monitor is said to steal the eggs from crocodiles' nests even though these are guarded by the mother.

Termite nest incubator

Monitors usually lay their eggs in nests in the ground or in hollow trees. The Indian monitor digs a hole about 1 ft deep with its forelegs then turns and backs in to lay its eggs. After laying it fills the nest hole by breaking down the sides with its snout and claws and tamping down the soil. In South Africa, Nile monitors lay their eggs in termite nests. They tear holes in the sides of the nests, lay their eggs in an enlarged chamber in the centre then leave the termites to repair the damage and so cover the eggs. Between 16 and 34 white leathery eggs are laid. The termites' nest provides heat for incubation and safety from enemies until the monitors hatch 5 months later. As the eggs hatch fluid escapes and softens the hard walls surrounding the nest. This enables the baby monitors to wriggle out of the eggs and then dig their way upwards. On reaching the surface they are reluctant to leave for several days, but eventually scuttle into nearby undergrowth.

Giant relatives

The monitors are among the oldest lizards, dating back some 130 million years. At this time other families of lizards that are now extinct were flourishing. Three families were closely related to the monitors: the aigialosaurs, dolichosaurs and mosasaurs. The latter two had taken to life in the sea, but the snakelike dolichosaurs did not last long. The mosasaurs were much more successful. The tail was flattened for swimming and the limbs formed broad paddles. The jaws were long and able to open very wide. Some mosasaurs reached a length of over 30 ft and preyed on fish and other reptiles that they seized in their large mouths with their sharp curved teeth.

The first fossil mosasaur was discovered in Maastricht in 1780 and consisted of a head over 3 ft long. The head attracted a considerable amount of attention and when the French attacked Maastricht in 1795 instructions were given to safeguard the house where it was thought that the fossil reposed. When the fortress fell it could not be found but a reward of 600 bottles of wine for its discovery soon led to 12 soldiers bearing the huge limestone block

into the camp. Since that time mosasaur skeletons have been found all over the world. Many of them have fractured bones but it is a matter of debate whether these wounds were caused by fights with predators or in territorial battles.

class	**Reptilia**
order	**Squamata**
suborder	**Sauria**
family	**Varanidae**
genus & species	*Varanus bengalensis* Indian monitor *V. exanthematicus* a South African monitor *V. giganteus* perenty *V. gouldii* Gould's monitor *V. griseus* desert monitor *V. niloticus* Nile monitor *V. rudicollis* rough-necked monitor *V. salvator* water monitor *V. varius* lace monitor others

Night lizard

Night lizards look rather like geckos, and they also have a permanent 'spectacle', composed of a transparent scale, covering each eye. The night lizards are a family found only in America. One genus **Xantusia** *is found in the United States where some species are quite common in certain localities. The desert night lizard is found in the deserts of California, Nevada, Utah, Arizona and Baja California where it lives in cover provided by Joshua trees and other species of Yucca. The maximum head and body length is 1¾ in. for males and 2 in. for females. Both have tails a little longer than the combined head and body length. The velvety skin is covered with fine scales on the upperparts and large square scales on the underparts. The colour varies from yellowish or grey to green, with black speckling on top, and pale grey to very light green underneath. The desert night lizard changes colour daily, being paler during the day than at night. The granite night lizard lives in California and is yellowish with black speckling. The island night lizard is found only on three small islands off the coast of California. The fourth of the night lizards found in the United States is the Arizona night lizard. Night lizards of two other genera* **Gaigeia** *and* **Lepidophyma** *live in Mexico and Central America, and one species* **Cricosaura typica** *lives in Cuba.*

Living with wood rats

As their name implies night lizards are nocturnal, hiding by day and usually coming out to forage only at night. The desert night lizard is one of the commonest lizards in the southwest United States but until a short while ago it was regarded as being quite rare. This was before it was realised that desert night lizards were sheltering in Joshua trees. The fallen branches and dead clusters of leaves of Joshua trees present excellent cover in the desert from enemies and from the sun's rays. Other plants do not provide such good cover but on the fringes of the deserts night lizards hide under sagebrush. A favourite hiding place of desert night lizards is in the nests wood rats build at the bases of the Joshua trees. The nests consist of piles of sticks and leaves which may be 2 ft high and 4 ft across, so providing very good cover. The lizards may make their homes in them while the wood rats are still in residence. In the summer night lizards lie up under a log or pile of leaves usually in single pairs but in winter they may gather in groups of up to 40 or more.

Other night lizards live in rock crevices or among boulders. The granite night lizard lives under slabs that have flaked off the bedrock and the Cuban night lizard lives among loose limestone boulders.

Feeding in leaf litter

Joshua trees also supply the desert night lizard with a plentiful source of food because night lizards feed on small animals that live in leaf litter and under logs. Ants, beetles and flies are their favourite food but they also take moths, beetles, spiders and sometimes scorpions.

Egg-tube placenta

Night lizards are viviparous, their young being born alive. After fertilisation the eggs take 90–120 days to develop. During this time food passes to the developing embryos and excretory products pass back to the mother through a placenta formed from the joining of the embryonic membranes and the oviduct. The litter is very small consisting usually of two young and never more than three. They are born in September or October and measure just under 1 in.

Ideal life-style

The desert night lizard's habits of hiding under cover and emerging mainly at night would seem to be an ideal way of life for an animal living in hot, dry country, although most desert reptiles are active during the day and retire to shelter at night.

A close study of the desert night lizard has shown that it probably was once similar to other lizards in its habits. It has vertical pupils like those of day-living reptiles, and it reacts to temperature changes in the same way as the bearded lizard and other day-living reptiles. It still likes to bask in the sun, but as its habitat became hotter and drier it has taken to hiding during the day in the cover provided by the Joshua trees. These trees are now rapidly diminishing in numbers but fortunately land has been set aside to preserve the stands of Joshua trees, and with them, incidentally, one of North America's most unusual reptiles.

△ *A desert night lizard like all the other night lizards, lacks moveable eyelids. The eye is covered by a clear scale derived from the lower lid.*

△ *A granite night lizard crawls over a rock — its natural habitat.*
▽ *An island night lizard with the bluntly pointed head that is typical of these lizards.*

class	**Reptilia**
order	**Squamata**
suborder	**Sauria**
family	**Xantusidae**
genera & species	**Cricosaura typica** *Cuban night lizard* **Xantusia vigilis** *desert night lizard* **X. henshawi** *granite night lizard* **X. arizonae** *Arizona night lizard* **X. riversiana** *island night lizard*

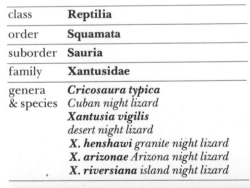

191

Sand lizard

The sand lizard belongs to the family Lacertidae that are usually considered as typical lizards. The family is confined to the Old World and includes such lizards as the viviparous lizard or common lizard as it is known in Britain, the wall lizard and the green lizard. They are a good choice as typical lizards, as none has the specialised or bizarre forms that are found in other lizard families. Their bodies are slender, their tails long and tapering and their limbs well developed.

The sand lizard, which is sometimes called the European fence lizard, is light brown or grey above with three rows of irregular dark brown or black spots running down its back. Each spot has a white centre and may be edged with white, and sometimes adjacent spots are joined to

Not so agile lizard

The name sand lizard is appropriate in England where it is confined to dry sandy heaths in the south and sand dunes in the northwest. On the European continent it has a wider range of habitats and is found in woodland clearings and hedgerows, and along the borders of fields as well as on dunes and heaths. These habitats are reflected in the names of the sand lizard in French *lezard des souches* (lizard of tree stumps) and in German *Zauneidesche* (hedge lizard). Wherever it is found the sand lizard prefers dry places such as banks rather than flat ground and often lives in colonies. Sand lizards can dig well and make their own holes in sandy ground, although they sometimes take over abandoned runs of mice or voles. They are timid and dash for the safety of their holes at the slightest disturbance; but they can neither climb so well nor run so fast as some of their relatives and so do not deserve their scientific name of *Lacerta agilis* any more than their common name.

Preferred food

Sand lizards feed mainly on insects and spiders but also eat worms, slugs, centipedes and woodlice. Before it is eaten the prey is killed by shaking it vigorously. Larger animals such as grasshoppers and beetles have their wings and legs removed first and are then torn into little pieces which are swallowed separately.

Territorial fights

Hibernation ends in March and sand lizards start mating in late April, the peak coming in May. During the mating season there is considerable rivalry between males, who defend small territories. Arguments occur if a male enters another's territory. If one lizard is larger than its rival the latter quickly retreats, but if evenly matched the two will fight and blood may flow. Sometimes the fighting is prefaced by posturing like that of rival tom cats meeting. The sand lizards arch their backs, puff out their necks and lower their heads. They circle

form a continuous line. The underparts are white or cream, sometimes with black spots. Adult males are tinged with green on the flanks and underparts and this becomes brighter during the breeding season. Females have brown flanks. The maximum size recorded for a sand lizard is just over 7½ in. Males are slightly larger than females.

Sand lizards are found over most of central Europe and they extend eastwards to Central Asia. In the British Isles they are restricted mainly to parts of southern and eastern England.

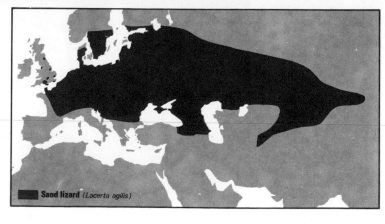

Sand lizard *(Lacerta agilis)*

△ *A sand lizard crawls out of its old skin. Like other reptiles, it sheds its skin at intervals as it grows. Although often considered a typical lizard, sand lizards are not aptly named as they are neither agile nor are they found only in sand. In Germany they are called hedge lizards, and in France, lizards of tree stumps.*

about, facing each other, then attack, rolling over and shaking one another in their jaws. Finally one breaks away and runs off.

Courtship is almost as rough as fighting. The females visit the males in their territories and are seized by the males and shaken. Mating then follows. The female lays 6—13 eggs, the size of the clutch depending on the size of the female. The eggs are deposited in a shallow pit dug by the female and afterwards covered by leaves or sand. The eggs are laid in June and July and hatch a month later. The young lizards are brown when they first hatch and before they hibernate in October they have grown from 2½ to 3 in. They become sexually mature at just under 2 years of age and are full grown at 4—5 years.

Trusting lizards

Although so timid in the wild, sand lizards are easily tamed. The French zoologist Rollinat has described how he kept lizards on a rockery in his garden. The sand lizards became much tamer than the wall lizards. In 5 days some were tame enough to take food from his fingers and learned to come from their holes when he beat on a tin. Later the sand lizards would climb over his body and take food from his lips. They did not mind Rollinat moving or even passing them around his friends. There have been a few people who have claimed to be able to call sand lizards out of their burrows, whenever they wished to do so, by making a particular high-pitched whistle. Others who have tried various whistlings

△ *A sand lizard curves its way through ling.*

have achieved no success. Perhaps it has to be a sound that resembles the one made by Rollinat's tin. In any case, it is odd since sand lizards do not seem to use a voice themselves.

class	**Reptilia**
order	**Squamata**
suborder	**Sauria**
family	**Lacertidae**
genus & species	*Lacerta agilis*

Skink

Skinks have none of the frills or decorations found in other lizard families; they all have an ordinary 'lizard shape' with a rather heavy tail and very often limbs that are reduced or missing. These are adaptations to the burrowing way of life which is characteristic of skinks and many spend most of their lives underground. Skinks are usually only a few inches long, the largest being the giant skink of the Solomon Islands, which is 2 ft long. The skink family contains over 600 species, and they are found all over the warmer parts of the world. In some areas, such as the forests of Africa, they are the most abundant lizards.

Within the skink family there are all gradations from a running to a burrowing way of life. The little brown skink of the southeastern United States has well-developed legs and toes and is a surface dweller; the burrowing Florida sand skink is almost limbless. In the **Scelotes** genus of Africa there is a whole range of limb reduction. Bojer's skink of Mauritius has well-developed legs; the black-sided skink of Madagascar has very short legs; others have lost their forelegs altogether and have a reduced number of toes on the hindlegs; and the plain skink of South Africa has completely lost all its legs.

Other adaptations for burrowing include the streamlining of the scales, the provision of a transparent 'spectacle' over the eye and the sinking of the eardrum into a narrow tube.

Diverse habits

Skinks are found in a variety of habitats, both on the ground and beneath the surface, from the damp soil of forests to the sands of deserts. A few live in trees, but only one has any adaptation for aboreal life. This is the giant skink which has a prehensile tail. Some skinks, such as the keel-bearing skinks, named after the projections on their scales, live on the banks of streams and dive into the water if alarmed. Some of the snake-eyed skinks live among rocks on the shore and feed on sea creatures such as small crabs and marine worms.

▷ A young **Eumeces skiltonianus**. Like many other lizards skinks can shed their tails when they are attacked by a predator. The young of some skinks, including the type shown, have bright blue tails as an added safety device. When attacked the tail is broken off and it bounds continually; as it is the most conspicuous thing in sight, the predator is confused and the skink can scuttle safely away while the predator pursues the bounding tail. The tail is bright blue only when the skink is young, when the hazards of life are greatest. The blue-tailed Polynesian skink is exceptional in retaining its blue tail throughout its life.

◁ Foot-long mother **Tiliqua rugosa** and enormous newly-born.

◁ ▽ *The largest of the skinks – the prehensile-tailed giant skink of the Solomon Islands.*

Teeth to fit the diet

The main food of skinks is insects and other small animals, including young mice and birds' eggs. The insect-eating skinks have pointed teeth with which they crush their hard-bodied prey and some types of skink which feed on earthworms have backwardly curving teeth which prevent the worms from escaping as they are being swallowed. The larger skinks are vegetarians and have broad, flat-topped teeth used for chewing.

Some lay eggs

Skinks lack the wattles and fans which other lizards use to display their superiority to rivals, but some male skinks develop bright colours during the breeding season. When they meet the males fight vigorously and may wound each other. Courtship is simple: the male follows a female, who allows him to catch her if she is ready to breed.

About half the skinks lay eggs; the others bear their young alive, the eggs being hatched just before they leave the mother's body. The eggs are usually laid under a log or rock and some skinks such as the five-lined skink of North America guard their eggs. The female curls around the eggs and stays with them until they hatch 4–6 weeks later, only leaving them to feed. As with other reptiles which stay with their eggs, it is difficult to decide what function they are performing. There is no evidence that skinks incubate the eggs and they desert them if disturbed, but it is known that skinks regularly turn their eggs which may be to prevent them from rotting.

Swimming in the sand

Some of the desert skinks are called sand-fish from the way they appear to swim through the sand. Their legs are well-developed but they are held close into the body when moving. Propulsion comes from the flattened tail which is reminiscent of the tails of amphibians or aquatic reptiles such as the marine iguana (page 184). Another adaptation is a sharp chisel-like snout that can cleave a way through the sand. Like other lizards, skinks have flexible skulls but their heads are strengthened for sand-swimming and burrowing by the fusing of the scales on the head.

class	**Reptilia**
order	**Squamata**
suborder	**Sauria**
family	**Scincidae**
genera & species	**Corucia zebrata** *giant skink* **Eumeces fasciatus** *five-lined skink* **Lygosoma laterale** *little brown skink* **Neoseps reynoldsi** *Florida sand skink* **Scelotes bojeri** *Bojer's skink* **S. inornatus** *plain skink* **S. melanopleura** *black-sided skink* *others*

Slow-worm

The snake-like slow-worm, alternatively known as the blind-worm or dead adder, is in fact a legless lizard. Internally there are vestigial shoulder- and hip-girdles, evidence that its ancestors once moved on four legs. A slow-worm has eyelids like other lizards, the two halves of its lower jaw are joined in front, another lizard characteristic, and its tongue is notched, not forked like that of a snake. An average large slow-worm is about 1 ft long, the record is a 20⅗ in. female.

The head of a slow-worm is small and short, not so broad as the body immediately behind it and larger in the male than the female. Fully-grown males are more or less uniform in colour above and on the flanks. They may be light or dark brown, grey, chestnut, bronze or brick red and one variety is even copper-coloured. The belly usually has a dark mottling of blackish or dark grey. The female often has a thin dark line down the centre of the back and another on the upper part

underground ensures fairly constant temperature conditions.

The slow-worm is not inappropriately named. More often than not when we come upon it, it will lie motionless, making no attempt to escape. At most it may move away in a leisurely manner and generally its actions are slow and deliberate. Occasionally, however, by contrast, it will move with astonishing speed.

In October the slow-worm hibernates in an underground burrow, in a hollow beneath a large stone, or even beneath a pile of dead leaves. As many as 20 may be found in one hibernaculum, the largest being underneath, the smallest on top.

Slow-worms cast their skins or, more correctly, their cuticle, about four times a year. The frequency of sloughing depends upon whether or not it is a good slug year, the chief food of the slow-worm, the shedding being in response to the need for more space for the growing body. The skin is shed whole as in snakes. Although a slow-worm readily sheds its tail the new tail is shorter and never as perfect as the old one. There is usually a ragged end to the old part, the narrower new part appearing as if thrust inside the fringe of old scales.

moment of birth or shortly afterwards. Litters of 6–12 – although as few as 4 or as many as 19 young have been recorded – are born in late August or September, but if the weather is cold this may be delayed until October or later. The young are up to 3½ in. long, silver or golden in colour with black underparts and a thin black line running down the middle of the back. Very active, they are able to fend for themselves from the moment of birth, catching insects, but showing a marked preference for any slugs small enough to eat.

Slow-worms have been known to live in captivity for up to 30 years or more, the record being held by one that lived in the Copenhagen Museum for 54 years.

Numerous enemies

Probably thousands of slow-worms are killed each year by man under the impression they are young adders. The slow-worm has many enemies, especially when young. Its main enemies are hedgehogs and adders. Frogs, toads, lizards and small snakes also eat it, as well as foxes, badgers and rats, and many birds, particularly birds-of-prey; and even the mistlethrush has been seen to take one.

▽ *Spritely youngsters: black-striped and golden or silver coloured, young slow-worms are able to fend for themselves from birth.*

of each flank, and her belly is usually black.

The slow-worm is found throughout Europe including the British Isles and eastwards into the Caucasus, Asia Minor and northern Iran. In Scandinavia and Finland it extends as far as latitude 65°N. It is also found in North Africa.

A variety of the slow-worm, known as the blue-spotted slow-worm, is widely distributed over Europe including the southern counties of England. The colour which may vary from a light blue to deep ultramarine may be present in spots or stripes, sometimes so closely set that the animal appears blue all over. All blue-spotted slow-worms are males.

Name not inappropriate

The slow-worm lives in open woodlands, commons and heathland. It is seldom seen during daylight apart from the spring and late summer or autumn. It spends the daytime under flat stones or logs or in burrows sometimes as deep as a foot below the surface, often lying in the earth completely buried except for its head. Life

The gardener's friend

The slow-worm eats spiders, small earthworms and tiny insects. There is a marked preference for the small white slug *Agriolimax agrestis* so often a pest on tender green vegetables. This is consumed in quantity, but where this slug is missing the slow-worm takes others. The prey is seized in the middle and chewed from end to end. The slow-worm also eats snails. The principal feeding time is soon after sunset, or after rain, when the slugs themselves come out to feed.

Ovoviviparous female

Mating is from late April to June, when there is a great deal of fighting between the males, each trying to seize the other by the head or neck. Once a hold has been obtained there is much writhing and rolling together. In mating the male seizes the female by the neck and twines his body around hers. The female is ovoviviparous, the eggs hatching within the body. On rare occasions the eggs are deposited before hatching. The young are enclosed within a membranous envelope which is punctured by a feebly developed egg-tooth, either at the

Deceptive appearance

Since the slow-worm's snake-like appearance can so easily deceive us, it is possible that other animals it is likely to encounter in the wild can make a similar mistake. Alfred Leutscher, writing in the *Illustrated London News* for June 3, 1950, tells the story of how he once placed a slow-worm in a vivarium containing three tame common frogs. They made repeated attempts to swallow the 'worm'. 'Suddenly these frogs began to behave as if frantic with fear, making every attempt to escape and dashing madly against the glass sides of their enclosure.' He came to the conclusion that the frogs had at first taken the slow-worm for a likely meal and had then mistaken it for a snake.

class	**Reptilia**
order	**Squamata**
suborder	**Sauria**
family	**Anguidae**
genus & species	***Anguis fragilis***

Teiid lizard

Because only a minority of this family have common names it is customary to speak of them with an anglicized form of their scientific name. The Teiidae is a family of American lizards. The 200 or so species in the family are very varied, particularly in the form of their scales, but there are no really bizarre types. Their ways of life are also very varied and teiids are found in a great number of habitats, from the high Andes to the seashore.

The largest teiid is the 4ft caiman lizard, which has a flattened tail and is amphibious. One foot smaller is the tegu of Brazil. Apart from a few giants such as these, teiids are usually 1 ft or less in length, the smallest being 3—4 in. long. Most of the teiids have a typical lizard form but some have almost lost their legs and live by burrowing.

The family is most numerous in the American tropics but one lives as far south as central Chile and the racerunners and

whiptails are distributed over most of the United States except the far north. One of these, the six-lined racerunner, is the best known of the teiids. It is the smallest species in the United States, growing up to 10 in. long, of which half is tail. The skin is dark brown and there are six narrow lines running down the body. Other race-runners and whiptails have yellowish lines or spots but they often lose them when they are fully grown. The male of the six-lined racerunner has a bluish belly while that of the female is whitish. As the name suggests, racerunners can move fast and they are reported as being able to run at 18 mph over short distances.

Must live in the open

As might be expected of a member of a predominantly tropical family, the six-lined raccrunner is active only in warm weather and may stay in its burrow on cloudy days. Similarly it spends a greater part of the year hibernating than other lizards living in the same area, being inactive for $\frac{1}{2}$—$\frac{2}{3}$ of the year. Racerunners live

△ *Whip-tailed and splay-footed **Cnemido-phorus maximus**, one of the many variations within the 200 species of the family Teiidae.*

in colonies on open, sandy soil, from which they disappear if the cover is increased, by agriculture, for instance. On warm days the lizards can be seen foraging, basking, chasing rivals or courting.

Each racerunner has a home range of $\frac{1}{5}$—$\frac{1}{4}$ acre, over which it forages. The range is not the same as a territory as it is not defended and the ranges of several individuals overlap. The frequent chasing and biting that can be seen in a colony are the result of a social hierarchy. One or two members of the colony are more aggressive than the others and the smallest lizards are harassed most. Within its range each race-runner has a burrow which it does defend. It may dig its own burrow or use the abandoned burrow of a mouse or vole. The burrow is used as a shelter from enemies and extremes of temperature.

The habitat of the six-lined racerunner is an average habitat for the teiid family as some live in deserts and others, such as the caiman lizard, are amphibious. The worm teiids and the snake teiid burrow in leaf mould. The Guiana earless teiid has minute legs on which it can walk slowly, but it wriggles like a snake when disturbed or even throws itself forward with a flick of its tail.

Teeth tell teiid's diet
Teiid lizards have a variety of diets as well as habits. This is reflected in their teeth. The front teeth are always conical but those in the side of the mouth may be conical, cusped or flattened. The caiman lizard has flattened teeth with which it crushes snail shells. The racerunners and the ameivas of Central America have cusped teeth and feed mainly on insects. The six-lined racerunner can catch active insects like grasshoppers but also digs in the soil for insects which it locates by scent. The tegu feeds on insects, frogs and lizards and occasionally raids poultry runs for eggs and chicks. It also eats fruit and some teiids eat almost nothing but plant food.

Blue-tailed babies
The few teiid species whose reproduction has been studied are egg-layers and this is likely to be the case throughout the family. Detailed studies have been made on the six-lined racerunner and one of the ameivas. The males in a colony fight each other and mate with any females that are responsive. When courting the male rubs his pelvis against the ground then, having found a receptive partner, rubs her with his pelvis and hindlegs. Racerunners lay one or two clutches a year, with 1—6 eggs in each clutch. The eggs are laid in sandy soil or under rocks and hatch in 8—10 weeks. The hatchlings are 1½ in. long and have blue tails at birth.

Unusual teiids
The tegu sometimes lays its eggs in termite nests built in trees. The walls of the nests are extremely hard and it must be very difficult for the female tegu to force her way in, let alone for the baby tegus to get out, for the termites repair the damage caused by the female's entry and so quickly seal the eggs in.

The tegu eggs are undoubtedly safe inside the termite nest, whereas most reptile eggs are very vulnerable to predators. The adult teiids are also eaten by a number of predators such as snakes, armadillos and coyotes, but the rough teiids of the tropical American rain forests are protected because their slender, rough bodies make them look like dead sticks on the forest floor. Furthermore if touched they become as rigid as a stick. Another teiid *Proctoporus shrevei* indulges in advertisement rather than concealment. It lives in caves on Trinidad and the males have a row of spots on each flank which glow in the dark.

class	**Reptilia**
order	**Squamata**
suborder	**Sauria**
family	**Teiidae**
genera & species	*Ameiva spp.* ameivas *Bachia cophias* earless teiid *Cnemidophorus sexlineatus* six-lined racerunner *Dracaena guianensis* caiman lizard *Tupinambis nigropunctatus* tegu

▽ *More snake-like than lizard:* **Euspondylus**. *Some teiid lizards resemble snakes even to the extent of losing their legs.*

Viviparous lizard

The viviparous or common lizard could be said to be a typical lizard. It has a slender body with a long tapering tail and well-developed limbs, a short, flat tongue, not deeply forked, external ear openings and the two halves of the lower jaw are firmly connected. The teeth are very small and conical, unfitted to deal with hard substances. It averages 5 in. in length, the female being slightly longer, with a maximum of about 7 in. The female is more heavily built, the male being the more graceful, his tail tapering gradually to a very fine tip. Although the tail is equal in length to the head and body in both sexes, that of the female appears shorter, owing to its sudden tapering beyond the thick basal portion.

It varies from yellow-grey to purple-brown above, with dark spots forming more or less broken longitudinal lines. There is sometimes a blackish line following the backbone to just behind the hips and a dark band edged with yellow along the sides. On the underside the males are orange or red, spotted with black. The females are orange, yellow or pale greenish, with or without black spots, or sometimes with only a few small grey dots. All-black, melanistic individuals occasionally occur.

The viviparous lizard lives farther north than any other European reptile. It ranges over most of Europe and Asia, except for southern and southeast Asia. It is found over the whole of the British Isles, including the Isle of Man, and is the only reptile found in Ireland.

Variety of habitat

The viviparous lizard, found in a wide variety of climates and habitats, is one of the hardiest reptiles. It lives as high as 8 000 ft in the Balkans and extends north of the Arctic Circle in Lapland. Elsewhere it is common on heaths, in open woods, in hedgerows, gardens and on sand dunes. It frequently basks in the sun and individuals have favourite spots such as a patch of sand or on an old wall. Sometimes as many as 50 have been seen lying together, basking, with their bodies flattened and limbs extended to catch as much sun as possible. Yet the viviparous lizard is intolerant of excessive heat. Indeed, in southern Europe it is found only in the mountain districts where it can keep cool.

The lizard is agile and graceful. Its movements are almost too quick for the eye to follow; and it is even more difficult to catch. It runs with a nimble glide, shooting forward in short dashes from one tuft of herbage to the next, the body and tail scarcely lifted from the ground. It can also run easily over the tops of heather shoots, spreading its toes out to cover the gaps between the foliage. The claws are used to ascend vertical walls or even posts with smooth surfaces. The lizard can also swim well and will pursue prey in water. It has good hearing and is said to respond to some musical sounds. A few people have claimed they can attract it from its hiding place by a particular whistle. In the British Isles hibernation begins in October, the adults going before the young ones which, in a warm autumn, have been seen out in the south of England as late as November. It is one of the first reptiles to reappear in the spring. In the southern parts of its range this may be as early as February but usually it is in March, the males and young coming out first, the females some weeks later.

Fond of spiders

Viviparous lizards feed mainly on insects, including flies, beetles and moths, as well as ants and their larvae, and they are particularly fond of spiders. Small caterpillars are swallowed whole, large ones chewed, the insides swallowed and the skin rejected.

▽ *Vantage point: a viviparous lizard seeks the warmest point on a rock. Although they enjoy basking in the sun, these reptiles cannot tolerate excessive heat.*

They locate insects by sound and will spend several minutes looking for one after hearing the rustle of the insect among grass or dry leaves. In captivity the viviparous lizard has been seen to enter a large bowl of water to seize an insect that had fallen onto the surface of the water. On rare occasions it has been seen in the wild swimming, apparently for the same purpose.

Living young

Mating takes place in April and May with no obvious courtship but with some fighting between the males. Gestation is about 3 months. As the name *vivipara* implies, the female retains her eggs until they are fully developed and ready to hatch. Thus the young are born free from the egg-membrane or else the membrane is broken either during or immediately after leaving her body. When kept in captivity the mother makes no attempt at a nest or concealment and seems to take no interest in her young. In the wild, however, she digs a shallow pit, preferably well concealed in moist soil, into which she deposits her young, in July or August. There are 5–8 at a birth, exceptionally 4 or 10. The baby lizards are $1\frac{1}{2}$–2 in.

long at birth. Most of them are bronze-brown but a few are born black and change to bronze-brown within a week. The underparts are greyish-brown and the back and sides are often speckled with gold. Within a few hours they begin to feed, hunting small soft-bodied insects such as aphides. From the first they are agile and skilful in the search for food. Males reach sexual maturity at 21 months.

Self-mutilation for safety

Large numbers of viviparous lizards fall victim to snakes, birds and other predators. Like many other species of lizards they are able to cast off the tail in order to elude an enemy and then grow a new one.

When attempting to catch a lizard, it is best to grasp it by the shoulders. If the tail is held instead, it will probably come away in the hand, snapping readily at a joint near the base. Another tail will grow from the stump if the lizard lives long enough, but it is always a poor, ungraceful affair compared with the original. General opinion is that the tail snaps off as a result of the mechanical pressure exerted in grasping it. In fact, the lizard actually throws off its tail. For example, it can happen that the lizard is held by the body, yet the tail comes away, nevertheless. Conversely, tame lizards accustomed to being handled will not lose their tails even when held by them. The autotomy (self-cutting), as the operation is called, is governed by a nervous reflex and a special breaking point in the tail. At that point, there is a line of weakness through one of the vertebrae, almost cutting it in two. Opposite this point each blood vessel and nerve is narrowed as in the waist of an hour-glass. So everything is ready for the tail to be thrown off by muscular contraction with the least damage and shock to the animal itself. The narrow neck in each blood vessel at this point serves as a natural ligature and keeps bleeding to a minimum when the break comes.

When cast off, the tail continues to lash violently, so it twists and bounces in a truly startling manner. The predator's eye is held by this unusual spectacle, while the former owner glides like lightning into the nearest cover. It is easy to imagine how successfully the antics of the severed tail can divert attention from the escaping lizard.

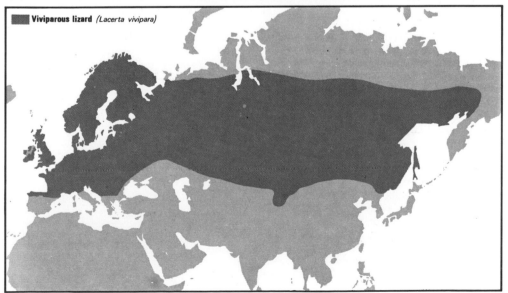

◁ △ *The first steps of a live-born viviparous lizard watched by its parent. The egg-membranes of the other young have not yet ruptured, and the remains of the yolk may be seen inside them as well as the forms of the baby lizards.*
◁ *The viviparous lizard is quite widely distributed in northern and central Europe and temperate Asia. In the Alpine and northern Balkan countries it occurs mainly as a mountain dweller, ascending to 9 000 ft. It is the only reptile found in Ireland.*

■ **Viviparous lizard** *(Lacerta vivipara)*

class	**Reptilia**
order	**Squamata**
suborder	**Sauria**
family	**Lacertidae**
genus & species	*Lacerta vivipara*

Wall lizard

The wall lizard got its name originally from its habit of living in the walls separating fields. The adult male grows to a length of 8 in. including a tail of up to 5½ in. The female is slightly shorter. It has an elegant appearance, with a slender body and tail, a narrow, pointed head, and well-developed limbs with long, slender toes. The numerous small scales on the back are granular and there are six rows of larger scales on the abdomen. As in nearly all lizards, the tail is very brittle and readily shed, but can be regenerated. The wall lizard presents such an amazing variation in colour that it is almost impossible to give anything but the most general description. The ground colour varies from grey to red-brown or black, sometimes with a bronze or greenish tinge and with lines or a series of white, yellow or green spots along each flank. The lower flanks are spotted with blue, green or white. The underparts vary from a milky white to copper-red, often spotted with black. The male's throat is usually cream, bordered with reddish-brown or blue. In addition, the brightness and variety of their colours change as the sunlight flashes on them.

Up to 14 subspecies or local races of the wall lizard have been described, usually distinguished only by their colours. The wall lizard is found in central and southern Europe from Holland, Germany and Poland to the countries bordering on both sides of the Mediterranean as far east as Asia Minor. It is also found in the Channel Islands. Some 200 wall lizards were liberated in southwest England in 1937, where the climate is very similar to that of the Channel Islands. Although they were seen for some years they did not flourish and are thought now to be extinct.

Lively and agile

The wall lizard lives in dry regions among rocks, walls and old buildings and can sometimes be found in gardens, especially in rockeries. It is very lively and active, running so fast that it comes and goes in a flash. It is an expert climber, even up perpendicular walls. It sees and hears well and is very inquisitive, investigating anything out of the ordinary. Although it will swim if necessary it will drown if it does not reach the bank quickly. Like all lizards, the wall lizards love to bask in the sun but will retire to crannies or holes in the rocks in cloudy or rainy weather. Each has its favourite spot on a rock or wall where it may be found regularly. In southern Europe wall lizards can be seen in large numbers lying in the sun on almost every wall, rock or ruined building and at times they can become quite tame.

In the northern part of its range the wall lizard hibernates from October to March among stones or rocks or in holes in the ground. In the south the period of hibernation is much shorter.

△ *Both male (left) and female wall lizards have their own regular basking places.*

Opportunist feeders

Wall lizards feed mainly on flies and other small insects or their larvae as well as on other small invertebrates. They will occasionally feed on fruit and soft plants. Like the European robin and other small birds, they will sometimes follow anyone working in the fields or garden to pick up the insects disturbed by the digging, and they have even been known to scramble about at the feet of picnickers, picking up any scraps of food.

Two or three clutches

In the wild the wall lizard mates usually in April, the female laying 3–9 oval white eggs in a hole dug in the soil. These hatch after about 2 months. There may be 2 or 3 clutches in one season. On hatching the young wall lizards are 1½–2 in. long. In captivity wall lizards live up to 3 years.

Attractive pet

With their beautiful colours and lively inquisitive ways wall lizards make charming pets. They are among the most popular of vivarium animals and every year thousands are exported from southern Europe. If kept in a vivarium it should be large and able to contain as many lizards as possible as wall lizards seem to like each other's company, running around seemingly playing with each other. The bottom of the vivarium should be covered in sand and there should be rocks and stones for the lizards to climb over and crevices where they can hide. There should also be some small plants and always a dish of water. They thrive on small earthworms, mealworms and other small soft insects and their larvae.

Colour preferences

Lizards will search for prey that eludes them and disappears from sight, making what look like purposive attempts to find it. They are helped by having keen eyesight and by an acute sense of hearing. A wall lizard living in a vivarium with a floor of dead leaves will search for a mealworm that crawls under the leaves, standing and turning its head from one side to the other, as if listening to the very slight, almost inaudible rustling. Then it will scrape over the leaves with its forefeet and pounce on the mealworm the moment it sees it.

Most lizards seem to show a preference for green, the commonest colour in their environment. Wall lizards living among rocks seem to be conditioned to preferring yellow, as well as orange and red, which may also be linked with their liking for fruit. They seem especially fond of the flesh of oranges, yellow plums and strawberries. When the lizard is in a vivarium, separated experimentally by glass from these fruits—the whole being so arranged that the lizard cannot receive the odour from them—it will make deliberate movements to reach the fruit, such as scratching the glass with its front feet.

class	**Reptilia**
order	**Squamata**
suborder	**Sauria**
family	**Lacertidae**
genus & species	***Lacerta muralis***

Adder

A snake, member of the viper family, the adder has a relatively stout body and a short tail. The average male is 21 in. long, the female 2 ft – the record length is 2 ft 8 in. The head is flat, broadening behind the eyes to form an arrow-head shape.

The colour and body-markings vary considerably; adders are among the few snakes in which male and female are coloured differently. Generally the ground colour is a shade of brown, olive, grey or cream; but black varieties in which all patterning is obliterated are fairly common. The most characteristic marking is the dark zig-zag line down the back with a series of spots on either side; the head carries a pair of dark bands, often forming an X or a V.

It is often possible to distinguish the sex of an adder by its colour. Those which are cream, dirty yellow, silvery or pale grey, or light olive, with black markings, are usually males; females are red, reddish brown or gold, with darker red or brown markings. The throat of the male is black, or whitish with the scales spotted or edged with black; females have a yellowish-white chin sometimes tinged with red.

Distribution and habits

The adder ranges throughout Europe and across Asia to Sakhalin Island, north of Japan. In the British Isles it is absent from Ireland and the northern isles. It is usually to be seen in dry places such as sandy heaths, moors and the sunny slopes of hills where it often basks in the sun on hedge-banks, logs and piles of stones. It is, however, also found in damp situations.

Its tolerance of cold allows the adder to live as far north as Finland, beyond the Arctic Circle. It escapes cold weather by hibernation, which starts when the shade temperature falls below 9°C/49°F. It emerges again when the air temperature rises above 8°C/46°F – even coming out onto snow –

△ *The adder's tongue looks menacing but is harmless. It is a smell-taste organ, picking up particles from the air and withdrawing them for analysis in the mouth.*

▽ *The hedgehog is one of the adder's arch-enemies. It is protected by its spines while it alternately bites and rolls up, until the adder is dead.*

but a cold spell will send it in again. The duration of hibernation depends, therefore, on climate: in northern Europe it may last up to 275 days, whereas in the south it may be as little as 105 days. In Britain, adders usually hibernate for about 135 days in October-March, depending on the weather.

Unlike many other snakes adders do not burrow but seek out crevices and holes where they lie up for the winter. The depth at which they hibernate depends, like duration, on the climate: in Britain the average depth is 10−12 in., but in Denmark, where winters are more severe, adders are found at depths of 4 ft.

Very often many adders will be found in one den, or hibernaculum. As many as 40 have been found coiled up together, along with a number of toads and lizards. This massing together is a method of preventing heat loss, but it is not known how the adders come to congregate in the hibernacula, which are used year after year. It may be that they can detect the scent left from previous years.

It is uncertain whether adders are nocturnal or diurnal. Their eyes are typical of nocturnal animals in that they are rich in the very sensitive rod cells: such eyes will see well at night, but during the day they need protection, and the adder's slit pupils cut down the intensity of light. On the other hand, despite these adaptations, adders are often active during the day. Courtship and some feeding are definitely diurnal; feeding depends on how hungry the adder is.

Rodent killer
The adder's main prey is lizards, mice, voles and shrews. Young adders subsist at first

A black adder. Adders range in colour from cream, through dirty yellow to silvery grey or olive (male); and from red to gold (female).

on insects and worms. Larger victims are killed by a poisonous bite, the effects of which vary with the size of the prey. A lizard will be dead within a few minutes, or even within 30 seconds; but an adder's bite is rarely fatal to humans. There were only seven authenticated records of fatalities through snakebite in England and Wales in the first half of this century, and four of these were children.

The adder's method of hunting is to follow its prey by scent, then poison it with a quick strike of the head. While the venom acts, the victim may have time to escape to cover, in which case the snake will wait for a while then follow to eat its dead prey.

Dance of the adders
The mating period is from the end of March to early May, though it has been known to last until autumn. In the north of Europe the summer is too short for the eggs to mature in one year, so breeding takes place in alternate years.

At the beginning of the breeding season, there is a good deal of territorial rivalry between males, culminating in the 'dance of the adders'. Two males face each other with head erect and the forepart of the body held off the ground. They sway from side to side, then with bodies entwined each attempts to force the other to the ground by pushing and thrusting. They do not attempt to bite each other.

Finally one gives up and departs. The female, who is frequently waiting close at hand, will accept any victorious male, if she is ready, and a male will mate with any female. He crawls up behind her and loops his coils over her body, rubbing his chin (which has especially sensitive skin) on her back until he reaches the back of her neck, and mating takes place.

Adders are ovoviviparous: that is, the eggs remain inside the mother's body until they are fully developed, and the young are born coiled up in a membrane which is ruptured by their convulsive movements. They have an egg tooth, which in other animals is used to rupture the egg membranes, but in adders it is degenerate as they have no need of it, and the tooth is so situated that it is of no use for this purpose. It is shed a few days after birth.

The young are born in August or September and the number ranges from five to 20: 10-14 are most common, each measuring 6-8 inches in length. They are immediately capable of independent existence, but often they appear to stay with the mother. Young adders disappear so quickly when disturbed that there is an ancient legend, an account of which appears in Holinshed's Chronicle of 1577, that in times of danger the mother adder swallows her offspring. This legend could be due to early observers cutting up an ovoviviparous mother and finding unborn adders inside. Not knowing that adders hatch from the egg inside the parent they would think she had swallowed them.

△ *Male (left) and female adders are always differently coloured.*

▽ *Adder with day-old young.*

The adder has no external ear or ear drum, but picks up vibrations from the ground through its lower jaw. The vertical slit pupil gives quick perception of horizontal movement.

Enemies although poisonous
Like most animals—even those well capable of defending themselves—adders are most likely to flee if confronted with danger, and they usually bite only if suddenly frightened. But, despite not having the excuse of self-defence, man is their chief enemy. However, the killing of adders on sight has not led to their decline, although nowadays increased urbanisation is destroying their habitat.

Undoubtedly many carnivores will take adders. Foxes and badgers kill them, and they have been found in the stomachs of pike and eels. Surprisingly, perhaps, the hedgehog is a great adversary of adders: one reason is that it can tolerate large doses of venom without harm. Its method of killing is to bite the adder, then curl up leaving nothing but a palisade of spines for the snake to strike at. It repeats the process of biting and curling until the snake is dead, after which the hedgehog eats it.

A confusion of names
The Anglo-Saxon name for the adder was *naedre*, which became 'a nadder' or 'a nedder' in Middle English. Later the *n* was transposed, so that we now have 'an adder'. The alternative name viper comes from the Anglo-Saxon *vipere* or *vipre*, itself derived from the Latin *vipera*. This was a contraction of *vivipara*, from *vivus* (alive) and *parere* (to bring forth)—alluding to the animal's method of reproduction. In general 'viper' was used to mean any venomous snake. There being only one such snake in England, viper and adder became synonymous for the one species (viper also being used to describe a venomous or spiteful person).

The two words have spread with the English language all over the world, being used not only for snakes of the genus *Vipera*. There are the near relatives such as the gaboon viper, more distant, like the pit vipers and mole vipers, and the death adder, which is not even in the viper family.

class	**Reptilia**
order	**Squamata**
suborder	**Serpentes**
family	**Viperidae**
genus & species	***Vipera berus***

Anaconda

The largest snakes are to be found in the boa family, and the largest of these is **Eunectes murinus**, *the anaconda or water boa. Probably no animal has been the subject of such exaggeration in respect of size. The name itself is said to come from the Tamil words* **anai** *for elephant and* **kolra** *for killer. Properly this name must have originally referred to the anaconda's relative, the Indian python. Claims for 140-ft anacondas have been made and 40 ft often occurs in travel literature. The famous explorer, Colonel Fawcett, claimed to have killed a 62-ft anaconda and was pronounced 'an utter liar' by London opinion. In fact, a 20-ft anaconda is a large specimen, although it must be presumed that larger individuals do occur. It is difficult to find an authentic record for the largest anacondas. The measurement of 37½ ft for one specimen has been widely accepted by scientists but not by all. Long ago, the New York Zoological Society offered a prize of 5,000 dollars for a 30-ft anaconda. This has never been won.*

The anaconda is olive green with large, round black spots along the length of its body and two light longitudinal stripes on the head. It lives throughout tropical South America, east of the Andes, mainly in the Amazon and Orinoco basins, and in the Guianas. It extends north to Trinidad. The species is variable in colour and size giving rise to numerous sub-specific names. However, these can be regarded as merely geographical variations. The closely related **Eunectes notaeus** *of Paraguay is known as the Paraguayan or southern anaconda.*

Life by jungle streams and swamps

Water boa is a good alternative name for the anaconda, the most aquatic of the boas. It is apparently never found far from water; sluggish or still waters being preferred to rapid streams. It is this preference that limits the species to the basins east of the Andes. Swamps are a favourite haunt.

Anacondas have, as a rule, fixed hunting grounds and generally live alone, but they are occasionally seen in groups.

Largely nocturnal in habit, anacondas lie up during the day in the shallows or sun-bathe on low branches, usually over water. On land they are relatively sluggish, but they are able to swim rapidly and often float motionless, allowing the current to carry them downstream.

Killing by constriction

Anacondas usually lie in wait for their prey to come down to the water's edge to drink, whereupon they strike quickly with the head, grabbing the luckless prey and dragging it underwater so that it drowns. At other times anacondas may actively hunt prey on land.

The usual prey caught by lying in wait are birds and small mammals—deer, peccaries

Anaconda is the largest of snakes, reaching up to 37 ft, although exaggerated claims give lengths of 140 ft. They kill their prey by constricting. Each time the victim breathes out, the anaconda tightens its coils until the animal dies of suffocation.

and large rodents such as agoutis. Fish also form a large part of the diet, a fact not surprising in so aquatic an animal. More surprisingly, turtles and caimans are sometimes attacked. There is a record of a 25-ft anaconda killing a 6-ft caiman. The special jaw attachment that snakes have allows an anaconda to swallow such a large victim. After a meal of this size, which will suffice an anaconda for several weeks, the snake rests for a week or more until digestion has taken place. Normally the diet will consist of more frequent smaller meals.

Most snakes are adapted for swallowing prey wider than themselves: the upper and lower jaws are only loosely attached, and the brain protected from pressure by massive bones. Also a valve on the breathing tube allows the snake to breathe while swallowing.

The method of killing the prey is the same as in other constricting snakes such as the pythons. The prey is not crushed, but merely contained; each time the victim exhales, the coils of the anaconda tighten around its chest so that the ribs cannot expand, thus preventing inhalation until it suffocates. Stories in travelogues refer to anacondas' prey having every bone in the body broken and being squashed to pulp. In reality, bones are rarely broken during the process just described, which is one of strangulation. The fallacy is due to confusion between freshly-killed and regurgitated prey. This is covered with mucus, smear their prey with saliva to facilitate swallowing.

Breeding

Few observations have been made on the breeding cycle of the anaconda. Males of southern anacondas studied in captivity were apparently aroused by the scent of the females. The male moves up alongside the female, flicking his tongue over her, until his head is resting over her neck. When in this position, he erects his spurs, two claw-like projections which are the last visible remnants of the hind limbs. The spurs are moved backwards and forwards against the female's skin and when the cloacal regions are in opposition, a hemipenis is inserted and copulation takes place.

Anacondas, like other boas, are viviparous. From 20—40, sometimes up to 100 young are born in the early part of the year. Each baby is 2—3 ft long.

Anacondas in folklore

It is not surprising that such a large, and malevolent-looking creature should be the subject of folklore and fallacy. The South American Indians have numerous stories about the anaconda, from the belief that it turns itself into a boat with white sails at night, to the mythology of the Taruma Indians who claimed to be descended from an anaconda. Several factors have led to tales of giant snakes. For one thing size is notoriously difficult to estimate unless a comparison can be made with something of known dimensions. Exaggeration is more likely if the animal is moving and writhing around, or if the observer has had a shock, as he might well have on suddenly seeing an anaconda Secondly, snake skins stretch very easily when being prepared so that the length of a skin gives no concrete evidence. It is not therefore difficult to see how stories of giant snakes could have arisen, and, once started, how this has led to unwitting or deliberate embroidery. Along with stories of venomous qualities and body size, there is exaggeration about the danger involved in meeting an anaconda. This is not unique; all large carnivorous animals become surrounded by stories of their man-eating habits. Many accounts are pure fiction. Only a few years ago a book was published describing a 140-ft anaconda, and how the author narrowly escaped from a 45-ft specimen by shooting its head off.

Other stories are reported truthfully but are not evidence of man-eating habits, but of self-defence, for when man blunders into an animal it is not surprising that it tries to defend itself. There are, however, remarkably few authentic stories of people killed and eaten. Rolf Blomberg, who has made many searches for record-sized specimens, has been able to find only two fairly definite instances of anacondas killing human beings. In only one case was it claimed that the victim, a 13-year-old boy, was eaten. Even this was somewhat doubtful because the story goes that he disappeared while bathing with friends. On discovering his absence, one of them dived down to search and saw an anaconda. The victim's father then hunted down the snake and shot it. Blomberg states that the boy's body had been vomited up but does not say whether,

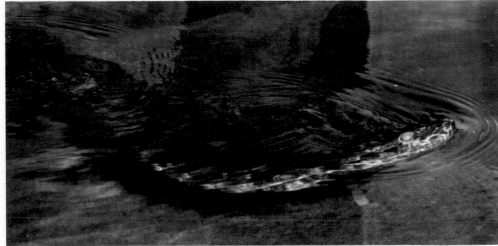

△ *An alternative name for the anaconda is water boa as it is never found far from the sluggish forest streams or swamps. Anacondas move relatively slowly on land but can swim rapidly and often float motionless, allowing the current to carry them downstream.*

▽ *Anacondas often lie up during the day in branches over the water's edge and wait for their prey to come down at night to drink, when they strike quickly with the head, grab the prey in their coils, often dragging it down into the water, to drown.*

in fact, it was recovered or whether this was only surmise. In the other incident a grown man was captured by an anaconda while swimming and was drowned. His body, when later found, had distinct marks of having been subjected to a powerful squeeze, but there was no indication of his having been swallowed.

Here then are two reports of the death of human beings, caused by anacondas. As we have seen, there is scme doubt about one of them and in the second the man may have been killed but there is nothing to show he was eaten. In fact, few anacondas would be large enough to swallow a man. Nevertheless, such stories, perhaps in a garbled form, would travel through the country, so giving the impression that anacondas are man-eaters. After this, anyone who disappeared

and was last seen at the water's edge would be presumed to have been eaten by the anaconda, especially if one of these large snakes was seen in the vicinity. Such stories are so sensational that nobody asks for details or unequivocal evidence and the travellers would then take home a supposedly authentic story to relate to eager and uncritical audiences.

class	**Reptilia**
order	**Squamata**
suborder	**Serpentes**
family	**Boidae**
genus & species	***Eunectes murinus*** ***E. notaeus***

Asp

The asp, aspic viper or June viper, closely related to the common adder is a member of the family Viperidae. This is not stating the obvious because there are snakes called vipers that do not belong, and are not true vipers. In colour the two are also rather similar, the ground colour of the asp being lighter, usually grey, grey-brown, coppery red or orange. The underparts are grey, dirty yellow or blackish, with a sulphur yellow or orange red patch under the tip of the tail. The upper part of the body is often marked with transverse dark brown or black bars, sometimes zig-zags, and occasionally there is an inverted V on the head.

Differences in size and colour are very much less marked than in the adder.

The neck of the asp is more slender than that of the adder and the species rarely attains a length of more than 2 ft, the largest on record being 2 ft 2½ in.

Immediate distinction between the adder and the asp can be made by looking closely at the head. The shields on the asp's head are small, and the iris of the eye is shiny yellow, as compared with the coppery-red of the adder. Furthermore, the tip of the asp's snout is turned up to make a small spike. This feature is more conspicuous in two related species, the long-nosed viper of southern Europe and Lataste's viper of Spain and north-west Africa.

Distribution and habits

The asp is common in many parts of Europe, generally farther south than the adder, but where the two overlap it is often difficult to decide to which species a specimen belongs. Hilly or low mountainous country is especially favoured, often at high levels. They have been recorded at 9 700 ft in the Alps. Their distribution is quite wide-spread throughout Europe as shown in the map overleaf.

The habitat of the asp is generally warmer and drier than that of the adder. It frequents rocks, waste land, hedges and scrub, rather than sandy heaths, like the adder. Each individual has a small home range of several square yards which it rarely leaves. Asps are active by day and night, retiring at irregular intervals to a hole in the earth or between rocks. In winter they hibernate,

*Asp **Vipera aspis** showing the tip of its snout turning up to make a small spike.*

sometimes several individuals coiling together in one hibernaculum.

The asp is a slow-moving snake, but it is aggressive and is more dangerous to man than the adder. Accidents are fairly common especially in the south of France where the animal is common, and bites have proved fatal. Nevertheless, even in the south of France, where there are probably more cases of snake bite than anywhere else in Europe, venomous snakes are not such a danger to the public as in tropical regions.

Carnivorous feeders
Small mammals such as mice and voles, young birds and lizards make up the bulk of the asp's food. The very young eat earthworms and insects.

Ritual breeding battles
Pairing takes place in April and May. Males indulge in a ritual battle, while the females watch. First, the males attempt to intimidate each other by rearing up in an S-shape, then, if neither retreats, they chase each other and try to coil round each other's bodies. They never attempt to bite and neither is ever harmed.

Asps are ovoviviparous, the eggs being retained in the mother's body until they are due to hatch. Sometimes the egg-membrane ruptures while still in the oviduct and the young are born alive. A female produces 4—18 young, measuring 7—8 in.

Cleopatra's asp
Asps are best known for being the kind of snake with which Cleopatra killed herself. Yet it is hardly likely that she would have used the asp *Vipera aspis* as this species does not live in Egypt. The reason for Cleopatra's snake being called an asp is that in past times the name was given to any kind of venomous snake, much in the same way as 'serpent' is used to describe any snake.

The drawback to a member of the viper family being employed for suicide is that, even when deliberately encouraged, their bites are not often fatal. What is more, the effects of viper venom are usually painful and messy. The venom of vipers is a systemic poison, which clots the blood and destroys the lining of the blood vessels. The venom of cobras, on the other hand, is a quick-acting poison that interferes with the action of nerves and muscles. Herpetologists, specialists in the study of reptiles, have argued that Cleopatra's asp was most likely to have been the Egyptian cobra, *Naja haje*. This snake has been known for a long time as being able to kill quickly and painlessly, and was often offered to political prisoners as an alternative to more painful and dishonourable ways of dying.

As final support to this argument, it is the Egyptian cobra that is depicted on the headdresses in ancient works of art.

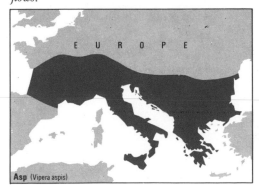

△ *Cleopatra with row of snakes on top of headdress. Although the asp is usually said to be the snake with which Cleopatra killed herself, it was most likely to have been the Egyptian cobra, which kills painlessly and quickly.*
▷ *Viper skull showing wide gape and the curved front fangs through which the venom flows.*

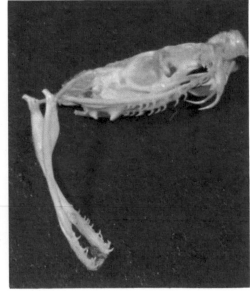

Asp (Vipera aspis)

class	**Reptilia**
order	**Squamata**
suborder	**Serpentes**
family	**Viperidae**
genus & species	***Vipera aspis***

Blind snake

The family Typhlopidae includes over two hundred species of small, non-poisonous snakes. They are usually 6—7 in. long but some species reach lengths of 1—2 ft, and the South African Schlegel's blind snake has reached 3 ft. In form they are worm-like with blunt heads, long, cylindrical bodies and short tails. The eyes are minute and can do no more than distinguish between light and dark.

It has been suggested, on the basis of characters of the skull, that blind snakes are lizards rather than snakes and that they have lost their legs and taken to slithering on their bellies like the slow-worm. There are still the vestiges of a pelvis showing their descent from a walking animal.

The family Leptotyphlopidae are also known as blind snakes. They are very similar to the Typhlopidae in outward appearance and habits but are not related. Alternative names are thread snakes, worm snakes or slender blind snakes.

Blind snakes are found in most warm parts of the world, but not in the Pacific Islands. In America they range from southern Mexico to Paraguay.

One species lives in Greece and the Balkans, in Europe. Another species, the natural range of which is from Arabia to Indonesia, has been spread to other parts of the world, under the name of flower-pot snake, because it is found among the roots of pot plants. It has reached South Africa, Hawaii and Mexico with exported plants.

Blind snake or worm snake **Typhlops blanfordi** from Ethiopia. Its head is protected by a large scale covering the snout and it lives underground so very little is known of its habits.

Strengthened skull for burrowing life

Like most other animals that live underground, such as moles and mole rats, blind snakes have minute eyes. There is little use for sight in the shallow burrows in soil and sand or under logs and rocks, where blind snakes live. They prefer moist situations and during the dry season they burrow deeper, perhaps as much as 2 ft. After rain they come to the surface, and during the monsoons they may be washed out of their shallow burrows.

The skulls of most snakes and lizards are not at all suited for burrowing. They are made up of many small bones that are only loosely attached to each other. Without limbs to dig the soil out of the way, blind snakes must dig by forcing the head into the ground. So it is not surprising that they, and the similar thread snakes, have strong skulls with the individual bones fused together. The head is also protected by a large scale covering the snout. The tail of blind snakes ends in a sharp spike which the animal drives into the ground so that the body has something firm to push against. In many ways the bodies of blind snakes have become adapted for burrowing in the same way as those of another kind of lizard, the amphisbaena.

Few teeth for eating termites

Blind snakes live on worms, insects and other small animals living in the soil or under rocks or logs. Many species live mainly on ants or termites and some even live in their nests.

We have seen how mammals which eat ants and termites, such as the aardvarks and aardwolves, have only a few, weak teeth, and this trait is paralleled in the reptiles. Blind snakes have teeth only in the upper jaw, except for one American genus, which has one tooth on each side of its lower jaw, and the thread snakes have teeth only in the lower jaw.

This strange creature could be snake or lizard.

Corkscrew mating technique

As they live underground and are so difficult to observe, the breeding habits are not well known. Some species are viviparous (see adder, page 203), but most lay eggs.

In mating, the male wraps his body like a corkscrew around the female. She lays a variable number of eggs, depending on her age. Young females of Schlegel's blind snake lay about a dozen eggs, while old individuals lay up to 60. The eggs are large in comparison with the size of the mother's body. Bibron's blind snake, which is some 15 in. long when mature, lays up to eight eggs, each ¾ in. long and ⅓ in. in diameter.

Snakes eat snakes

Blind snakes probably have few enemies except when flushed out of their burrows by floods, when they are sitting targets for any flesh-eater or scavenger. Otherwise, snakes seem to be their main enemies. The remains of a blind snake 9½ in. long were found in the stomach of a burrowing mole-viper, a species that itself rarely grows to more than 1½ ft.

Snakes on tap

In some parts of Africa blind snakes are regarded as the army ants' cows as they have been seen crawling along in the middle of a column of army ants. It is more likely that the relationship is the other way round, that the blind snakes are feeding on the army ants.

Another local belief is that the sharp, claw-like scale on the tail is a sting, so this harmless snake has the reputation of being dangerous. The idea is probably reinforced by a blind snake's attempts to stick the scale into the hand of anyone holding it, but this is to provide leverage to wriggle out of the grasp rather than to inject venom.

Whether they thought blind snakes were harmless or not, there was an occasion many years ago when some of the citizens of Calcutta had a nasty shock from the sudden appearance of blind snakes, and this shock can well be imagined. After some very wet weather large numbers of flower-pot snakes were washed out of their shallow burrows and into the water supply to reappear through taps all over the city.

class	**Reptilia**
order	**Squamata**
suborder	**Serpentes**
family	**Typhlopidae**
genus	*Typhlops*

Boa

The boa constrictor is one of the stock dangerous animals that the explorers of romantic tales meet. Several snakes of the family Boidae are called boas in ordinary language but none is so well-known as the boa constrictor, although this name has also come to mean any large snake. The boa constrictor is not even the largest of the boa family, being dwarfed by the anaconda (see page 205). Sizes of most snakes have been exaggerated but there is a reliable record of a boa constrictor 18½ ft long. A 15 ft specimen is considered to be very long.

The boa constrictor is found in the warmest parts of America, from the north of Mexico to Argentina, as well as on the West Indian islands of Trinidad and a few other islands of the Lesser Antilles.

Nocturnal hunter in jungle and desert

Although the boa constrictor is virtually harmless to man it may cause great alarm when found near human habitation. Yet boas are not venomous and, like most animals, they will flee rather than stand and fight. Even if provoked into attacking, most boa constrictors are probably not large enough to kill a man by constriction – that is, throwing a series of strangulatory loops around him. In the event of an attack, the man can easily escape by running, for boas are not swift over the ground. The rosy boa of California, a smaller species, has been recorded as travelling at ¼ mph, with spurts of twice that speed.

The fear inspired by the boa constrictor is shown by a story of how a boa constrictor entered a village in Colombia, presumably in search of food. The villagers fled and asked a white man to seek it out and shoot it. He eventually found it asleep on a bed in one of the houses and duly shot it, but the villagers were still reluctant to return, for, they said, its mate was bound to come looking for it. Unlike its relative the anaconda, which stays near water, the boa constrictor lives in many types of country. In Mexico, it is found in semi-arid parts, on the fringes of deserts, while in tropical America boas live in the dense, wet jungles, but as they seldom enter water they do not compete with the anaconda for food. Furthermore, the boa constrictor spends more time in the trees; the anaconda does little climbing. The boa constrictor is mainly nocturnal but it has been seen hunting during the day.

Crops and plantations are also a haunt of boas and they will come into villages in search of food.

Tall stories

The boa that entered the Colombian village was probably in search of dogs or hens. Apart from this robbing of man, boa constrictors feed on a variety of animals. Terrifying tales of the boa constricting large animals, including man, are numerous. The majority are very tall stories and the rest grossly exaggerated. Most of the time the boa satisfies its hunger by taking large lizards and birds, such as antbirds. On one occasion a boa was found to have only the tail of a lizard in its stomach. This is interesting evidence of the value of the lizard's ability to shed its tail when caught at its rear end. Only occasionally are largish mammals taken, a 30–40 lb ocelot was found once in a 10 ft specimen. Normally squirrels, opossums, and spiny rats are the mammals eaten.

If boas are such slow movers it is obvious that they cannot chase swiftly moving prey. Rather, they lie in wait or creep up stealthily on an unsuspecting animal. Less prey will be caught by this slow method, but as snakes need food only at long intervals speed is not necessary. When they are inactive they use up little energy and can survive long periods without eating. Even when supplied with plenty of food, some boa constrictors eat very little. One small pet boa ate only 55 white mice in 18 months. This is a very small intake of food compared with that of a flesh-eating mammal, one of a size comparable with the boa being more likely to eat one mouse a day at least.

The boa constrictor's method of killing its prey is, as its name suggests, by constriction. This is not the same as crushing and is fully described for anacondas (see page 205).

The power of a boa constrictor's digestive juices is demonstrated by the boa that ate a porcupine. A few quills were stuck in the mouth, otherwise it had been digested except for some hair and the claws. A series of X-ray photographs were taken of a boa constrictor to show how it digested its prey. A rat was held in the stomach for four days and photographs showed that the bones were gradually being dissolved. During this period the digested products had been released into the intestine to be absorbed.

Breeding

Both males and females of the boas and pythons have a pair of spurs, one either side of the cloaca, the genital and excretory opening. These spurs are the last visible remains of the hind limbs, although these snakes have vestigial pelvic girdles. The male's spurs are longer than the female's and he uses them to stimulate her to mating by scratching her body, especially around the cloaca. Eventually the female raises her tail allowing the male to wrap his tail round her, and mating takes place.

The details of reproduction are not wellknown. Mating has been recorded from December to March in Trinidad. Young are born alive with an average length of 20 in. There are usually 20–60 young in each brood. They may double their length in the first year, the rate of growth depending very much on temperature and food supply, and some mature when 2 or 3 years old.

Flees from danger

When young, boas have many enemies amongst flesh-eating animals, but as they grow larger fewer of these are able to tackle them. A jungle racer, a notorious snakeeating snake, has been recorded as killing a young boa constrictor.

The boa's reaction to danger is either to flee or to threaten by hissing, a noise like

△ *Emerald tree boa anchored to the branch by its prehensile tail, waiting for a bird or small mammal to come within striking range.*

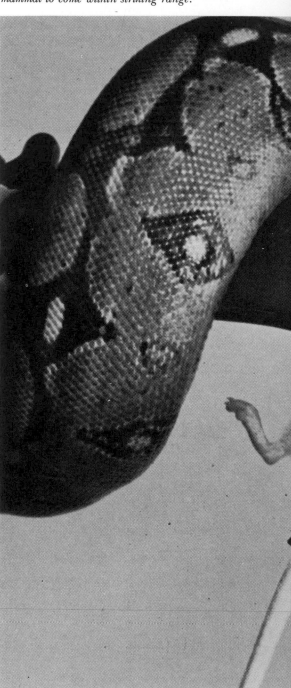

△ Only a few boas live outside the New World and one of them is this sand boa of Africa and Asia.
▽ Boa constrictor engulfing a rat. The boa is often overrated as to size, but they are still big snakes, the record being 18½ ft long. Specimens over 10 ft long are rare.

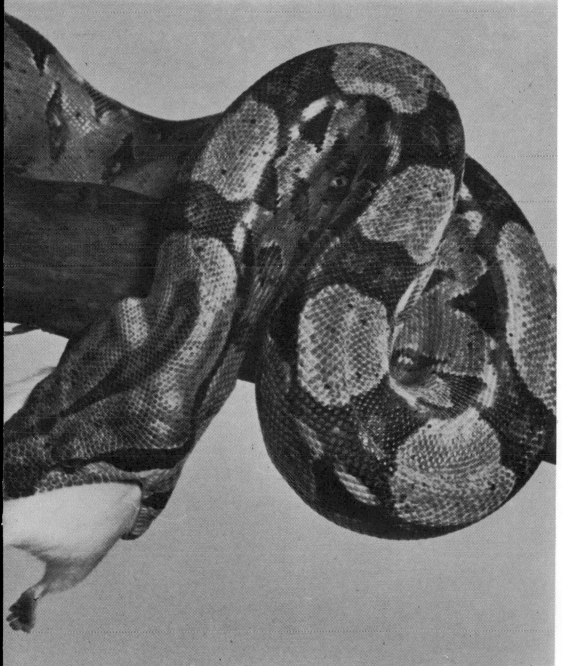

escaping steam that can be heard over a distance of 100 ft. Despite all the hair-raising stories told about boas, they prefer to live a quiet life and only as a last resort defend themselves by biting.

Clues to past history

Were it not for the boas and pythons we should have no direct evidence that the ancestors of snakes had limbs. That would have been a reasonable assumption based on their many lizard-like features but the constrictor snakes actually have the clear remains of a pelvis (or hipbone) and vestiges of hind legs. The pelvis has the same number of bones as in lizards, but they are smaller and not joined to the backbone. The limbs are represented by one, sometimes two bones and a claw, on each side of the body. There are three other kinds of snakes that show vestiges of hind limbs, or a pelvis. Blind snakes (page 209) have a rod of cartilage where the pelvis should be, and thread snakes have a small pelvis and a pair of claw-shaped hind limbs. The cylinder snakes also possess vestigial limbs and pelvis.

There are many vestigial organs known, in both animals and ourselves. The appendix, the blind tube attached to our intestine, which was once a large sac for digesting vegetable matter, is the vestigial organ that most readily springs to mind as it often leads to emergency operations. With this, as with so many others, it is wrong to say, as is often said, that it is useless. Vestigial organs have so often been found to have taken on a new function. The hind limbs of the boa offer a case in point. From being locomotory organs they have degenerated, and are now used for stimulating the female to mate.

class	**Reptilia**
order	**Squamata**
suborder	**Serpentes**
family	**Boidae**
genus & species	***Boa constrictor***

Unlike the related anaconda, the boa shows little preference for water. It is found from the Mexican desert to dense American jungles

Boa (Boa constrictor)

211

Boomslang

The boomslang is one of the rear-fanged snakes in which some of the teeth in the back part of the upper jaw are enlarged and have grooves running down their front surfaces to carry venom. In general, rear-fanged snakes are not dangerous to man, but the boomslang is an exception.

Boomslang is the Afrikaans word for tree snake but is applied to only one of many tree-dwelling snakes. Boomslangs grow up to 6 ft in length but average around 4 ft. The body is slender, the tail long and a distinguishing feature is the round, blunt head and large eyes with round or occasionally slit-like pupil. The coloration of the body is bright green, sometimes with black patches. Females are almost always a uniform light or dark brown. The variation in colour often causes boomslangs to be confused with other species, especially mambas.

Fatal perch

The boomslang is a very agile snake amongst the trees, where it slides gracefully through the branches, aided by a prehensile tail. It often comes down to the ground, however, in search of food or a place to lay its eggs, where it can travel very rapidly, flashing back to cover if disturbed.

Much of its time is spent immobile, coiled on a branch or poised with the front part of the body raised in the air. When immobile it is very difficult to see, its green or green and black body merging with the foliage. Birds, which figure largely in its diet, have been known to perch on it.

Prey held while venom kills

The prey of boomslangs is chameleons and other tree lizards and snakes, together with birds, small mammals and frogs. An animal is seized in the jaws and held firmly while the venom trickles down the grooves in the teeth and acts on the victim. In the case of the larger reptiles it catches, this takes about 15 minutes. This is quite a slow death but the venom is very toxic, only minute quantities being needed to ensure eventual death. A pigeon succumbs after injection with only 0·0002 mg (less than one ten-thousandth of an ounce) of boomslang venom.

The eggs and fledglings of birds are often snatched from their nests and a boomslang may be mobbed by furious, yet still cautious, parent birds if they find it near their nest. Eggs are swallowed whole and the shells dissolved by the strong digestive juices.

Breeding in trees

Unlike most other snakes, boomslangs mate in trees. The eggs, 8–23 in number, are laid in early summer, 4 months after mating. The female seeks out a hollow in which to lay her eggs, perhaps a woodpecker hole in a tree or hollow in a sandy bank, wherever it is warm and moist. The eggs hatch out after 4–7 months and the newly-emerged young measure about 15 in.

Enemies

Usually boomslangs retreat from danger but if threatened or provoked they will inflate the neck and front part of the body with air, so that they look like a cobra with its hood inflated. The distension of the body in this manner separates the scales and shows the brilliantly coloured skin between them, giving a frightening effect. Their natural enemies are therefore few. Boomslangs are, however, cannibalistic, and one can eat another nearly its own size.

Several snakes have been credited with being the most dangerous to man, notably the mamba, the cobra and the krait, but it is very difficult to find an outright winner because so many factors are involved. A snake with a very potent poison may not really be dangerous because it lives in inaccessible places, whereas another with mild venom may habitually haunt dwellings where it is a constant hazard. Sea snakes in Asia cause many deaths among fishermen who walk barefoot through their catch which may harbour a snake.

The boomslang is very hard to place in a hierarchy of dangerous snakes. Its pure venom is very toxic, acting both on the nervous system and on the blood system, dissolving the walls of blood vessels and destroying blood cells. The venom is more toxic, weight for weight, than that of mambas and cobras, yet each boomslang secretes only a very small amount. Added to this, boomslangs are shy and only bite if handled.

They also take some time to inject the venom, having to chew at the wound to allow the venom to penetrate. So if the snake is knocked away immediately, the bite may not be very severe. Donald Broadley, a Rhodesian herpetologist (a snake specialist), records how he was bitten on the finger by a boomslang while demonstrating snakes in the Salisbury Snake Park. He immediately pulled it off and cut incisions around the bite and encouraged a flow of blood. An hour later he developed a splitting headache and was taken to hospital. The next day blood transfusions were started to replace the destroyed blood cells and the bleeding from gums and stomach. Later, blood appeared in the urine and it was only after 16 pints of blood had been transfused in the following week that the bleeding stopped. During this time he had felt no pain, only a weakness from loss of blood.

Another herpetologist was luckier. He was bitten through his shirt and very little venom entered his body. However, he was very ill for a few days. Both these men knew what to do in the event of snakebite and had access to antidotes and medical aid, but where there is neither knowledge nor medication, boomslang bites can prove fatal.

Few birds or tree-climbing lizards are safe from the deadly poisonous boomslang which is very agile amongst the trees and can glide gracefully to the tips of the most slender branches.

class	**Reptilia**
order	**Squamata**
suborder	**Serpentes**
family	**Colubridae**
genus	
& species	***Dispholidus typus***

Cobra

Immortalised in Kipling's story of the hardy mongoose Rikki-Tikki-Tavi, the true cobras of the genus **Naja**, from the Sanskrit word 'naga' for snake, are medium-sized snakes. Several species average 6 or 7 ft. The Indian cobra has a dark body encircled by a series of light rings, and like all cobras, it has the characteristic hood behind the neck. The neck is flattened horizontally by long, moveable ribs being swung out to stretch the loose skin of the neck, rather like the ribs of an umbrella stretching out the fabric. The cobra rears up and expands the hood when frightened or excited, and, in the Indian cobra, this displays the distinctive spectacled pattern

the hood has the typical 'spectacle' markings, but towards the eastern side of India a single ring-like marking becomes more common, while in the Kashmir and Caspian region the hood is marked with black transverse bars.

There are four species in Africa, the black-and-white cobra, the Cape cobra, the spitting cobra and the Egyptian cobra, which is also found in Asia.

Some cobras, such as the Egyptian cobra, are diurnal, others nocturnal like the Indian cobra, retiring by day to a favoured shelter in a burrow or under rocks. Some are found only near water.

Inoculating nerve-poisons

The cobra's venom is secreted from glands which lie just behind the eyes. It runs down

The Indian cobra is regarded by many experts as being one of the most dangerous snakes and death has been recorded as little as 15 minutes after the bite. Figures of 10 000 deaths a year have been given for India, which represents 1 in 30 000 of the population. Snakebite is so common in Asia and Africa because so many of the country people go about barefooted. Some cobras, notably the spitting cobra, of Africa, defend themselves by spitting venom over a distance of up to 12 ft. They aim for the face and the venom causes great pain and temporary blindness if it gets in the eyes.

Cobra venom has a different effect on the body than that of vipers which acts principally on the blood system, destroying tissues. Some tissue damage is done by cobra venom causing swelling and haemorr-

One of the four African species, the Cape cobra eats snakes as well as rodents, and is not averse to cannibalism.

Indian cobra, with its distinctive pattern. A cobra's hood works like an umbrella, with long, flexible ribs spreading the thin skin.

as the scales slide apart. The pattern is on the back of the neck but it can be seen from the front as the stretched skin is translucent.

Another well-known species is the Egyptian cobra, depicted on Ancient Egyptian headdresses rearing up with its hood inflated. Average length of adults is $5\frac{1}{2}$–6 ft and there are reports of their reaching 10 ft, although the longest reliable measurement is over 8 ft. The body is yellowish to almost black, the lighter forms often having darker spots.

Cobras are found in Africa and Asia, although fossils have been found in Europe, presumably dating from a time when the climate was warmer. There are two or four species in Asia, the number depending on different authorities' methods of classification. One of these is the Indian cobra that is found from the Caspian across Asia, south of the Himalayas to southern China and the Philippines, and south to Bali in Indonesia. Throughout its range, the markings vary. In the west

ducts to the fangs that grow from the front of the upper jaw. Each fang has a canal along the front edge, and in some species the sides of the canal fold over to form a hollow tube like a hypodermic needle, so resembling the hollow fangs of vipers. The cobra strikes upwards, with the snout curled back so that the fangs protrude. As soon as they pierce the victim's flesh, venom is squirted down the fangs by muscles that squeeze the venom gland. When a very aggressive cobra tightens these muscles too early venom dribbles from its mouth.

Cobras' fangs are fairly short, but after it has struck the snake hangs on, chewing at the wound and injecting large quantities of venom. The seriousness of the bite depends very much on how long the cobra is allowed to chew. If it is struck off immediately, the bite will probably not be too serious. It is always difficult to assess the dangers of snake bite. Even where good medical records are kept, some of the less severe cases will probably not be reported, and the severity depends so much on the condition of the victim. Young and old people and those who are sick, especially with weak hearts, are most likely to succumb.

hage, but the principal ingredients are neurotoxins acting on the nervous system causing paralysis, nausea, difficulty in breathing and, perhaps, eventually death through heart and breathing failure.

Rat-catching snakes

Cobras eat mainly rodents, coming into homes after rats, which is a cause of many accidents. Frogs, toads and birds are also eaten, the cobras climbing trees to plunder nests. The Egyptian cobra often raids poultry runs. The Cape cobra often eats snakes, including its fellows, and the black-and-white cobra is reported to hunt fish. When food is short they will eat grasshoppers and other large insects.

Cobras' mating dance

Before mating, the pair 'dance', raising their heads a foot or more off the ground and weaving to and fro. This may continue for an hour before mating takes place, when the male presses his cloaca to the female's and ripples run through his body.

The Cape cobra mates between September and October and the eggs are laid a month later. These dates vary through the cobras' range as they mate and lay eggs at the season most likely to provide abundant food for the young. Eggs number 8–20, and are laid in a hole in the ground or in a tree. The female may stand guard and during the breeding period is irritable and aggressive. She is liable to attack without provocation with dire results for passers-by if her nest is near a footpath. Newly-hatched cobras measure about 10 in.

Enemies

The traditional enemies of cobras are the mongooses, but genets also attack them. The mongoose's tactics are to leap backwards and forwards, around the cobra, keeping it continually on the alert until it tires and cannot hold its body raised in striking position. The mongoose is protected by the speed of its movements and by being very resistant to the cobra's venom. Mongooses do not always win, however. It has been suggested that the inflated hood serves as a protection, making it difficult for any enemy to bite the cobra's neck. Cobras also sham dead, going limp until danger passes.

Snake-charmer's bluff

Cobras, especially the Indian and Egyptian species, are the favourite performers in the snake-charmer's act. It is perhaps fairly common knowledge now that the snakes are not reacting to the music but to the rhythmic movements of the charmer. The pipe is merely a stage prop, and is not used by all performers, because snakes are deaf, or, in other words, they cannot perceive airborne vibrations. They have no eardrum that in most other terrestrial animals vibrates in time to the airborne waves, and

The legendary 'asp' or Egyptian cobra may grow to a length of 8 ft; and length for length it is much heavier than the Indian cobra.

they do not have the systems of bones and ducts that convey the vibrations from the eardrum to the sense cells of the inner ear. They can, however, detect vibrations through the earth.

The explanation of the cobras' dance is that the basket is suddenly opened, exposing the snakes to the glare of daylight. Half-blinded and somewhat shocked, they rear up in the defensive position with hoods inflated. Their attention is caught by the first moving object they see, which is the swaying snake-charmer, whose actions they follow.

Part of the act consists of the cobras being handled and even kissed on the head. This is not such a dare-devil act of bravado as it may seem for it is said that cobras cannot strike accurately in the full light of day, and, anyway, their fangs will have been

drawn or their lips sewn up. If this has not been done, the chances are that the charmer is immune to their venom.

class	Reptilia
order	Squamata
suborder	Serpentes
family	Elapidae
genus & species	*Naja naja* Indian cobra *N. haje* Egyptian cobra *N. nivea* Cape cobra *N. nigricollis* spitting cobra *N. melanoleuca* black-and-white cobra others

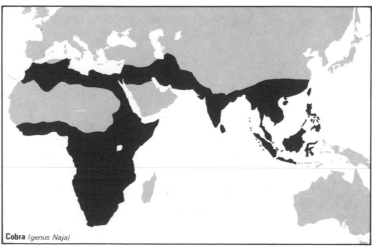

Cobra (genus Naja)

△ When cobras 'dance' for snake-charmers it is because, shocked and half-blinded by sudden exposure to daylight, they rear into their typical defensive position with their attention fixed on the first moving object they see — the hand or pipe of the snake-charmer.

Coral snake

*Coral snake is the name given to many strikingly-coloured snakes with patterns of rings running round the body and tail. The body is slender, and there is no pronounced distinction between head and neck, as in the vipers. In North and South America there are several genera of true coral snakes, which are close relatives of the cobras, as are the Oriental coral snakes belonging to the genus **Maticora**. In South Africa some members of the genus **Aspidelaps** are called coral snakes, and they are very similar in appearance and habits to their American relatives.*

The two North American coral snakes have prominent rings round the body in the same sequence of black, yellow or white, and red. The Arizona or Sonora coral snake is small, having a maximum recorded length of $19\frac{1}{2}$ in. The larger common coral snake occasionally reaches over $3\frac{1}{2}$ ft. Some tropical species reach 4 or 5 ft.

*Brightly-coloured banding is not constant in coral snakes. Members of the genus **Leptomicrurus** have long thin bodies and short tails, which are dark on the upper side and have yellow spots underneath.*

Of the many species of New World coral snakes, only two extend as far north as the United States. The common coral snake extends north from Mexico, through eastern Texas to the low-lying country of Kentucky and North Carolina and south to Florida. The Arizona coral snake lives in the arid lands of Arizona, New Mexico and northern Mexico. Other coral snakes range south to northern Argentina.

Poisonous but rarely dangerous

Coral snakes do not strike like a cobra, but approach their victim slowly, sliding their head over its body. The fangs are short and to inject a lethal quantity of venom the snake chews the flesh, lacerating the skin and so forcing in a large amount of poison, which acts on the nervous system and has a very powerful effect. In Mexico the common coral snake is called the '20-minute snake' as its bite is supposed to be fatal within that time. But 24 hours is a more likely time. Surprisingly few deaths have been reported.

Coral snakes are nocturnal, lying up during the day in runs under stones or bark or in mossy clumps, but they are sometimes active during the day if it has been raining. They trouble people little because of their secretive habits. When man is abroad during the day, coral snakes are resting away from the danger of being trodden on, which would cause them to bite. Occasionally there are reports of coral snake bites but these are usually due to people carelessly handling them.

Snake eaters

The jaws of coral snakes do not open very wide and they can eat only slender prey, which consists mainly of small lizards, other snakes and probably insects.

Technicolor warning technique. Bright colours do for the coral what the dry, sinister rattle does for the rattlesnake: they warn potential attackers not to try their luck.

Breeding

The common coral snake lays 3—14 soft, elongated eggs in May or June, in a hollow in the earth or under a log. When they hatch, after 10—12 weeks, the young snakes measure 7—8 in. and have pale skins, the colours of which become more intense as they get older.

Enemies

Snake-eaters themselves, coral snakes are preyed upon by other snake-eaters such as the king snake, which is resistant to the effects of coral snake venom. On Trinidad, mongooses, which were introduced to keep down the numbers of snakes, have not affected the coral snake population.

One unusual report is that of a large bullfrog eating a 17in. coral snake. Although the narrow-jawed snake could not have swallowed the bullfrog, it is strange that it was not able either to escape or to poison its adversary.

First-class animal puzzle

Parallels can be drawn between the brightly-coloured coral snake, perhaps the most gaudy of animals, apart from some of the birds and fishes, and the bright stripes of bees and wasps. Conspicuous colouring is a feature of many animals that are poisonous, whether the poison is transmitted by stings, fangs or merely by being set free when the body is eaten, as in the burnet moth.

In the insect world, some harmless insects, such as hoverflies, mimic the colour patterns of the harmful bees and wasps, gaining protection because birds and other predators learn to connect the colour with an unpleasant taste. It is suggested that the coral snakes also have their mimics, for in America, Africa and Asia there are non-poisonous snakes with brightly-coloured rings. In the United States some reports of coral snakes in unusual places have been due to two non-poisonous snakes, the scarlet snake and the scarlet king snake. These, however, have a different sequence of bands. In the coral snakes the red band has

yellow or white on either side. In the mimics the red band has a black band on either side. This is put another way by Drs Boys and Smith in their book on recognising poisonous amphibians and reptiles and treating their bites:

> 'Red on yellow (or white)
> Kill a fellow (or might);
> Red on black
> Venom lack'

This distinction does not hold elsewhere in America. The false coral snake of South America has no yellow bands.

The trouble with the theory of the coral snake's bright colours being a warning is that it is nocturnal, so enemies are unlikely to see the colour and therefore are unlikely to learn that a bright-banded snake is dangerous. How then are the mimicking snakes, who are also secretive, to profit? One habit shared by many ringed snakes, both venomous and harmless, is to coil themselves up with the head underneath and wave the tail, which looks rather like the head in these species. Perhaps this leads an enemy to attack a less vulnerable part of the snake. However, one animal who does notice bright colour is man, and because he will kill any snake that might be poisonous, the harmless mimics actually suffer from looking like a venomous snake.

It has been suggested that the banding on coral snakes, perhaps also on their mimics, is in the nature of a disruptive pattern, breaking up the outline of the body, so making the animal less readily seen by predators. This still leaves unexplained the presence of typical warning colours in the patterns.

class	**Reptilia**
order	**Squamata**
suborder	**Serpentes**
family	**Elapidae**
genera	*Micruroides* *Micrurus* *Leptomicrurus* others

215

Egg-eating snake

Although many snakes eat eggs, only the Indian and African egg-eating snakes live almost exclusively on eggs and have a remarkable device for dealing with them.

There are five species of egg-eating snake in Africa, and one, related to them, in India. They are slender with blunt, rounded snouts and narrow heads not distinct from the neck, as are the arrowhead-shaped heads of many other snakes.

The common egg-eating snake, found in many places from Egypt to South Africa, is usually around 2½ ft long, a 3ft one being a large specimen. Its colour varies from slate-grey to olive-brown, with large, square black patches on the back that sometimes form a zig-zag line. The East African egg-eating snake, about the same size, ranges from the southern borders of Kenya to Mozambique. It is pinkish to reddish-brown with darker Vs and transverse bars running down the back. The largest species is the southern egg-eating snake. This averages 3 ft, and there are records of individuals of 3¾ ft.

Egg-eating snakes are mainly active at night and spend much of their time gliding through the foliage of trees, searching for birds' nests. They are harmless to man; they have no venom and only a few weak teeth at the back of the mouth. These are incapable of breaking the skin — not that the snakes will even attempt to bite.

Egg-crushing throats

An egg-eating snake, with a head and neck the diameter of a man's finger, can swallow whole a chicken's egg with a diameter of $1\frac{3}{4}$ in. It is a characteristic of snakes that they are able to swallow objects wider than themselves. Their jaws are specially hinged to engulf their prey (anaconda, page 205) and their throats can expand to accommodate the food. When swallowing an egg, the scales on the head and neck get pulled apart as the skin underneath becomes stretched to tissue-paper thickness.

The snakes seek out eggs by smell. On finding an egg, a snake investigates it carefully with its tongue, rejecting it if it is addled, and, if the egg is large, measuring its size by running the head and neck over it. Satisfied with its find, the snake then coils itself around the egg to hold it steady, yawns a few times as if limbering up and proceeds to engulf the egg from one end, drawing it in with slow, deliberate gulps.

Having swallowed the egg (which may take ¼ hour) the snake breaks it open with a most remarkable device that grips and saws through the shell. Along the roof of the throat there are about 30 teeth which are projections from the backbone that stick through the skin of the throat. The first 17 or 18 of these teeth are long and knife-shaped, the next few are broad and flat and the remaining 6 or 7 are stout pegs projecting forwards. The egg is held against the teeth by throat muscles contracting around either end. The snake then raises its head off the ground and bends it backwards and forwards so the long teeth saw through the shell, releasing the contents. Next, the snake arches its neck upwards, so the shell is forced against the flat middle teeth which fold the shell into a rolled-up, boat-shaped sausage. The contents of the egg are swallowed and a valve in front of the stomach closes to keep them in while the snake wriggles and contorts to eject the empty shell.

In the tropical forests, egg-eating snakes will have a plentiful supply of food as birds nest all the year round, but in South Africa or northern India their food supply is seasonal. It is very likely that egg-eating snakes in these regions have to fast for the greater part of the year, living on fat stored up during the birds' nesting season.

△ *The big swallow: after a few experimental yawns to limber up, the snake lets out its elongated jaw hinges and begins to work the egg down its throat towards the 'teeth'. These saw through the shell which then rapidly collapses under the onslaught of repeated throat spasms. When the egg's contents have been swallowed, the flattened shell is regurgitated, with the sharp fragments (still attached to the membrane beneath the shell) wadded together into a neat pellet.*

▷ *Blue-grey version of the egg-eating snake, draped tastefully in the branches. Colour variations run from slate-grey to olive-brown.*

▽ *How the snake goes to work on an egg: these 'teeth' are in fact projections from the spine which grow down through the skin of the throat.*

Egg-laying

Because so much of the egg-eating snake's behaviour is unique, attention has been directed to that and their breeding habits have been largely overlooked. They lay 12–15 eggs which hatch in 3 to 4 months.

The newly-hatched young measure 9–10 in. It would be interesting to know whether they are able to swallow eggs when still small. Presumably they would have to select the smallest of birds' eggs.

Putting on a fierce front

Although egg-eating snakes are not venomous, their behaviour when disturbed is sufficient to deter any enemy that did not know better. At the first sign of danger an egg-eating snake inflates the front part of its body and hisses violently. Then it coils itself up and strikes at its adversary, for all the world like a cobra or other venomous snake, but cannot inflict any damage.

The body does not coil properly. Instead it is thrown into parallel folds which curve round in a C-shape, and are continually moving so that the scales hiss as they rasp against each other.

Many disguises

The common egg-eating snake is further protected by its resemblance to venomous snakes. This is more than coincidence, because throughout its range from Egypt to the Cape this snake varies in colour to match different venomous snakes in each area. In Egypt it resembles the brown saw-scaled viper whose venom is the most powerful of all vipers. It also hisses by rubbing its scales together in the same way as the egg-eating snake. Farther south, in Tanzania, the egg-eating snake mimics the young of the lowland viper, and in the southern half of Africa three snakes are mimicked. In Southwest Africa the horned adder is the model, and in South Africa the egg-eating snakes can be mistaken for a Cape mountain adder. In many parts they resemble night adders, which have the same dark squarish marks running down the back. In one part of Rhodesia night adders lose their dark markings, and here the egg-eating snake also has a uniform colour.

Mimicking poisonous snakes may well help to deter such enemies as baboons or warthogs, but may not work against predatory snakes such as the boomslang. Against man, the mimicry is positively disadvantageous. The usual reaction is to kill any snake in case it should prove dangerous, and to resemble known dangerous snakes is to provoke this reaction.

class	**Reptilia**
order	**Squamata**
suborder	**Serpentes**
family	**Colubridae**
genera & species	***Dasypeltis scabra*** *common African egg-eating snake* **D. medici** *East African egg-eating snake* **D. inornata** *southern egg-eating snake* **Elachistodon westermanni** *Indian egg-eating snake*

Fer de lance

*The deadly fer de lance was given its name by French settlers on the island of Martinique because of its lance-shaped head and body. In Latin America it is called **barba amarillo** (yellow beard) after its yellow chin. The fer de lance belongs to the family of pit vipers, like moccasins and rattlesnakes. It is one of about 3 dozen species in a genus that is found only in central and southern America. The largest specimens reach nearly 8 ft but the average is 4–5 ft. The body is brown or dark grey with a characteristic pattern of black-edged diamonds running down the body. The range of the fer de lance covers the hot tropical coasts of America from northern Mexico to Argentina. It is found in both wet and dry country, in forests and open country. The fer de lance is also found on Trinidad, Tobago, Martinique and Santa Lucia in the West Indies.*

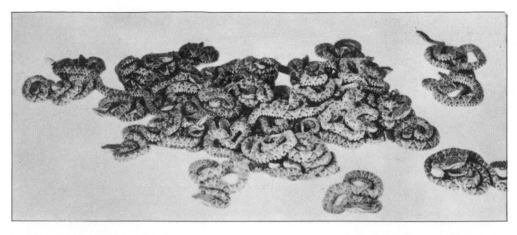

Were they used as weapons?

The fer de lance is a snake which is very much feared. It is very common and often encountered by agricultural workers as they clear away undergrowth or work in plantations. The fer de lance also has an unpleasant habit of coming out at night to lie on warm roads and footpaths. Its evil reputation is enhanced by its long fangs, and there is a good deal of justification for its bad name. Its venom is very potent and accidents are quite common because its habits often bring it into contact with man.

There are two legends as to how the fer de lance came to Martinique and Santa Lucia, islands several hundred miles from the snake's mainland home. One is that the plantation owners brought them from the mainland and released them in the woods to induce their slaves to stay on the plantations and not try to escape. An earlier tradition, recounted by a European historian in 1667, has it that the Arawaks, a tribe living on the mainland, brought basket loads of poisonous snakes to bedevil the Caribs with whom they were at war. The snakes could well have been fer de lances. This primitive form of biological warfare is not without precedent.

In 186 BC the King of Bithynia overcame the Pergamenian fleet by ordering jars of poisonous snakes to be thrown into the enemy ships.

They lurk in poor dwellings

Fer de lances feed on small animals such as opossums, frogs, lizards, small snakes and rodents. Their search for rats and mice brings them once again into contact with man, because they frequent poor dwellings and outhouses which are usually infested with rodents.

Venomous babies

The young are born alive in litters of 60–80, sometimes more. The number in a litter and the size of the young snakes at birth depend on the size of the mother. A 6 ft fer de lance bears young 1 ft long. The young snakes are born with the venom apparatus fully developed and are dangerous from the start.

The large numbers of fer de lances in one litter are usually cited as the explanation for the species being so common. This may be so, but the number of eggs or babies that an animal produces is usually proportional to its mortality rate, so numbers entering the population balance the numbers lost, independently of whether the species is common or rare. The fer de lance is probably common because it is adaptable and can live in a variety of habitats.

When snake eats snake

A fer de lance can no doubt defend itself against many predators by its poisonous bite, and by rapidly vibrating its tail when disturbed. It does not have a rattle like its relatives the rattlesnakes but the vibrating tail rustles against the leaves and presumably acts as a deterrent.

Neither warning nor venom are proof against the mussurana, however. Ditmars in his *Snakes of the World* describes how he put this snake-eating snake into an enclosure with a fer de lance. The mussurana nosed the fer de lance then grabbed its neck and quickly coiled its body round it. The fer de lance bit the mussurana, but this had no effect and the latter was able to contort its body until it was firmly wrapped around the fer de lance like a spring. It then grasped the fer de lance just behind the head so it was helpless, while the mussurana chewed away injecting large quantities of venom. After 20 minutes the mussurana pushed its mouth over the fer de lance's head and slowly swallowed it. The mastery of the mussurana over the fer de lance is shown by the 6½ft mussurana that was cut open to reveal a 6ft fer de lance in its stomach.

Mongooses that failed

Late in the 19th century a plan was made to solve two of the problems afflicting the sugar cane plantations of Santa Lucia and other Caribbean islands. Rats were eating the crop before it could be harvested and the fer de lances were making harvesting hazardous. Accordingly it was decided to import mongooses from India. Mongooses eat rats and they also had the reputation of being valiant hunters of venomous snakes. While it is true that they will kill venomous snakes, this is only a sideline, as was soon discovered in the West Indies. There was some reduction in the number of fer de lances, but the plan has largely failed. The mongooses attacked rats but they also killed the snakes, both harmless and dangerous to man, that killed rats. The mongooses also attacked other animals, especially ground-nesting birds. So this attempt at biological pest control has ended with the establishment of a new pest. Mongooses have even been known to eat sugar cane!

class	**Reptilia**
order	**Squamata**
suborder	**Serpentes**
family	**Crotalidae**
genus & species	*Bothrops atrox*

*Above left: A brood of deadly fer de lance babies. A parent 6 ft long bears some 60–80 miniatures 1 ft long – all dangerous from birth. But these large families are not the most likely reason for the spread of the fer de lance; it is probably as common as it is because it has managed to adapt to a number of habitats. In the adult (right and above) the poison fangs grow long, and the dangerous **Bothrops atrox** is much feared by sugar cane workers on plantations. Below left: Artist's impression of a 19th century sugar cane plantation shows just how close workers can get to the snake's habitat – and helps to explain how the fer de lance achieved its notoriety.*

Garter snake

Garter snakes are the commonest and most familiar snakes of the United States and Canada. They also occur in Mexico. They are found farther north than any other reptile in the Western Hemisphere, the common garter snake as far north as 67 degrees latitude, in the Yukon. Garter snakes are non-venomous, slender, marked with longitudinal stripes, commonly 2 ft, sometimes 3 ft long, the record being 5 ft. The common garter snake may be black, brown or olive with three yellowish, orange or red stripes. The stripes may be vivid or dull. The belly is usually yellow or greenish. All-black individuals may occur. One species, known as the ribbon snake, has three golden-yellow stripes, and its scales are more markedly keeled than in other garter snakes. It lives in southeastern Canada and the United States east of the Mississippi, especially in marshy areas, and takes readily to water. Another subspecies, the western ribbon snake **Thamnophis sauritus proximus**, *lives west of the Mississippi.*

From sea level to the Rockies

Garter snakes live in a variety of habitats from sea level to high up in the Rockies. The mountain garter snake is the only reptile in the Rocky Mountain National Park. The Mexican garter snake is found up to 13 000 ft. They are, however, often restricted to the neighbourhood of streams and lakes in the western half of the United States but are found almost everywhere in the humid eastern half. The plains garter snake is found even in the suburbs of towns such as New York and Chicago, where they hibernate in cracks in the ground near the bases of buildings.

They are the last reptiles to go into winter quarters and the first to come out, as early as March, from a hibernaculum which may be as deep as 3 ft underground. A saying of one tribe of North American Indians is that the first clap of thunder brings them out of hibernation.

It is said there is one or another subspecies of garter snake in every state, and in places the species overlap. Where they do there is no competition. The different species tend to occupy slightly different habitats, one preferring damper ground than the other, for example, and usually they show slightly different food preferences. They also tend to breed at different times.

Early food is worms

Young garter snakes feed almost entirely on earthworms in their first year. After that, although worms are the chief item in their diet, they also eat frogs, toads and salamanders, sometimes fish and occasionally birds' eggs. Large garter snakes may eat mice.

Very large litters

Mating takes place near the winter quarters, soon after the snakes come out in late winter. The male has tiny barbels on his chin which

he passes along the female's back as he prepares to mate with her. Once mating is over the snakes disperse to their summer ranges. The young are born alive in summer in litters of usually 50–60 but the number may vary from 12 to 78. The newly-born garter snake is 6 in. long. It grows a foot a year for the first 2–3 years, is mature at 2 years old, is ready to mate in its third spring and may live 12 years. There is, however, a very heavy death-rate during the first few months, due mainly to predators and starvation.

Killed in error

Their enemies are snake-eating snakes, hawks, owls, skunks and domestic cats. All-black individuals, or those with indistinct stripes, are apt to be killed by people in mistake for poisonous snakes. They are also killed in large numbers on the roads.

A garter snake's defence is to give out an obnoxious fluid from a pore on either side of the vent. It may bite but this has little effect on the human skin.

Some snakes lay eggs; others, such as garter snakes, bear their young alive. The first is called ovipary, the second is ovo-vivipary and in this the eggs remain inside the mother until they hatch. In both, the eggs contain yolk for feeding the developing embryo but in ovoviviparous snakes oxygen for breathing and moisture must be supplied by the maternal tissues, so the shells must be very thin, virtually no more than a transparent membrane in most cases. In garter snakes, as well as European adders, sea snakes and the Australian copperheads, a sort of placenta is formed to carry nourishment from mother to developing young. It is a very simple affair, nothing like as efficient as the placenta of mammals,

but it is enough to supplement the yolk supply already in the egg.

The main advantages of ovovivipary are that there is no chance of the eggs drying up and the temperature remains fairly constant. The mother can choose basking areas with suitable temperatures. This is important in latitudes where summers are short and where even summer temperatures are not high. Add to this the advantages of having even a simple placenta and it is easy to see why garter snakes can live so far north. The disadvantages of ovovivipary are that the mother is encumbered, less agile and therefore handicapped in hunting and in dodging enemies. In most species this is minimized by the broods carried being small in numbers. It is the more remarkable, therefore, that garter snakes should commonly have 50—60, even 78 young in a brood.

△ *Colourful version of the common garter, with three stripes of vivid yellow.*
◁ *Garter snakes take readily to water; this wandering garter has hunted down a small speckled dace and is dragging it onto a stretch of floating algae before tucking in.*

class	**Reptilia**
order	**Squamata**
suborder	**Serpentes**
family	**Colubridae**
genus & species	***Thamnophis sirtalis*** *common garter snake* **T. elegans** *mountain garter snake* **T. elegans vagrans** *wandering garter snake* **T. radix** *plains garter snake* **T. sauritus** *ribbon snake, others*

Garter snakes
(Genus *Thamnophis*)

Grass snake

Until the beginning of this century this non-poisonous reptile was known as the ringed snake. A third name, one at least as appropriate although seldom used, is water snake.

Grass snakes are usually 2½–3 ft long but occasionally longer ones are recorded. These are females, which are larger than the males. The colour is usually olive brown, grey or green along the back with two rows of small black spots arranged alternately. Along the flanks are black vertical bars. The most obvious feature by which the snake can be recognized is the yellowish patch either side of the neck forming an incomplete collar or ring. This may sometimes be orange, pink or white.

The ringed snake ranges from Britain, through Europe (south of latitude 65 degrees). There are 75 related species of water snake, most of them in the Old World, a few in North America, all similar, except for details of colouring.

A master swimmer

The grass snake is usually found near ponds and streams, on marshy ground or in damp woodlands, rarely on sandy heaths or on dry ground. It is active by day and especially in spring can be seen basking on banks or on logs. A good climber, it may go up into shrubs or low trees but never more than a few feet from the ground. It readily enters water, swimming strongly with side-to-side movements of the body, holding the head well clear of the water and moving it from side to side as if searching. One grass snake was found 20 miles from land in the Bay of Biscay, still heading out to sea. Grass snakes hibernate from October to April, but the period varies according to latitude, being shorter in the south. Usually many come together in holes in the ground, but smaller numbers may pass the winter under logs, boulders or piles of brushwood.

Big meals at long intervals

Grass snakes' main food used to be frogs. In Britain at least these are now rare compared with a quarter of a century ago, so presumably most grass snakes must be feeding mainly on other animals. Newts were their second preference, and after this fish and tadpoles. A few eat toads, but the majority, to avoid the toads' poison, refuse them. Lizards and slowworms, shrews, mice, voles, and young birds are also taken occasionally. One grass snake was seen eating honey bees but insects are not in the normal diet. Much of the food is caught in the water, smaller prey being swallowed while the snake is still submerged, larger prey being brought to land to be eaten. The main feeding time seems to be early morning, and when food is plentiful large meals are taken, for example, 17 newts one after the other, a 7in. gudgeon swallowed in the usual way, head-first. Young grass snakes feed on earthworms, slugs, tadpoles, newt larvae and small fish.

Bundles of eggs

Mating takes place in April and May. The male glides up to the female and places his chin on her back near the base of her tail. With his tongue flicking in and out rapidly, he caresses her back with his chin as his head moves towards the back of her head. Then, throwing his body in loops over her, coupling is completed. Eggs are laid in June or July, under heaps of decaying leaves or rotting vegetation, under hayricks or heaps of sawdust in sawmills, in compost or manure heaps. The number of eggs laid at a time is usually 30–40 but may vary from 8 to 53, each oval and up to 1 in. long. They stick together and as they dry and the 'glue' hardens they lose their glistening appearance and become matt white. Sometimes several females lay in the same place, as in North Wales in 1901 when 40 bundles of eggs totalling well over a thousand were found in a hole in an old wall near a row of cottages.

The eggs hatch in 6–10 weeks, the baby snakes slitting the parchment-like shell with the egg-tooth on the snout. On hatching they measure about 7 in. Grass snakes have lived for 9 years in captivity.

Defence: a nasty taste

There is not a great deal of positive information on enemies. Badgers and hedgehogs have been seen to eat adult grass snakes, and birds of prey have been watched flying up with them. The greatest mortality is among the babies. From 7 in. when first hatched they grow to 10–12 in. at a year old. Many are probably eaten by large and small flesh-eaters, possibly at times because of their worm-like appearance. More precise information is needed, however, because although a toad will seize a baby grass snake in its mouth it quickly rejects it and shows every sign of having a nasty taste in the mouth. Among other things the toad wipes its lips vigorously with first one front foot, then the other. This unpleasant taste may well protect young grass snakes from some other flesh-eaters.

Shamming dead

An adult grass snake uses an unpleasant secretion from its vent as the second line of defence. Its first line is to strike as any poisonous snake would, but the grass snake does so with the mouth shut. At the same time it blows up its body and hisses. This is pure bluff. It is soon followed by the unpleasant secretion, as evil-smelling as a skunk's, but not in such quantity. The third line of defence is to sham dead. The grass snake quickly turns onto its back, opens its mouth, lets the tongue loll, and holds itself rigid. It is a realistic performance. The snake looks quite dead. If, at this point, you turn the snake over onto its belly and close its mouth, it turns onto its back as soon as you take your hands away, opens its mouth and lets its tongue loll. You can keep on doing this and each time the snake flips over, goes into what looks like a death posture, as if it were determined to look dead, come what may.

class	**Reptilia**
order	**Squamata**
suborder	**Serpentes**
family	**Colubridae**
genus & species	*Natrix natrix* others

▽ *Best way to identify a grass snake is by the collar patches – yellow, orange-pink, or white.*   ▽ *Shamming dead, with head askew and jaws gaping.*

Hog-nosed snake

The three species of hog-nosed snakes are named after the sharply upturned tip of their snouts, like those of farmyard hogs. The head is short and broad, the tail short and the body thick. The colour is very variable, commonly olive green, brownish, grey or slate. There is usually a row of dark bars or blotches and a row of spots along either side. In darker animals the blotches and spots are obscured. The underside is yellowish or whitish mottled with brown or grey. The overall colour of individual hog-nosed snakes depends on their habitat. Those living in woodland are generally darker than those living in dry sandy places.

The eastern hog-nosed snake is the largest species, usually 18–30 in. long, with a record of 48 in. It is found from Ontario in Canada to Florida and Texas. The western hog-nosed snake is usually 16–21 in. long, and lives on sandy prairies from Alberta to Central Mexico. In southeastern United States there is the southern hog-nosed snake, the smallest of them all at 12–27 in. long.

Eating frogs and toads

The hog-nosed snake's snout is apparently used as a shovel when the snake burrows through loose soil. It prefers dry, sandy country in the prairie districts of North America, but it can also be found in orchards and swamps. As far as is known its prey consists largely of frogs and toads—mainly the latter—but as it burrows through the soil it would be surprising if young snakes did not take worms and other soil-dwelling animals. It has been known to eat small mammals, birds, lizards and snakes. Prey is seized and swallowed head first, assisted by long fang-like teeth in the back of the mouth. It has been suggested that the snakes use these teeth to puncture the skins of toads that have inflated themselves in self-defence. In Michigan, however, observations showed that hog-nosed snakes fed entirely on toads, and where the toads' habitat was being destroyed by drainage and building the snakes were becoming rare.

Eggs swell before hatching

Eggs are laid in a damp place, such as under a rotting log, in June or July. Each female lays 12–30 white, leathery eggs, occasionally more. As they develop, the eggs swell and, just before hatching, they are nearly spherical and have increased in volume by one-third. Newly-hatched eastern hog-nosed snakes measure 6–8 in. and are grey rather than brownish like the parents, but they have the rows of dark markings.

Two-line defence

Hog-nosed snakes belong to the family Colubridae. Most of the snakes in this family are harmless but some have developed means of deterring enemies. The grass snake (opposite) feigns death and the egg-eating snake (page 216) mimics poisonous snakes or pretends to be dangerous by inflating the front part of its body, coiling up, hissing and even striking. This is enough to convince most enemies that it is well to keep clear, especially as the egg-eating snake resembles venomous vipers. The false coral snakes (page 225), of a different family, also mimic poisonous snakes. The hog-nosed snakes too are impostors with a variety of acts. Some of them resemble the poisonous massasanga rattlesnake. Moreover, if disturbed, they show off the markings on the skin by inflating the front half of the body and neck by spreading their ribs and adjusting the jaw bones until there is a hood like that of an angry cobra (page 213). In all their next step is to hiss and strike at the adversary, but with the mouth shut. This behaviour has led to such names as 'spreading adder' and 'hissing sand snake'.

If this impressive display of ferocity fails to send an enemy fleeing, the hog-nosed snake abruptly changes its tactics and rolls over, limp, with mouth open and tongue hanging out, even giving a realistic final death twitch. Like the grass snake that has the same trick, the hog-nosed snake will persist in rolling onto its back whenever it is turned onto its belly.

Yet another bluff?

Hog-nosed snakes may have been double-crossing people all along. It is firmly stated that they are not venomous. Yet a person's hand has been known to swell up and become painful after a bite from a hog-nosed snake. The long teeth in the back of its mouth do not have grooves down which poison could flow, as in poisonous members of the Colubridae, but the secretions from their parotid glands, the modified salivary glands, which in snakes produce venom, could still be toxic and their poison be painful if it got into an open wound. Some species of oriental grass snakes have poisonous salivary glands. In considering 'borderline' cases like this, it must be remembered that animals are still evolving; in a million years from now, several of the 'harmless' snakes could well have an efficient venom apparatus.

△ Eastern hog-nosed snake, largest of the three species.
▽ Hog-nosed snakes are found in nearly every state in the eastern half of North America, from Canada to the Gulf of Mexico.

Overleaf: A western hog-nosed snake. These snakes are usually from 16 to 21 in. long, and live on sandy prairies from Alberta to Central Mexico.

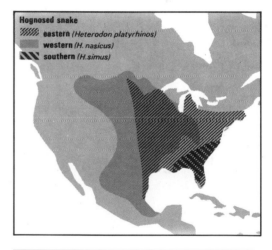

Hognosed snake
////// eastern (*Heterodon platyrhinos*)
western (*H. nasicus*)
\\\\ southern (*H.simus*)

class	**Reptilia**
order	**Squamata**
suborder	**Serpentes**
family	**Colubridae**
genus & species	*Heterodon nasicus* western hog-nosed snake *H. platyrhinos* eastern hog-nosed snake *H. simus* southern hog-nosed snake

King snake

These are North American snakes, harmless to man—as are most members of their large family, the Colubridae. A special feature of king snakes—and the reason why they are so named—is that they eat other snakes, including venomous species like rattlesnakes. Another feature is that they show many colour varieties.

The common king snake, also known as the chain snake or thunder snake, is up to 6 ft long. The typical form, along the east coast area of the United States, is shiny black, criss-crossed by bands of yellow or white forming a chain-like pattern on its sides. Its underside is black with white or yellow blotches. The head is narrow and there is a slightly marked neck. In the Mississippi Valley the king snake is greenish with white or yellow speckling. In Georgia, Alabama and Florida it is black or dark brown marked with yellow. The Californian subspecies is in two colour phases: one with yellow rings, the other with yellow stripes, the background colour of both being black or brown. These and other species and subspecies range over most of the United States northwards into southern Canada and southwards into Mexico. The milk snakes, up to 3½ ft long, are closely related to the king snakes. Their name is sometimes applied to king snakes in different localities.

Some king snakes are ringed red, yellow and black and look very like the venomous coral snakes. So they are sometimes called false coral snakes, a name also given to other colubrid snakes such as the rear-fanged **Erythrolamprus** *of South America, red with black rings.*

△ **Lampropeltis getulus splendida**, *Sonora king snake, has distinctive black marks along its back.*

▽ **Lampropeltis doliata amaura**, *Louisiana milk snake or 'false coral snake' as it is sometimes called.*

Terrorising the rattlers

King snakes, active especially in afternoon and evening, do not pursue other snakes. They eat small mammals, usually rodents, as well as lizards and frogs, caught in meadows and wooded areas. Should one of them meet another snake, however, it will eat it. It strikes it with its teeth and grasps the neck of its victim, at the same time throwing its body round the other snake, killing it by suffocation, just as pythons and boas kill their prey. King snakes are immune to snake venom, even that of rattlesnakes and copperheads, and the danger they represent to other snakes is shown by the behaviour of a rattlesnake in the presence of a king snake. Instead of coiling its body, raising its head to strike with its teeth, and raising its tail to shake its rattle, it keeps its head and neck on the ground and raises part of its body in a high loop, trying to beat off its attacker by blows from this loop.

The smaller milk snakes of North America take similar prey but the snakes they eat are younger and smaller. They are named for an alleged habit of taking milk from cows. This same story is current in parts of the world for other species of snakes. Not only is there no evidence to support it but the way a snake's teeth work make it virtually impossible to believe that any snake could take a cow's teat into its mouth without lacerating it badly.

Brightly coloured babies

Mating takes place in spring, the female laying 10–30 white parchment-shelled eggs in summer. Sometimes these are laid on the ground, more usually they are under leaves and plant litter. In some species, she may coil her body around the eggs for the first day or so, but afterwards leaves them. They hatch in 4–6 weeks, the baby snakes being 7–8 in. long, coloured like the parents but with the colours brighter.

Snake eats snake

There are many stories, and photographs have appeared in the Press, of one snake swallowing another. This happens in zoos when two snakes seize the same food. Sooner or later their noses touch as they both try to swallow the same thing, and the one with the larger gape swallows the other. There was a case of a 38 in. king snake eating a 40 in. corn snake, a 15 in. grass snake and an 8 in. Dekay's snake all in one day. Doubtless this happens in the wild also, but rarely. There are, however, snakes like the European smooth snake *Coronella austriaca* which, besides eating frogs, lizards and mice, also eats snakes. One of the lizards it eats is the legless and snake-like slowworm,

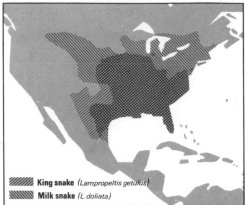

King snake *(Lampropeltis getulus)*
Milk snake *(L. doliata)*

but smooth snakes, themselves only 18 in. long, will also eat young adders. Other snakes are snake-eaters to the extent of being famous for this habit, like the file snakes *Mehelya* of Africa. They behave like king snakes, in constricting their prey, and seem also to be immune to poison. The mussurana *Clelia clelia* of tropical America is another snake-eater. One mussurana (see page 218) 6½ ft long that looked unduly swollen was found to have swallowed a 6 ft fer-de-lance, the dreaded poisonous snake. The most famous snake-eater is perhaps the king cobra or hamadryad *Naja hannah*, of southeast Asia. It does not constrict its victims and it is not immune to poison, which is why it usually eats non-venomous snakes. It will, however, eat the other kind – including smaller king cobras.

Were it possible to know the truth we should doubtless find that many snake-eating snakes are cannibalistic, if only by accident. A snake is a snake to a snake-eating snake, whatever its species. Even more bizarre things than this have been seen. FW Fitzsimons, the distinguished South African specialist in snakes, tells of a Cape file snake that intervened when two deadly night adders had each seized a leg of a frog. The file snake settled the argument by swallowing all three. Then there was Dudly-Duplex, the two-headed king snake of San Diego Zoo. One night one head tried to swallow the other. This was rescued the following morning. Later, the aggrieved head tried to take revenge—with fatal results for the two heads and the body to which they belonged.

class	**Reptilia**
order	**Squamata**
suborder	**Serpentes**
family	**Colubridae**
genus & species	***Lampropeltis getulus*** common king snake *** L. doliata*** milk snake, others

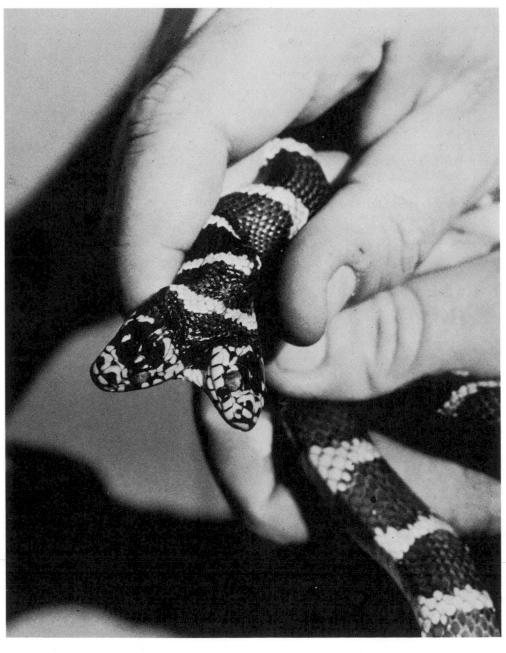

△ *The green mamba, contrary to popular opinion, leads a quiet existence of its own in the trees, and is rarely aggressive.*

Mamba

Feared throughout Africa for its deadly venom and remarkable agility, the mamba is one of the most dangerous snakes in the world. The largest is the black or blackmouthed mamba, not in fact black, but dark brown. The usual length is 8−9 ft but it may go up to 14 ft. The green mamba never exceeds 9 ft and is usually about 6 ft long. It is shy and elusive, seldom aggressive and its venom is barely half as poisonous as that of the black mamba. The two mambas were once thought to be colour varieties of one species.

The black mamba ranges from the east of Zaire and southern Ethiopia southwards to Natal and South West Africa. One species of green mamba is found on the eastern side of Africa, from Kenya to southern Natal, another two across East Africa and into West Africa. Stories of crested mambas come from older black mambas; their skin is often incompletely moulted and old skin remains attached, especially to the head. The black mamba lives in dry open bush, from lowlands to 4 000 ft, the green mamba lives in trees.

Retreat in anger

Black mambas live on the ground, sometimes wandering far afield, hunting or seeking a mate, but soon returning to a 'home' in a hole in the ground, among rocks or under a fallen tree trunk. The holes are usually aardvark burrows and cavities in termite mounds. If disturbed, they make for home, attacking anything in the way.

Besides the relatively high speed with which it moves the black mamba can strike accurately in any direction, even while travelling fast, with its head raised off the ground, mouth open and tongue flicking. It also expands the neck to form a slight hood and when disturbed gives a hollow-sounding hiss. In striking it can throw its head upwards from the ground for about two-fifths the length of its body. Its speed is legendary, and has been variously estimated at 10, 20 or 30 mph on the flat and higher estimates have been based on a mamba travelling down a slope. These arc completely unrealistic. As a cold-blooded creature with somewhat inefficient circulation, a mamba would not be capable of the effort needed to reach and sustain such speeds. Eyewitness accounts of high speed are sure to be inaccurate; few people would stay and objectively observe a mamba at full speed across rough country. The black mamba is, however, thc fastest of snakes,

with an accurately recorded speed of 7 mph. Speeds of about 15 mph may be possible in short bursts. Mambas are at a disadvantage on a smooth surface and black mambas are often run over when crossing roads, especially those with tarred surfaces.

Black mambas will climb into low trees but are more given to climbing rocks, where they lie sunning themselves. The green mamba is a tree-dweller and seldom found outside forests or thick bush. It is slightly less nervous than the black mamba.

Bird snatcher

The black mamba's prey is almost solely warm-blooded animals, such as birds and small mammals, including dassies or rock hyraxes and rodents. It digests food quickly, a large rat being completely digested in 8−10 hours. RM Isemonger, in *Snakes of Africa*, has written about three mambas that basked on a large boulder covered with red-flowered creeper whosc blossoms attracted small sugarbirds. As these gathered nectar from the flowers a mamba would suddenly seize one in the air. Within two minutes the bird ceased to struggle and the snake would either swallow it at once or, more often, it would drop the bird on the rock and flicker its tongue over it before eating it. Isemonger also saw a dassie struck as it stopped on the rock to scratch its ear. The dassie ran for cover and after a few minutes the mamba reached into the cover of the vines, seized the corpse, dropped it onto the rock, and, after an inspection with the tongue, swallowed it.

The green mamba eats birds and their eggs, chameleons, geckos and other tree lizards, as well as small mammals.

Rapid growth

Both mambas lay eggs, those of the green mamba being slightly the smaller. The breeding season is spring and early summer. A female black mamba lays 9—14 eggs, oval and 3 in. long. The newly hatched young are 15—24 in. long and able to kill mice or rats. Growth is rapid and one black mamba grew to 6 ft long in a year. A further indication that growth is rapid is that those best acquainted with these reptiles say that a mamba less than 6 ft long is rare. Young black mambas are greyish green to olive green at birth, gradually getting darker as they grow. Baby green mambas are bluish but become brighter green as they grow.

Striking at soft skin

Mambas' main enemies are mongooses, but only while they are young. Eagles and secretary birds kill them and young ones may be eaten by snake-eating snakes. Interesting sidelights are supplied by PW Willis of South Africa on how a mamba kills, and indirectly, on the value of a mongoose's coat as a shield. Willis has had five dogs killed by black mambas and he noticed that in every case the snake struck deliberately and unhurriedly at places where there is soft skin exposed with a minimum of hair, such as behind the ear, on the cheek below the eye or in the 'armpit'. A mongoose, with the exception of the face, lacks these vulnerable spots. Another interesting point in Willis' account is that he said that within a

▽ *World's fastest snake: black mamba at speed.*

▷ *Black mamba in right hand, pythons in left. Venom is 'milked' from mambas for research into antidotes and other medical uses.*

few hours each carcase had turned colour and putrefied slightly. This may indicate that the venom is an aid to digestion.

Know your snake!

There are stories about the green mamba lying in wait on branches overhanging paths through the bush, harmonising with the green foliage around it and ready to attack. It is even said to cry out with a weird noise to lure people into its ambush. Then, raising its head and body high, it strikes, sinking its poisonous fangs into the throat of its victim, who drops to the ground paralysed and is dead within seconds. Such stories contrast with what we know of this shy, elusive and unaggressive snake that feeds on lizards and small birds and their eggs. Perhaps it is as well that the green mamba is relatively inoffensive because it is often mistaken for other tree snakes, including harmless species and this misled a student of snakes who parked his car under some trees near Nairobi. On his return he saw a small green snake on top of the car. His thoughts being elsewhere at the moment, he picked up the snake and put it in his pocket. He was horrified to discover later that he had been carrying a green mamba almost next to his skin.

class	**Reptilia**
order	**Squamata**
suborder	**Serpentes**
family	**Elapidae**
genus & species	***Dendroaspis angusticeps*** *green mamba* ***D. polylepis*** *black mamba, others*

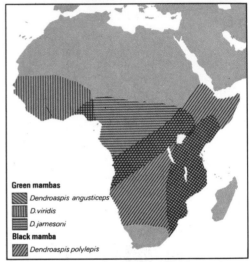

Green mambas
- *Dendroaspis angusticeps*
- *D. viridis*
- *D. jamesoni*

Black mamba
- *Dendroaspis polylepis*

Pit viper

Some of the most-feared snakes are to be found among the 60 species of pit vipers (family Crotalidae) including well known forms like the fer de lance, which has already been dealt with (page 218), and the sidewinder and the rattlesnakes, which we shall come to later. Here we shall consider others, such as the American water moccasin, copperhead and bushmaster, as well as the Asiatic pit vipers. Pit vipers are a diverse group with several interesting specializations, which is why we have given them three entries. Here, while dealing with the family in general terms, we pay special attention to what has been called their sixth sense, the two pits on the head that give them their name.

*Pit vipers are solenoglyph. That is, they have fangs which fold back and are erected when about to be used. Most pit vipers are land-living, some are tree-dwellers, a few have taken to water and others lead a partially burrowing life. Water moccasins are heavy-bodied, up to 5 ft long, and while living on land they readily take to water when disturbed and they hunt in water. They are slate black to olive or tan with indistinct brown bands. The copperhead, a brown snake with hourglass markings along the back, is up to 3 ft long. It lives in rocky outcrops and quarries and among piles of rotting logs. The bushmaster is the longest of the American pit vipers, up to 12 ft, mainly grey and brown with large diamond blotches along the back. It has large venom glands and unusually long fangs. Its generic name **Lachesis** is from one of the Fates that influenced the length of life of people – a grim pun by the scientist who named it, for the bushmaster is one of the most dangerous of snakes. The Asiatic pit vipers are of two kinds, tree-dwelling and ground-living, the first having prehensile tails that assist their climbing. The Himalayan pit viper lives at altitudes of 7 000–16 000 ft, sometimes being found even at the foot of glaciers.*

The Asiatic pit vipers are found mainly in eastern and southeast Asia with one species extending as far west as the mouth of the River Volga. Wagler's pit viper is kept in large numbers in the Snake Temple in Penang. The water moccasin and the copperhead are widespread over the eastern and middle United States, the bushmaster ranges from Costa Rica and Panama to northern South America.

The warning posture of the water moccasin, mouth open showing its white lining, gives it the alternative name of cottonmouth. It also vibrates its tail at the same time, like its relatives the rattlesnakes, although it has no rattle to make a warning sound. Pit vipers, apart from their pits, are very

△ *Trimeresurus gramineus.*
▷ *Overleaf: Pit viper Bothrops schlegeli.*

ordinary snakes. Some take a wide range of foods, like the water moccasin which eats rabbits, muskrats, ducks, fish, frogs, other snakes, birds' eggs, and nestlings. The copperhead eats small rodents, especially the woodmouse, other snakes, frogs, toads, and insects, including caterpillars and cicadas. The bushmaster, by contrast, takes mainly mammals, and pit vipers generally tend to hunt warm-blooded animals more than cold-blooded, as one would expect from snakes with heat-detector pits. They have one on each side of the head between the eye and the nostril. Using these a pit viper can pick up the trail of a warm-blooded animal.

'Seeing' heat

Each pit is $\frac{1}{8}$ in. across and $\frac{1}{4}$ in. deep. A thin membrane is stretched near the bottom and temperature receptors, 500–1 500 per sq mm, are packed within this membrane. These receptors are so sensitive they can respond to changes as small as 0·002 of a C°, and they allow a snake to locate objects 0·1 of a C° warmer or cooler than the surroundings. In more understandable terms a pit viper could detect the warmth of the human hand held a foot from its head. The membrane with its receptors can be compared to an eye with its retina. The overhanging lip of the pit casts 'heat shadows' onto it, so the snake is aware of direction, and since the 'fields of view' of the two pits overlap there is the equivalent of stereoscopic vision, giving a rangefinder. A pit viper hunting by day has the advantage of being able to follow an animal's heat trail through low vegetation after the animal has passed out of sight. It could, of course, do this equally well by scent. The facial pits come into their own in night hunting, when prey can be tracked by scent with the facial pits guiding the final strike. At first it was thought they had something to do with an accessory aid to smell or as an organ of hearing—snakes have no ears. Another suggestion was that they might be organs for picking up low-frequency air vibrations. Then, as late as 1892, it was noticed that a rattlesnake, one

of the pit vipers, was attracted to a lighted match. Then came the discovery that pythons have pits on their lips that are sensitive to heat. The first experiments on pit vipers were made in 1937, and left no doubt that the pits are heat detectors and further studies since have shown just how delicate they are.

Snakes in cold climates

Pit vipers usually bear living young. There are a few exceptions, the bushmaster being one, and that lives in the tropics. Pit vipers extend from the Volga across Asia and across America. There may be a direct connection between these two facts. One of the advantages of bearing living young, as against laying eggs, is that the offspring are protected not only against enemies but also against low temperatures until they are at an advanced stage of development. At some time pit vipers must have crossed the land bridge that used to exist where the Bering Straits are now. This is well north, and it would have been far easier for snakes able to bear live young to survive in these latitudes and so make the crossing. It probably explains also why the Himalayan pit viper can live so near glaciers, and why the most southerly of all snakes is a pit viper named Bothrops ammodytoides, living in the Santa Cruz province of Argentina.

class	**Reptilia**
order	**Squamata**
suborder	**Serpentes**
family	**Crotalidae**
genera & species	**Ancistrodon contortrix** copperhead **A. himalayanus** Himalayan pit viper **A. piscivorus** water moccasin **Trimeresurus wagleri** Wagler's pit viper

Puff adder

There are 8 species of puff adder in Africa and they range in size from the Peringuey's desert adder, 1 ft long, to the Gaboon viper, 6 ft or more long. They are stout bodied snakes with short tails. The head is very broad compared with the neck, and is covered with small overlapping scales. There is a deep pit of unknown function above the nostrils, and in many species one or more erectile scales on the snout form 'horns', as in the rhinoceros viper. Not all puff adders are given this name, although they all belong to the same genus, and they fall into two groups. These are the highly coloured Gaboon viper and rhinoceros viper, of the tropical African forests, and the sombrely coloured brown and grey puff adders of the savannah and deserts. One of this second group, the common puff adder, is yellow to brown with darker bars or chevrons on the back. It ranges from Morocco southwards across the Sahara to the Cape and is also found in Arabia. The others have less extensive ranges, the Cape puff adder, for example, being found only in the mountains of Cape Province, South Africa.

Melting into the background

Savannah and desert puff adders, with their duller colourings, tend to harmonize with the differently coloured soils on which they are living. So also do the Gaboon and rhinoceros vipers in spite of their bright colours, for their colour patterns are disruptive. The Gaboon viper has a gaudy pattern of yellow, purple and brown arranged in geometric forms. The rhinoceros viper, even more brilliantly coloured with more purple, and blue as well, has green triangles margined with black and blue on its sides. But both snakes are virtually invisible on the carpet of dead and green leaves on the forest floor. The smaller species of puff adder live on sandy soils. Several of these smaller adders are able to climb into bushes, but generally puff adders keep to the ground, hunting mainly during the night.

Inoffensive yet deadly

The broad head of the puff adder houses the large venom glands and although the effect of this snake's bite is less rapid than that of a mamba or a cobra it is just as deadly. Fortunately, these snakes strike only to disable prey or in self-defence, and need a fair amount of provocation to make them hit back. Africans are said to be more afraid of harmless geckos than of the Gaboon viper, and Herbert Lang tells of a small boy dragging a 5 ft live specimen into his camp to sell it to him. If their venom is slow-acting it is nonetheless potent. R Marlin Perkins, curator of reptiles in the St Louis Zoological Gardens, nearly died from the bite of a Gaboon viper. Some years

◁ *The attractive 'horned' head of the rhinoceros viper is deceptive; it houses the venom glands.*

later, in 1964, the Director of the Salt Lake City Zoo died from a puff adder bite received while handling the snake. Puff adders can give out as much as 15 drops of venom at a time—4 drops are enough to kill a man. But usually snakes give a first warning by hissing. The hissing sound is produced by forcing air from the lungs and windpipe through the glottis. Puff adders have an especially loud hiss. Their puff makes a sound more like the noise of a horse when it forces air through its lips.

Beckoning their food

The food of puff adders varies widely between the species. Small prey, such as a frog, is grabbed and swallowed without being poisoned. Larger prey is struck with the fangs and allowed to run away to die. The snake later follows its trail to eat it. The carcase is dragged into the snake's mouth by the teeth in the lower jaw. Once part of the victim has reached the throat, muscular swallowing movements carry it down, the snake holding its head up to assist this. Some scientists claim that the long fangs, which may be 2 in. long in a 5ft Gaboon viper, are used to drag the victim into the snake's mouth. South African herpetologists do not support this, but suggest the long fangs make it possible to inject the venom deeply.

The common puff adder and the Gaboon viper eat rats and mice, ground-living birds, frogs, toads and lizards. The Cape Mountain adder feeds on the same but is known to eat other snakes. The many-horned adder and the horned puff adder bury themselves in the sand, except for the eyes and snout, to catch lizards. The horned puff adder leaves the tip of its tail sticking out of the sand and waggles it to attract its victims within striking distance.

An enemy to many small animals, the puff adder has few adversaries itself, mainly birds of prey, mongooses and warthogs, and man. Puff adders can store large quantities of fat and this is sold by African herbalists as a cure for rheumatism.

Large families

Puff adders are ovoviviparous. That is, the eggs are hatched inside the mother so the young are born alive or else they wriggle out of the egg capsule soon after it is laid. Mating is usually from October to December, the young being born in March and April. The young from a mother 3 ft long, are about 8 in. at birth. There are 8–15 in the litter of the smallest species, 70–80 or more in the large puff adders.

Fasting to grow

The paradoxical frog (page 106) is named for the paradox that the tadpole is much greater than the froglet into which it changes. The puzzle is, where does all the spare flesh go? The situation is reversed in the baby puff adder. As soon as it is born it can kill and eat small mice although it moults first before looking for food. It can, however, happily go without food for as much as 3 months. The ability to fast is not unusual. What is extraordinary is that the baby puff adder still grows 25% in length and increases its girth by a quarter while doing so.

△ Sedate mating, two love-locked common puff adders, the male is on the right. Mating usually takes place from October to December. Fertilisation is internal and sperm may survive inside the female for long periods. Most reptiles lay their eggs but puff adders are ovoviviparous, the female retains the eggs until the young are ready or nearly ready to hatch 5—6 months later.

◁ Submerged for the day, a small Peringuey's puff adder spends the day well hidden. Alerted by the photographer the snake raises its head so giving its position away. But its sandy colouring blends well with the soil making the snake very inconspicuous.

class	**Reptilia**
order	**Squamata**
suborder	**Serpentes**
family	**Viperidae**
genus & species	**Bitis arietans** common puff adder
	B. atropos Cape Mountain adder
	B. caudalis horned puff adder
	B. cornuta manyhorned adder
	B. gabonica Gaboon viper
	B. inornata Cape puff adder
	B. nasicornis rhinoceros viper
	B. peringueyi Peringuey's puff adder

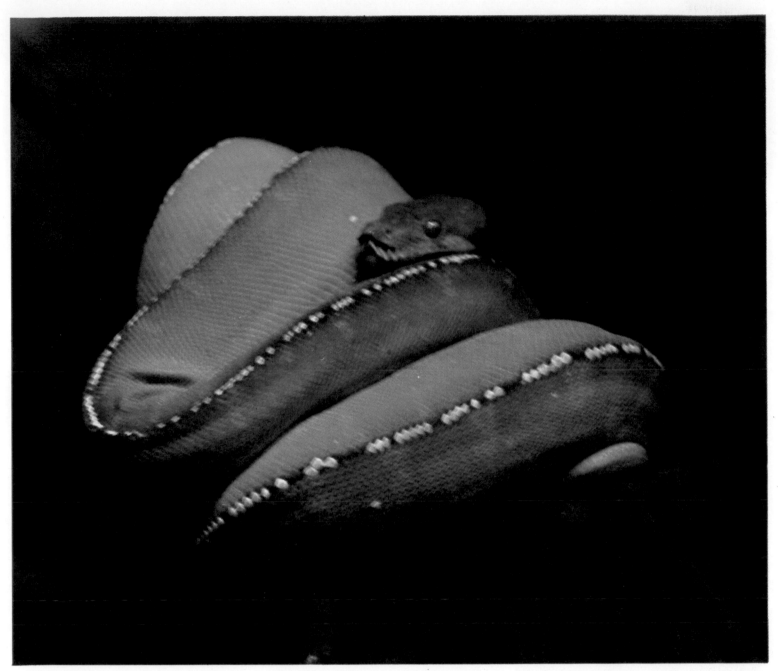

Python

Pythons are the Old World equivalent of the New World boas. Like the boas they have small spurs that represent the vestiges of hind limbs. The largest and best-known pythons belong to the genus **Python.** Not only are these large pythons at home in jungles, climbing trees, but they are often found near water. The African rock python which reaches about 32 ft long is not quite as long as the accepted record figure for the anaconda, the largest of the boas (page 205). It lives in most parts of Africa in open country except the deserts. The other African pythons are the ball python and Angolan python of West Africa. There are no pythons in southwest Asia but several species are found from India to China and the East Indies. The Indian python reaches about 20 ft and ranges through southeast Asia from India to China and on some of the islands of the East Indies. The reticulated python,

reaching a length of 33 ft, has a more easterly distribution, from Burma to the Philippine Islands and Timor. The short-tailed python lives in the Malayan Peninsula, Borneo and Sumatra and the Timor python lives on the islands of Timor and Flores in Indonesia.

As well as the true pythons there are several other genera of pythons, including the carpet snake, that are found in the East Indies and Australia. Of the rock pythons the largest is the 20ft amethystine rock python or scrub python. A smaller group is the Australian womas which eat other snakes. The green tree python of New Guinea hunts in trees. The burrowing python, which lives in West Africa, in Liberia and throughout the rain forest of Zaire, spends its time underground chasing rodents and shrews.

Good travellers

The large pythons are often found near water and the Indian python is almost semi-aquatic. They also live in jungles and

△ *A green tree python wraps its coils around itself as it waits for some unsuspecting prey which it grasps with its enlarged front teeth. Its leaf-green colour with white spots along its back and its extremely prehensile tail, make it admirably adapted for life in the trees.*

climb trees, except for the African python which prefers open country. The reticulated python shows a preference for living near human settlements. At one time it was a regular inhabitant of Bangkok, hiding up by day and coming out at night to feed on rats, cats, dogs and poultry. One individual was caught in the King's palace. This habit of associating with buildings must account for its turning up in ships' cargoes. One reached London in good condition; but it is a good traveller under its own steam. It swims out to sea and was one of the first reptiles to reach the island of Krakatoa in the Malay archipelago, after it erupted in 1888, destroying all life.

Any live prey accepted

Pythons kill their prey by constriction, wrapping themselves around the body of the

235

prey so that it cannot breathe. The coils then hold the body steady while the python works it into its mouth. Prey is caught by ambush; the python lies in wait then springs out knocking the animal with its head and seizing it with its jaws until it can wrap its body round it. The list of animals eaten by pythons is too long to enumerate. Mammals are preferred, followed by birds, but young rock pythons have been caught in fish traps. African pythons eat many small antelopes such as duikers, gazelle, impala and bushbuck. A large python can swallow prey weighing up to 120 lb but this is exceptional and usually smaller animals are taken such as dassies, hares, rats, pigeons and ducks. Jackals and monkeys are sometimes eaten and one 18 ft African python is known to have eaten a leopard, with very little damage being sustained in the process of catching it. Pythons sometimes suffer from their meals. They have been found with porcupine quills and antelope horns sticking through their stomach wall. Usually such dangerous projections are digested before causing any serious damage.

A large animal will last a python for a long time but they sometimes kill several small animals in quick succession. An African python has been credited with capturing and eating three jackals and a small python was seen to kill two sparrows in quick succession, then pin down a third with its tail.

There are a few authentic accounts of men being attacked by pythons, and there is good reason to believe the case of the 14 year old Malay boy attacked and eaten on the island of Salebabu.

Devoted mother pythons

The courtship of pythons is less lively than that of smaller snakes. The male crawls after the female, trying to climb over her and sometimes they rear up and sway to and fro. The spurs or vestigial limbs that lie either side of the cloaca are used by the male to scratch the female and stimulate her to raise her body so that he can wrap his body around hers and bring the two cloacas together. The eggs, 100 in a single clutch, are laid 3–4 months after mating. The female gathers the eggs into a pile and wraps herself around them, brooding them throughout the 2–3 month incubation period, only leaving them for occasional visits to water and more rarely to eat. Most pythons merely guard their eggs but the Indian python incubates them by keeping her body a few degrees above that of the surrounding air. Reticulated pythons are 2–2½ ft long when they hatch and for the first few years they grow rapidly at a rate of about 2 ft or more a year. An Indian python nearly trebled its length in its first year of life. Pythons may live for over 20 years.

Courageous otters

Even the great snakes are not free from enemies. Young pythons have many enemies but as they grow larger fewer animals can overcome them. Crocodiles, hyaenas and tigers have been found with the remains of pythons in their stomachs and Jim Corbett writes of finding a 17ft Indian python killed by a pair of otters which had apparently attacked from either side, avoiding harm by their agility. When the ball python of Africa is molested it rolls itself into a tight, almost uniformly round ball, its head tucked well inside.

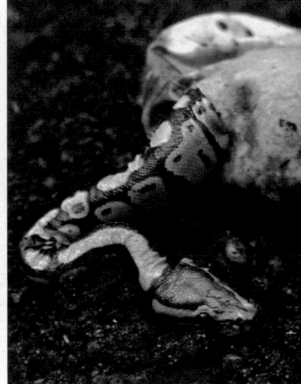

Beating elephants

Both African and Indian pythons were well known to the Greeks and Romans and have taken their place in folklore and religion. They are, for instance, responsible for one of the many dragon legends. Dragon is derived from the Greek word for snake, and the ancient writers were obviously talking about big snakes. It was mediaeval naturalists who turned them into fabulous creatures. Edward Topsell has left us a delightful description of how dragons capture elephants. In his *Historie of Serpentes* 1608 he writes how they 'hide themselves in trees covering their head and letting the other part hang down like a rope. In those trees they watch until the Elephant comes to eat and croppe off the branches, then suddainly, before he be aware, they leape into his face and digge out his eyes, and with their tayles or hinder partes, beate and vexe the Elephant, untill they have made him breathlesse, for they strangle him with theyr foreparts, as they beat him with the hinder.' Apart from the impracticability of an elephant being attacked, this is a reasonable account of a python killing its prey.

◁ *Strangled! A flying fox, caught in the jaws of a scrub python, is being strangled to death by the python's tightening coils.*

△ *A carpet python* **Morelia spilotes** *curls over and around her eggs, rarely leaving them. The temperature within her coils is up to 12F° warmer than the surrounding atmosphere.*

▷△ *A ball python emerges from its egg, after an incubation period of up to 80 days. It may be one of a hundred snakes in the clutch.*

▷ *Superfluous legs. The two claws (arrowed) on either side of the anal vent of this African python are vestigial hind limbs, reminding us that snakes evolved from legged reptiles.*

▽ *The African python's skull shows the typical arrangement of teeth of a non-poisonous snake. The even sized teeth all point backwards, which ensures a firm and fatal grip on their prey.*

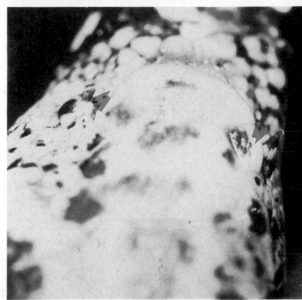

class	**Reptilia**
order	**Squamata**
suborder	**Serpentes**
family	**Pythonidae**
genera & species	***Calabaria reinhardti*** burrowing python ***Chondropython viridis*** green tree python ***Liasis amethystinus*** amethystine rock python ***Morelia argus*** carpet snake ***Python anchietae*** Angolan python ***P. curtus*** short-tailed python ***P. molurus*** Indian python ***P. regius*** ball python ***P. reticulatus*** reticulated python ***P. sebae*** African python ***P. timorensis*** Timor python

Racer

Racers are closely related to whip snakes. They have slender streamlined bodies with relatively large heads, small curved teeth, and large eyes. All racers are paler on the belly but, depending on the species, of which there are more than 20, they can be black, olive, brown or reddish on the back. Generally, racers living in humid areas are darker than those found in drier parts. The striped racer has a marked yellow stripe on its side. Black racers, the largest species, are often over 3½ ft long. The females are larger than the males. The young are usually brighter than the adults and are checkered with alternating blotches of pale olive and darker brown.

They are not poisonous or constrictor snakes but catch their prey by pinning it to the ground with their bodies.

Racers are found throughout most of the United States, Mexico, southern Europe, North Africa and southwest Asia.

Prefer open scrubland

Racers are usually found in scrubland, pastures or among crops, but the larger species also live in open woodland. They live on the ground but climb into bushes or trees, or even swim, to escape danger. They tend to remain 'homebased' all their lives, often not travelling out of an area of about 25 acres. Local movements may be made, for instance, escaping out of a crop at harvest time, or to find suitable places for hibernation.

They hibernate in crevices in rocks or in the disused burrows of pocket gophers or other animals. Sometimes they hibernate entwined in small groups with other snakes, not necessarily racers. They are usually found where the temperature is between 10°C/50°F and 0°C/32°F, but they can survive slightly lower temperatures for short periods. As much as 6 months may be spent in hibernation.

In the summer months racers control their body temperature by basking in the sun or seeking shade. They can tolerate a higher temperature than most other snakes and seem happiest in temperatures of around 26°C/79°F.

Eating according to size

Racers use eyesight to catch prey and they often course through dense cover in active search of food. Smell may also play a part as they are known to catch some animals in their burrows. When the prey is caught the racer works its jaws towards the head and swallows the animal whole, head first. The type of food eaten depends very largely on the size of the racer. Young snakes feed mainly on insects, lizards, frogs and grasshoppers but larger snakes will eat mice, voles, birds and other smaller snakes. Black racers eat mainly rats, weasels and young rabbits which they swallow whole. Racers are said also to eat the young of their own species but the only time EA Liner, who studied blue racers, actually saw this happen it almost seemed to be by mistake: two racers were attempting to swallow the same lizard. One succeeded and proceeded to swallow the other racer which was still clinging stubbornly to the lizard.

Promiscuous snakes

The courtship of the racer is like that of the garter snake (page 220). A male finds a receptive female in early spring and lies alongside

238

◁ *The black racer is not all that its name implies. It moves at a maximum speed of 3½ mph compared with 10 mph for a black mamba.*
△ *A united couple. Mating black racers, with their large heads and streamlined bodies, lie side by side in the grass, the male rippling spasmodically until mating is finished.*

her, rippling spasmodically. The female sometimes moves off but this seems only to increase the male's interest. Two male racers may court the same female simultaneously. Racers lay eggs in clutches of 10−20. The number depends largely on the size of the female. The eggs are white and leathery and may be buried over a foot deep in an abandoned pocket gopher or ground squirrel hole, or, in humid climates, they may be near the surface just under some loose soil or a piece of wood. Development takes about 2 months and depends on the humidity and warmth of the environment. The young snakes usually hatch in August or September and break out of their eggs by means of an egg tooth which they lose a few days after hatching. The young are about 10 in. long and increase to about 17 in. before they hibernate in October.

Will fight if provoked

The natural enemies of racers are hawks, owls, skunks and other snake-eating snakes. The racer's eggs are very vulnerable, not only to predators, but also to drying out and flooding. The death rate among the first year young is again very high. Probably about 50% die in their first active year before they have reached mature size. Modern farming has reduced numbers drastically as farm machinery now moves too rapidly to permit escape and deep ploughing turns up racer eggs, while the cutting of crops forces many racers to seek new 'homes'. If disturbed a racer escapes as quickly as possible, zig-zagging silently away in the undergrowth often using a downhill slope to increase its speed. Sometimes it just coils itself passively and exudes musk or thrashes its tail excitedly to attract attention to a certain spot and then glides away quickly, often returning to the same spot by another route. It will also shed its tail, leaving it thrashing on the ground while the rest of the snake escapes. The racer sometimes puts up a spirited fight if cornered. It raises its head about a foot and strikes repeatedly at its enemy, lacerating the skin with its teeth.

Racer in name only?

It is commonly accepted that the racer is one of the swiftest of snakes and this is how it got its name. Yet the fastest reliable recorded speed for this same snake is only a little over 3½ mph, no more than a good walking pace for a man. The speed of snakes is probably exaggerated because of the ease with which they slide through the undergrowth, disappearing in a trice. Compared with the black mamba (page 227) whose maximum speed is 10 mph, the racer turns out to be not at all fast. Even the European grass snake (page 222) can travel at 5 mph.

class	**Reptilia**		
order	**Squamata**		
suborder	**Serpentes**		
family	**Colubridae**		
genus & species	*Coluber constrictor constrictor* black racer *C. constrictor flaviventris* blue racer *C. flagellum piceus* red racer *C. lateralis* striped racer, others		

Rat snake

Rat snakes are non-venomous and are related to the European grass snake. The common name refers to the habit of eating rodents, and some are also called chicken snakes. Most rat snakes belong to the genus **Elaphe**, with which we are mainly concerned here, but the name does cover snakes with the same habits in other genera. Rat snakes have stout bodies, square heads and extremely flat bellies. The scales of the belly have slight keels which help in tree climbing.

There are six species of rat snake in America which range from Ontario to Central America. The black rat snake, also known as the black chicken snake or pilot black snake, grows to 5 ft with a record length of over 8 ft. The back and head are black but the tips of the scales are edged with white and the chin and belly are white turning to grey towards the rear. The name pilot black snake is derived from an unfounded idea that it warns poisonous snakes of danger and guides them to safety. The black rat snake ranges from Ontario to Florida and Texas. The yellow rat snake, yellow chicken snake or striped house snake averages 5 ft. As its name suggests, it is bright yellow with four dark stripes and lives in the south-eastern United States. The fox snakes are so-called because they secrete an odour like that of foxes. They are stouter than their relatives and are yellowish brown with dark brown blotches. The copper-coloured head sometimes causes them to be confused with copperhead snakes. They may grow to 6 ft. Asian rat snakes include the Indian rat snake and the keeled rat snake. A European representative of the genus is the Aesculapian snake of south-east Europe and Asia Minor.

▽ An unnerving sight—a large, brightly coloured yellow rat snake crosses a track in the Everglades, Florida, USA.

Evidence of the good climbing ability of rat snakes: yellow rat snake.

Aesculapius, Greek god of medicine, and symbol, Aesculapian snake.

Adaptable snakes

Rat snakes are found in a variety of habitats, from woodlands and scrub to arid country and lakes and marshes. For example, some are found in the deserts of Mexico, while fox snakes, which are seldom found far from water, swim well and can be found sunbathing on rocks near water. In colder parts of North America and in eastern Europe rat snakes hibernate, emerging during early spring.

Although mainly ground dwellers, some rat snakes are good climbers, their green colour and the keels on the belly scales being typical of climbing snakes. The corn snake and the black rat snake for instance climb the trunks of large trees by wedging themselves into crevices in the bark gaining extra grip with the keels.

Snakes are usually very conservative in habit but the keeled rat snake of Malaya and Indonesia, which grows up to 12 ft, has become adapted to living with man. In wild country it is diurnal but around villages and farms it hunts at night for rodents.

Varied diet

Rat snakes are constrictors, trapping and strangling their prey in coils of their bodies. The diet is unusually varied for snakes, that of the Indian keeled snake including frogs, lizards, other snakes, birds and mammals, but rodents such as rats, mice, voles and squirrels form the bulk of the diet. The fox snakes also eat earthworms and tree-climbing rat snakes plunder birds' nests.

Twining courtship

In the Aesculapian snake, as in many others, courtship takes the form of a chase followed by a dance. The male chases the female until he can coil around her. They continue in this position, then the pair rear up and dance for up to an hour or more before copulation takes place. Some rat snakes are oviparous, laying clutches of about 20 eggs in burrows in loose earth or decaying logs. The eggs are laid in midsummer and the female sometimes stays with them until they hatch about 9 weeks later and then leaves.

Foul defence

The rat snake's first line of defence is to emit a foul-smelling fluid from glands at the base of the tail, similar to that of the grass snake (page 222). Some species vibrate their tails when annoyed. The fox snake was once called the 'hardwood rattler'. Unfortunately this habit does not protect them from man who is even more likely to brand them as dangerous and to destroy them on sight. If handled, rat snakes will bite and draw blood, but there is no poison in these bites.

Beneficial snakes

The Aesculapian snake is believed to be the snake on the symbol of Aesculapius, the Greek god of medicine. The original temple of Aesculapius was at his supposed birthplace at Epidaurus in Greece and was frequented by large, easily tamed snakes that have been identified as Aesculapian snakes. They were thought to be incarnations of the god and to have healing powers. The Romans later took over many of the Greek myths, including that of the Aesculapian snake. Furthermore, they took the snake with them on their travels, which accounts for isolated colonies of Aesculapian snakes as far north as Germany.

class	**Reptilia**
order	**Squamata**
suborder	**Serpentes**
family	**Colubridae**
genera & species	***Elaphe guttata*** *corn snake* ***E. longissima*** *Aesculapian snake* ***E. obsoleta*** *black rat snake* ***E. quadrivittata*** *yellow rat snake* ***E. vulpina*** *fox snake* ***Ptyas mucosus*** *Indian rat snake* ***Zaocys carinatus*** *keeled rat snake* *others*

241

Rattlesnake

These are heavy-bodied and usually highly venomous snakes, best known for the rattle, sometimes called a bell, cloche, buzzer or whirrer, on the tail. When disturbed the rattlesnake vibrates its tail, or rattle, as if giving warning that it is about to strike. Rattlesnakes are found almost entirely in North America, from southern Canada to Mexico, where there are 30 species and over 60 subspecies, with one species in South America.

*There are two groups of rattlesnakes, each represented by one genus: the pygmy rattlesnakes **Sistrurus** have short slender tails and very tiny rattles, and they never exceed 2 ft in length; and the rattlesnakes proper **Crotalus**, which are usually around 3½–5 ft but exceptionally grow to 8 ft or more. The timber or banded rattlesnake of the eastern States is marked with dark chevrons on the back. In the prairie rattlesnake the markings are irregularly oblong. Most others have diamond markings. Rattlesnakes share with other pit vipers (page 229) a tolerance of low temperatures. The Mexican dusky rattlesnake lives at altitudes of up to 14 500 ft.*

Sound varies with size

The rattle is made up of a number of loosely interlocked shells each of which was the scale originally covering the tip of the tail. Usually in snakes this scale is a simple hollow cone which is shed with the rest of the skin at each moult. In rattlesnakes it is larger than usual, much thicker and has one or two constrictions. Except at the first moult, the scale is not shed but remains loosely attached to the new scale, and at each moult a new one is added. The rattle does not grow in length indefinitely. The end scales tend to wear out, so there can be a different number of segments to the rattle in different individuals of the same age, depending on how much the end of the rattle is abraded. It seldom exceeds 14 segments in wild rattlesnakes no matter how old they may be, but snakes in zoos, leading a more untroubled life, and not rubbing the rattle on hard objects, may have as many as 29 pieces in a rattle. The longer the rattle the more the sound is deadened, 8 being the most effective number to give the loudest noise. The volume of sound not only varies with the size of the snake and the length of the rattle, but it also varies from species to species. At best it can be heard only a few feet away.

◁ *Threatening tiger rattlesnake. Between its coils is a large rattle, a unique organ composed of horny segments of unshed skin. The fact that rattlesnakes shed their skin three or four times a year during the first years of their lives disposes of the popular idea that the number of rattles corresponds to the years of the snake's age. The best reason to be found for the evolution of the rattle in an animal that is deaf is that it acts as a warning device to large animals that may molest or tread on the snake.*

243

Rattlers not all black

It is hard to generalize on the size and effectiveness of the rattle as it is on any other feature of rattlesnakes. For example, these snakes have a reputation for attacking people, and of being bad tempered. It applies only to some of them. Unless provoked or roughly treated the red diamond rattlesnake may make no attempt to strike when handled. It may not even sound its rattle. The eastern and western diamond backs, by contrast, not only rattle a warning but they will also pursue an intruder, lunging at it again and again. How poisonous a snake is also depends on several things, such as its age – the younger it is the less the amount of poison it can inject – and whether it has recently struck at another victim, when the amount of venom it can use will be reduced. Cases are known in which a snake has taken nearly two months to replenish its venom to full capacity. Rattlesnakes of the same species from one part of the range may be more venomous than those from another part. Prairie rattlesnakes of the plains are about three times as venomous as those of California, and half as poisonous again as those of the Grand Canyon.

Waterproof skin

Rattlesnakes feed on much the same prey as other pit vipers (page 229), mainly small warm-blooded animals and especially rodents, cottontail rabbits and young jack rabbits. Young rattlesnakes, including the pygmy rattlesnakes, take a larger proportion of coldblooded animals, such as frogs, salamanders and lizards. Studies have also been made on how much rattlesnakes drink, and the remarks that follow probably apply to all snakes. Their needs are not as great as those of active and warm-blooded animals because the water loss from the body is not high. They need about one-tenth as much water as a mammal of similar size. In one test it was found that twice as much water is lost from a rattlesnake's head, and this mainly in its breath, as from the whole of the rest of its body, which suggests that its skin is almost waterproof. When it does drink it sucks up water from a pond or stream. There is no evidence that it laps it with the tongue, as is sometimes stated, or that it drinks dew.

Two years to be born

All rattlesnakes give birth to live young. Whether they have one litter a year or less depends on the climate. The prairie rattlesnake has one litter a year in the southern part of its range, but in the northern part it may be two years before the young are ready to be born. Mating is in spring and the number in a litter may vary from 1 to 60 according to the size of the mother, the usual number being between 10 and 20.

Slaughter of infants

Their venom does not spare rattlesnakes from being killed and eaten. Hawks of all kinds kill them, so do skunks and snake-eating snakes. Pigs, deer and other hoofed animals trample them, especially the young ones, and many die of cold or excessive heat, or from starvation. Indeed few from a litter survive their first year.

Sensitive eyes

Snakes are known to be deaf yet they often seem to be reacting to sounds. In fact, they seem at first glance to be able to hear but there is more to it than this, as Laurence Klauber found in his celebrated tests on rattlesnakes. First, having placed a rattlesnake under a table, he clapped two sticks together making sure his hands and the sticks could not be seen by the snake. It reacted, apparently to the sound. Puzzled at first, Klauber finally found the reason. He was sitting on a stool, his feet dangling, and every time he clapped the sticks together his feet moved and the snake reacted to sight of them. So he put a screen between the snake and his feet, and still the snake reacted when he clapped the sticks – it was seeing a reflection of Klauber's feet in a nearby window.

He found his red diamond rattler highly sensitive to footsteps on a concrete floor 15 ft away, and it still reacted to footsteps that distance away after he had placed it on a blanket. He decided to test this further. He put the snake in a fibreboard box, suspended this by a rubber band from a stick held each end on a pillow, to insulate it from vibrations through the ground. It still reacted to clapped sticks and to the radio. It was, in fact, as Klauber finally found, picking up the heat from the valves of the radio as these warmed up, and it was reacting to vibrations in the floor and sides of the fibreboard box, against which its body rested. So the box was changed for a Chinese woven bamboo basket hung from the same stick. Still the snake appeared to react to sound, but further tests showed it was reacting to Klauber's hand movements seen through the very tiny cracks between the bamboo withies. Apart from anything else, these experiments show how hard it can sometimes be to test a particular animal sense. They also show, among other things, how sensitive a snake's eyes are to small movements.

class	**Reptilia**
order	**Squamata**
suborder	**Serpentes**
family	**Crotalidae**
genus & species	*Crotalus adamanteus* eastern diamond back *C. atrox* western diamond back *C. horridus* timber or banded rattlesnake *C. pusillus* Mexican dusky rattlesnake *C. ruber* red diamond back *C. tigris* tiger rattlesnake *C. viridis* prairie rattlesnake

◁ *Sparring partners – two western diamond back rattlesnakes engage in combat. Although it is difficult to observe both snakes simultaneously during the fight it seems that the twining of the necks is a manoeuvre for an advantageous position from which one snake may forcefully throw his opponent.*

Suspended in space, a motionless African vine snake. Its black-tipped, red tongue is thought to act as a lure to attract birds and other prey.

Rearfanged snake

*The rearfanged snakes, also known as backfanged snakes, have two or three grooved teeth on each side of the upper jaw at the rear. These teeth conduct poison from the salivary glands into prey held in the mouth. They are not harmful to people, as a rule, although the booms-lang, which belongs to the same sub-family, the Boiginae, is dangerous. The subfamily takes its name from the man-grove snake or yellow-ringed cat snake, which is up to 7 ft long, black with bright yellow markings, and lives in southeast Asia. Like many rearfanged snakes its head is short and broad and its body long and slender. Other rearfanged snakes living in trees have very long heads, like the longnosed tree snake of southeast Asia, the vine snakes of Africa, and the rearfanged tree snakes **Oxybelis** in tropical America. The African sand snakes also belong to this subfamily.*

It is likely that the subfamily Boiginae is artificial and that the snakes placed in it have only the one common feature, of having the fangs at the rear of the jaw. Moreover, other snakes are called rear-fanged although they belong to other related subfamilies. There are, for example, the aquatic rearfanged snakes of the subfamily Homalopsinae, dwelling largely in mudflats.

Snake-charmer's dupe

The mangrove snake lives in lowland forest or mangrove swamps and is called a cat snake because each pupil has a vertical slit, as in a cat's eye. This snake is readily tamed and is sometimes used by snake-charmers who pretend it is the dangerous krait. The African vine snake, also known as the twig snake or bird snake, lives from tropical Africa to the Cape, and is up to 4½ ft long with an exceptionally long, slender tail, which makes up nearly half the snake's total length. Its colour is grey to pinkish brown with dark markings and its head is green to mauve or violet. It is very like the longnosed tree snake of southeast Asia, and the two can be taken as typical of tree-dwelling rearfanged snakes. They lie along branches with the front third of the body held in space and unsupported, rigidly motionless for long periods on end. Their pupils have horizontal slits, hourglass-shaped, which are said to give them a binocular vision. They move swiftly through the trees and can also move rapidly over the ground.

Climbing and gliding

Other southeast Asian species are the paradise tree snakes. One has a green spot on each scale and a row of four-petalled red spots along the back. These snakes can climb straight up the vertical trunk of a rough-barked tree. They can descend by 'flying', simply by launching themselves into space and hollowing the underside of the body so a cushion of air is trapped beneath it and they come to no harm.

Sand snakes

The African sand snakes are usually some shade of grey, sometimes with dark or pale stripes, and often spotted on the front part of the body. They match the colours of sandy or stony ground over which they move swiftly. They are found in sandy areas throughout Africa, and related to them is the 20 in. hooded snake which is brown with black spots on the neck, and lives in North Africa and the Iberian peninsula. Other rearfanged snakes that range into southern or southeastern Europe are the Montpellier snake, which is up to 6 ft long, coloured in various shades of grey with rows of spots or stripes on the back, and the 3 ft European cat snake, which is grey with black markings.

Eating bats and hummingbirds

Rearfanged snakes agree closely in their food. They eat mainly lizards; in the Old World, geckos and chameleons are taken by the tree-dwellers; in America, anole lizards. They will sometimes take birds in tropical America, chiefly the hummingbird, and on the ground they hunt frogs and toads, and other smaller snakes. The man-grove snake is also said to catch bats. It is believed that some species, by flicking their brightly coloured tongue in and out, excite the curiosity of their prey and so lure them to their doom. They can, however, pursue the prey swiftly, and partly for the speed of their movement, partly for their long slender bodies, they are credited in some parts of the world with being able to drive straight through a man's body, like a lance.

245

Bagpipes

Since rearfanged snakes are a diverse group there is little that can be said briefly about their breeding except that, as in other groups of snakes, some species lay eggs and some bear live young. Not a great deal is known about their enemies. That they do have natural enemies is clear from the behaviour of some of them, which blow out their throat so exposing the coloured skin between the scales. How they do this is not known for certain but it seems to be due to the snake inflating its windpipe. As a rule, this is strengthened by rings of cartilage and can no more be blown up than could a piece of garden hose. In the rearfanged snakes these rings are incomplete. They are little more than half rings on the underside of the windpipe so that the upper part can be made to balloon out.

Snail-eating snakes

The aquatic rearfanged snakes of the subfamily Homalopsinae live largely on mudflats, feeding on frogs, rodents, and even fish and crabs where the mudflats are tidal. The poison of one species has little effect on frogs or rodents but has a very strong effect on crabs. It is somewhat remarkable that snakes should eat crabs; and there are American water snakes that eat crayfishes, and the red-bellied snake *Storeria* of North America often feeds on slugs. There are snakes, however, in both tropical America and southeast Asia, which eat snails. The bones of their chin are so arranged that the snakes can insert the lower jaw into a snail's shell, give it a sharp twist in order to hook their front teeth firmly into the snail's body and then pull the snail right out of its shell.

class	**Reptilia**
order	**Squamata**
suborder	**Serpentes**
family	**Colubridae**
genera & species	**Boiga dendrophila** *mangrove snake* **Chrysopelea paradisi** *paradise tree snake* **Dryophis nasuta** *longnosed tree snake* **Malpolon monspessulana** *Montpellier snake* **Psammophis spp** *African sand snakes* **Telescopus fallax** *European cat snake* **Thelotornis kirtlandi** *African vine snake, others*

Twig snake or bird snake – two other appropriate common names for the African vine snake, a tree-dweller like its close relative the boomslang. This snake may be up to 4½ ft long, with an exceptionally long, slender tail.

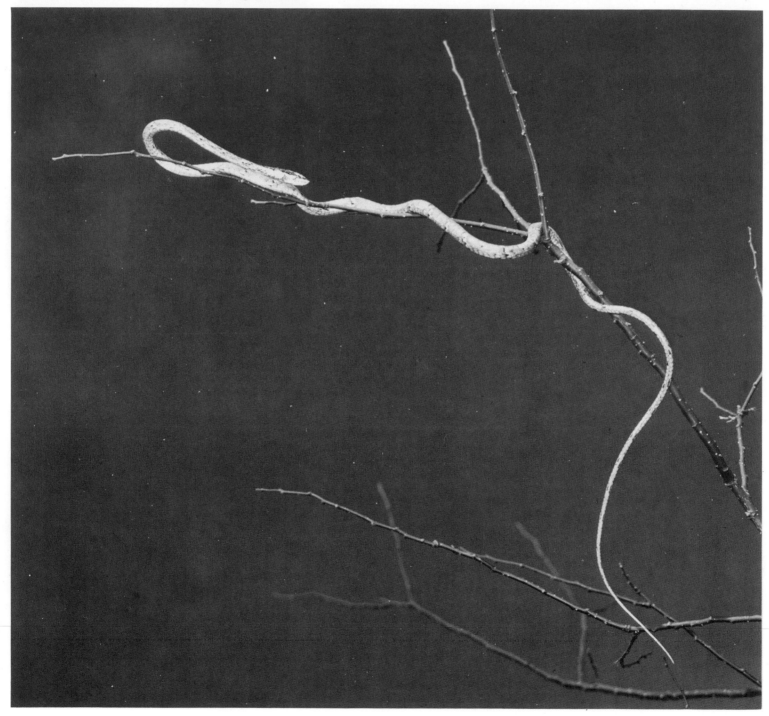

Sidewinder

Also known as the horned rattlesnake, the sidewinder is named after its peculiar form of locomotion which allows it to move over soft sand. Sidewinders are small rattlesnakes, the adults being only 1½–2 ft long. The females are usually larger than the males, whereas in other rattlesnakes it is the reverse. The body is stout, tapering to a narrow neck with a broad head like an arrowhead. Above each eye there is a scale that projects as a small horn. There is a dark stripe running backwards from each eye. The body is pale grey or light brown with a row of large dark brown spots running down the back and smaller ones on each side. The tail is marked with alternate light and dark bands and the underparts of the body and tail are white.

The single species of sidewinder lives in the deserts of the southwest United States, including Nevada, Utah, California, Arizona and in the northern part of the state of Baja California in Mexico.

The sidewinder is a small squat rattlesnake that is perfectly adapted for living in deserts.

Sand snake

Sidewinders are most common in areas of loose, windblown sand and although they can be found among rocks or on compacted sand there is usually loose sand nearby. Although other rattlesnakes live in deserts and can be found on loose sand, the sidewinder is the most characteristic of this type of habitat. It is likely that in this habitat the sidewinder has an advantage over the other snakes. By adapting to life in moving sand the sidewinder does not compete with other snakes. These can move over sand by the usual eel-like wriggling. The sidewinder's unusual looping movement enables it to get a good grip on loose sand and so move faster.

Sidewinders are most active in the early part of the night when air temperatures are not dangerously high and when their prey is also active. They spend the day in mouseholes or buried in sand, usually under the shelter of a creosote bush or a yucca. They bury themselves by shovelling sand over themselves with looping movements of the body until they are coiled like springs, flush with the surface of the sand. Their mottled brown colour makes them very difficult to see as they lie there half buried.

Desert prey

The shallow saucers in the sand where sidewinders have been resting are often found near mouse and rat burrows as the sidewinders are probably attracted to these areas where they will find prey plentiful. Their main food is small rodents, such as deer mice, kangaroo rats and spiny pocket mice, and lizards such as the tree-climbing utas and other sand-dwelling iguanids. Sidewinders also eat a few snakes, such as the glossy snake and even other sidewinders, and a few small birds.

The breeding habits of sidewinders are the same as those of other rattlesnakes (page 243). Mating takes place when they emerge from hibernation in spring and the young are born alive.

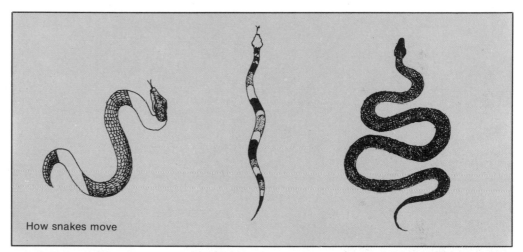

How snakes move

Sidewinding is like a coiled wire rolled along the sand making a series of oblique parallel tracks. Only the white areas touch the ground.

In serpentine movement the body literally skates along in a series of shallow curves which get a grip on any projecting object.

Concertina movement: with the tail anchored the head and neck dart forward, the neck grips the ground and the rest of the body is then pulled up.

Sidewinding

Many snakes will perform 'sidewinding' movements if placed on a sheet of glass, throwing their bodies into loops to get a grip on the smooth surface. The sidewinder, and the horned viper and puff adder of African deserts, make a habit of sidewinding, leaving characteristic tracks in the sand. These are a series of parallel, wavering lines each with a hook at one end made by the sidewinder's tail.

It is very difficult to see how the track is made without seeing a sidewinder in action. In normal, or rectilinear, movement, a series of waves passes down a snake's body, pushing against the ground and driving the snake in the opposite direction to the waves. Sidewinding is very different; it is more like a coil spring being rolled or the movement of the tracks of a caterpillar tractor. The snake throws its body into curves and, when moving, only two points of the body touch

the ground. These two points remain stationary while the raised parts move at an angle to the direction of the waves that pass along its body. As the snake progresses the part of the body immediately behind is raised, so that the body is laid down and taken up like a caterpillar track. When the point of contact reaches the tip of the tail, a new point is started at the head end and the snake moves along a series of parallel tracks.

class	**Reptilia**
order	**Sauria**
suborder	**Serpentes**
family	**Crotalidae**
genus & species	***Crotalus cerastes***

Tree snake

Many snakes live in trees. Some, like the boomslang (page 212) and several of the rearfanged snakes (page 245), have already been dealt with. Attention is given here to the tree snakes of southern and southeast Asia which are not only the most adept at climbing among trees but have also earned the name of 'flying snakes'.

One of the best known is the paradise tree snake of Malaya. It is black but there is a bright green spot on each of its scales, so it seems to have a regular pattern of green spots. It also has a row of four-petalled red spots along its back. Its underside is yellowish green. The golden tree snake **Chrysopelea ornata** *ranges from Sri Lanka through southeast Asia to the Philippines. It is black with golden yellow to orange markings and red spots on its back. Tree snakes are up to 5 ft long and are very slender, with a tail that is nearly half the length of the head and body.*

Expanding ribs

Tree snakes are most accomplished climbers, able to go up almost vertical walls or tree trunks by making use of every little irregularity in the surface. They are helped in this by a well marked angularity along each side of the body and tail. They can also spring across gaps of 3–4 ft, in an almost vertical position. This remarkable feat is performed by the snake coiling itself loosely over a branch then straightening explosively. The most famous exploit of tree snakes is, however, to drop through the air in a glide, either from bough to bough or from tree to ground. The snake holds its body rigid and launches itself into the air, and at the same time it 'draws in its belly'. Part of this action involves spreading the outer ends of the ribs. On each side of the ventral scales is a suture and by muscular contraction the outer ends of each scale are drawn down and slightly in, so the whole lower surface becomes concave, trapping a cushion of air beneath it. The effect is similar to that of dropping a stick of bamboo split lengthwise. The split bamboo falls more slowly than a comparable piece of bamboo stem that is intact, and it descends more nearly in the horizontal position. The tree snakes are even said to help the forward movement of the glide by alternately inflating and drawing in their belly.

Hunting by sight

When actively hunting a tree snake glides slowly and almost noiselessly to the top of a tree then slides slowly down to the lower branches, looking for lizards, geckos and similar prey. In such hunting sight is the best way of locating a target. Related snakes, belonging to the same subfamily, are known to use binocular vision. They have a long horizontal pupil and the sides of the snout are hollowed out in front of the eyes, forming grooves. Light from objects directly in front of the snout travels along the groove, enters the front of each eye and strikes the retina on the other side of the eye. This almost certainly gives binocular and stereoscopic vision, demonstrated by the way such snakes turn their heads to follow the movements of anything they are investigating.

Females store sperm

A related North American snake *Leptodeira annulata*, known as the cat-eyed snake, is remarkable for the behaviour of one member of its species which laid a clutch of fertile eggs after having been kept on its own for 6 years. There are other examples of a female snake in captivity producing several clutches of fertile eggs at intervals of about a month. Presumably, therefore, some female snakes can store sperm inside their bodies for use over long periods. Whether this is general for tree snakes is not known. In fact, in spite of their being numerous and widespread, and known for a long time, we are very ignorant of their breeding habits except to say that they lay eggs.

Ignorance dispelled

This is not the only aspect of their way of life that has suffered from lack of knowledge. The 'flying' habit is another. As is usual when information is lacking legend and folklore take the upper hand. In Malaya and Indonesia it was believed that to get from tree to tree the snake changed into a bird and flew. Moreover, it remained in this guise until a real bird alighted nearby, when it immediately changed back to a snake and seized the bird. Zoologists were not taken in by such stories, nor were they prepared to believe the snake could fly, or even glide, until Major Stanley Flower kept some tree snakes in captivity. It is not easy to induce a tree snake to throw itself through the air, but Major Flower finally induced his pets to leap from the top windows of his house to the lower branches of a tree several yards away.

A green tree snake **Philothamnus irregularis** *winds its way through an African tree.*

class	**Reptilia**
order	**Squamata**
suborder	**Serpentes**
family	**Colubridae**
genus & species	***Chrysopelea ornata*** *golden tree snake* ***C. paradisi*** *paradise tree snake others*

A green lizard provides a substantial meal for a dark green whip snake—a large yet agile hunter.

Whip snake

The whip snakes are, as their name suggests, extremely slender with long tapering tails. The name has been applied to very close relatives of the racers (page 238) of North America and Eurasia, to other snakes of the family Colubridae that live in the Orient and to Australian members of the family Elapidae. The name is most commonly used for the European or dark green whip snake and its relatives. They are found mainly around the Mediterranean from the Atlantic coast of France to the Persian Gulf and through North Africa. One species can be found as far north as Poland.

The dark green whip snake is the largest European snake, growing to over 6 ft and occasionally up to 8 ft, one third of this length being tail. The head is fairly prominent and the eyes are large. The colour is, typically, yellowish-brown or pale olive with black bars and spots at the front end and yellowish-white underparts. One of the commonest snakes around the Adriatic, it ranges from southern France and northern Spain through Switzerland and Italy to Asia Minor. Close relatives of the dark green whip snake are Dahl's whip snake and the brown whip snake, both ranging from the Balkans into western Asia.

Of the Oriental whip snakes, the pencil-slim common green whip snake may grow to 6 ft or more but is usually 3 – 4 ft. The tail is long, the eyes large with horizontal pupils and the snout is long and pointed. The body is bright green, but the green is made up of minute spots of yellow on a blue blackground. It lives in India and Southeast Asia. The brown speckled whip snake is very similar in appearance except that it is brown. It lives in southern India and Ceylon.

The Australian whip snakes belong to the family Elapidae and are venomous. The yellow-faced whip snake of all states except Tasmania may be 3 – 4 ft long and its bite has an effect similar to that of a bad wasp sting. The black whip snake grows to 6 ft or more and has a more severe, sometimes dangerous, bite.

Difficult to capture

The common characteristic of the three kinds of whip snake, apart from their slender bodies, is their ability to move fast, although this may be more apparent than real, as in the racers (p 1896). They can, however, disappear into undergrowth or under stones with remarkable speed and are very difficult to capture. The French authority on snakes, Lataste, tells how he saw a certain whip snake at a particular spot many times over a period of two years but was never able to catch it.

The whip snakes of the Mediterranean region usually live on the ground in dry places among shrubs and stones, although they sometimes climb among bushes. The Oriental whip snakes, however, spend most of their time in trees and are sometimes called tree snakes. Because of their colour and shape they are easily mistaken for hanging vines or twigs. The Australian whip snakes live on the ground in dry areas.

Good vision

Whip snakes feed mainly on small reptiles especially skinks and other lizards which they chase and swallow alive, instead of enveloping them in their coils. Voles, mice and large insects such as locusts are also eaten. Tree-living whip snakes take large numbers of tree frogs and also catch birds up to the size of a dove. The horseshoe whip snake enters houses in Spain and Algeria where it preys on mice and robs the nests of sparrows.

The Oriental whip snakes are unusual in having horizontal pupils that appear as long slits. There is also a groove running along the snout to each eye which probably allows each eye to see objects in front of the head and allows stereoscopic vision, as the eyes' field of vision overlaps. The Oriental whip snakes are among the few snakes which can detect motionless prey.

Eggs or live young

Mediterranean whip snakes lay their eggs in holes or crevices in the ground or under stones. The eggs vary in number from 3 in the horseshoe whip snake to about 15 in the dark green whip snake. The Australian whip snakes also lay eggs, varying from 3 to 6 in number, but the Oriental whip snakes give birth to 3 – 22 live young.

St Paul's viper

Most descriptions of Mediterranean and Oriental whip snakes emphasise their ferocity. At one time the Mediterranean species had the generic name of *Zamenis*, alluding to its aggressiveness, while the green whip snake of India and Ceylon is popularly believed to strike at the eyes and in Singhalese is called the 'eye plucker'. The name is well earned for, although whip snakes do not necessarily aim at the eyes, they strike aggressively with the mouth open, even attempting to strike through the window of a cage. They inflict painful bites, but no venom is injected although the saliva of the green whip snake can cause a local swelling. It has been suggested that the dark green whip snake, which is common on many of the Mediterranean islands from Corsica and Sardinia eastwards, was the 'viper' that bit and clung to St Paul's hand after he had been shipwrecked on Malta. According to the story in the Acts of the Apostles the Maltese were surprised that St Paul came to no harm and 'said that he was a god'. One might expect that the local people would know which animals were dangerous but in several parts of the world snakes, geckos and various insects are supposed to be deadly when they are in fact harmless.

class	**Reptilia**		
order	**Squamata**		
suborder	**Serpentes**		
family	**Colubridae**		
genera & species	*Coluber hippocrepis* horseshoe whip snake *C. jugularis* brown whip snake *C. najadum* Dahl's whip snake *C. viridiflavus* dark green whip snake *Ahaetulla mycterizans* green whip snake *A. pulverulentus* brown speckled whip snake		
family	**Elapidae**		
genus & species	*Demansia olivacea* black whip snake *D. psammophis* yellow-faced whip snake, others		

Index

Acknowledgments

This book is adapted from 'Purnell's Encyclopedia of Animal Life', published in the United States under the title of 'International Wild Life'.
AFA: Geoffrey Kinns; Heather Angel; Ronald Austing; M E Bacchus; Bavaria: W Harstrick, Pfletschinger, P Reiserer, Rohdich; S C Bisserot; Alice Brown; Maurice Burton; H R Bustard; Colin G Butler; Carolina Biological Supply Co; A Christiansen; John Clegg; M J Coe; Ben Cropp; Gerald Cubitt; D Davis; Kev Deacon; G T Dunger; G Dunn; J Mason; Andre Fatras; Harry & Claudy Frauca; Carl Gans; G S Giacomelli; Peter J Green; W D Haacke; H Hansen; Roy A Harris & K R Duff; Robert Hermes; Peter Hill; M J Hirons; E S Hobson; Eric Hosking; Chris Howell-Jones; David Hughes; Jacana: Brosset, P H Vasserot; Walter Jarchow; Denys A Kempson; A B Klots; E F Kilian; G Kinns; G E Kirkpatrick; Yves Lanceau; Henning Lender; Lim Boo Liat; E Lindsey; Peter Livesley; Michael Lyster; The Mansell Collection; Marineland of Florida; John Markham; J Mason/G Dunn; Meston; Carl Mills; Lorus & Margery Milne; John Moore; P Morris; Natural History Museum; K B Newman; NHPA: Anthony Bannister, Joe Blossom, Stephen Dalton, E Elkan, Graham Pizzey, Gordon F Woods; John Norris Wood; Okapia; Klaus Paysan; B Pengilley; Photo Library Inc; Photo Res.: Des Bartlett, Jane Burton, C Ciapanna, Jack Dermid, Michael Freeman, Sven Gillsater, Vincent Serventy, J R Simon, Howard E Uible; Photographic Library of Australia; Popperfoto; Roebild; Ronan Picture Library; Root/Okapia; L Lee Rue III; Gunter Senfft; Fritz Siedel; M F Soper; A J Southward; Helmut Stellrecht; John Tashjian at Fort Worth Zoo and Steinhart Aquarium; John Visser; Peter Ward; John Warham; Constance P Warner; D P Wilson; WWF: Van Nostrand; Nolly Zaloumis; Zoological Society of London.